ELEGY BY W. S.

A Study in Attribution

Donald W. Foster

DELAWARE

Newark: University of Delaware Press
London and Toronto: Associated University Presses

Associated University Presses
440 Forsgate Drive
Cranbury, NJ 08512

Associated University Presses
25 Sicilian Avenue
London WC1A 2QH, England

Associated University Presses
P.O. Box 488, Port Credit
Mississauga, Ontario
Canada L5G 4M2

The paper used in this publication meets the requirements
of the American National Standard for Permanence of Paper
for Printed Library Materials Z39.48-1984.

Library of Congress Cataloging-in-Publication Data

Foster, Donald W., 1950–
    Elegy by W.S.

    Originally presented as the author's thesis (Ph.D.—
University of California)
    Includes bibliographies and index.
    1. W. S. Funerall elegye in memory of the late
virtuous master William Peeter of Whipton neere Exetour.
2. Shakespeare, William, 1564–1616—Authorship.
3. Strachey, William, 1572?–1621—Authorship.
4. Peter, William, 1582–1612, in fiction, drama, poetry,
etc.   5. Elegiac poetry, English—History and criticism.
I. W. S. Funerall elegye in memory of the late virtuous
master William Peeter of Whipton neere Exetour.
II. Title.
PR2199.F863F67   1989   321'.3   87-40427
ISBN 0-87413-335-1 (alk. paper)

PRINTED IN THE UNITED STATES OF AMERICA

CONTENTS

PREFACE

THIS book is about a poem that was first printed in 1612 and that has never, until now, been printed again, a poem that may be by Shakespeare. Such an announcement is likely to excite both interest and skepticism—perhaps intense interest, at least in those not experienced enough to know better, and surely intense skepticism. Both responses are appropriate. Shakespeare is the English national poet, the greatest poet in our language, by many accounts the greatest poet of any language. The discovery of a new poem by him would of course interest all who love English literature—could his authorship be proven. But so many poems have been ascribed to Shakespeare over the years, only to be rejected, that the chances are slim and perhaps nil that any new attribution will win general favor.

The recent commotion over "Shall I die, shall I fly"—in which the editors of the Oxford Shakespeare announced the discovery of a "new" Shakespeare poem—should give us pause. As it turned out, the ascription of that unfortunate lyric to "William Shakespeare" was old news and, in the judgment of most readers, wrong as well. After a brief debate, the attribution was widely discredited and the poem all but forgotten. Yet the controversy was not altogether without profit if it served to remind us of how little progress has been made in testing the accuracy of doubtful attributions. The usual technique, in a study such as this, has been to begin with a private conclusion that this or that author wrote this or that text; to produce proofs, like rabbits, from out of one's hat; and then to express astonishment and indignation when the world fails to perceive the obvious.

That W. S.'s *Funeral Elegy* for William Peter was written by William Shakespeare is more than I know. That it should be added at once to the Shakespeare canon, and to the reading list of sophomore English classes, is more than I desire. Nor do I expect anyone else to succeed where I have failed in proving that the *Elegy* is indeed Shakespeare's. There is simply no way of knowing with certainty. An attributional study such as this is nevertheless worth doing: W. S.'s *Elegy* is of some interest in itself. There is a possibility, perhaps even a strong possibility, that it was written by Shakespeare. And the poem may serve as a case study by which to

7

examine the much larger problem of what constitutes an "author"—to examine what it is that makes Shakespeare *Shakespeare*.

It gives me great pleasure to set down here the names of those who helped me to bring this project to fruition. My research was generously funded by the University of California at Santa Barbara, whose assistance included two travel research grants and two graduate fellowships. The staffs of the Bodleian, British, and Huntington libraries, and of the Balliol College and Exeter College libraries, aided my research. I owe much also to the staffs of the Public Record Office, London, and of the Devon Record Office. For permission to reproduce the 1612 Quarto I wish to thank the Master and Fellows of Balliol College, Oxford. And I acknowledge with thanks a grant from the Lucy Maynard Salmon Fund of Vassar College toward the publication of this book.

This book began as a doctoral dissertation at the University of California, under the direction of Mark Rose, Richard Helgerson, Garrett Stewart, Michael O'Connell, and Bert O. States. I am deeply grateful for their patient and painstaking support. Their expert advice and cautious skepticism saved me from numerous pratfalls. I owe much also to the helpful advice of press readers G. Blakemore Evans, Arthur Kinney, and George T. Wright, and to the cheerful assistance of my editors, especially Beth Gianfagna of Associated University Presses. I am, of course, fully responsible for whatever errors or eccentricities have survived the scrutiny of my early readers. Nor should their generous help be confused with an endorsement of my thesis that William Shakespeare may have written this elegy by W. S.

I owe most to my wife Gwen, who is perhaps the only woman ever widowed, for a time, by a funeral elegy. Without her daily assistance this book could not have been completed. To Gwen this book is affectionately dedicated.

ABBREVIATIONS

Arber   Arber, Edward, ed. *A Transcript of the Registers of the Company of Stationers of London, 1554–1640.* 5 vols. London, 1875–77.

D.A.P.   Halkett, Samuel, and John Laing. *A Dictionary of Anonymous and Pseudonymous Publications in the English Language, 1475–1640.* 3d ed. rev. Edited by John Horden. Harlow, Eng.: Longman, 1980.

E.D.C.   John Tucker Murray. *The English Dramatic Companies, 1158–1642.* 2 vols. London: Constable, 1910.

E.S.   E. K. Chambers. *The Elizabethan Stage.* 4 vols. Oxford: Clarendon, 1923.

F1   William Shakespeare. *Comedies, Histories, and Tragedies* [First Folio]. London, 1623.

FQ   Edmund Spenser. *The Faerie Queene.*

H & S   *Ben Jonson.* Edited by C. H. Herford and Percy and Evelyn Simpson. 11 vols. London, 1875.

NQ   *Notes and Queries.*

PL   John Milton. *Paradise Lost.*

PRO   Public Record Office, London.

Puttenham   George Puttenham, *The Arte of English Poesie.* London, 1589.

RES   *Review of English Studies.*

SQ   *Shakespeare Quarterly.*

STC   Pollard, A. W., and G. R. Redgrave, *A Short-Title Catalogue of Books Printed in England, Scotland, and Ireland and of English Books Printed Abroad: 1475–1640.* 2 vols. 2d ed. rev. and enlarged. Edited by W. A. Jackson, F. S. Ferguson, and

     Katharine F. Pantzer. London: The Bibliographical Society, 1976.

Williams Franklin B. Williams, ed. *Index of Dedications and Commendatory Verses in English Books before 1641.* London: The Bibliographical Society, 1962.

W.S.   E. K. Chambers. *William Shakespeare.* 2 vols. Oxford: Clarendon, 1930.

A KILLING AT EXETER

ON Saturday, the twenty-fifth of January, at 7:00 P.M., William Peter was murdered. The year was 1612.

Early in the day, about ten in the morning, John and Edward Drew of Broadclyst, accompanied by their Irish footman, rode forth from their Killerton estate for an afternoon of midwinter revels in nearby Exeter. As they made their way toward town, the brothers were the picture of Renaissance gallants, John dressed all in black, his elder brother Edward in a white cloak and white hat. Both men carried swords at their sides, and both were excellent riders.

When they arrived at the Oxford Inn, just outside the East Gate, the Drews alighted for a drink. As they lingered, the host, Giles Geal, offered to sell the elder Drew a fine-looking pony. Edward, who had a passion for buying and selling horses, asked to take her for a ride, and Geal complied. As he mounted, his brother John asked him where he would ride. Edward answered that he would ride to Will Peter's and "make a quarrel with him about the buying of a horse."

Edward galloped away, riding again past St. Anne's Chapel, then up the broad road of St. Sidwell toward the Peter residence, some two miles to the east, called "Whipton House." When he arrived, William Johns, a servant, opened the gate for him. The Peters were still at dinner, but upon learning that he had a visitor, Master Peter arose, went to the door, and asked him in. Drew urged his friend to ride with him into Exeter. So while the servant Johns got ready his horse, Peter put on his riding boots, rapier, and cloak, then bade his wife farewell and accompanied Drew into town. When they came again to Geal's house outside the East Gate, John Drew was gone. He had ridden into town, wearing the white cloak left behind by Edward at the inn. After stopping at Alexander Osborne's house to conduct some necessary business there, he had proceeded to the cutler's thinking to exchange his sword for a rapier. But he failed to agree with the cutler upon a price and finally returned to the Oxford, where he found his brother and Will Peter having a drink together.

After three-quarters of an hour, Peter and the two Drews rode into the city to Peter Chapman's, where they ordered another round of drinks. Edward, who admired Will Peter's horse, suggested they make an exchange, but Peter refused to sell. They paid their bill and rode next to the

11

sign of the Bear, on Southgate Street at the lower corner of Bear Lane. Rather than enter the dining room, Peter and the Drews proceeded to the cellar, where they called for a quart of canary wine. Alice Drake, the hostess, brought the wine along with two biscuit cakes. She was about to serve them when Edward Drew "swore a great oath" and said that if she put the cakes on the table, he would throw them to the floor. Peter, apparently embarrassed by his friend's behavior, said, "I will eat a piece of biscuit, for I love it."

Mrs. Drake served him one cake, broke it, and took the other away. Upon her return some few minutes later, the elder Drew began to "talk very wantonly" with her, wherewith, as she said later, she was "not well pleased." Peter again intervened, saying, "Take you no unkindness, for he is an idle gentleman"—at which point Edward suddenly got up from his seat and started for the door. His two companions rose with him. But when Peter asked if they would not first drink up the wine, John returned and sat down. His elder brother stormed out the front door, quietly shaking his head and "looking somewhat eagerly." It was at about this time that he commanded his Irish footman to return home to Killerton. Peter, meanwhile, stayed with the younger Drew in Mrs. Drake's cellar to finish the wine. He then paid the bill and left with John by the rear door. Edward, returning to the cellar moments later to find that his companions had left, followed them to the stables.

Upon retrieving their horses, the three friends rode to the Dolphin, just down Billeter Lane. Peter stopped first at the Mermaid across the way to ask John Rowell, one of the servants there, to walk his horse. The Drews in the meantime entered the Dolphin. They greeted the host, George Northvale, and went upstairs to one of the large rooms reserved for "persons of quality," where they found Sir Edward Seymour engaged at cards with some friends.

Peter and the Drews stayed at the Dolphin for almost an hour. They drank another pot or two of beer and shared some wine with Sir Edward. Then, as they were about to depart, the elder Drew noticed William Short, one of Northvale's servants, building a house of cards. Drew walked up, took a last swig of beer, and spewed it onto the table, knocking down the cards, then left the room laughing. This, apparently, drew another rebuke from Will Peter: on their way out, the two men were seen pushing one another on the staircase.

Peter crossed the street to the Mermaid to retrieve his horse from Rowell while the Drews entered Northvale's courtyard to retrieve theirs. The Mermaid, then kept by John Garland, was another famed meeting place for "Devon's Worthies." It was an old inn already in 1612, and had a colorful history. It was here, for example, that Sir Gawen and Sir Peter Carew came in 1549, with their company of knights and squires, after confronting the Catholic insurgents at St. Mary's Clyst. According to local legend, when the inn was first established a long consultation on the choice of an appropriate sign ended in the observation that the "Mermaid" would sing catches to the youths of the parish.

It was almost 7:00 P.M. when Will Peter strode past the sign of the Mermaid and into the courtyard. He tipped Rowell for walking his horse, mounted, and was about to leave when he met Mr. Harries, an acquaintance, also on horseback. As Peter and Harries chatted by lamplight in the yard of the inn, they were joined by John and Edward Drew, who, when they rode into Garland's court, called for two more pots of beer. The beer was brought, and they drank the first pot with Peter and Harries, all four men remaining on horseback. But Drew and Peter, without speaking, crossed their horses a dozen times or more, to prevent one another from going—which caused certain of those standing about to suppose there was some "discontentment" between them. After only a few minutes, they turned to go, leaving the second pot of beer untouched.

As they headed toward home, Will Peter was in the lead, followed by John and Edward. It was quite dark, but they galloped through the city at a furious pace, up High Street and out the East Gate. Edward called out to his brother, saying, "He rideth fast, but I will ride faster, and will give him a nick before he gets home."

Alarmed, John shouted, "No, brother, do not hurt him." But Edward only spurred his horse faster up the broad road of St. Sidwell. John, too, quickened his pace, but could not keep up. There was just enough light, as Edward caught up with Will Peter near St. Anne's Chapel, for John to see his brother's drawn sword before he vanished in the darkness.

Moments later, he heard a crash as Peter and his horse tumbled off the causey into the dirt.

Up the road a stretch, Edward stopped his horse. He waited for John to catch up, then said, ingenuously, "I think Will Peter is fallen." Since it was too dark to see, they called out Peter's name. No one answered. Not far away, though, near St. Anne's Chapel, someone stood before a doorway with a lighted candle, where a few persons were gathered in the dark. John, hoping one of them to be Peter, suggested that they ride near to investigate. But while John approached the lighted doorway—still wearing his brother's white cloak—Edward lurked in the shadows beside a large crucifix that stood by the chapel. Or, if we may believe Edward's later testimony, it was he who drew near, wearing his own cloak, while John stayed behind. In the web of lies that followed, both brothers laid claim to the part.

The house belonged to a Mrs. Stuckeys. The man at the door with the candle was her son, John Rogers. George Seleg, a local husbandman, had come to inquire of Mrs. Stuckeys whether his wife was there, but the old woman had received no visitors that night. It was while Seleg, Mrs. Stuckeys, and her son John were speaking that one of the two Drews approached (though which one, they could not later say), and without dismounting asked if a gentleman was within. They told him, "No." But neither John nor his brother Edward, as they later told the story, did "desire the said candle to look what was become of Will Peter." Instead they rode on toward Whipton. Along the way, just before the turning on the causey near Whipton House, they came upon Peter's horse, standing in the road. John suggested that they go back once again to look for their friend. "Did you not see Will Peter," asked Edward, "lying on the ground as you passed by?" John had not. "*I* did," said Edward. John asked whether they should not help him. Edward replied, "Let him alone!"—and John, who feared his elder brother, obeyed. Taking the bridle in his hand, Edward led Peter's horse to Whipton House. "If they shall ask for Master Peter," said John, "what answer will you make?"

"Let them seek him," said Edward.

Arriving at Whipton House, Edward Drew knocked at the gate with his boot, without dismounting. This time it was certainly brother John who stayed in the shadows, not wishing to be seen. When William Johns answered, he saw only his master's riderless horse, and Edward Drew alongside. Johns asked where his master was. Drew replied, "He will come by and by." He then turned, spurred his horse, and rode away.

When Edward caught up with brother John, the two men rode home in silence to their Killerton estate. But after they were in bed and the light put out, Edward said he wished that Will Peter were not dead, and that if he were not dead, he was perhaps gone back to Sir Edward Seymour. John asked why he had struck Peter down. Edward snapped, "What is that to you?"—but added, some minutes later, "I pray God Master Peter be well."

Peter's body was found later that evening, alongside the causey, and was brought into Roger Fishmore's house, where it was promptly covered up. The commotion in the neighborhood lasted most of the night. Robert White brought word to his neighbors, the Stockmans. Someone else rode into town with the news. A small crowd gathered. The corpse was not uncovered, though, till after 4:00 A.M., when John Garland, host of the Mermaid, appeared and asked if there were any visible wounds. The young Bowyer brought a candle, pulled back the blanket, and lifted Peter's head. He had no difficulty finding the wound: Drew had stabbed his friend in the back of the head, driving the point of his short-sword right through Peter's skull. Agnes Stockman said later that the floor was awash in blood.

In the morning, after conferring with William Johns, a constable came round to Killerton. He knocked at the gate, and asked for Edward Drew. Inside, brother John asked him what he would do if Will Peter were dead.

Edward answered with a veiled threat: "Brother," he said, "be advised, and discover by no means your knowledge in this business." He then walked silently outside, where he was arrested and his horse sent for. John, thinking it best to accompany them, fetched his horse as well—and in the orchard, before they came away, Edward said to him, as if by way of belated revelation, "Me*thought* I saw Will Peter lying on the ground!" John held his peace.

The verdict of the twenty men who sat on the Coroner's jury was a charge of willful murder against the elder Drew, with John Drew named as an accessory after the fact. What happened thereafter remains unclear. Scanty evidence suggests that Edward, at least, escaped custody, to spend the rest of his days as a fugitive from justice. He died in 1637 and was buried at Broadhembury, an estate then owned by his eldest brother Thomas. John died in 1614, and was buried at nearby Broadclyst. A poor likeness of John, and perhaps of Edward as well, is preserved in the family monument at Broadclyst Church, erected by Thomas in 1622: the figures of Bridgett Drew and of Edward Drew, senior, Sergeant-at-Law, lie beside one another. At their feet are the kneeling figures of four sons and three daughters, in bas-relief. One of their five sons was omitted from the sculpture, perhaps William, the eldest, who died shortly before his father in 1598. More likely, it was Edward for whom brother Thomas could find no place in the family monument.

There was a story told soon after Peter's death, and reported by Tristram Risdon in his *Survey of Devon* (written over a period of years from 1605 to 1630), that Will Peter's portrait fell from the wall shortly before his death, causing his head to be broken in the very place where he later received his death wound. The legendary painting has not survived. Nevertheless, two other portraits of Will Peter have been preserved, the first carved in stone in the Peter family monument, which was erected in 1608 to the memory of his father, Otho. The memorial still stands in the Peamore Chapel of St. Martin's Church, Exminster, some three miles from Bowhay. The tomb is surmounted by three coats of arms, Peter at the west end, Southcott at the east, and in the center Peter impaling Southcott. Below left, facing the center, are the kneeling figures of Otho Peter and his two sons, John and William. On the right, facing them, are the figures of his wife Frances (n. Southcott) and daughter Elizabeth. Two cherubic female figures kneel above, at the top of the tomb, over a brass inscription on which the arms of Peter are again displayed, along with some Latin verses that play on the Peter name. Unfortunately, all seven effigies are stock figures, inexpertly carved, and their features are badly worn. The figure farthest to the left, representing Otho's younger son William, is missing its hands and lower legs.

The other portrait to have survived of William Peter was done in ink. It is not, however, a drawing, but rather a poem, a memorial in verse written to preserve the memory of a young man whose many excellent qualities were partially obscured by the circumstances surrounding his death. *A Funeral Elegy in Memory of the Late Virtuous Master William Peter* was written by one "W. S.," an acquaintance of Peter during his nine years at Oxford.

The existence of this poem is as much a mystery in its own way as Peter's death. Most Renaissance elegies, if not written for wealthy patrons, were penned for great celebrities. William Peter was neither. All other surviving elegies of two hundred lines or more were composed by well-known, if sometimes uninspired, poets, most of them men who made their writing a lifetime career. Yet the author of this 578-line poem offers us no clue to his identity but a set of initials. Most surprising of all is that this poem, which was written in just a few days' time, is remarkably well-done. The early seventeenth century is not a period distinguished for its elegiac verse. Every major poet of the age but Shakespeare is known to have tried his hand at writing an elegy or two—Webster, Tourneur, Jonson, Heywood, Ford, Drayton, Davies, Campion, Beaumont, and dozens of others—yet their memorial verse is, for the most part, as lifeless and stiff as their respective subjects. Excepting those by Jonson and Donne, most Jacobean elegies have gathered dust in the Special Collections of university libraries. Few have ever been reprinted—and their neglect, in most cases, is well deserved. Yet now and then, when wandering through volumes long forgotten, one stumbles upon a work of unusual merit. Such is the Peter elegy, a poem never until now reprinted, and never (as far as I can tell) so much as mentioned in print. It is not, to be sure, among the greatest poems in our literature. In many respects, the poem is all too ordinary. Yet there is a distinct possibility, as we shall see, that this *Funeral Elegy* was written by William Shakespeare.

A NOTE ON THE TEXT

THE text of the *Elegy* is provided by the Quarto of 1612, printed by George Eld for Thomas Thorp. Despite what appears to have been a rather small, private printing, two copies have survived, both at Oxford, one in the Bodleian and one in the Balliol College Library. In all probability, the Bodleian received its copy as part of the agreement in 1610 between Thomas Bodley and the Stationers' Company, by which the library was to receive a copy of every book printed. It has been bound together with five contemporaneous publications.[1] The Balliol copy (photographically reproduced on pp. 24–66 below) has been rebound with twenty-eight other works in a volume now titled *Miscellaneous Poems,* containing verse by Arthur Brett, Alexander Brome, Abraham Cowley, Sir William Davenant, John Denham, John Dryden, and others. There is no record of how the library came to acquire the collection. A bookworm of discriminating taste has eaten a small hole through the upper inside margin of the Balliol text, yet the print is generally more legible than in the Bodleian copy and four misprints have been corrected—*rumor* has been changed to *rumor'd* (421), *withour* to *without* (469), *'m* to *'em* (552), and an auxiliary *have,* missing in the Bodleian copy, has been supplied. The two surviving copies of the Quarto are identical in other respects, having been printed from the same setting of type throughout.

The 1612 Quarto was apparently set from copy supplied by the author himself, although it appears that W. S. took no part in proofreading the printed text, for it contains several obvious misprints—an uncapitalized *w* (187), *Sot* for *Sat* (60), *goood* for *good* (477), the omitted *t* in *invitemens* (284), and *witnesles* for *witnesses* (540)—that remain uncorrected even in the Balliol copy. In my edited text, obvious misprints have been quietly corrected. In addition, I have made two emendations in the Quarto text (the first of which was kindly suggested by G. Blakemore Evans): Line 8 of the Quarto reads, "Sith as it euer hee maintain'd the same," which is ungrammatical and makes little sense. Where "it" appears, one should expect to find "that," since *that,* in Elizabethan verse, was used frequently as a conjunctional affix following *as.* It seems likely that the compositor simply misread the author's "yt" (= *that*) for "yt" (= *it*). These are often confused in Renaissance texts (but the line as emended may still be corrupt; the *OED* offers various precedents for both *sith that* and *as that,*

17

but none for *sith as*).[2] Second, in line 441, "prophane" seems to be a misprint for "prophand" in the author's manuscript: thus "profan'd" in my edited text.

The manuscript from which the Quarto was typeset appears to have been very lightly punctuated. Given the complexities of syntax in this poem, it is easy to see how a compositor working from such a manuscript could be misled and confuse the sense by adding incorrect punctuation intended as clarification, but in the case of the Peter elegy the judgment of the compositor or scribe was unusually poor. Even given the oddities of contemporaneous practice, the insertion of misplaced end-punctuation, semicolons, and marks of parenthesis frequently mangle the sense so badly as to make the thought unintelligible. For example:

> they doe intend,
> (According to the tenour of the Saw
> Mistooke, if not obseru'd, writ long agoe)
> When men were onely led by *Reasons* law,
> *That such as is the end, the life prooues so.*

(362–66)

When correctly punctuated, the sentence makes perfect sense:

> they do intend,
> According to the tenor of the saw
> Mistook, if not observ'd (writ long ago
> When men were only led by reason's law),
> That "Such as is the end, the life proves so."

(362–66)

My working principle in preparing a modern text of the *Elegy* has been to keep the pointing light. Unnecessary punctuation, as in the original Quarto, may only confuse the sense or deplete the verse of a multiple meaning. The frequent and unnecessary use of italics in the Quarto, which is typical of Renaissance publications, has been abandoned. In those instances where italics are used to indicate a quotation, I have substituted quotation marks. Similarly, rather than make arbitrary decisions about which words W. S. might or might not wish to see capitalized in this edition, I have followed modern convention and capitalized only the pronoun *I,* the interjection *O,* proper nouns, the first letter of every sentence, and the first letter of every verse line. Personified nouns such as *death, truth, time,* and *reason,* I have left in lower case, not in supposed conformity to the poet's own practice, but because personification is a matter of interpretation best left to the individual reader and not to the poet's original compositor; the same goes for possible puns on proper names (*will, rock, ridgway, drew*) and for biblical nouns (*hell, deity, angels*). Spelling has been made to conform with modern usage, though I have retained archaic variants where they represent Jacobean alternatives in the form, and not merely in the spelling, of words. Examples are *sith, conster, disgest, adventers, strook,* and the frequent elision of participles (e.g., *Rememb'ring, sund'red*).

Notes

1. Francis Rollenson, *Twelve Prophetical Legacies* (London, 1612); Francis Tomlinson, *The Holy Salutation of the Blessed Apostle St. Jude* (London, 1612); Thomas Tuke, *A Discourse of Death, Bodily, Ghostly, and Eternall* (London, 1613); Hugh Broughton, *Observations upon the First Ten Fathers* (London, 1612); and Anthony Nixon, *Londons Dove* (London, 1612).

2. The "thorn," written and printed in Shakespeare's day as a *y,* stood for *th-;* y^t was thus a standard abbreviation for *that,* even as ye could stand for *the.* This practice often led to confusion in printed texts, especially between *ye* and *the, it* and *that.*

ELEGY BY W. S.

The Text

A
FVNERALL
Elegye

In memory of the late Vertuous
Maister VVilliam Peeter
of Whipton neere
Excester.

(13)

By *W. S.*

Imprinted at London by *G. Eld.*   6
1612.

A FUNERAL ELEGY

In Memory of the Late Virtuous
Master William Peter
of Whipton near
Excester

By W. S.

TO MAISTER
Iohn Peter of *Boohaye*
in Deuon. Esq.

He loue I bore to your brother, and will doe to his memory, hath crau'd from me this laſt duty of a friend; I am heerein but a ſecond to the priuiledge of *Truth* who can warrant more in his behalfe, then I vndertooke to deliuer. Exerciſe in this kind I will little affect, and am leſſe adicted to, but there muſt be miracle in that labour, which to witneſſe my re-

A 2   membrance

TO MASTER JOHN PETER

of Bowhay in Devon, Esq.

The love I bore to your brother, and will do to his memory, hath crav'd from me this last duty of a friend; I am herein but a second to the privilege of *truth,* who can warrant more in his behalf than I undertook to deliver. Exercise in this kind I will little affect, and am less addicted to, but there must be a miracle in that labor which, to witness my remembrance

membrance to this departed Gentleman, I would not willingly vndergoe : yet what-ſoeuer is heere done, is done to him , and to him onely . For whom, and whoſe ſake, I will not forget to remember any friendly reſpects to you, or to any of thoſe that haue lou'd him for himſelfe, and himſelfe for his deſerts.

W .S.

to this departed gentleman, I would not willingly undergo. Yet whatsoever is here done, is done to him and to him only. For whom and whose sake I will not forget to remember any friendly respects to you, or to any of those that have lov'd him for himself, and himself for his deserts.

W. S.

A Funerall Elegie.

Since *Time*, and his predestinated end,
  Abridg'd the circuit of his hope-full dayes;
Whiles both his *Youth* and *Vertue* did intend,
The good indeuor's, of deseruing praise :
What memorable monument can last,
Whereon to build his neuer blemisht name?
But his owne worth, wherein his life was grac't?
Sith as it euer hee maintain'd the same.
Obliuion in the darkest day to come,
When sinne shall tread on merit in the dust;
Cannot rase out the lamentable tombe
Of his *Short-liu'd desert's* : but still they must
Euen in the hearts and memories of men,
Claime fit *Respect*; that they, in euery lim,
Remembring what he was, with comfort then
May patterne out, *One truly good* by him.
For hee was truly good; if honest care,
Of harmlesse conuersation, may commend
A life free from such staines, as follyes are;
Ill recompenced onely in his end.
Nor ean the toung of him who lou'd him least,
(If there ean bee minority of loue,
To one superlatiue aboue the rest,
Of many men in steddy faith) reproue
His constant temper, in the equall weight
Of *thankfulnesse*, and *kindnesse*: *Truth* doth leaue
Sufficient proofe, he was in euery right,
As kinde to *giue*, as thankfull to *receaue*.
The curious eye, of a quick brain'd suruey,
Could scantly find a mote amidst the sun,

A 3

A FUNERAL ELEGY

Since time, and his predestinated end,
Abridg'd the circuit of his hopeful days,
Whiles both his youth and virtue did intend
The good endeavors of deserving praise,
5   What memorable monument can last
Whereon to build his never-blemish'd name
But his own worth, wherein his life was grac'd—
Sith as [that] ever he maintain'd the same?
Oblivion in the darkest day to come,
10   When sin shall tread on merit in the dust,
Cannot rase out the lamentable tomb
Of his short-liv'd deserts; but still they must,
Even in the hearts and memories of men,
Claim fit respect, that they, in every limb
15   Rememb'ring what he was, with comfort then
May pattern out one truly good, by him.
For he was truly good, if honest care
Of harmless conversation may commend
A life free from such stains as follies are,
20   Ill recompensed only in his end.
Nor can the tongue of him who lov'd him least
(If there can be minority of love
To one superlative above the rest
Of many men in steady faith) reprove
25   His constant temper, in the equal weight
Of thankfulness and kindness: Truth doth leave
Sufficient proof, he was in every right
As kind to give, as thankful to receive.
The curious eye of a quick-brain'd survey
30   Could scantly find a mote amidst the sun

8 *Sith*] since   that] it Q

Of his too-shortned dayes : or make a prey
Of any faulty errors he had done.
Not that he was aboue the spleenfull sence
And spight of mallice; but for that he had
Warrant enough in his owne innocence,
Against the sting of some in nature bad.
Yet who is hee so absolutely blest,
That liues incompast in a mortall frame?
Some-time in reputation not opprest?
By some in nothing famous but defame?
Such in the *By-path* and the *Ridg-way* lurke
That leades to ruine; in a smooth pretence
Of what they doe, to be a speciall worke,
Of singlenesse, not tending to offence.
Whose very vertues are not to detract,
Whiles hope remaines of gaine (base fee of slaues)
Despising chiefly, men in fortunes wrackt,
But death to such giues vnremembred graues.
Now therein liu'd he happy, if to bee
Free from detraction, happinesse it bee.
His yonger yeares, gaue comfortable hope
To hope for comfort, in his riper youth;
Which (haruest-like) did yeeld againe the crop
Of *Education*, betterd, in his truth :
Those noble twins of heauen infused races,
Learning and *wit*, refined in their kind :
Did ioyntly both, in their peculiar graces,
Enrich the curious temple of his mind.
Indeed a temple, in whose precious white,
Sot *Reason* by *Religion* ouer-swayd:
Teaching his other senses, with delight,
How *Piety* and *Zeale* should bee obey'd.

Not

Of his too-short'ned days, or make a prey
Of any faulty errors he had done—
Not that he was above the spleenful sense
And spite of malice, but for that he had
35 Warrant enough in his own innocence
Against the sting of some in nature bad.
Yet who is he so absolutely blest
That lives encompass'd in a mortal frame,
Sometime in reputation not oppress'd
40 By some in nothing famous but defame?
Such in the bypath and the ridgway lurk
That leads to ruin, in a smooth pretense
Of what they do to be a special work
Of singleness, not tending to offense;
45 Whose very virtues are, not to detract
Whiles hope remains of gain (base fee of slaves),
Despising chiefly men in fortunes wrack'd—
But death to such gives unrememb'red graves.
     Now therein liv'd he happy, if to be
50   Free from detraction happiness it be.
His younger years gave comfortable hope
To hope for comfort in his riper youth,
Which, harvest-like, did yield again the crop
Of education, better'd in his truth.
55 Those noble twins of heaven-infused races,
Learning and wit, refined in their kind
Did jointly both, in their peculiar graces,
Enrich the curious temple of his mind;
Indeed a temple, in whose precious white
60 Sat reason by religion oversway'd,
Teaching his other senses, with delight,
How piety and zeal should be obey'd—

44 *singleness*] sincerity

Not fruitlesly in prodigall expence,
Wasting his best of time: but so content
With *Reasons golden Meane* to make defence,
Against the assault of youth's incouragement:
As not the tide of this surrounding age,
(When now his Fathers death had freed his will)
Could make him subiect to the drunken rage,
Of such whose onely glory is their ill.
Hee from the happy knowledge of the wise,
Drawes vertue to reprooue secured fooles;
And shuns the glad sleights of insnaring vice,
To spend his spring of dayes in sacred schooles.
Heere gaue hee dyet to the sick desires,
That day by day, assault the weaker man;
And with fit moderation still retires,
From what doth batter Vertue now and than.
But that I not intend in full discourse,
To progresse out his life; I could display,
A *Good man* in each part exact; and force
The common voyce to warrant what I say.
For if his fate and heauen had decreed,
That full of dayes hee might haue liu'd to see
The graue in peace; the times that should succeed
Had been best-speaking witnesses with mee.
Whose conuersation so vntoucht, did moue
Respect most in it selfe, as who would scan
His Honesty and Worth, by them might prooue,
Hee was a kind, true, perfect, gentleman.
Not in the out-side of disgracefull folly
Courting Opinion, with vnfit disguise;
Affecting fashions; nor addicted wholy
To vnbeseeming blushlesse vanities:

Bu

Not fruitlessly in prodigal expense
Wasting his best of time, but so content
65   With reason's golden mean to make defense
Against the assault of youth's encouragement;
As not the tide of this surrounding age
(When now his father's death had freed his will)
Could make him subject to the drunken rage
70   Of such whose only glory is their ill.
He from the happy knowledge of the wise
Draws virtue to reprove secured fools
And shuns the glad sleights of ensnaring vice
To spend his spring of days in sacred schools.
75   Here gave he diet to the sick desires
That day by day assault the weaker man,
And with fit moderation still retires
From what doth batter virtue now and then.
But that I not intend in full discourse
80   To progress out his life, I could display
A good man in each part exact and force
The common voice to warrant what I say.
For if his fate and heaven had decreed
That full of days he might have liv'd to see
85   The grave in peace, the times that should succeed
Had been best-speaking witnesses with me;
Whose conversation so untouch'd did move
Respect most in itself, as who would scan
His honesty and worth, by them might prove
90   He was a kind, true, perfect gentleman—
Not in the outside of disgraceful folly,
Courting opinion with unfit disguise,
Affecting fashions, nor addicted wholly
To unbeseeming blushless vanities,

78 then] than Q; again at 434

,,But futing fo his habit and defire,
,,As that his *Vertue* was his beft *Attire.*
Not in the waft of many idle words
Car'd hee to be heard talke; nor in the flote
Of fond conceit (fuch as this age affordes)
By vaine difcourfe vpon himfelfe to dote.
For his becomming filence,gaue fuch grace
To his iudicious parts; as what hee fpake
Seem'd rather anfwers (which the wife imbrace)
Then bufie queftions,fuch as talkers make.
And though his qualities might well deferue
Iuft commendation, yet his furnifht mind
Such harmony of goodneffe did preferue,
As Nature neuer built in better kind.
Knowing the beft, and therefore not prefuming
In knowing,but for that it was the beft :
Euer within himfelfe free choyce refuming
Of true perfection,in a perfect breft.
So that his Minde and Body made an In,
The one to lodge the other,both like fram'd
For faire conditions; guefts that fooneft win
Applaufe,in generality well fam'd,
If trim behauiour , geftures mild, difcreet
Endeuors ; modeft fpeech ; befeeming mirth;
True friendfhip ; actiue grace ; perfwafion fweete;
Delightfull loue,innated from his birth;
Acquaintance vnfamiliar; carriage iuft;
Offenceleffe refolution ; wifht fobriety ;
Cleane-temper'd Moderation ; fteddy Truft;
Vnburthen'd confcience ; vnfain'd Piety ;
If thefe,or all of thefe,knit faft in one
Can merit praife : then iuftly may wee fay,

Not

95   But suiting so his habit and desire
       As that his virtue was his best attire.
       Not in the waste of many idle words
       Car'd he to be heard talk, nor in the float
       Of fond conceit, such as this age affords,
100   By vain discourse upon himself to dote;
       For his becoming silence gave such grace
       To his judicious parts, as what he spake
       Seem'd rather answers which the wise embrace
       Than busy questions such as talkers make.
105   And though his qualities might well deserve
       Just commendation, yet his furnish'd mind
       Such harmony of goodness did preserve
       As nature never built in better kind;
       Knowing the best, and therefore not presuming
110   In knowing, but for that it was the best,
       Ever within himself free choice resuming
       Of true perfection, in a perfect breast;
       So that his mind and body made an inn,
       The one to lodge the other, both like fram'd
115   For fair conditions, guests that soonest win
       Applause; in generality, well fam'd,
       If trim behavior, gestures mild, discreet
       Endeavors, modest speech, beseeming mirth,
       True friendship, active grace, persuasion sweet,
120   Delightful love innated from his birth,
       Acquaintance unfamiliar, carriage just,
       Offenseless resolution, wish'd sobriety,
       Clean-temper'd moderation, steady trust,
       Unburthen'd conscience, unfeign'd piety;
125   If these, or all of these, knit fast in one
       Can merit praise: then justly may we say,

121 *unfamiliar*] uncommon   *carriage*] behavior toward others

Not any from this frailer stage is gon,
Whose name is like to liue a longer day.
Though not in eminent courts, or places great,
For popular concourse; yet in that soile
Where hee inioy'd his birth, life, death, and seat,
Which now sits mourning his vntimely spoile.
And as much glory is it to be good;
For priuate persons, in their priuate home;
As those descended from illustrious bloud,
In publick view of greatnesse: whence they come.
Though I rewarded with some sadder taste,
Of knowing shame; by feeling it haue prou'd
My countries thanklesse misconstruction; cast
Vpon my name and credit, both vnlou'd
By some, whose fortunes sunck into the wane
Of Plenty and Desert, haue stroue to win
Iustice by wrong; and sifted to imbane
My reputation, with a witlesse sinne,
Yet Time, the Father of vnblushing Truth,
May one day lay ope malice which hath crost it:
And right the hopes of my indangered youth,
Purchasing credit in the place I lost it.
Euen in which place, the subiect of the verse
(Vnhappy matter of a mourning stile)
Which now that subiects merits doth rehearse,
Had education, and new beeing: while
By faire demeanor, he had wonne repute
Amongst the All of all that liued there:
For that his actions did so wholy sute
With worthynesse, still memorable here.
The many houres till the day of doome,
Will not consume his life and haplesse end:

B   For

Not any from this frailer stage is gone
Whose name is like to live a longer day—
Though not in eminent courts or places great
130   For popular concourse, yet in that soil
Where he enjoy'd his birth, life, death, and seat
Which now sits mourning his untimely spoil.
And as much glory is it to be good
For private persons, in their private home,
135   As those descended from illustrious blood
In public view of greatness, whence they come.
Though I, rewarded with some sadder taste
Of knowing shame, by feeling it have prov'd
My country's thankless misconstruction cast
140   Upon my name and credit, both unlov'd
By some whose fortunes, sunk into the wane
Of plenty and desert, have strove to win
Justice by wrong, and sifted to embane
My reputation with a witless sin;
145   Yet time, the father of unblushing truth,
May one day lay ope malice which hath cross'd it,
And right the hopes of my endangered youth,
Purchasing credit in the place I lost it—
Even in which place the subject of the verse
150   (Unhappy matter of a mourning style
Which now that subject's merits doth rehearse)
Had education and new being; while
By fair demeanor he had won repute
Amongst the all of all that lived there,
155   For that his actions did so wholly suit
With worthiness, still memorable here.
The many hours till the day of doom
Will not consume his life and hapless end,

143 *sifted to embane*] searched out how to poison

For should he lye obscur'd without a toombe,
Time would to time his honesty commend.
Whiles Parents to their children will make known,
And they to their posterity impart,
How such a man was sadly ouerthrowne,
By a hand guided by a cruell heart.
,,Whereof as many as shall heare that sadnesse,
,,Wil blame ẙ ones hard fate, the others madnesse.
Whiles such as doe recount that tale of woe,
Told by remembrance of the wisest heades,
Will in the end conclude the matter so,
As they will all goe weeping to their bedds.
For when the world lies winterd in the stormes
Of fearefull consummation; and layes downe,
Th'vnsteddie change of his fantastick formes,
Expecting euer to be ouer-throwne:
When the proud height of much affected sinne
Shall ripen to a head, and in that pride,
End in the miseries it did begin,
And fall amidst the glory of his tide:
Then in a booke where euery worke is writ,
Shall this man's actions bee reueal'd; to shew
The gainfull fruit of well-imployed wit,
Which payed to heauen the debt that it did owe:
Heere shall be reckoned vp the constant faith,
Neuer vntrue, where once he loue profest;
Which is a miracle in men (one saith)
Long sought, though rarely found: and he is best
,,who cã mak freindship, in those times of change,
,,Admired more, for being firme then strange.
When those weake houses of our brittle flesh,
Shall ruin'd bee by death; our grace, and strength,

Youth

For should he lie obscur'd without a tomb,
160   Time would to time his honesty commend;
Whiles parents to their children will make known,
And they to their posterity impart,
How such a man was sadly overthrown
By a hand guided by a cruel heart,
165   Whereof as many as shall hear that sadness
Will blame the one's hard fate, the other's madness;
Whiles such as do recount that tale of woe,
Told by remembrance of the wisest heads,
Will in the end conclude the matter so,
170   As they will all go weeping to their beds.
For when the world lies winter'd in the storms
Of fearful consummation, and lays down
Th'unsteady change of his fantastic forms,
Expecting ever to be overthrown;
175   When the proud height of much affected sin
Shall ripen to a head, and in that pride
End in the miseries it did begin
And fall amidst the glory of his tide;
Then in a book where every work is writ
180   Shall this man's actions be reveal'd, to show
The gainful fruit of well-employed wit,
Which paid to heaven the debt that it did owe.
Here shall be reckon'd up the constant faith,
Never untrue, where once he love profess'd;
185   Which is a miracle in men, one saith,
Long sought though rarely found, and he is best
        Who can make friendship, in those times of change,
        Admired more for being firm than strange.
When those weak houses of our brittle flesh
190   Shall ruin'd be by death, our grace and strength,

Youth, memory and shape, that made vs fresh,
Cast downe, and vtterly decay'd at length:
Whe all shall turne to dust from whence we came,
And we low leueld in a narrow graue,
What can we leaue behind vs but a name?
Which by a life well led may honour haue?
Such honor, ô thou youth vntimely lost,
Thou didst deserue and hast; for though thy soule
Hath tooke her flight to a diuiner coast,
Yet here on earth thy fame liues euer whole.
In euery heart seald vp, in euery toung
Fit matter to discourse; no day preuented,
That pitties not thy sad and suddaine wrong,
Of all alike beloued and lamented.
And I here to thy memorable worth,
In this last act of friendship, sacrifice
My loue to Thee; which I could not set forth
In any other habit of disguise.
Although I could not learne (whiles yet thou wert)
To speake the language of a seruile breath:
My truth stole from my toung into my hart,
Which shall not thence be sundred, but in death.
And I confesse my loue was too remisse,   (thee:
That had not made thee know, how much I pris'd
But that mine error was, as yet it is,
To thinke loue best in silence: for I siz'd thee
By what I would haue been; not onely ready
In telling I was thine; but beeing so,
By some effect to shew it: Hee is steddy
Who seemes lesse then hee is, in open shew.
Since then I stil reseru'd to trye the worst,
Which hardest fate and time thus can lay on mee.

B 2   T'inlarge

Youth, memory and shape that made us fresh
Cast down, and utterly decay'd at length;
When all shall turn to dust from whence we came
And we low-level'd in a narrow grave,
195 What can we leave behind us but a name,
Which, by a life well led, may honor have?
Such honor, O thou youth untimely lost,
Thou didst deserve and hast; for though thy soul
Hath took her flight to a diviner coast,
200 Yet here on earth thy fame lives ever whole,
In every heart seal'd up, in every tongue
Fit matter to discourse, no day prevented
That pities not thy sad and sudden wrong,
Of all alike beloved and lamented.
205 And I here to thy memorable worth,
In this last act of friendship, sacrifice
My love to thee, which I could not set forth
In any other habit of disguise.
Although I could not learn, whiles yet thou wert,
210 To speak the language of a servile breath,
My truth stole from my tongue into my heart,
Which shall not thence be sund'red, but in death.
And I confess my love was too remiss
That had not made thee know how much I priz'd thee,
215 But that mine error was, as yet it is,
To think love best in silence: for I siz'd thee
By what I would have been, not only ready
In telling I was thine, but being so,
By some effect to show it. He is steady
220 Who seems less than he is, in open show.
Since then I still reserv'd to try the worst
Which hardest fate and time thus can lay on me.

T'inlarge my thoughts, was hindered at firſt,
While thou hadſt life: I tooke this taske vpon me,
To regiſter with mine vnhappy Pen,
Such duties as it owes to thy deſert;
And ſet thee as a Preſident to Men,
And Limne thee to the world but as thou wert.
Not hir'd, as heauen can witneſſe in my ſoule,
By vaine conceit, to pleaſe ſuch ones as know it;
Nor ſeruile to be lik't; free from controule;
Which paine to many men I doe not owe it.
But here I truſt, I haue diſcharged now
(Faire louely branch too ſoone cut off) to Thee,
My conſtant and irrefragable vow,
As had it chanc't thou might'ſt haue done to mee.
But that no merit ſtrong enough of mine,
Had yeelded ſtore to thy well-abled quill:
Whereby t'enrole my name, as this of thine,
How ſ'ere inritched by thy plenteous skil.
Heere then I offer vp to Memory,
The value of my tallent (precious man)
Whereby if thou liue to Poſterity,
Though't be not as I would, tis as I can :
"In minds from whence endeauor doth proceed,
"A ready will is taken for the deed.
Yet ere I take my longeſt laſt farewell,
From thee, faire marke of ſorrow; let me frame
Some ampler work of thanke, wherein to tel
What more thou didſt deſerue, then in thy name,
And free thee from the ſcandall of ſuch ſenſes,
As in the rancour of vnhappy ſpleene,
Meaſure thy courſe of life (with falſe pretences)
Comparing by thy death, what thou haſt beene.

So

T'enlarge my thoughts was hindered at first,
While thou hadst life; I took this task upon me,
225   To register with mine unhappy pen
Such duties as it owes to thy desert,
And set thee as a president to men,
And limn thee to the world but as thou wert—
Not hir'd, as heaven can witness in my soul,
230   By vain conceit, to please such ones as know it,
Nor servile to be lik'd, free from control,
Which, pain to many men, I do not owe it.
But here I trust I have discharged now
(Fair lovely branch too soon cut off) to thee,
235   My constant and irrefragable vow,
As, had it chanc'd, thou mightst have done to me—
But that no merit strong enough of mine
Had yielded store to thy well-abled quill
Whereby t'enroll my name, as this of thine,
240   How s'ere enriched by thy plenteous skill.
Here, then, I offer up to memory
The value of my talent, precious man,
Whereby if thou live to posterity,
Though't be not as I would, 'tis as I can:
245   In minds from whence endeavor doth proceed,
A ready will is taken for the deed.
Yet ere I take my longest last farewell
From thee, fair mark of sorrow, let me frame
Some ampler work of thank, wherein to tell
250   What more thou didst deserve than in thy name,
And free thee from the scandal of such senses
As in the rancor of unhappy spleen
Measure thy course of life, with false pretenses
Comparing by thy death what thou hast been.

228 *limn*] depict or delineate
232 *owe it*] acknowledge it (servile behavior) as my obligation

„ So in his mifchiefes is the world accurſt,
„ It picks out matter to informe the worſt.
The wilfull blindneſſe that hood-winkes the eyes
Of men in-wrapped in an earthy vayle,
Makes them moſt ignorantly exerciſe,
And yeeld to humor, when it doth aſſaile;
Whereby the candle, and the bodies light
Darken's the inward eye-ſight of the mind :
Preſuming ſtill it ſees, euen in the night
Of that ſame ignorance which makes them blind.
Hence conſter they with corrupt Commentaries,
Proceeding from a nature as corrupt,
The text of malice; which ſo often varies,
As 'tis by ſeeming reaſon vnder-propt.
O ! whether tends the lamentable ſpight
Of this worlds teen-full apprehenſion ?
Which vnderſtands all things amiſſe; whoſe light
Shines not amidſt the darke of their diſſention ?
True 'tis, this man (whiles yet he was a man)
Sooth'd not the current of beſotted faſhion :
Nor could diſgeſt as ſome looſe Mimicks can,
An empty ſound of ouer-weening paſſion :
So much to bee made ſeruant to the baſe,
And ſenſuall aptneſſe of diſ-vnion'd vices :
To purchaſe commendation by diſgrace,
Whereto the world and heate of ſinne intices.
But in a ſafer contemplation,
Secure in what he knew, he euer choſe
The ready way to commendation,
By ſhunning all inuitemens ſtrang, of thoſe
Whoſe illneſſe is the neceſſary praiſe,
Muſt waite vpon their actions : onely rare

In

255   So in his mischiefs is the world accurs'd:
        It picks out matter to inform the worst.
        The willful blindness that hoodwinks the eyes
        Of men enwrapped in an earthy veil
        Makes them most ignorantly exercise
260   And yield to humor when it doth assail,
        Whereby the candle and the body's light
        Darkens the inward eyesight of the mind,
        Presuming still it sees, even in the night
        Of that same ignorance which makes them blind.
265   Hence conster they with corrupt commentaries,
        Proceeding from a nature as corrupt,
        The text of malice, which so often varies
        As 'tis by seeming reason underpropp'd.
        O, whither tends the lamentable spite
270   Of this world's teenful apprehension,
        Which understands all things amiss, whose light
        Shines not amidst the dark of their dissension?
        True 'tis, this man, whiles yet he was a man,
        Sooth'd not the current of besotted fashion,
275   Nor could disgest, as some loose mimics can,
        An empty sound of overweening passion,
        So much to be made servant to the base
        And sensual aptness of disunion'd vices,
        To purchase commendation by disgrace,
280   Whereto the world and heat of sin entices.
        But in a safer contemplation,
        Secure in what he knew, he ever chose
        The ready way to commendation,
        By shunning all invitements strange, of those
285   Whose illness is, the necessary praise
        Must wait upon their actions; only rare

255 *his*] i.e., its
256 *to inform*] to report as an accusation
265 *conster*] construe
270 *teenful*] grievous
275 *disgest*] 1. (to) stomach, or 2. (to) bring slowly to a state of perfection
286 *rare*] extraordinary

In beeing rare in fhame, which ftriues to raife
Their name by dooing what they do not care.
As if the free commiffion of their ill,
Were euen as boundleffe as their prompt defires:
Only like Lords, like fubiects to their will,
Which their fond dotage euer-more admires.
Hee was not fo; but in a ferious awe,
Ruling the little ordered common-wealth,
Of his *owne felfe* with honour to the law,
That gaue peace to his bread, bread to his health.
Which euer hee maintaind in fweet content,
And pleafurable reft; wherein he ioyd
A Monarchy of comforts gouernment,
Neuer vntill his laft to bee deftroyd.
For in the *Vineyard* of heauen-fauoured learning,
(Where hee was double honor'd in degree)
His obferuation and difcreet difcerning,
Had taught him in both fortunes to bee free.
Whence now retir'd home; to a home indeed;
The home of his condition and eftate;
Hee well prouided gainft the hand of need,
Whence yong-men fome time grow vnfortunate.
His difpofition, by the bonds of vnity,
So faftned to his reafon; that it ftroue,
With vnderftandings graue immunity,
To purchafe from all hearts a fteddy loue.
Wherein not any one thing comprehends,
Proportionable note of what hee was,
Then that hee was fo conftant to his friends,
As hee would no occafion ouer-paffe,
Which might make knowne his vnaffected care,
In all refpects of triall, to vnlock

His

In being rare in shame (which strives to raise
Their name by doing what they do not care),
As if the free commission of their ill
290   Were even as boundless as their prompt desires;
Only like lords, like subjects to their will,
Which their fond dotage ever more admires.
He was not so: but in a serious awe,
Ruling the little ordered commonwealth
295   Of his own self, with honor to the law
That gave peace to his bread, bread to his health;
Which ever he maintain'd in sweet content
And pleasurable rest, wherein he joy'd
A monarchy of comfort's government,
300   Never until his last to be destroy'd.
For in the vineyard of heaven-favored learning
Where he was double-honor'd in degree,
His observation and discreet discerning
Had taught him in both fortunes to be free;
305   Whence now retir'd home, to a home indeed
The home of his condition and estate,
He well provided 'gainst the hand of need,
Whence young men sometime grow unfortunate;
His disposition, by the bonds of unity,
310   So fast'ned to his reason that it strove
With understanding's grave immunity
To purchase from all hearts a steady love;
Wherein not any one thing comprehends
Proportionable note of what he was,
315   Than that he was so constant to his friends
As he would no occasion overpass
Which might make known his unaffected care,
In all respects of trial, to unlock

287 *rare in shame*] seldom remorseful
291 i.e., in appearance like lords, yet enslaved to their own will
301 *vineyard*] i.e., Oxford

His bofome and his ftore which did declare,
That Chrift was his, and he was *Frendſhips Rock:*
A Rock of *Frendſhip* figured in his name,
Fore-fhewing what he was, and what fhould be,
Moft true prefage, and he difchargd the fame,
In euery act of perfect amitye:
Though in the complementall phrafe of words,
He neuer was addicted to the vaine
Of boaft, fuch as the common breath affoords,
He was in vfe moft faft in tongue moft plaine,
Nor amongft all thofe virtues, that for euer,
Adorn'd his reputation, will be found
One greater then his *Faith* : which did perfeuer,
Where once it was protefted alway found.
Hence fprung the deadly fuell that reuiu'd
The rage which wrought his end; for had he been
Slacker in loue, he had beene longer liu'd,
And not oppreft by wraths vnhappy finne.
By wrathes vnhappy finne, which vnaduif'd
Gaue death for free good wil and wounds for
Pitty it was that blood had not beene prif'd (loue
At higher rate, and reafon fet aboue
Moft vniuft choller, which vntimely *Drew*
Deftruction on it felfe: and moft vniuft,
Robd virtue of a follower fo trew,
As time can boaft of both for *loue* and *truſt,*
„So henceforth all(great glory to his blood)
„Shall be but Seconds to him being good .
„The wicked end their honor with their finne,
„In death, which only then the good begin.
Loe heere a leffon by experience taught,
For men whofe pure fimplicity hath drawne,
                                        Their

His bosom and his store, which did declare
320 That Christ was his, and he was friendship's rock:
A rock of friendship figured in his name,
Foreshowing what he was, and what should be,
Most true presage; and he discharg'd the same
In every act of perfect amity—
325 Though in the complemental phrase of words
He never was addicted to the vain
Of boast, such as the common breath affords;
He was in use most fast, in tongue most plain,
Nor amongst all those virtues that for ever
330 Adorn'd his reputation will be found
One greater than his faith, which did persever,
Where once it was protested, alway sound.
Hence sprung the deadly fuel that reviv'd
The rage which wrought his end, for had he been
335 Slacker in love, he had been longer liv'd
And not oppress'd by wrath's unhappy sin—
By wrath's unhappy sin, which unadvis'd
Gave death for free good will, and wounds for love.
Pity it was that blood had not been priz'd
340 At higher rate, and reason set above
Most unjust choler, which untimely drew
Destruction on itself; and most unjust,
Robb'd virtue of a follower so true
As time can boast of, both for love and trust:
345 So henceforth all (great glory to his blood)
Shall be but seconds to him, being good.
The wicked end their honor with their sin
In death, which only then the good begin.
Lo, here a lesson by experience taught
350 For men whose pure simplicity hath drawn

321 *rock*] i.e., Peter, from Greek *petros,* rock
326–27 *vain / Of boast*] vanity of boasting; perhaps also boastful vein
328 *in use most fast*] of steadfast behavior
339 *that*] his
349 *taught*] i.e., is taught

'Their truſt to bee betrayd by beeing caught
Within the ſnares of making truth a pawne.
Whiles it not doubting whereinto it enters,
Without true proofe and knowledge of a friend,
Sincere in ſingleneſſe of heart, aduenters
To giue fit cauſe, ere loue begin, to end.
,,His vnfain'd friendſhip where it leaſt was ſought,
,,Him to a fatall time-leſſe ruine brought.
Whereby the life that purity adorn'd
With reall merit, by this ſudaine end,
Is in the mouth of ſome in manners ſcorn'd,
Made queſtionable, for they doe intend,
(According to the tenour of the Saw
Miſtooke, if not obſeru'd, writ long agoe)
When men were onely led by *Reaſons* law,
That ſuch as is the end, the life prooues ſo.
Thus *Hee*, who to the vniuerſall lapſe
Gaue ſweete redemption, offring vp his bloud,
To conquer death by death; and looſe the traps
Of Hell, euen in the triumph that it ſtood.
Hee thus, for that his guiltleſſe life was ſpilt
By death, which was made ſubiect to the curſe;
Might in like manner bee reprou'd of guilt,
In his pure life, for that his end was worſe.
But ô farre bee it, our vnholy lips
Should ſo prophane the Deity aboue:
As theerby to ordaine reuenging whips,
Againſt the day of *Iudgment* and of *Loue*:
The hand that lends vs honour in our dayes,
May ſhorten when it pleaſe; and iuſtly take
Our honour from vs, many ſundry wayes,
As beſt becomes that wiſedome did vs make.

The

Their trust to be betray'd by being caught
Within the snares of making truth a pawn;
Whiles it, not doubting whereinto it enters,
Without true proof and knowledge of a friend,
355 Sincere in singleness of heart, adventers
To give fit cause, ere love begin to end:
His unfeign'd friendship where it least was sought,
Him to a fatal timeless ruin brought;
Whereby the life that purity adorn'd
360 With real merit, by this sudden end
Is in the mouth of some in manners scorn'd,
Made questionable, for they do intend,
According to the tenor of the saw
Mistook, if not observ'd (writ long ago
365 When men were only led by reason's law),
That "Such as is the end, the life proves so."
Thus he, who to the universal lapse
Gave sweet redemption, off'ring up his blood
To conquer death by death, and loose the traps
370 Of hell, even in the triumph that it stood:
He thus, for that his guiltless life was spilt
By death, which was made subject to the curse,
Might in like manner be reprov'd of guilt
In his pure life, for that his end was worse.
375 But O far be it, our unholy lips
Should so profane the deity above
As thereby to ordain revenging whips
Against the day of judgment and of love.
The hand that lends us honor in our days
380 May shorten when it please, and justly take
Our honor from us many sundry ways,
As best becomes that wisdom did us make.

353 *it*] their trust
356 begin to end] begin, to end Q
378 *Against*] for the coming
382 *did us make*] that created us

The fecond brother who was next begot,
Of all that euer were begotten yet;
Was by a hand in vengeance rude and hot,
Sent innocent to be in heauen fet.
Whofe fame the Angels in melodious quiers,
Still witneffe to the world; then why fhould hee,
Well-profited in excellent defires,
Bee more rebuk'd,who had like deftiny?
Thofe Saints before the euer-lafting throne,
Who fit with crownes of glory on their heads,
Wafht white in bloud,from earth hence haue not
All to their ioyes,in quiet on their beds;   (gone,
But tafted of the fower-bitter fcourge,
Of torture and affliction,ere they gained,
Thofe bleffings which their fufferance did vrge.
Whereby the grace fore-promif'd they attained.
Let then the falfe fuggeftions of the froward
Building large Caftles in the empty ayre ,
By fuppofitions fond and thoughts vntoward,
(Iffues of difcontent and fick defpaire)
Rebound groffe arguments,vpon their heart;
That may difproue their malice : and confound
Vnciuill loofe opinions, which infert
Their foules into the roule,that doth vnfound
Betraying pollicies : and fhew their braines
Vnto their fhame ridiculous: whofe fcope
Is enuie,whofe indeuors fruitleffe paines,
In nothing furely profperous,but hope.
And that fame hope,fo lame,fo vnpreuailing,
It buries felfe conceit in weake opinion ;
Which beeing croft,giues matter of bewayling
Their vain defignes,on whom want hath dominiõ.

C   Such

The second brother, who was next begot
Of all that ever were begotten yet,
385   Was by a hand in vengeance rude and hot
Sent innocent to be in heaven set—
Whose fame the angels in melodious quires
Still witness to the world. Then why should he,
Well-profited in excellent desires,
390   Be more rebuk'd, who had like destiny?
Those saints before the everlasting throne
Who sit with crowns of glory on their heads,
Wash'd white in blood, from earth hence have not gone
All to their joys in quiet on their beds,
395   But tasted of the sour-bitter scourge
Of torture and affliction ere they gained
Those blessings which their sufferance did urge,
Whereby the grace fore-promis'd they attained.
Let then the false suggestions of the froward,
400   Building large castles in the empty air,
By suppositions fond and thoughts untoward
(Issues of discontent and sick despair)
Rebound gross arguments upon their heart
That may disprove their malice, and confound
405   Uncivil loose opinions which insert
Their souls into the roll that doth unsound
Betraying policies, and show their brains,
Unto their shame, ridiculous; whose scope
Is envy, whose endeavors fruitless pains,
410   In nothing surely prosperous, but hope—
And that same hope, so lame, so unprevailing,
It buries self-conceit in weak opinion;
Which, being cross'd, gives matter of bewailing
Their vain designs, on whom want hath dominion.

387 *quires*] i.e., choirs
406 roll] roule Q, a frequent Jacobean spelling for both *roll* and *role*
    unsound] 1. prove as unsound; 2. silence
409 *whose endeavors*] i.e., whose endeavors are
412 *in weak opinion*] in the weakness of their suppositions
414 *on whom want hath dominion*] over which dearth has dominion

Such, and of such condition may deuife,
Which way to wound with defamations fpirit,
(Clofe lurking whifpers hidden forgeries)
His taintleffe goodneffe, his defertfull merit.
But whiles the minds of men can iudge fincerely,
Vpon affured kno vledge : his repute
And eftimation, fhall be rumor'd cleerly,
In equall worth, Time fhall to time renew't.
The Graue, that in his euer empty wombe,
For euer clofes vp the vnrefpected,
Who when they dye, dye all ; fhall not intombe,
His pleading beft perfections as neglected.
They to his notice in fucceeding yeeres,
Shall fpeake for him, when Hee fhall lye below ;
When nothing but his memory appeares,
Of what hee was ; then fhall his vertues grow.
His beeing but a priuate man in ranke,
(And yet not rank't beneath a Gentleman)
Shall not abridge the commendable thanke,
Which wife pofteritie fhall giue him than :
For *Nature*, and his therein happy *Fate*,
Ordain'd that by his quality of minde,
T'ennoble that beft part, although his ftate
Were to a lower bleffedneffe confin'd.
Blood, pompe, ftate, honour, glory and command,
Without fit ornaments of difpofition,
Are in themfelues but heathnifh and prophane,[1]
And much more peacefull is a meane condition,
Which vnderneath the roofe of fate content,
Feeds on the bread of reft : and takes delight,
To looke vpon the labours it hath fpent,
For it's owne fuftenance, both day and night.

Whiles

415 Such, and of such condition, may devise
Which way to wound with defamation's spirit
(Close-lurking whisper's hidden forgeries)
His taintless goodness, his desertful merit.
But whiles the minds of men can judge sincerely,
420 Upon assured knowledge, his repute
And estimation shall be rumor'd clearly
In equal worth—time shall to time renew't.
The grave, that in his ever-empty womb
For ever closes up the unrespected,
425 Who, when they die, die all, shall not entomb
His pleading best perfections as neglected.
They to his notice in succeeding years
Shall speak for him when he shall lie below;
When nothing but his memory appears
430 Of what he was, then shall his virtues grow.
His being but a private man in rank
(And yet not rank'd beneath a gentleman)
Shall not abridge the commendable thank
Which wise posterity shall give him then;
435 For nature, and his therein happy fate,
Ordain'd that by his quality of mind
T'ennoble that best part, although his state
Were to a lower blessedness confin'd.
Blood, pomp, state, honor, glory and command,
440 Without fit ornaments of disposition,
Are in themselves but heathenish and profan'd,
And much more peaceful is a mean condition
Which, underneath the roof of fate content,
Feeds on the bread of rest, and takes delight
445 To look upon the labors it hath spent
For its own sustenance, both day and night;

439 *state*] high status
441 profan'd] prophane Q

Whiles others plotting which way to bee great,
How to augment their portion and ambition,
Doe toile their giddie braines, and euer fweat,
For popular applaufe, and power's commiffion.
But one in honour's like a feeled Doue,
Whofe inward eyes are dim'd with dignity;
Do's thinke moft fafety doth remaine aboue,
And feekes to be fecure, by mounting high:
,, Whence when he fals, who did ere while afpire,
,, Fal's deeper downe, for that he climed higher.
Now men who in a lower region liue,
Exempt from danger of authority,
Haue fitteft times in *Reafons rules* to thriue,
Not vext with enuy of prioritie.
,, And thofe are much more noble in the mind,
,, Then many that haue noblenesse by kind.
Birth, blood, and ancefters, are none of ours,
Nor can we make a proper challenge to them:
But vertues and perfections in our powers,
Proceed moft truly from vs, if we doe them.
Refpectiue titles or a gracious ftile,
With all what men in eminence poffeffe,
Are, without ornaments to praife them, vile:
The beauty of the mind, is noblenesse.
And fuch as haue that beauty, well deferue
Eternall characters, that after death
Remembrance of their worth, we may preferue,
So that their glory die not with their breath.
Elfe what auailes it in a goodly ftrife,
Vpon this face of earth heere to contend,
The goood t'exceed the wicked in their life,
Should both be like obfcured in their end?

Whiles others, plotting which way to be great,
How to augment their portion and ambition,
Do toil their giddy brains, and ever sweat
450 For popular applause and power's commission.
But one in honors, like a seeled dove
Whose inward eyes are dimm'd with dignity,
Does think most safety doth remain above,
And seeks to be secure by mounting high:
455　　Whence, when he falls, who did erewhile aspire,
　　　Falls deeper down, for that he climbed higher.
Now men who in a lower region live
Exempt from danger of authority
Have fittest times in reason's rules to thrive,
460 Not vex'd with envy of priority,
　　　And those are much more noble in the mind
　　　Than many that have nobleness by kind.
Birth, blood, and ancestors, are none of ours,
Nor can we make a proper challenge to them,
465 But virtues and perfections in our powers
Proceed most truly from us, if we do them.
Respective titles or a gracious style,
With all what men in eminence possess,
Are, without ornaments to praise them, vile:
470 The beauty of the mind is nobleness.
And such as have that beauty, well deserve
Eternal characters, that after death
Remembrance of their worth we may preserve,
So that their glory die not with their breath.
475 Else what avails it in a goodly strife
Upon this face of earth here to contend,
The good t'exceed the wicked in their life,
Should both be like obscured in their end?

451 *seeled dove*] in falconry, a pigeon with its eyes stitched shut so as to make it climb higher
460 *priority*] precedence in rank
462 *by kind*] by natural descent
472 *Eternal characters*] monumental inscriptions

Vntill which end,there is none rightly can
Bee termed happy,since the happinesse
D:pends vpon the *goodnesse* of the man,
Which afterwards his praises will expresse.
Looke hither then,you that inioy the youth
Of your best dayes ; and see how vnexpected
Death can betray your iollity to ruth ?
When death you thinke is least to be respected ?
The person of this modell here set out,
Had all that youth & happy dayes could giue him:
Yet could not all encompasse him about,
Against th'assault of death,who to relieue him
Strooke home but to the fraile and mortall parts,
Of his humanity : but could not touch
His flourishing and faire long-liu'd deserts,
Aboue fates reach,his singlenesse was such.
So that he dyes but once,but doubly liues,
Once in his proper *selfe*,then in his *name* :
Predestinated *Time*,who all depriues,
Could neuer yet depriue him of the same.
And had the *Genius* which attended on him,
Beene possibilited to keepe him safe,
Against the rigour that hath ouer-gone him,
He had beene to the publick vse a staffe :
Leading by his example in the path ,
Which guides to doing well,wherein so few
The pronesse of this age, to error hath
Informed rightly in the courses trew.
As then the losse of one,whose inclination
Stroue to win loue in generall, is sad,
So specially his friends, in soft compassion
Do feele the greatest losse they could haue had.
                                          Amongst.

Until which end, there is none rightly can
480 Be termed happy, since the happiness
Depends upon the goodness of the man,
Which afterwards his praises will express.
Look hither then, you that enjoy the youth
Of your best days, and see how unexpected
485 Death can betray your jollity to ruth
When death you think is least to be respected!
The person of this model here set out
Had all that youth and happy days could give him,
Yet could not all-encompass him about
490 Against th'assault of death, who to relieve him
Strook home but to the frail and mortal parts
Of his humanity, but could not touch
His flourishing and fair long-liv'd deserts,
Above fate's reach, his singleness was such—
495 So that he dies but once, but doubly lives,
Once in his proper self, then in his name;
Predestinated time, who all deprives,
Could never yet deprive him of the same.
And had the genius which attended on him
500 Been possibilited to keep him safe
Against the rigor that hath overgone him,
He had been to the public use a staff,
Leading by his example in the path
Which guides to doing well, wherein so few
505 The proneness of this age to error hath
Informed rightly in the courses true.
As then the loss of one, whose inclination
Strove to win love in general, is sad,
So specially his friends, in soft compassion
510 Do feel the greatest loss they could have had.

499 *genius*] tutelary god or attendant spirit

Amongst them all she who those nine of yeares
Liu'd fellow to his counsailes, and his bed;
Hath the most share in losse: for I in hers,
Feele what distemperature this chance hath bred.
The chast imbracements of coniugall loue,
Who in a mutuall harmony consent;
Are so impatient of a strange remoue,
As meager Death it selfe seemes to lament.
And weep vpon those cheeks, which nature fram'd
To be delightfull orbes, in whom the force
Of liuely sweetnesse playes, so that asham'd
Death often pitties his vnkind diuorce.
Such was the separation here constraind,
(Well-worthy to be termed a *rudenesse* rather)
For in his life his loue was so vnfain'd,
As hee was both an husband and a father.
The one in firme affection, and the other
In carefull prouidence, which euer stroue
With ioynt assistance to grace one another,
With euery helpfull furtherance of loue.
But since the summe of all that can be said
Can bee but said that *Hee was good*: which wholy
Includes all excellence can be displaide,
In praise of Vertue and reproach of Folly:
　　His due deserts, this sentence on him giues,
　　Hee dy'de in life, yet in his death hee liues:
Now run's the method of this dolefull song,
In accents breefe to thee; *O thou deceast* !
To whom those paines do onely all belong,
As witnesles I did not loue thee least.
For could my worthlesse braine find out but how,
To raise thee from the Sepulcher of dust;
　　　　　C 3　　　　Vndoub-

Amongst them all, she who those nine of years
Liv'd fellow to his counsels and his bed
Hath the most share in loss; for I in hers
Feel what distemperature this chance hath bred.
515   The chaste embracements of conjugal love,
Who in a mutual harmony consent,
Are so impatient of a strange remove
As meager death itself seems to lament,
And weep upon those cheeks which nature fram'd
520   To be delightful orbs in whom the force
Of lively sweetness plays, so that asham'd
Death often pities his unkind divorce.
Such was the separation here constrain'd
(Well-worthy to be term'd a rudeness rather),
525   For in his life his love was so unfeign'd
As he was both an husband and a father—
The one in firm affection and the other
In careful providence, which ever strove
With joint assistance to grace one another
530   With every helpful furtherance of love.
But since the sum of all that can be said
Can be but said that "He was good" (which wholly
Includes all excellence can be display'd
In praise of virtue and reproach of folly),
535   His due deserts, this sentence on him gives,
"He died in life, yet in his death he lives."
Now runs the method of this doleful song
In accents brief to thee, O thou deceas'd!
To whom those pains do only all belong
540   As witnesses I did not love thee least.
For could my worthless brain find out but how
To raise thee from the sepulcher of dust,

514 *distemperature*] distempered condition   *chance*] mishap
520 *whom*] i.e., which
524 *rudeness*] violence
533 *can be*] i.e., that can be
540 witnesses] witnesles Q

Vndoubtedly thou shouldst haue partage now,
Of life with mee; and heauen bee counted iust :
If to a supplicating soule, it would
Giue life a new, by giuing life againe
Where life is mist : whereby discomfort should
Right his old griefes, and former ioyes retaine.
Which now with thee are leapt into thy toombe,
And buried in that hollow vault of woe :
Expecting yet a more seuerer doome,
Then times strickt flinty hand will let 'em know.
And now if I haue leuel'd mine account,
And reckon'd vp in a true measured score,
Those perfect graces which were euer wont
To wait on thee aliue, I aske no more.
But shall heereafter in a poore content,
Immure those imputations I sustaine,
Learning my dayes of youth so to preuent,
As not to be cast downe by them againe:
Only those hopes, which fate denies to grant,
In full possession to a captiue hart :
Who if it were in plenty, still would want,
Before it may inioy his better part :
From which detain'd, and banisht in th'exile
Of dimme misfortune, ha's none other prop,
Whereon to leane and rest it selfe the while,
But the weake comfort of the haplesse *Hope*.
And *Hope* must in despight of fearfull change,
Play in the strongest closet of my brest:
Although perhaps I ignorantly range,
And court opinion in my deep'st vnrest.
But whether doth the streame of my mischance
Driue me beyond my selfe: fast friend, soone lost,

Long

Undoubtedly thou shouldst have partage now
Of life with me, and heaven be counted just
545 If to a supplicating soul it would
Give life anew, by giving life again
Where life is miss'd; whereby discomfort should
Right his old griefs, and former joys retain
Which now with thee are leapt into thy tomb
550 And buried in that hollow vault of woe,
Expecting yet a more severer doom
Than time's strict flinty hand will let 'em know.
And now if I have level'd mine account
And reckon'd up in a true measured score
555 Those perfect graces which were ever wont
To wait on thee alive, I ask no more
(But shall hereafter in a poor content
Immure those imputations I sustain,
Learning my days of youth so to prevent
560 As not to be cast down by them again)—
Only those hopes which fate denies to grant
In full possession to a captive heart
Who, if it were in plenty, still would want
Before it may enjoy his better part;
565 From which detain'd, and banish'd in th'exile
Of dim misfortune, has none other prop
Whereon to lean and rest itself the while
But the weak comfort of the hapless, hope.
And hope must in despite of fearful change
570 Play in the strongest closet of my breast,
Although perhaps I ignorantly range
And court opinion in my deep'st unrest.
But whether doth the stream of my mischance
Drive me beyond myself, fast friend, soon lost,

546 *Give life anew*] i.e., to the poet
546 *giving life again*] i.e., to the deceased
557 *content*] 1. satisfaction; 2. matter contained in writing
556–64 The sense here seems to be "I ask no more . . . except for those hopes
which fate denies to grant," etc. Hence the added marks of parenthesis in
lines 557–60, though the syntax remains problematic.
559 *prevent*] circumvent
563 *Who*] a captive heart   *it*] hopes [*sic*]
564 *it*] heart
566 *has none*] i.e., the heart has none
570 *closet*] 1. a strongbox for valuables; 2. private chamber
572 *court opinion*] pursue public favor; cf. line 92
573 *whether doth*] even if

Long may thy worthinesse thy name aduance,
Amongst the vertuous, and deseruing most.
Who herein hast for euer happy prou'd,
In *life* thou liu'dst, in *death* thou dyed'st *belou'd.*

FINIS.

575   Long may thy worthiness thy name advance
       Amongst the virtuous and deserving most,
          Who herein hast for ever happy prov'd:
          In life thou liv'dst, in death thou died'st belov'd.

                    FINIS

577 *Who*] thou who

Commentary

INTRODUCTION

The Subject: William Peter, 1582–1612

WILLIAM Peter, the second son of Otho Peter, gent., was christened in Devonshire on 31 December 1582 in the parish church of Shillingford St. George. He grew up on the Peters's Bowhay estate, in an elegant manor house built by his grandfather, John Peter, who was three times mayor of Exeter. Nothing else is known of William's childhood until 13 July 1599, when he entered Exeter College, Oxford (the school endowed by his great-uncle, Sir William). He matriculated three months later, on 26 October, and spent most of the ensuing decade at the University, though with several extended leaves of absence.

In the autumn of 1608—a year after his father's death and two years after completing his Master's degree—Peter finally withdrew from Oxford and returned to Bowhay, whereupon his thoughts turned to marriage. On 9 January following, he took to wife Margaret Brewton, the daughter of wealthy parents of Exeter and Whipton. Their marriage was brief. On 25 January 1612 Peter was slain by Edward Drew while riding home from an afternoon of carousing in nearby Exeter. His body was laid to rest on 1 February, in the church of St. Martin's, Exminster.

In addition to the *Elegy* itself, various documents concerning Peter's life have been preserved at Exeter, Oxford, and London, from which I have pieced together a fairly complete, if sketchy, biography. The coroner's inquest following his murder is of particular interest, since it provides a detailed account of Peter's last hours.[1] This and the other surviving records contain a good deal of useful information about William Peter, including a few notable surprises, yet there is nothing that cannot await publication elsewhere. My principal interest here lies rather in the *Funeral Elegy,* and in that W. S. who wrote the poem in February 1612. I shall, however, return to the circumstances of Peter's life as the need arises.

The Circumstances of Publication

On Thursday, 13 February 1612, just nineteen days after William Peter's death, the following entry was made in the Stationers' Register, at the Stationers' Hall in London:

Thomas Thorpe. Entred for his Copye vnder th'[h]andes of the wardens, A booke to be printed when it is further
aucthorized called, *A funerall Elegye in memory of the
late virtuous master WILLIAM PEETER of Whipton
neere Exetour . . .* vj d.[2]

Thomas Thorp, an affable and devout London stationer, was made a
freeman of the Company on 4 February 1594, upon completion of a nine-
year apprenticeship. His first independent publication came in 1600, with
a reprint of Lucan's first book as translated by Christopher Marlowe—
Thorp having acquired the rights to it from friend and fellow stationer,
Edward Blount. Since he had neither the wealth nor the influence to
acquire his own press, all of the fifty publications in which Thorp had a
hand were printed by other stationers; yet, though his booklist is rather
small when compared to that, say, of Edward Blount or Richard Field, he
was on friendly terms with many of the best writers of the age and
preserved for posterity some of their best work. Already by 1612 Thorp
had published four plays by George Chapman; two by John Marston; two
plays and three masques by Ben Jonson; *Eastward, Ho!* by Jonson,
Chapman, and Marston; Marlowe's translation of Lucan; Shakespeare's
Sonnets; John Healey's translations of Epictetus, Cebes, and Augustine;
plus a variety of devotional tracts, newssheets, satires, and the like; to
which he added, in February of 1612, this funeral elegy for Willam Peter,
by an author who chose not to place his name on the title page.

One of the first things worth noting about W. S.'s *Elegy* for William
Peter is that the poem is almost entirely without precedent. When it came
to publishing memorial verses, neither lack of talent nor lack of a famous
subject prevented any poem from going to the press, so long as the poet or
his patron had cash in hand. There is, however, only one example, prior to
the Peter elegy, of anyone having printed as an independent quarto a
memorial poem for a virtual unknown like William Peter. In 1595, in
Edinburgh, there appeared a pamphlet entitled, *A Memorial of the Life
and Death of Two Worthye Christians, Robert Campbel . . . and His Wife
Elizabeth,* by J. D. But this poem (written in 1574) is less an elegy than a
devotional tract, "a little treatise . . . brought to light" by the author (John
Davidson) for the purpose of "stirring up of the zeal of God's people
among us"—"God's people," in this case, referring to the followers of John
Knox. In addition, George Whetstone in 1577 published *A Remembraunce
of George Gaskoigne,* in tribute to a man of no rank who had nevertheless
been one of England's most influential and popular poets. There are,
finally, a few instances of broadside (single-sheet) epitaphs for London
merchants and other persons of no rank having been printed at private
expense. But apart from these few exceptions, there were no independent
publications, prior to 1612, in memory of anyone below the rank of knight,

or, in the ecclesiastical hierarchy, below the rank of bishop. If we exclude also memorial tributes to important public officials and to a few famed knights like Drake and Sidney, and a brief volume of epitaphs, privately printed, in memory of Sir William Buttes, no such work in English had ever before been printed for anyone outside the peerage.

The reason that elegies for persons of small fame are so rare during this era is simply that there was no money in it for either poet or stationer. Poetry may have sold better in 1612 than it does today, but that says little for the aesthetic sensibilities of the average book-buyer in King James's England. It is clear from the number and variety of surviving publications that most poetry sold well or poorly according to its subject matter, not according to its merits as literature. And since London booksellers were therefore not interested in helping to memorialize persons of no fame, no matter how great the verse, Renaissance poets craving success in the marketplace generally reserved their elegiac labors for departed celebrities; or, if dead celebrities were in short supply, for the deceased family members of likely patrons.

That the Peter elegy was privately printed is indicated first of all by the nature of its content—an elegy for a provincial gentleman of no obvious interest to London bookmen. Nor is there an "Epistle to the Reader," signed by the author or publisher, commending the book to the London reading public. Most telling of all, though the printer is identified as was (nominally) required—"Imprinted at London by G. Eld./1612"—the stationer's name nowhere appears in the volume, nor do the words "to be sold" appear on the title page. Apart from surreptitious or illegal publications, or works sold by subscription, the usual practice, almost without exception, was for the stationer to be identified in the front matter of all texts offered for public sale, even when the author's name was not, followed usually by the bookseller's address or sign. In most cases, if a stationer hired out the printing of a text, both his own name or initials and that of his printer are provided. This information appears usually on the title page, extra copies of which were customarily used by stationers for the purpose of advertisement.

Thomas Thorp never owned his own shop except perhaps as a minority shareholder. All of his commercial ventures were sold for him by other booksellers, most of them by his senior partners William Aspley at the Parrot (1603–9) and John Wright at Christ Church gate (1609–24), or by his friends Edward Blount and Walter Burre—yet he nevertheless took care always to assert his reproduction rights either on the title page, in the publisher's epistle, or both. The Peter elegy is one of only two instances in Thorp's twenty-five years as an active publisher of his having neglected to do so, the second being John Taylor's *Eighth Wonder of the World* (1613), which was probably one of many such projects financed by Taylor himself.

That neither Thorp's own name nor the address or sign of a bookseller is provided in the front matter of the *Elegy,* when taken together with the other evidence, points conclusively to a private printing.

Most other contemporaneous publications that lack the endorsement of a stationer appear, like the Peter elegy, to have been printed at a customer's expense, though these represent only a small portion of all works printed in Great Britain in the years 1570–1630. Of some two hundred separate publications of elegiac verse during these six decades, only thirty-four lack the usual marks of a book offered for public sale.[3] The example most closely analogous to the Peter elegy is *The Muses Mourning, or Funerall Sonnets for the Death of John Moray, Esq.* Moray, an untitled gentleman who died in prison in 1615, is as unlikely a candidate for a printed elegy as William Peter, except that the tribute was written by his "much beloved friend," John Taylor, who was fast becoming one of England's most financially successful poets. Like the Peter elegy, Taylor's poem is a rare exception in having been written for a person of no rank or fame. It, too, is the work of a single author and is numbered among those few works that bear no sign of having been designed for public consumption. In having such a work printed, Taylor was perhaps influenced by the earlier example of W. S.

If indeed W. S. paid for the printing of his *Elegy,* it is remarkable that we find no hint in the dedication, and none in the poem itself, that he expects to be reimbursed, much less rewarded for his labors. It was customary, when offering one's work to a prospective patron, to express one's hope of its receiving "favor and protection," or in similar euphemistic language to suggest that a gratuity would be much appreciated. This is especially true of those authors who paid the printer out of pocket. In any case, it would have been rather unusual for a poet to expect the patronage of a country squire like John Peter. Persons below the rank of knight were not, for the most part, literary patrons, nor was their patronage usually sought by writers who ventured their own capital. Under the circumstances, it seems reasonable to believe that William Peter was indeed the "fast friend" of W. S., that the poet wrote the poem of his own volition upon receiving news of his friend's death (as he professes in his text), and that he paid for the printing out of his own purse without expecting reimbursement.

AUTHORSHIP

ANY attempt to determine who wrote this *Funeral Elegy* for William Peter must doubtless begin with the initials, W. S., on the title page, and the first thing we must ask is whether the initials are not simply *wrong*. The answer is almost certainly no. There are a few known instances of Renaissance poems or plays having been issued, perhaps for the sake of improving sales, under the name or initials of a popular writer, even when the said writer had little or no part in the work. In none of Thomas Thorp's other publications is he guilty of such a practice, and there would be little cause for him to begin here, especially if, as appears to be the case, he never made any effort to market the volume for public distribution.

Scholarly investigation has shown that the use of false or transposed initials on printed works was the exception even when there was an apparent desire for anonymity, and then only when there appears to have been a good reason for concealing the author's identity, as in the case of a scurrilous satire or an unauthorized religious tract.[1] In the case of memorial verse the use of incorrect initials is unheard of, no matter who the publisher.

Nor was it in the least unusual, in Renaissance publications, to print only the author's initials when his identity was known to the persons for whom the work was printed or, in the case of books offered for public sale, when his identity was known to the London reading public—as, for example, in Spenser's *Daphnaida* ("By Ed. Sp."), Marlowe's Ovid ("By C. M.") or John Donne's posthumous *Poems* ("By J. D."). In the case of elegiac poems, it was quite ordinary for poets of the day merely to initial their verse or even to omit their name altogether; this was a practice mandated, perhaps, by a shared sense of decorum, since memorial verses were written, ostensibly, to honor the deceased and not to enhance the poet's own fame or income. Whether the W. S. who wrote the Peter elegy was famous or a complete unknown, there is nothing unusual in his failure to sign his full name to the work.

That the title page of the *Elegy* is followed by the author's own epistle to John Peter, a dedication again subscribed by "W. S.," makes it a virtual certainty that these were, indeed, the poet's correct initials. We may therefore ask what living individual with the initials "W. S." could have written this poem. "W. S.: a Checklist" (in appendix A of this text) attempts to provide the bibliographical data for all contemporaneous writers with the initials W. S., excluding only William Shakespeare (for whom a similar list is readily available in the *STC*) and William Strachey (whose works are listed in appendix B). The Checklist, based largely on the *STC* and on Williams's *Index of Dedications and Commendatory Verses,* embraces all relevant works of poetry or prose printed in the years 1570–1630, to which I have added the indexed manuscript verse in the Huntington, Bodleian, and British Libraries by any contemporaneous poet with these initials. During these six decades, about fifty published authors, bore the initials W. S. A majority of these were writers of devotional pamphlets and religious polemics; a few were dead by 1612 or under the age of fifteen. Yet even among those published W. S.'s who were certainly alive in 1612, I find it impossible to establish any direct ties to the Peters of Bowhay—unlike, say, the direct link between William Peter and Sir Arthur Gorges (a Dunchideok neighbor) or between the Peters and John Ford (a probable friend). Indirect ties may, however, be traced to three authors in the Checklist—William Slatyer, William Strachey, and William Shakespeare—all three of whom wrote poetry. We must consider also W. Shute, who translated Guillaume du Vair's *Holy Meditations Upon Seaven Penitentiall Psalmes,* a prose pamphlet printed for Thomas Thorp in 1612. Otherwise, the only remaining poets with these initials who were certainly alive in 1612 are William Segar, Wentworth Smith (a hack playwright who worked for Philip Henslowe from 1601 to 1603), the W. Smith (possibly Wentworth) who in 1613 wrote a play called *The Hector of Germany,* and the authors of a few scattered prefatory verses. To choose the likeliest candidate from among this group will not, of course, prove the authorship of the *Funeral Elegy,* for one may hypothesize, in addition to these, any number of poetic W. S.'s altogether unknown to us. But we can at least narrow the field.

   The work of William Segar and the two Smiths is discussed briefly in appendix A. Of these three, none can have had any connection with the Peter elegy. Slatyer, Shute, Strachey, and Shakespeare, however—all of whom have possible ties to William Peter, to Thomas Thorp, or both— invite a somewhat closer scrutiny. Slatyer deserves mention if only because his years at Oxford overlap with Peter's, and he is the only poet listed, apart from Strachey and Shakespeare, who is likely to have known persons within Peter's circle. He was born at Tykeham, near Bristol, and sometime later moved with his family to Somerset. On 6 February 1600, at age thirteen, he matriculated to St. Mary's Hall, Oxford. Peter at the time was a nineteen-year-old student at Exeter College. In 1607 Slatyer transferred to Brasenose, from which he graduated B.A. on 23 February 1609. He was made a fellow in 1611 and took his M.A. on 13 November of that year. In 1617 he served, first as treasurer of the Cathedral Church of St.

Davids, then as rector of Romany New Church. He began publishing poetry in 1619, took his B.D. and D.D. in December 1623, and was rector of Herden, Kent, from 1625 until his death on 14 February 1646.

Slatyer's first volume of poetry was a tribute to Queen Anne, entitled *Threnodia* (1619). The volume consists mostly of shape poems and acrostic verses of no value, and several epitaphs, the briefest of which is as follows (this and all quotations following are taken from the original publications, but are reproduced here in modernized spelling and punctuation, lest intrinsic merit should be obscured by illegibility):

EPITAPHIUM

Here lies entombed fair England's Queen,
Whose peer, earth now doth here avow t'have been scarce seen.

Few works of poetry are longer than Slatyer's *Palae-Olbion* (1621), a verse history of Great Britain, in which he traces two thousand years of English history. His epic grinds to a halt after some twelve thousand lines of doggerel, half in English, half in Latin. But his labored verse has no obvious affinities with the Peter elegy. Nor is there any external link between Slatyer and the Peter family, apart from Slatyer's presence in Oxford from 1600 to 1608.

Sometime early in 1612, in London, there was printed a devotional book for Thomas Thorp entitled, *Holy Meditations upon Seaven Penitentiall Psalmes,* composed "by G.D.V." [Guillaume du Vair], and Englished by one "W. Shute." This little volume conveys an extreme intensity of religious feeling. It begins thus in purple prose and continues so for three hundred pages:

Lay not upon me, O Lord, the arm of thy severe judgment. It would throw me like a torrent into the depth of death and eternal damnation. It would devour me like fire, and the remainder of my body would fly away into ashes. What eye is able to endure, without perishing for fear, the only look of thine angry countenance when casting thine eye upon us? Thou piercest the very bottom of our hearts and discoverest the secrets of our impure consciences. Our abominable sins will draw down thy just anger upon our heads, and thy enkindled wrath will throw us headlong into the gulf of pain, torments, and misery. . . .

The author ends on a consolatory note, looking forward to that day when he shall witness, with his own eyes, the wrath of God meted out to the strong and wealthy men of this earth, while he achieves the salvation denied to so many others. The translator, W. Shute, tells of his long "hours of melancholy bestowed on these holy meditations, with much satisfaction." Finding the work to be of great merit, he resolved at last to translate it for the edification of Sir Peter Manwood of Kent, Knight of the Order of the Bath.

Because Shute is one of only three W. S.'s represented in Thomas Thorp's booklist—together with Strachey and Shakespeare—he must be considered as a candidate for authorship of the Peter elegy. Unfortunately, little else is known of him. He published no poetry and no original prose works, only three translations from the French, the first of which was Thomas de Fougasses's *General Historie of Venice,* a twelve-hundred-page chronicle in two folio volumes. It was first entered in the Stationers' Register on 4 May 1611 to William Stansby, entered again on 12 August, and published by Stansby the following year. Next came his translation of du Vair's *Meditations,* entered to Thorp on 2 December 1611 and printed early in 1612. Upon completion of the *Meditations,* Shute fell to work on *The Triumphs of Nassau,* a chronicle by J. J. Orlers and H. de Haestens. He finished the project in only a few months' time. It was registered to stationer Adam Islip in April 1612 (three months after the death of William Peter) and published in 1613 as a four-hundred-page folio text.

After 1613, nothing more is heard of W. Shute. What little we know of him comes from the front matter of his three books, in which his name is printed a total of seven times, appearing each time as "W. Shute" or as "W. Shute, gent." He dedicates to Sir Peter Manwood his edition of du Vair's *Meditations,* and promises to "strive hereafter to present you with matter of some other subject," an effort that appears not to have been forthcoming; perhaps he was rebuffed by Manwood in his request for patronage. His two historical works—both of them rather dry, encyclopedic narratives—are dedicated to Lords Philip and William Herbert. Since both Peter Manwood and Philip Herbert were from Kent, it may be that Shute was a Kentishman as well. He appears to have been well-educated and, given his command of the French tongue, may have spent some years on the continent. It seems likely that he studied at Cambridge University, since there are eight unidentified Shutes who attended Cambridge in the years 1550–1615. There is no W. Shute, nor any unidentified person of this surname, who attended Oxford prior to 1662. Shute's dedications—his only surviving original work—are written in a mannered prose that has no obvious similarities to the Peter elegy, but it is impossible to say what his poetry might look like, should he have undertaken to write in verse. That he was hard at work on his translation of Orlers and de Haestens at the time of Will Peter's death does not preclude the possibility of his having taken time off from that project to work on a poem—any man who could translate two thousand pages of French prose in less than two years could, presumably, write a six-hundred line elegy in two weeks—yet the only evidence I have been able to muster in support of his authorship is the appearance in his works of isolated words that appear also in the *Elegy,* as for example *oblivion, zeal, limn, apprehension, genius, ornament, endeavors, diviner* and *compass about.* To conclude that he wrote the elegy for William Peter would require, without more evidence than this, an unadvised leap of faith, yet he cannot be flatly ruled out.

William Strachey and William Shakespeare require a more detailed consideration than either of these. Strachey is a little-known poet who composed several brief commendatory verses between 1604 and 1616. He is best known for his prose epistle from Virginia (written in 1610), which served as one of Shakespeare's sources for *The Tempest,* the elder poet having read it in manuscript (though it did not appear in print until 1625). There is no proof that either Strachey or Shakespeare was a close friend of William Peter, but both are able poets and both are associated with persons belonging to Peter's circle. Whether either of these men wrote the *Elegy* is more than I can say with certainty. I have chosen rather to play the advocate first for one, then for the other, presenting the available evidence for each—while keeping in mind that there were many W. S.'s living in England in 1612 besides William Strachey and William Shakespeare.

THE CASE FOR WILLIAM SHAKESPEARE

T HAT the *Elegy* for William Peter may have been written by William
Shakespeare is partly suggested by its frequent echoing of Shakespeare's plays and love poems. We shall look at some of the more striking
verbal parallels further along. But even if all readers were at once per-
suaded that the *Elegy* sounds like Shakespeare, such unanimity of intui-
tion would fail to serve as "proof" that William Shakespeare wrote it.
What is wanted rather is the closest possible scrutiny of the available
evidence for Shakespeare's authorship, together with all possible contrary
evidence. Nor is it enough simply to demonstrate that the poem has
certain Shakespearean qualities. It has to be shown that such qualities, at
least in this particular combination, are found nowhere *but* in Shakespeare, a formidable task. Lastly, it must be demonstrated that there is at
least a remote possibility that Shakespeare knew William Peter. It seems at
first quite unlikely, and perhaps altogether unbelievable, that a forty-seven-
year-old London playwright, comfortably well-to-do and thinking about an
early retirement, should take the time or trouble to write a funeral elegy
for a man almost twenty years his junior who lived more than one hundred
miles away.

To the end of comparing W. S.'s *Elegy* for William Peter with similar
efforts by other writers. I have compiled an exhaustive bibliography of all
the elegiac and sepulchral verse printed in the years 1570–1630 (totaling
81,602 lines), excluding poetry from unprinted manuscripts and all poetry
in a language other than English. I have doubtless missed a few stray
elegiac verses in this or that miscellany, but the bibliography (hereafter
referred to as the "Memorial Verse") is substantially complete, and is
printed, in its entirety, in appendix A.

For the purpose of more detailed comparison, I have, in addition,
abstracted from the Memorial Verse a "Cross-Sample" restricted to those
poems, of at least fifty lines, composed and printed in the years 1610–13 (a
quadrennium that has as its approximate midpoint the composition in
February 1612 of W. S.'s *Elegy* for William Peter); and to obtain the
broadest possible cross-sample of the best English poets, I have included
three additional poems—two by Francis Beaumont and one by Sir Arthur

80

Gorges—that were written during this four-year period but not immediately printed (these three being the only unprinted manuscripts included in the bibliography).

The Cross-Sample includes elegiac verse by such noted poets as Campion, Chapman, Davies, Donne, Heywood, Tourneur, Webster, Edward Herbert, and Richard Niccols. This wealth is due in large part to the death in November 1612 of Henry, Prince of Wales, the best-loved member of the royal family. His death submerged the nation in grief and stimulated a great outpouring of elegiac verse. Few years in English history have seen a greater volume of elegiac poetry than the years 1610–13. In addition to the many tributes to England's Prince Henry, the Sample includes Davies's funeral elegy for Elizabeth Dutton; Richard Johnson's memorial for the Earl of Salisbury; an anonymous elegy for Henry IV, King of France, and another translated from the French by Josuah Sylvester; Donne's elegy and two anniversaries for Elizabeth Drury; the lament of William Primrose for the Puritan divine Hugh Broughton; Beaumont's tributes to Lady Penelope Clifton and to Lady Manners, Countess of Rutland; and three short pieces by the Scotsman David Murray. I shall return to these as the need arises.

In presenting a case for William Shakespeare's authorship of the Peter elegy, we may begin with the dedication, since this short epistle to John Peter of Bowhay is not the only dedication that may have been penned by Shakespeare. We have also the dedications of *Lucrece* and *Venus and Adonis*, both addressed to the Earl of Southampton, and when we compare the *Elegy* dedication to that of *Lucrece,* we find that the two are remarkably similar in language and format. The one begins: "The love I dedicate to your Lordship is without end"; and the other: "The love I bore to your brother, and will do to his memory, hath crav'd from me this last duty of a friend." The poet goes on in each case to minimize the value of his work (a conventional feature of the Renaissance book-dedication): *Lucrece* "is but a superfluous moiety" of the author's devotion, and the *Elegy* is "but a second to the privilege of truth." Next comes a short disclaimer, or statement of intent. In *Lucrece* we read, "What I have done is yours, what I have to do is yours"; and in the *Elegy,* "Whatever is here done is done to him and to him only." Both dedications conclude with a promise—a promise to Southampton of continued duty, and to Peter's kin, a vow of remembrance and friendly respects.

In a fairly exhaustive search, I have not been able to find another dedication that so closely approximates Shakespeare's model. The striking likeness of these two epistles cannot be attributed solely to the dictates of convention. If this dedication was not written by William Shakespeare, it appears at least that the "real" W. S. has sought to imitate him. Nor is Shakespeare's dedication of *Venus and Adonis* without interest here, for its controlling metaphors (a friend as a strong prop, a harvest of worth, and a settling of accounts) are all three to be found again in the *Elegy,* where they are expressed in much the same language. The dedications are alike also in that all three are shorter than most Renaissance epistles (*Ven.,* 152 words; *Luc.,* 112 words; *Elegy,* 137 words); and all three lack the usual epigraph wishing happiness in this life and eternal life hereafter (or an equivalent phrase). Shakespeare prefers the simple form, "To [name and title]" for his epigraphs, as does W. S.

Prosody

W. S.'s *Elegy* for William Peter has some formal affinity with the Sonnets, for we find in it the same *abab cdcd efef* rhyme scheme and, frequently, the same syntactical organization of the quatrains, as in the "For when . . . / When . . . / Then . . ." series beginning in line 171 of the *Elegy* (cf. Sonnets 12, 15). We find moreover a rhymed couplet marking every major rhetorical shift—so that one might describe the resulting structure as a sequence of twelve expanded or contracted Shakespearean sonnets. If indeed Shakespeare wrote the *Elegy,* it is only natural that he should use a form more congenial to him than continuous couplets, for the couplet was always too confining for the extended and interlaced patterns of his verse. In fact, here as in the Sonnets, the couplets tend on the whole to be less successful than the quatrains—the first and third couplets in particular seem weak—so that even the poem's least resonant lines may seem to bear, ironically, the signature of William Shakespeare.

There can be little doubt where W. S. got the idea for using this particular format for a funeral elegy. Excluding sonnets, only three poems in the Memorial Verse, 1570–1630, are written in continuous quatrains—Samuel Daniel's "Funerall Poeme upon the Death of the Late Noble Earle of Devonshire," and John Cooper's "Funeral Tears" for the same man, both printed in 1606, before W. S.'s *Elegy*; and John Davies, "The Muses Teares" (1613). Of these three, only Daniel inserts couplets, sporadically, between the quatrains as is done here, and there are in addition several clear verbal echoes of Daniel's poem to be found in the Peter elegy. This in itself is of interest, since Shakespeare looked always to Daniel as one of his principal mentors. His debt was obvious even to his contemporaries, as is evident, for example, in the Cambridge *Parnassus* plays, wherein "Sweete Mr. Shakspeare" is charged with the "monstrous theft" of plagiarizing Daniel's verse wholesale. "I thinke," says Ingenioso, "he will runn throughe a whole book of Samuell Daniells."[1]

Daniel, however, in his lament for the Earl of Devonshire, did not make the mistake of calling his poem an "elegy." Renaissance elegies after

Spenser are typically written in rhymed couplets throughout, as in Donne, Drayton, and Jonson. This is especially true of university men. Already by 1600 there was nearly universal agreement among educated Englishmen that poets should follow the classical model, not Spenser's, if they wished to call their memorial verses by the name of "elegy." George Puttenham in his *Arte of English Poesie* (1589) describes the "distick," or couplet, as appropriate to elegy, epitaph, and epigram, three forms that are not to be "harmonically entertangled, as some other songs of more delicate musick be." Alternative labels included such terms as *funeral sonnets, funeral tears, complaint, lay, anniversary,* and the pastoral *eclogue,* though the classical influence is everywhere apparent, especially after 1600. Of those poems in the Memorial Verse called by some other name than *elegy,* nearly half are in couplets, many of them in hexameter, or in a pattern of alternating line-length, in obvious imitation of the classical "elegiac couplet," a model recommended by Puttenham, since "a limping *Pentameter* after a lusty *Exameter* [makes] it go dolourously more then any other meeter."[2]

Of more than five hundred poems in the Memorial Verse, only seven are clearly labeled as "elegies" which are not in rhymed couplets: Spenser's "Astrophel: A Pastoral Elegie" and, in the same volume, Roydon's "Elegie . . . for His Astrophill" (1587); Thomas Rogers's "Celestiall Elegies" for the Countess of Hereford (1598); the *Elegy* for William Peter, by W. S. (1612); *Two Elegies, Consecrated to . . . Henry Prince of Wales* (1613), the first by Christopher Brooke and the second by William Browne, both of whom greatly admired Spenser; and, lastly, William Slatyer's inept verses for Queen Anne, entitled "Elegia" (1619). That the author of this "Funerall Elegye" for William Peter risked the scorn of his better-educated contemporaries suggests that he, like William Shakespeare, was little moved by the disapproval of the classicists.

More important is the extraordinary frequency in the *Elegy* of enjambed, or "run-on," lines. W. S. is quite remarkable in this respect. But first some clarification is needed, since scholars frequently disagree in their definition of what constitutes a "run-on line." Enjambment, strictly speaking, does not depend on the vagaries of punctuation. If there is a syntactic break at the end of the line, even where no punctuation or pause is required, the line is not "enjambed." A standard measure of run-on lines in Shakespeare has therefore proven elusive. Some scholars (Marco Mincoff, for example), counting only syntactic enjambment, arrive at lower figures across the board than those scholars who count all unstopped lines as "run-on" (such as D. L. Chambers).[3]

As a measure of style, any reasonable definition is adequate so long as the same criterion is used throughout. In the ensuing tabulations for W. S., Shakespeare, and for the 1610–1613 Cross-Sample, I have sought objectivity by adopting a slightly different index than is usually employed, counting as "open" or "unstopped" all those verse lines that by today's standards require no end-punctuation, and that are not followed, in the line succeeding, by a parenthesis—regardless of whatever end-punctuation may appear in the original printed text. This has rendered much less arduous the task of evaluating some 128,000 lines of English verse. It should, however, be noted that the frequency of syntactically enjambed lines in Shakespeare, W. S., and in the Cross-Sample, is somewhat lower than the figures given below.

By anyone's measure, all poets tend to be more or less consistent in their "open" lines from one work to the next (except, of course, in very short poems). John Donne, for example, in his *First Anniversary* (1611), *Second Anniversary* (1612), and "Elegy on the Untimely Death of the Incomparable Prince, Henry" (1613), has in the three publications a percentage of unstopped lines, respectively, of 32.8, 32.8, and 32.7; or, as printed in the original quartos, 27.8, 28.1, and 28.6. The two elegies by John Davies included in the Cross-Sample have an index of 34.7 and 32.6, or, as first printed, 28.7 and 27.4; and so for almost any of Shakespeare's contemporaries.

In the Peter elegy there is an extraordinarily high incidence of open lines: 266 of 578 lines, or 46.0 percent, as against 45.9 percent in *Cymbeline,* 46.5 in *Winter's Tale,* 45.5 in *The Tempest,* 52.2 and 60.6, respectively, in Shakespeare's supposed portion of *Henry VIII* and *The Two Noble Kinsmen.*[4] Shakespeare is the only known poet living in 1612 (of any initials) whose frequency of unstopped lines ranges quite consistently above 40 percent. Though the general tendency in the literature of the period was an increased preference for enjambment, there are few poems or plays by any author in the years 1608–13 with an incidence approaching that found in Shakespeare, and these, almost without exception, are by poets in the London dramatic circle, most of them by Tourneur, Webster, Ford, Middleton, and Beaumont.[5] Even these five men, all of whom emulate Shakespeare in many ways, rarely exceed 45 percent in their frequency of open lines, and none prior to 1615 sustains a frequency comparable to that of Shakespeare's late plays.

Nor did Shakespeare himself learn overnight to master the art of enjambment. The remarkably high incidence of open lines in his last plays marks the culmination of a career-long trend, a pattern evident in table 1.1, which indexes unstopped lines in Shakespeare from the least frequency to the greatest (for a more reliable comparison, I have disregarded all but pentameter lines).[6] As with other such indices, this one fails to produce the precise order in which the plays were written, for there are, as always, intervening variables, such as the average speech-length. A play like *Othello,* with a great number of one- or two-line speeches in verse, tends

TABLE 1.1 / UNSTOPPED LINES				
Title	approximate date	pentameter lines	open lines	%
Err.	1591/2	1607	144	9.0
Shr.	1592/3	2045	214	10.5
Ven.	1592	1194	136	11.4
3H6	1591	2865	333	11.6
2H6	1591	2478	325	13.1
1H6	1592	2659	366	13.8
LLL	1595	1431	199	13.9
Tit.	1591/2	2427	347	14.3
MND	1595/6	1414	213	15.1
TGV	1592/3	1358	206	15.2
Rom.	1595	2555	398	15.6
R3	1592/3	3423	540	15.8
PhT	—	67	11	16.4
Luc.	1593	1855	322	17.4
Son.	—	2154	374	17.4
Jn.	1595	2560	452	17.7
Wiv.	1597	228	43	18.9
Ado	1598	660	131	19.8
JC	1599	2147	436	20.3
R2	1595/6	2757	570	20.7
LC	—	329	69	21.0
AYL	1599	983	216	22.0
Ham.	1600	2769	670	24.2
Oth.	1603/4	2284	556	24.3
TN	1600/1	782	192	24.6
MV	1597	2068	511	24.7
H5	1599	1795	466	26.0
2H4	1598	1495	400	26.8
Tro.	1601/2	1956	527	26.9
1H4	1597	1646	456	27.7
Tim.	1606/8	1541	430	27.9
MM	1604	1356	383	28.2
Lr.	1605	2055	609	29.6
Mac.	1606	1830	571	31.2
Per. 3-5	1607/8	880	280	31.8
AWW	1603/5	1364	461	33.8
Ant.	1606/7	2484	1014	40.8
Cor.	1607/8	2447	1071	43.8
Tmp.	1611	1410	642	45.5
Cym.	1609	2677	1228	45.9
WT	1610	2117	985	46.5
H8 (Sh.)	1613	1474	769	52.2
TNK (Sh.)	1613	1041	631	60.6

Mac. (Mid.)	—	49	13	26.4
Per. 1-2	—	645	125	19.4
H8 (Fl.)	1613	768	256	33.3
H8 (?)	1613	449	168	37.4
TNK (Fl.)	1613	1434	396	27.6
"Shall I die"	(Yale)	36	2	5.6

to have more end-stopped lines than might otherwise be expected, given its date, while those like *1 Henry IV,* with few one-line speeches in verse, tend to register a relatively greater use of enjambment. Nor is the index for a play written mostly in prose, such as *Merry Wives,* as significant statistically as that for a play with a great number of verse lines, such as *3 Henry VI* or *Cymbeline.* Lastly, blank verse has usually a slightly higher frequency of open lines than rhymed verse by the same author. But if we allow in Shakespeare's works a margin of error of just 2 percent in either direction there are few chronological anomalies—and with a margin of 5 percent there are none at all.

Shakespeare's gradual increase in unstopped lines is nearly imperceptible when one reads the plays in chronological order; yet his index triples in the first twenty years of his career, after which—beginning about 1608 with *Antony and Cleopatra*—he seems to have begun making a conscious effort to avoid end-stopped lines. Each of the last seven plays (including Shakespeare's supposed portion of *Henry VIII* and *The Two Noble Kinsmen*), has a frequency of open lines far above that normally found in contemporaneous works by other authors. Nor does any single poem in the Cross-Sample fall within the expected range for a work of this date by Shakespeare. The only three that come close are the elegies of Cyril Tourneur (42.3%, or 31.4% as originally printed in 1613), John Webster (42.1%, or 35.1% as first printed in 1612), and Francis Beaumont (43.3%, or 29.4% as first printed). All three were London playwrights, which suggests that the W. S. who wrote the *Elegy* may have been a playwright as well. There was, after all, no better exercise than the writing of blank verse by which to acquire the art of enjambment.

The first systematic study of Shakespeare's versification was done by Charles Bathurst (who, coincidentally, was descended from William Peter's elder brother John). In his *Remarks on Shakespeare's Versification* (1857), Bathurst points out the increasing frequency of enjambed lines in Shakespeare, and notes also the relatively high percentage in Shakespeare of feminine endings (Bathurst calls them "double endings"), most notably in the blank verse of the late plays, but true everywhere. There is little rhymed verse in the late plays with which to compare the Peter elegy, but feminine endings in Shakespeare's nondramatic verse fall within a very narrow range, from a low of 7.7 percent in the *Sonnets* to a high of 15.7 percent in *Venus and Adonis* (see table 1.2).[7] The mean frequency for the collected poems is 10.5 percent, excluding in every case end-words such as *power, field,* or *fuel,* which may be pronounced as a single syllable. Most other poets of the age rarely exceed 5 to 7 percent, though there are, of course, exceptions. Hugh Holland's 162-line elegy for the Prince (1613) has 114 feminine endings, or 70.4 percent (versus 77.9% in his elegy for King James, twelve years later). Of the thirty-six poets represented in the Cross-Sample, only three (Allyn, Burton, and Taylor) have a frequency within two points of Shakespeare's mean of 10.5 percent. Fifteen of the thirty-six poets studiously avoid feminine endings altogether, having a frequency of less than 1 percent. In W. S.'s elegy, 67 of 578 lines have feminine endings, for a frequency of 11.6 percent.[8]

TABLE 1.2 / FEMININE ENDINGS			
Title	Total lines	Feminine endings	%
Ven,	1194	188	15.7
Luc.	1855	198	10.7
PhT	67	6	9.0
Son.	2154	165	7.7
LC	329	29	8.8
Total	5599	586	10.5

Most feminine endings in the *Elegy* find close parallels in Shakespeare. A few examples:[9]

About him were a press of gaping faces, . . . /
All jointly list'ning, but with several graces,
As if some mermaid did their ears entice, . . .

(*Luc.* 1408–11)

Those noble twins of heaven-infused races, . . . /
Did jointly both, in their peculiar graces,
Enrich the curious temple of his mind; . . .

(*Elegy* 55–58)

But sorrow that is couch'd in seeming gladness
Is like that mirth fate turns to sudden sadness.

(*Tro.* 1.1.39–40)

Whereof as many as shall hear that sadness
Will blame the one's hard fate, the other's madness; . . .

(*Elegy* 165–66)

"I know not love," quoth he, "nor will not know it,
Unless it be a boar, and then I chase it;
'Tis much to borrow, and I will not owe it; . . ."

(*Ven.* 409–11)

Not hir'd, as heaven can witness in my soul,
By vain conceit, to please such ones as know it,
Nor servile to be lik'd, free from control,
Which, pain to many men, I do not owe it.

(*Elegy* 229–32)

Say thou art mine, and ever
My love, as it begins, shall so persever.

(*AWW* 4.2.36–37)

Nor amongst all those virtues that for ever
Adorn'd his reputation will be found
One greater than his faith, which did persever, . . .

(*Elegy* 329–31)

What's in the brain that ink may character
Which hath not figur'd to thee my true spirit?
What's new to speak, what now to register,
That may express my love, or thy dear merit?

(*Son.* 108.1–4)

Such, and of such condition, may devise
Which way to wound with defamation's spirit
(Close-lurking whisper's hidden forgeries)
His taintless goodness, his desertful merit.

(*Elegy* 415–18)

When most I wink, then do mine eyes best see,
For all the day they view things unrespected,
But when I sleep, in dreams they look on thee,
And darkly bright, are bright in dark directed.

(*Son.* 43.1–4)

The grave, that in his ever-empty womb
For ever closes up the unrespected,
Who, when they die, die all, shall not entomb
His pleading best perfections as neglected.

(*Elegy* 423–26)

W. S. is a skilled metrician. His elegy contains few irregular lines, and of these, none can be described as unfortunate. There are in the *Elegy* only two lines with an extra foot (122, 309), both of which are commensurate with Shakespeare's practice. For example, the elegist, in compiling a list of seventeen virtues that adorned William Peter, inserts in his iambic verse a single line of hexameter (122), as does Shakespeare in Timon's list of seventeen social goods (*Tim.* 4.1.15–21). In both cases the irregular line helps to vary the rhythm, breaking up the potential monotony of a list.

There are, of course, many Jacobean poets besides Shakespeare whose meter is as fluid as that found in the Peter elegy. But W. S. and Shakespeare are alike in that they both avoid frequent nonce-contractions to smooth out their meter after the fashion, say, of John Donne ("as t'her," "sh'was dead," "fitly'nd"). Especially worth notice in this respect is that Shakespeare and W. S., unlike most Jacobean poets, avoid nonce-contradictions in *'s* (= is). Barring the "standard" contractions with a pronoun or adverb (*he's, here's,* etc.), Shakespeare contracts *is* only four times in his combined nondramatic works. No examples may be found in the *Funeral Elegy.* By way of comparison, in an elegiac poem of comparable length—"The Muses Teares" of John Davies (630 lines)—*is* is contracted twenty-three times, and ten of these are nonce-contractions. Moreover, W. S., like Shakespeare in all of his nondramatic works, makes only sparing use of repetitious diction as a metrical device. Except for the purpose of dramatic dialogue, Shakespeare eschews the frequently repetitious diction of much Jacobean verse as is found, for example, in the poems of George Chapman and John Marston ("come, come"; "all, all"; "on, on"; "see, see"). And, like Shakespeare, W. S. avoids the regular but lickety-splickety rhythms of such poets as Josuah Sylvester and George Wither.

As has been illustrated at length by Dorothy Sipe, one of Shakespeare's primary metrical strategies is the use of syllabic variants.[10] Where John Donne writes such lines as this, "Nor could incomprehensibleness deter" (*First Anniversary* 469), Shakespeare would find a variant instead, or invent one, to normalize the meter. Whether or not Shakespeare wrote the *Elegy,* striking examples of Shakespeare's manner, as outlined by Sipe, are found throughout the poem. A few examples are given in table 1.3. I find no poet in the Cross-Sample whose metrical regularity depends as heavily on syllabic variants as does the verse of both William Shakespeare and W. S.

Rhyme

Both W. S. and Shakespeare, by means of run-on lines, act to suppress rhyme for the sake of a more natural syntax. This is a tendency not often found in contemporaneous verse. George Puttenham in 1589 advised that "the good maker will not wrench his word to help his rime, either by falsifying his accent or by untrue orthographie";[11] but most poets of the day were quite willing to wrench not just individual words, but entire sentences, into painful contortions for the sake of a rhyme, a practice

TABLE 1.3 / METRICAL VARIANTS		
W.S.	**line**	**variant**
memorable	5	memorial
comfortable	51	comforting
securèd	72	secure
blushless	94	unblushing
unblushing	145	blushless
ope	146	open
plenteous (2 sylls.)	240	plentiful
enwrapped	258	wrapped
conster	265	construe
disunion'd	278	disunited
invitements	284	invitations
content	297	contentment
joy'd	298	enjoy'd
pleasurable	298	pleasing
proportionable	314	proportionate
adventers	355	venters, ventures
timeless	358	untimely
made questionable	362	questioned
mistook	364	mistaken
writ	364	written
begot	383	begotten
fore-promised	398	promised
fruitless	409	unfruitful
taintless	418	untainted
repute	420	reputation
nobleness	462	nobility
specially	509	especially
worthless	541	unworthy
undoubtedly	543	doubtless
partage	543	partaking
supplicating	545	suppliant
more severer	551	more severe
in despite of	569	in spite of

everywhere evident in the 1610–13 Cross-Sample. One must constantly struggle with such sentences as this by Davies, "No crown, for prize, though it he touch'd, he found," in which normal syntax is mutilated for the sake of the rhyme.[12] By way of contrast, the rhymes in the Peter elegy are as unobtrusive as may be found anywhere in English verse prior to John Milton (including, even, the *Sonnets* of William Shakespeare).

The formation of rhyme in Renaissance poetry has long been a principal means (together with spelling) of ascertaining how our language was pronounced in the various parts of England. In the Peter elegy there are 289 end-rhymes, nearly a third of which are "imperfect" for the modern reader, yet virtually all of these (apparent) off-rhymes find parallels in Shakespeare, the majority of them in the identical word-pairs used here, as for example *care : are, reprove : love, strove : love, words : affords, great : seat, grave : have, tongue : wrong, blood : good, froward : untoward, spirit : merit, worth : forth, lost : most, parts : deserts, wert : heart,* and many other such. All of these pairs were, for Shakespeare, rhyming phonemes. The same appears to be true of W. S. It seems evident, for example, that both poets pronounce *wert, heart, parts* and *deserts* to rhyme with *art* or *arts* (cf. also *insert : heart* in lines 403–5 of the *Elegy* and, in Shakespeare, such rhymes as *art : convert, athwart : heart, convertest : departest*). W. S. rhymes *give him* with *relieve him,* while Shakespeare pairs *give me : relieve me* (in *Per.*), *lived* with *achieved* (in *H5*), *give* with *believe* (in *H8*), and so on. Unlike, say, Sir Arthur Gorges of Devonshire, both Shakespeare and W. S. appear to pronounce *relieve* and *achieve* with a shortened vowel.

That Shakespeare also pronounced such words as *strive, revive,* and *thrive* with a shortened vowel is worth note, for in this he differs from many of his contemporaries. Even so distinguished an authority as Fausto Cercignani finds it odd that Shakespeare should couple [to] *live : thrive (R2* 1.3.83–84) and *live : thrive : alive (AWW* 4.3.373–75). Lacking other examples, he concludes that "*live : thrive* is no rhyme at all."[13] But it seems clear that all such words in Shakespeare rest on a short vowel, as again in *live : contrive (JC* 2.3.15–16), *strives : gives : contrives (LC* 240–43), and in analogous combinations in which neither *live* nor *give* is a member. W. S.'s rhymes *live : thrive, liv'd : reviv'd,* and *lives : deprives* (457–599, 333–35, 495–97; cf. *lives : gives* 535–36). In this practice W. S. and Shakespeare differ markedly from such Devonshire poets as Arthur Gorges (1557–1625) and William Strode (1600–1645).

W. S.'s rhymes *remiss : is* (213–15) and *was : overpass* (314–16) are less noteworthy. For such words as *his, is,* and *was,* Cercignani "finds considerable fluctuation between *s* and *z* . . . in Shakespeare's day."[14] That Shakespeare pronounced these words with final *s* is attested by such rhymes as *his : kiss, is : amiss, this : bliss : is : kiss, was : grass,* and *was:pass.* But in this Shakespeare and W. S. are not unlike Ben Jonson, John Donne, George Chapman, and numerous other poets of the age.

For a more objective measure than is possible with any one of these particulars, we may divide W. S.'s end-rhymes into three categories: first, "identical" Shakespearean rhymes, that is, word-pairs in the *Elegy* that appear also in Shakespeare (excluding the same words in a different inflection); second, "analogous" rhymes, which have close Shakespearean parallels; and third, "unlikely" Shakespearean rhymes (that is, word-pairs without close analogues in Shakespeare's known verse).

Of the 289 word-pairs used by W. S., 129 have identical Shakespearean counterparts.[15] Of the remaining pairs, 158 find close analogues in Shakespeare. These include such typical examples as *prov'd:belov'd* in W. S. versus *approv'd:belov'd* in Shakespeare; *hers:years* in W. S. versus *hers:tears* in Shakespeare; *on me:upon me* versus *on you:upon you,* *taste:cast* versus *taste:fast* or *taste:last, days:ways* versus *day:way,* and so on. Only two rhymes in the *Elegy* may be described as "unlikely" Shakespearean rhymes—*command:profane* and *weight:right*—and neither of these is especially problematic. The first may be classed as an unlikely rhyme for any English poet, including W. S. himself. It is probably a misprint for *command:prophan'd,* which would be a perfect rhyme for most Jacobeans, Shakespeare included. Compare, for example, John Donne's *prophan'd:land* (*Lamentations of Jeremiah* 95–96), Spenser's *Diane:prophane* (*FQ* 4.10.30.1–3), or Chapman's *prophane:Plebian* (*Andromeda Liberata* 10–11). W. S.'s second "unlikely" Shakespearean rhyme, *weight:right,* is likewise improbable for most Jacobeans, including W. S., who elsehere rhymes *white:delight, light:night, spite:light, veil:assail,* and *constrain'd:unfeign'd.*[16] Clearly, neither off-rhyme suggests that W. S.'s pronunciation differed from that of Shakespeare (unlike, say, such rhymes in "Shall I die" as *shew:rue, plenty:scanty,* and *meadows:shadows).* I have nevertheless counted W. S.'s *weight:right* and *command:prophane* as "unlikely" Shakespearean rhymes, for a percentage of 0.69 percent. By way of comparison, we find nine "unlikely" Shakespearean rhymes in *Venus and Adonis* (1.51%), six in *The Rape of Lucrece* (0.75%), three in the *Sonnets* (0.28%), one in "A Lover's Complaint" (0.71%), and none in "The Phoenix and the Turtle."[17] In other words, W. S. has a lower percentage of "unlikely" Shakespearean rhymes than does Shakespeare himself in three of his five nondramatic works.

Any passage of English verse in the Southern tongue that contains at least fifty rhymes, randomly selected from Jacobean literature, is likely to have rhymes that are largely congruent with Shakespeare's practice. My own sampling suggests an expected range of 88–96 percent congruency with Shakespeare for any London poet in 1610–13, counting as "congruent" all rhymes that are identical or at least analogous to those found in the Shakespeare canon. W. S.'s *Elegy,* at 99.3 percent, has a greater concordance with Shakespeare than do most poems of comparable length by other authors. We may turn, for a comparison, to three passages of verse actually ascribed to Shakespeare in the seventeenth century that have been rejected as spurious by modern scholarship: first, the Hecate material in *Macbeth* (3.5.1–36 and 4.1.39–43, 125–32, including the full text of the two Middleton songs); second, the doubtful items in *The Passionate Pilgrim* (4, 6–14); and third, the lyric, "Shall I die, shall I fly." W. S.'s *Elegy* has a significantly greater concordance with Shakespeare than do any of these works (see table 1.4).[18]

TABLE 1.4 / RHYME					
Title	Total rhymes	Identical rhymes	Analogous rhymes	Likely Shakespeare rhymes	Unlikely Shakespeare rhymes
A Funeral Elegy	289	129 44.6%	158 54.7%	287 99.3%	2 0.7%
Macbeth Hecate passages	45	21 46.7%	22 48.9%	43 95.6%	2 4.4%
Passionate Pilgrim (4, 6-14)	78	30 38.4%	41 52.6%	71 91.0%	7 9.0%
"Shall I die"	74	26 35.1%	40 54.1%	66 89.2%	8 10.8%

Diction

Unlike any poem in the Cross-Sample, the Peter elegy has a remarkably high concordance with Shakespeare's cumulative vocabulary: of 4,318 words, the stems for all but four *(superlative, innated, conjugal, immunity)* may be found elsewhere in the poems and plays. W. S. registers as high a concordance with Shakespeare as Shakespeare himself. In fact, *Venus and Adonis, The Rape of Lucrece,* "The Phoenix and the Turtle," and "A Lover's Complaint" each registers a lower concordance with the Shakespeare canon elsewhere than does the *Elegy,* while the somewhat higher concordance found in the *Sonnets* is to be expected, since this is the longest of Shakespeare's nondramatic works, and since the sonnets were written over an extended period, unlike either the *Elegy* or the remaining canonical poems. The figures for Shakespeare are shown in table 1.5. The criteria used here to define "unique words"—words found in just one of Shakespeare's works—are those developed by Eliot Slater

TABLE 1.5 / UNIQUE WORDS			
Poem	Unique words	Total words	Unique words/ 1000
Ven.	101	9730	10.38
Luc.	149	14548	10.24
PhT	10	352	28.41
Son.	129	17520	7.36
LC	62	2563	24.19
Total	451	44713	10.08

and Alfred Hart.[19] If we apply the same criteria to the *Elegy,* we find forty-four unique words, for a frequency of 10.18/1000.

Even if we define a "word" (more narrowly than Hart and Slater) as a precise configuration of letters, there are in the *Elegy* only sixty-nine words not found in the canonical works. Twenty-five of these involve simply the addition or omission of an inflectional ending (*s* or *'s* for a noun, adverbial *-ly* or comparative *-er* for an adjective, or a different verb-ending) for words that otherwise appear in the plays or love poems. Nineteen are compounds ("sour-bitter," "harvest-like," and so on) in which both elements appear previously in Shakespeare. Eight involve the addition of a quantitative prefix or suffix: "*un*rememb'red," "*un*beseeming," "blush*less*," "*un*blushing," "gain*ful*," "teen*ful*," "*un*affected," "desert*ful*"; and four, the addition of a noun-suffix: "invite*ments*," "prone*ness*," "defam*ation*'s," "part*age*." "Adventers," "complemental," "pleasurable," and "possibilited" lack a Shakespearean precedent, though the stems in each case appear in Shakespeare, as in his use of "venter" and "adventerous" when a majority of writers in 1612 consistently use the modern form (with *-ur-* rather than *-er-*). This leaves us with nine words—"superlative," "surrounding," "innated," "concourse," "irrefragable," "disunion'd," "conjugal," "immunity," and "supplicating"—that might be cited as evidence against Shakespeare's authorship; but of these nine, at least seven—*conjugal* and *supplicating* are possible exceptions—appeared previously in works well known to Shakespeare, such as Holinshed's *Chronicles,* Camden's *Remains,* Daniel's *Cleopatra* and Florio's *Montaigne*; and all nine are of Latin derivation. Shakespeare in the last years of his career greatly expands his vocabulary. Apart from minor variations on previously used stems of the sort noted above, the vast majority of the new words are Latinate. It should be surprising therefore not to find in the *Elegy* at least a few such words not found earlier. We find, moreover, several Latin borrowings in the *Elegy* that belong certainly to Shakespeare's later vocabulary, as for example "eminence," "eminent," "misconstruction," "peculiar," "priority," and "questionable," none of which appears in his work until after 1600. "Judicious" (*Elegy,* 102) is thought to have made its first appearance in our literature in John Florio's *Giudicioso* (1598), but Shakespeare immediately adopted the word, and used it in *Merry Wives, Hamlet, Macbeth, King Lear,* and *Coriolanus.*

It is a commonplace observation that one of Shakespeare's characteristic means of adding words to our language, or at least to his own vocabulary, was with the *un-* prefix;[20] as in the *Elegy,* where we find "unrememb'red," "untouch'd," "unfit," "unbeseeming," "unfamiliar," "unburthen'd," "unfeign'd" (3x), "untimely" (3x), "unlov'd," "unblushing," "unhappy" (5x), "unsteady," "untrue," "unfortunate," "unaffected," "(to) unlock," "unadvis'd," "unjust" (2x), "unholy," "untoward," "uncivil," "(to) unsound," "unprevailing," "unrespected," "unexpected," "unkind," "undoubtedly," and "unrest"—an extraordinary number of *un-* words for a poem of less than 600 lines. Alfred Hart writes:

> The important group of words beginning with the prefix *un-* amounts to nearly four per cent. of Shakespeare's vocabulary; about a quarter are 'new' to literature. It follows logically, therefore, that we may expect to find in a play of Shakespeare's, and especially in a tragedy, a large number of words beginning with *un-,* a considerable number of them used by him for the first time. . . . Such are characteristics of almost all his plays, early or late.[21]

Hart notes that Chapman has in his twelve plays fewer "new" *un-* words than one finds in *Hamlet* alone. All ten of the "new" *un-* words in *The Two Noble Kinsmen* are in Shakespeare's portion, and the relative frequency of the *un-* prefix is four times higher in Shakespeare's than in Fletcher's portion. "None of his contemporaries or predecessors," concludes Hart, "approaches Shakespeare in the number of coined words of this type."

It appears that Hart has overestimated the actual percentage of *un-* words in Shakespeare's vocabulary. Spevack's *Concordance* registers 29,066 different "words" in Shakespeare (with a "word" defined as any particular configuration of letters); of these 724 are *un-* words, or 2.5 percent, about half the figure cited by Hart (he has perhaps counted *until, unless, unto, uncle,* and words beginning in *uni-* or *under-*). Hart likewise overestimates Shakespeare's uniqueness in this respect, for I find several poets who approach Shakespeare in their frequency of *un-* words, including, for example, such prominent authors as Edmund Spenser, Thomas Kyd, and Thomas Heywood. It is nevertheless true that Shakespeare's vocabulary contains an unusually high percentage of *un-* words, even at 2.5 percent. The same is true of W. S. In the *Elegy* (including the epistle, in which no *un-* words appear) there are 4,445 words. Of the 1,420 "different words" (using Spevack's definition), 28 are (different) *un-* words, or 2.0 percent. W. S. thus comes closer to Shakespeare's mean than does Shakespeare himself in *Venus and Adonis* (0.9%), *The Rape of Lucrece* (1.4%), the *Sonnets* (1.2%), and "A Lover's Complaint" (0.7%).

Of W. S.'s *un-* words, several appear only rarely prior to Shakespeare, or not at all. The *OED* (which is not, of course, exhaustive) offers only one prior instance each of the adjectives "unblushing" (Daniel, 1595) and "unfamiliar" (Hooker, 1594); only one of "unburthen'd" prior to *King Lear,* and that in an obscure legal document, where it is spelled with a *d* and not, as Shakespeare spells it, with a *th.* (Compare *unburthens* [*2H6* 3.1.156], *unburthen* [*MV* 1.1.133], *unburthen'd* [*Lr.* 1.1.41], and 57 occurrences in Shakespeare of *burthen-.*) The *OED* offers one instance of "unexpected" prior to *King John* (Sidney, 1586), while "unrespected" makes an early appearance in the *Sonnets.* "Unprevailing" (*Elegy,* 411) may be one of many such Shakespearean coinages: I have discovered no instance of it prior to Hamlet's "unprevailing woe" (*Ham.* 1.2.107) or, indeed, any additional examples during Shakespeare's lifetime; and unlike many subsequent writers, both Shakespeare and W. S. use the word to mean *unavailing* rather than *unprevalent.*

As noted by Hart, Shakespeare also has an unusually high frequency of words with the quantitative suffix *-less* or *-ful,* and he introduced many such words into our literature. W. S.'s vocabulary in this respect, too, looks markedly Shakespearean. For example, we find in the *Elegy* such relatively new words as "disgraceful" (the earliest *OED* citation is to Shakespeare's *1H6*), "offenseless" (the earliest citation is to *Oth.*), and "spleenful" (the *OED*'s first two instances are both by Shakespeare, in *Tit.* and *2H6*). That the *OED* cites Shakespeare for many such words in the *Elegy* is unremarkable in itself, since Shakespeare's works were an important source in compiling the *OED.* But having made a thorough search among the leading poets and playwrights of the age, I find no one whose vocabulary so closely matches Shakespeare's in its overlap with the particular *un-, -less,* and *-ful* words used by W. S.; nor is there apparent any major author who matches Shakespeare's use of these words, as a percentage of total vocabulary, more closely than W. S. As registered in Spevack, for every 1,000 (different) words in Shakespeare's total vocabulary, 48 end in the suffix *-ful* and 58 in *-less.* The ratio in the nondramatic works is 68/1000 and 71/1000, respectively. W. S. has 14 different words in *-ful* and 11 in *-less,* or 99/1000 and 77/1000, respectively. These figures are higher than for most poets in the Cross-Sample but are well within the probable range for a Shakespeare poem.

W. S.'s use of hyphenation is of equal interest, since every poet has his characteristic frequency and distinctive method of forming compounds. George Wither, for example, uses hyphenation for emphatic repetition, as in "deep-deep," "half-half," "last-last," "sad-sad," and sometimes for rhyming repetition, as in "sure-pure" or "high-flying-crying-dying crimes," all these examples being taken from his elegy for Prince Henry. William Basse, in his brief elegy for the Prince, employs "angel-like," "earth-like," "flower-like," "maid-like," "man-like," "new-built," "sea-like," "sun-like," "three-fork'd," "widow-like." Here as elsewhere Basse flogs his poor verse with a string of (noun)-*like* compounds, while using few other compound words. Josuah Sylvester is especially fond of triple and quadruple compounds, many of which are simply bad puns, and most of which reflect the moralistic flavor of his poetry. In his tribute to the Prince he employs "all-admir'd," "all-desir'd," "all-vertuous," "bib-all-nights," "case-pride," "church-goods," "face-pride," "four-wheel'd," "French-Italiate," "horse-leach," "in-sin-newation," "Mach-Aretines" (for Englishmen who think like Machiavelli and Aretino), "sea-crabs," "shin-pride," "shoo-pride," "sice-sink-ap-asses," "sin-full," "tap-to-bac-conists," "too-too-oft," "top-bough," "top-gallant," "wide-wide-yawn-ing," and "wit-wantons." One doesn't need to read these elegies to know that they were written by someone other than William Shakespeare. It is enough simply to see a list of their hyphenated words.

In the *Elegy* by W. S., however, we find twenty-two compound words, for a net frequency of 5.1/1000 words, as opposed to 4.4 in *The Winter's Tale* and 5.5 in *The Tempest* (excluding in each case the few hyphenated proper nouns and non-compounds). W. S.'s manner of hyphenation is indistinguishable from that of Shakespeare, whose practice in his non-dramatic poetry is quite consistent. Excluding, once again, words that are not genuine compounds ("a-bed," "a-playing," "bow-wow," "Ca-Cal-iban," "to-day," and so on), there are in Shakespeare's collected non-dramatic works 241 compounds, of which 152, or 63.1 percent, have as their second element a past or present participle, a figure nearly twice the average for other poets of the age (including, for all poets, such para-synthetic formations as "beef-witted," "beetle-headed," and "big-bellied"). (See table 1.6.)

Of the forty items in the Cross-Sample, twelve have a frequency of compound words within Shakespeare's range of 3.6–6.7, but of these, only three—William Drummond (2.18), Richard Johnson (3.33), and John Webster (3.05)—have a frequency of participial compounds within the expected range for a poem by Shakespeare. Of the twenty-two compounds in the Peter elegy, fourteen have as their second element a past participle: "never-blemish'd," "short-liv'd," "quick-brain'd," "too-short'ned," "heaven-infused," "clean-temper'd," "well-employ'd," "low-level'd,"

TABLE 1.6 / HYPHENATION						
	Ven.	*Luc.*	PhT	*Son.*	LC	Tot./Av.
hyphenated compounds/1000 words	64 6.58	98 6.74	2 5.86	63 3.60	14 5.46	241 5.39
participial compounds/1000 words	42 4.32	59 4.06	2 5.86	38 2.17	11 4.29	152 3.40

"well-abled," "heaven-favored," "doubled-honor'd," "well-profited," "fore-promis'd," and "long-liv'd"; and two, "best-speaking" and "close-lurking," are formed with a present participle, for a combined frequency of 3.71, well within Shakespeare's range of 2.17–5.86.

All these compounds are as we should expect them to be in a poem by Shakespeare. The first two instances of "short-liv'd" given in the *OED* are both by Shakespeare, though we needn't suppose it to be a Shakespearean coinage; "long-liv'd" appears in the *Elegy,* as in Sonnet nineteen, but was introduced to the language some two centuries earlier. To W. S.'s "quick-brain'd," we may compare Shakespeare's "quick-witted," "clay-brain'd," "dull-brain'd," "fat-brain'd," "hare-brain'd," "mad-brain'd," and others; and to W. S.'s "clean-temper'd," Shakespeare's "best-temper'd," "ill-temper'd," and "strong-temper'd," in addition to "clean-timber'd" in *Love's Labor's Lost,* with a possible quibble on "clean-temper'd." The addition of *fore-* to a past participle ("fore-promis'd," 398) is characteristic of Shakespeare, as in "fore-bemoaned," "fore-betray'd," "fore-recited," "fore-wearied," and "fore-vouch'd," all presumed to be Shakespearean coinages. The coupling of noun or adverb to a participle is again typically Shakespearean: W. S.'s "heaven-infused" and "heaven-favor'd" find such antecedents as Shakespeare's "heaven-bred," "heaven-hu'd," "heaven-kissing," "heaven-moving." The elegist's "never-blemish'd" recalls Shakespeare's "ne'er-touch'd," "never-erring," "never-daunted," and so on for many others, while William Peter's "*well-abled* quill" recalls both the "*well-refined* pen" of the rival poet (Son. 85.8), and Shakespeare's "*all-unable* pen" in the epilogue to *Henry V.* "Best-speaking," "low-level'd," "double-honor'd," and "close-lurking" find their parallels in "false-speaking," "best-moving," "low-crooked," "low-declined," "double-henn'd," "all-honor'd," "fell-lurking," and many other such, too numerous to mention.

The four words most commonly employed by Shakespeare in the formation of compound words are *well-* (used 95 times, coupled with 66 different words), *-like* (93 times with 74 words), *self-* (53 times with 42 words, not counting "self-same," a word found frequently elsewhere), and *all-* (39 times with 37 words). More than half the compounds using *-like* appear in the last eleven plays, and from *Macbeth* onward, all the plays have a frequency of "(word)-*like*" compounds falling within the exceedingly narrow range of 0.17 to 0.30/1000 words, with a combined average of 0.21 (as compared, say, to Basse, whose elegy for the Prince has a frequency of 5.61, while half the poets in the Sample have a frequency of zero.) The frequency of *-like* in the *Elegy* is 0.23 ("harvest-like"). Though Shakespeare's index for his three other favorites (*well-, self-, all-*) lack the consistency of *-like,* all three are represented in the *Elegy* in W. S.'s "well-abled," "well-employ'd," "well-profited," "well-worthy," "self-conceit," and "all-encompass." The two remaining compounds found in W. S. are "ever-empty" and "sour-bitter," the first of which has Shakespearean parallels in "ever-angry," "ever-blinded," "ever-burning," and so through the alphabet to "ever-valiant"; and the linking of not-quite redundant adjectives, as in "sour-bitter," is a Shakespearean hallmark, as in "sour-cold," "ashy-pale," "pale-dead," "dead-cold," "cold-pale," "moody-mad," and countless others.

Then, too, Shakespeare often took more liberties with existing words than his contemporaries. One of his most characteristic devices is the substitution of one part of speech for another, a noun for an adjective, adjective for verb, and so on, examples of which may be found in all of his works. This interchange of grammatical forms was a recognized rhetorical figure, known in Latin as *permutatio.* It is very frequent in Shakespeare, as has been noted in numerous studies of Shakespearean style.[22] In the *Elegy* we find such examples as "defame" for *defamation* (40), "joy'd" for *enjoy'd* (298), "remove" for *separation* (317), and "boast" for *boastfulness* (327). All of these appear previously in Shakespeare, but they may be found also, with varying frequency, in non-Shakespearean texts. More interesting is W. S.'s use of the pronoun "all" as an absolute, with a definite article (154). The *OED* affords only one similar instance prior to Shakespeare's *Sonnets* ("God, the great All"), in a poem by Thomas Bastard.[23] Also noteworthy is W. S.'s use of "vain" for *vanity* (326). The *OED* lists only two similar occurrences between 1450 and 1742 (Josuah Sylvester [1606] and Owen Feltham [1628], to which may be added Shakespeare's *Measure for Measure* (2.4.12, with a pun on *vane*) and *Troilus and Cressida* (2.3.200 [*vaine* Q1, *veine* F1] and 5.3.32 [*vaine* Q, F1], with a pun on *vein* in both passages); and unlike either Sylvester or Feltham, both Shakespeare and W. S. appear to select "vain," rather than "vanity," for the sake of a pun. "Thank" for *thanks* or *thankfulness* is rare as well. The editors of the *OED* offer only two instances during Shakespeare's lifetime—one in George Gascoigne (1577) and one in the Douay Bible (1609)—to which may be added *Richard II* (2.3.65) and W. S.'s *Elegy* (433).

"Possibilited," a noun transfigured as a past participle (500), is unique to this text. It does not appear either in Shakespeare or, if the *OED* may be trusted, anywhere else. As the most extraordinary example in the *Elegy* of *permutatio,* it deserves further comment. Alfred Hart has found such formations to be markedly distinctive of Shakespeare's verse, particularly in the late plays. Hart writes,

> I find but seven unusual verbs of this kind in the sixteen plays of Marlowe, Greene, Peele, and Kyd, and can trace but one such instance in the twelve plays of Chapman. The last plays of Shakespeare teem with daringly brilliant metaphors due solely to this use of nouns and adjectives as verbs.[24]

Hart offers such late Shakespearean examples as "urn," "chapel," "corslet," "skiff'd," "niggard," "port," "jaw," "knee," "virgin'd," "mountebank," "bonnetted," "fisted," "feebling," "furnace," "disaster," "fever," "brooch'd," "tongue," "brain," "climate," "base," "oar'd," and others, all used as active verbs in the last plays, and he suggests that his list could easily be "trebled from these plays alone." But "Even Shakespeare's daring ingenuity," says Hart, "could not compel certain nouns to do duty as active verbs."

> He therefore transmuted them into participles used adjectively by adding *-ed* to them. Usually the "new" word so formed is in the passive voice. These formations are so numerous in the poet's plays that a large number of illustrative quotations is not necessary.[25]

Hart nevertheless goes on to provide such examples from the last plays as "servanted," "carbunkled," "token'd," "chalic'd," "dasied," "star'd," "fringed," "legg'd," "pioned," "twilled," "helmeted," "dregg'd," "scissor'd," "brimm'd," "mason'd," and others. Hart writes that

> The habitual use of these formations seems peculiar to Shakespeare; they are almost unknown to his predecessors and I have found three only in the twelve plays of Chapman.[26]

Hart finds that "The presence of six such 'new' words in Shakespeare's presumed portion of *The Two Noble Kinsmen*" (against none in Fletcher's portion) "gives additional support to the opinion that he wrote it."[27] The same may be said of "possibilited" in the *Elegy* by W. S.

Shakespeare is known also for preserving the form, while altering the meaning, of words. A characteristic example is his substitution of "memorable" for "commemorative," as in *Henry V,* wherein Fluellen wears a leek in his cap "as a *memorable* trophy of predeceas'd valor" (*H5* 5.1.72). Here "memorable" is employed to denote a "trophy" that is not itself something to be remembered, but that rather *aids* the memory. Again in the same play King Henry wears a leek for a "*memorable* honor" (4.7.104), to which may be compared W. S.'s "*memorable* monument" in line five of the *Elegy*. To use "memorable" in this sense is so extraordinary that it has not merited an entry in the *OED*. The only example I have found elsewhere of "memorable" approximating Shakespeare's usage is in *2 Tamburlaine*—"each shall retain a scroll / As memorable witness of our league" (1.1.145)—wherein the adjective may be taken to mean "memorial."

A related phenomenon, though perhaps less striking, is Shakespeare's use of "comfortable" where most contemporaries prefer "comforting." Characteristic Shakespearean examples include, "Be comfortable to my mother," "speak comfortable words," "his comfortable temper has forsook him," "No comfortable star did lend his light." The word appears thirteen times in Shakespeare, and all but once is used as an approximate synonym for "comforting" or "cheering." The sole exception is in *Pericles* 1.2.36, in a passage generally agreed to be the work of someone other than Shakespeare. Among the principal sixteenth- and seventeenth-century poets, only George Herbert uses "comfortable" as Shakespeare does to denote that which gives cheer, though there is perhaps a similar instance in Milton's "comfortable heat" in *Paradise Lost*. Spenser, Sidney, Marlowe, Jonson, and Donne, for example, all prefer either "cheerful," "comforting," or a suitable alternative. W. S., however, uses the word after Shakespeare's manner:

His younger years gave comfortable hope
To hope for comfort in his riper youth, . . .

(51–52)

Another noteworthy characteristic of W. S.'s diction is the relative sparsity in this poem of proper nouns and adjectives. Shakespeare in his dramatic works has fewer proper nouns, and far fewer classical allusions, than do most of his contemporaries. The same may be said of his nondramatic works. Apart from personified common nouns, we find in "A Lover's Complaint" (329 lines) only "May and April"; in "The Phoenix and the Turtle" (62 lines), only "Arabian." In *Venus and Adonis* (1,194 lines), apart from the names of the title characters and Cupid, we find only four proper nouns, each used once. In the *Sonnets* (2,154 lines), the names of the months are used seven times, the names of classical figures seven times, "Grecian" once, and "muse" (capitalized in some editions) seventeen times. The majority of Renaissance verse is far more heavily peppered with proper nouns. For example, in Ben Jonson's elegy for Shakespeare (again excluding personified common nouns) there are thirty-two proper nouns and adjectives in only eighty lines. In the 13,200 lines of the 1610–13 Cross-Sample there are 1,689 proper nouns, with a low of 0.72/100 lines (by Holland), a high of 60.83/100 lines (by Primrose), and a combined incidence of 12.80/100 lines. In the Peter elegy there is one proper noun in 578 lines, for an incidence of 0.17/100 lines, or a mere 1 percent of the Jacobean average, excluding Shakespeare.

W. S.'s subordinating conjunctions are of equal interest. We find here one instance of "sith," and several of "whiles." For adverbial use (excluding the use of "while" as a noun), "whiles" is often the preferred form in Shakespeare's printed works, despite the tendency of compositors to substitute, in such cases as this, the dominant form of the word. Moreover, the use here of "sith" and "whiles" suggests that the author of the Peter elegy may belong to the older generation of poets. "Sith" appears sporadically throughout the seventeenth century (though obsolete by 1700 except as a poetic archaism), and "whiles" survived in Scotland and the North Country well into the nineteenth century. Yet both words by 1612 were falling out of use in the Southern tongue. Of those poets in the Memorial Verse for whom such information is available, the median date of birth is 1579. Of these, the median birth-date for those who use "sith" is 1568, for those who use "whiles," 1566, and for those who use both, 1552. A few poets, like John Davies of Hereford (1565–1618), use "sith" almost exclusively. William Shakespeare, like W. S., uses "sith" and "since" more or less interchangably, but prefers the latter to either "sith" or "because"—and this, too is instructive, for Shakespeare over the course of his career gradually abandoned the use of "because." If one arranges the plays according to the ratio of "since" to "because," one arrives at an order similar to that in which they were written, from a low in *Titus Andronicus* (3/9), *1–2 Henry VI* (5/12 and 6/7), and *Two Gentlemen of Verona* (12/15), to a high in *Antony and Cleopatra* (15/1), *Cymbeline* (20/1), *Pericles* 3–5 (6/0), and *The Tempest* (18/0). If Shakespeare, shortly after writing *The Tempest,* were to write a poem 4,328 words long with an equivalent frequency for both words, we should expect to find four occurrences of "since," and none of "because," precisely what we find in the *Elegy.*

One peculiar feature of Elizabethan verse that all but vanishes from our literature by the middle of the seventeenth century is the use of "that" as a conjunctional affix. In Spenser's poetry, something like one in ten of the subordinating conjunctions is followed by a "that" that serves no necessary grammatical function, but only smoothes out the meter. In Milton, there are no such examples to be found. Examples of "that" as a conjunctional affix may be found in nearly ten percent of the poems listed in the Memorial Verse, being linked to "as," "because," "how," "if," "lest," "since," "sith," "when," "where," "while," "whilst," "whiles," and "until." Shakespeare uses redundant "that" with all of these, as well as with "besides," "though," "till," "unless," and "whether," albeit without any clear pattern. What makes this phenomenon especially worth notice is that the conjunctional affix rarely appears as late as 1612 except in works by the older generation then living. Still more important is that William Shakespeare and W. S. differ from those poets who by analogy came to add the affix to "for," a coordinating conjunction. Most poets who add "that" to "for" do so in precisely the same way that they add it to the subordinators, and for the same purpose of smoothing an otherwise irregular line, as in Henry Peacham's pastoral elegy for Prince Henry ("She Archon hight, *for that* she had no peer" [line 7]), or again in John Wilson's lament for the Prince:

> all the world doth
> Stand amaz'd, when they see a blazing star
> . . . .
> *For that* a comet, by experience known,
> Like to mishaps, doth never come alone.
>
> (1–6)

Similar examples of "for that" may be found in memorial poems by Samuel Daniel, Francis Hamilton, and Thomas Churchyard, in which the second word is extraneous—even where (as in the examples cited above) "for that" can be construed to mean *because*. One finds in addition poets who use the phrase, "for that," in such a way that the first word, "for," is the redundant element, as in James Maxwell's memorial to Prince Henry (1612). Comparing the deceased prince to Henry the saint, Maxwell writes,

> Both's fate it was to make this isle to shed
> Huge streams of tears, *for that* in youthful prime
> Such wights of worth should fall before their time.
>
> (178–80)

Here the weight of the sense is borne entirely by the second element, "that." The unnecessary "for" merely smoothes out the meter.

Shakespeare, somewhat differently from either of these, almost always uses "for that" as a substitute for "because," which word (as already noted) is often avoided, especially in the late works; and the phrase is indissoluble. For example, in the final scene of *Measure for Measure*, Angelo at his trial tells Duke Vincentio that his betrothal to Mariana

> . . . was broke off,
> Partly *for that* her promised proportions
> Came short of composition, but in chief

For that her reputation was disvalued
In levity.

(MM 5.1.218–22)

The Duke, unpersuaded, first reproves Angelo, then condemns him to die as Claudio died, professing that "like doth quit like"; but he absolves Mariana of guilt, saying,

I thought your marriage fit; else imputation,
For that he knew you, might reproach your life,
And choke your good to come.

(MM 5.1.420–22)

To such usage we may compare W. S.'s *Elegy,* in which "for that" is used in identical fashion, as in these lines:

He thus, *for that* his guiltless life was spilt
By death, which was made subject to the curse,
Might in like manner be reprov'd of guilt
In his pure life, *for that* his end was worse.

(Elegy 371–75)

Here, as in Shakespeare, "for that" is used as a substitute for "because," and neither "for" nor "that" is redundant. To remove either will not simply disrupt the meter, but confuse the sense. The substitution occurs four more times in the *Elegy* by W. S. (in lines 34, 110, 155, 456), and dozens of times in the plays and poems of William Shakespeare. Never in Shakespeare is there a redundant "for" in these constructions, and with one exception (*Mac.* 4.3.185), never after *Richard II* (1595) may the second element, "that," be removed. Both Shakespeare and W. S. use "for that" in effect as a single word, synonymous with "because"—which is all the more remarkable in that the substitution does simply nothing for the meter. "For that" and "because," both iambs, are metrically identical.[28]

There is much more that one might say concerning the affinities of diction between W. S. and William Shakespeare. For example, Shakespeare makes sparing use of "very" in his poetry—only eleven times in his combined nondramatic verse, for a relative frequency of 0.25/1000 words; as here where "very" appears only once (line 45), for a frequency of 0.23. And unlike his practice in the plays (where "very" is of course used conversationally), when Shakespeare does use "very" in his nondramatic verse, he reserves it for use as an adjective rather than as an adverb, as in "very smell," "very lists," "very eyes," "very part," "very birds," "very woe," "very refuse"; the only exceptions are "very late" in *Venus and*

Adonis, and "very same" (twice) in the *Sonnets.* Of the thirty-six poets represented in the Cross-Sample, only John Donne and George Wither use "very" as an adjective, Donne once in 1,248 lines, Wither eight times in 960 lines. In the *Elegy,* W. S.'s single "very" is an adjective modifying "virtues."

One might approach W. S.'s diction from the opposite angle by pointing out all the words characteristic of the age that are *missing* from the *Elegy*—"eft" (for *again*), "eke" (for *also*), "yer" (for *ere*), "ne" (for *never*), "enow" (for *enough*), "hight" (for *named* or *called*), "when as" (for *when*), "whereas" (for *where*), and many other such—which, though frequently used by other poets, are generally avoided by Shakespeare, as by W. S. The absence of such words is hardly conclusive, but their failure to appear in the Peter elegy does rule out a great number of other poets who use them continually, as is true also of un-Anglicized Greek and Latin words or phrases, which many poets affect as a means of displaying their erudition. It is also worth noting before moving on that W. S.'s *Elegy,* unlike a very substantial percentage of Renaissance verse, is markedly free of provincial words and phrases, and of noteworthy provincial spellings. If W. S. is from Devonshire, he shows no trace of a West-County dialect (unlike, say, Sir Arthur Gorges). W. S. appears rather to have spent much of his adult life in or near London, busily assimilating a vocabulary much like that of William Shakespeare.

Spelling

Spelling in Renaissance England was very much a personal affair, except in the classical languages and, to a lesser degree, in English words derived from classical roots. Native words were spelled phonetically, though not by any established system. Educated letter-writers not only could, but did, spell words any way they pleased. As a result, orthography in Jacobean manuscripts is largely the product of the author's pronunciation (which varied from county to county), coupled with his individual habits of representing the vowel sounds.

Of those contemporaneous authors for whom we have surviving manuscript copy, none is entirely consistent, though most abide by recognizable patterns, and most have a few consistent peculiarities of spelling not often found elsewhere. Were we to begin with an unsigned Jacobean manuscript, it might therefore be possible to identify the author largely on the basis of spelling, if the orthography closely matched that of a writer for whom sufficient manuscript copy has come to us—provided, of course, that the orthographic evidence was not contradicted by calligraphy, style, and substance.

In printed texts—such as the 1612 Quarto of the Peter elegy—orthography is of limited usefulness as a clue to authorship, since printers made no conscious effort to preserve original manuscript spellings. Compositors usually memorized a line of copy, set it up, then moved on to the next. In the process, the compositor's own habitual spelling tended to supersede the author's. Thus, for example, George Eld, who frequently substituted prefixal *in-* for manuscript *en-* (and *im-* for *em-*). Nevertheless, it has long been established that manuscript orthography (whether in Shakespeare's hand or in the hand of a scribe) exerted a persistent influence on compositors in the typesetting of Shakespearean texts (as is true also of virtually any contemporaneous author). Granted, we cannot be certain in any given instance that a word in the First Folio or in the best quartos represents the poet's original spelling. We may, however, take as authorial those spellings that appear consistently in a broad sample of the best texts—which is to say, in those plays and poems thought to have been typeset from Shakespeare's own papers, such as the early narrative poems, the first Quarto of *Richard II,* and the First Folio text of *Coriolanus.* We may assume also to be authorial a majority of those spellings that appear repeatedly and in more than one text (even if inconsistently) when these are incongruent with the respective printers' usual habits of normalization. By this means we have been able to agree on a surprising number of preferred Shakespearean spellings.

The *Elegy* Quarto of 1612 is remarkably congruent with what we know of Shakespeare's orthographical habits. To begin, the poem was obviously written by someone who spoke the Southern tongue, and probably by a long-time resident of London. More importantly, of those words that appear in the twenty-one pages of the *Elegy* Quarto and that appear also in the good quartos of Shakespeare's plays and poems, there is not a single spelling in the Quarto that lacks a Shakespearean counterpart.

Those spellings of W. S. that escaped normalization by Eld's compositor are found in all the best Shakespearean texts. W. S.'s "sunck," for example, is typical also of Shakespeare, as has been noted by Dover Wilson.[29] We find "bancks" in *Lucrece,* "sunck," "ranck," "winck," "banckes," "wrinckles" in the *Sonnets,* and numerous related instances in the dramatic quartos. Then, too, it is known that Shakespeare, like W. S., usually spelled such words as *public* or *fantastic* with a final *-ick* (rather than *-ique* or *-ike,* standard alternates); and it is thought that Shakespeare, like W. S., preferred *-ence* to *-ense* for such words as *defense, expense, pretense,* and *recompense.*

Shakespeare is one of many Renaissance authors who, like W. S., habitually wrote "spight" and "despight"; this, by way of a mistaken analogy with such native words as *light, night,* and *right,* even though *spite* is etymologically distinct, being derived from Old French *despit.* We know also, from the original printed texts of *Venus and Adonis, A Midsummer Night's Dream,* and *Coriolanus,* that Shakespeare, like W. S., spelled *dissension* in *-tion,* though *-cion* and *-sion* are more commonly found elsewhere. To these may be added numerous other, equally striking, examples. It is a virtual certainty that Shakespeare preferred the spellings "flote" (for *float*), "hart" (for *heart*), "mist" (for *missed*), "sute" (for *suit*), and "wast" (for either *waist* or *waste*); as well as "chast," "perswasion," "priuiledge," "reprooue," "stile," "wisht," and "sudaine" (alt., "sodaine"). All of these are found in the *Elegy,* even though Eld's compositors generally preferred "chaste," "float," "heart," "miss'd," "reprove," "waste," and "wish'd." With the remaining four (*persuasion, privilege, sudden,* and *suit*), it is not entirely clear what spelling prevailed among Eld's compositors.

Shakespeare usually wrote "then" for both *than* and *then.* The usual exception is when he wishes to rhyme either of these with another word ending in *-an,* at which times he uses "than" for both—as in *The Rape of Lucrece,* where Shakespeare rhymes "then" (Q: *than*) with "ran" and "began" (*Luc.* 1437–40). This is precisely the pattern followed by W. S., who uses "then" for both *than* and *then* except when rhyming "then" (Q: *than*) with "man" and "gentleman" (*Elegy,* 78, 434). Also noteworthy in the *Elegy,* though not extraordinary, is the doubling of consonants in polysyllabic words of foreign derivation, which Partridge finds everywhere characteristic of Shakespeare, and doubled *l* throughout except in conjunction with another consonant or before final *-e.* The doubled *l* appears to have been used almost exclusively by Shakespeare for all words of two or more syllables, and in the suffix *-full;* as is true also of W. S. (as in "choller," "cruell," "equall," "fatall," "hopefull," "mallice," "mortall," "pollicies," "thankfull," and so throughout the *Elegy* Quarto). W. S.'s "choller" is especially worth note, for Shakespeare's habitual spellings, "choller" and "chollerick," are quite unusual; both show a disregard of the Latin root, *cholera.* The *OED,* in one thousand years of the written language, offers 135 citations of *choler-* (including all words with this stem). Of these 135 examples, only 13 have a doubled consonant, and 5 of those 13 examples are supplied by Shakespeare. That "choller" was Shakespeare's preferred spelling is evident, for example, in Q2 of *Hamlet* (4 times) and in the First Folio text of *Coriolanus* (twice).

A notable exception to the double-consonant pattern in Shakespeare is the spelling, "adicted" (e.g., *Ham.* 2.1.19). This again reflects a disregard for its Latin root, *addictus;* to which may be compared W. S.'s "adicted" in the dedication to the *Elegy.* Among eighty-three instances of *addict-* recorded in the *OED,* the sole non-Shakespearean instance of *adict-* is found in John Marston (1598), who, unlike either Shakespeare or W. S., apparently spelled the word with an apostrophe ("adic't").

A. C. Partridge notes that Shakespeare tended to omit apostrophes when eliding preterits, though by 1600 the vogue of the printers was to use the full orthography -ed, or the conventional -'d, after both voiced and unvoiced stem-finals.[30] In the *Elegy*, as in the *Sonnets*, it appears from the rather haphazard refinement of marked elision that Eld's compositor worked from copy in which the apostrophes were largely or completely absent. Moreover, Shakespeare was one of many writers who tended to invert the endings of preterits with stems ending in unstressed -en or -er, as in *Lucrece*, where we find "fastned," "remembred," "battred," "falne," and (in the dedication) "lengthned"; as also in the *Elegy*, where we have "fastned," "unremembred," "sundred," and "shortned." To these may be added literally dozens of other spellings found in the *Elegy*— "doe," "goe," "loe," "heere," "neere," "theerby," "joynt(ly)," "foorth," "affoords," "becomming," "shew," "strooke," "(un)burthen(d)," "(un)fain(d)," "yeeld," "lim" (= *limb*), "sence," "toung," "vertue," and so on—none of which taken alone is extraordinary by contemporary standards, but which are known to be in agreement with Shakespeare's usual practice.

Were it certain that Shakespeare wrote the manuscript addition to *Sir Thomas More*, one might stress such spellings as "bloud," "hart," "strang," "trew," "whiles," "voyce," "choyce" in the *Elegy*, versus "bloud," "hart," "straing," "trewe," "whiles," "voyce," "noyce" in Hand *D* of *Sir Thomas More*; "adicion," "afoord," "banck," "grote" in Hand *D*, versus "adicted," "affoord," "sunck," "flote," in the *Elegy*; "then" for *than* in both; and so on for many similar examples. But since the attribution of Hand *D* is still disputed by some scholars (though I think wrongly), the orthography of that document has no certain bearing on the Peter elegy. We must depend rather on those spellings that, by reason of their consistency in the best texts, are unquestionably "preferred" Shakespearean spellings, irrespective of *Sir Thomas More*.

Accidence

Though every Renaissance author has a few peculiarities of grammatical accidence, the morphology and inflection of words in this *Elegy* by W. S. cannot be distinguished from Shakespeare's. To begin, there is a relatively high frequency of superlatives, a feature common to all the late plays. In the *Elegy* we find "strongest," "greatest," "least," "longest," "hardest," "last," "wisest," "the all of all," "deep'st," "best-speaking," "best perfections" (plus many more instances of "best" or "perfect"), "absolutely blest," "superlative," and so on, most of which appear in phrases with precise Shakespearean parallels. It might be supposed that the frequent use of superlatives in the *Elegy* is simply the result of a generic mandate to *praise,* but a second look shows that less than one in ten of the superlative constructions refers to William Peter.

Of special interest is W. S.'s use of the word *most.* Though not previously noted in the criticism, the frequency of *most* (excluding its use as a substantive) is one of the best indices for dating Shakespeare's work, and certainly one of the simplest. Using no other information but the frequency of adverbial or adjectival *most,* one arrives at the order shown in table 1.7 for the plays and poems. As is the case with almost any stylistic index, there are a few anomalies: *Merry Wives of Windsor,* written almost entirely in the "low" style, has a smaller frequency of *most* than should otherwise be expected, while *Hamlet* has a greater, and *Love's Labor's Lost* a far greater, incidence than one should expect, given their respective dates; and there is a surprising disparity between the two parts of *Henry IV.* In the case of *Love's Labor's Lost,* the anomalous frequency of *most* may be partly explained as Shakespeare's lampoon on the mannered language of academe, which was heavily peppered with superlatives (as, for example, in the prose of Gabriel Harvey, a scholar who has sometimes been seen in the figure of Don Armado). The habitual superlatives in the writing (and presumably in the speech) of contemporaneous scholars were due partly to the influence of classical models. But if Shakespeare in *Love's Labor's Lost* pokes fun at the "most vain" learning, "most fine" figures, "most maculate" thoughts, "most singular" epithets, "most serious" designs (etc.) of academics, he came nevertheless, over a period of years, to adopt the same mannerism without the benefit of having attended the university (*LLL* 1.1.72; 1.2.55, 92; 5.1.15, 99). Already by 1600 his frequency of *most* was as high, and by 1610, higher, than that of most Oxford wits. Since we know that the *Elegy* for William Peter was written in February 1612, we should expect to find in it a frequency of at least 1.3/1000 words if written by Shakespeare, as in all works written by him after 1600, and—though the index of a single word is necessarily less predictable in a short text than in a play of 16,036 words—ideally we should expect to find an incidence close to that of *The Tempest* (= 2.6). In the *Elegy* we find "most deserving," "most fast," "most ignorantly," "most in itself," "most plain," "most unjust" (twice), "most safety," "most share," "most true," and "most truly," for an identical incidence of 2.6.[31]

Even the grammatical "solecisms" are typically Shakespearean: "more severer" (551) takes its place beside "more better," "more bigger," "more bigger-look't," "most boldest," "more braver," "most bravest," "most busil'est," "more corrupter," "most coldest," "most dear'st," "more harder," "more headier," "most heaviest," "most most loving," "more worse," "most worst," "more worthier," and "most worthiest," all se-

TABLE 1.7 / ADV., ADJ. MOST		
Title	**absolute frequency**	**frequency 1000/words**
3H6	5	0.2
Shr.	7	0.3
Wiv.	9	0.4
Luc.	6	0.4
Tit.	9	0.5
TGV	9	0.5
1H4	12	0.5
Ven.	5	0.5
2H6	14	0.6
Rom.	16	0.7
Jn.	14	0.7
1H6	15	0.7
LC	2	0.8
R2	17	0.8
MV	18	0.9
Err.	13	0.9
R3	31	1.1
Ado	24	1.2
MND	20	1.2
Tro.	34	1.3
Son.	25	1.4
JC	28	1.5
Mac.	24	1.5
2H4	40	1.6
H5	42	1.6
TN	32	1.7
AYL	36	1.7
Cym.	46	1.7
TNK (Sh.)	17	1.7
AWW	41	1.8
Per. 3-5	20	1.9
Cor.	50	1.9
Tim.	36	2.0
Lr.	51	2.0
WT	50	2.0
Oth.	56	2.2
H8 (Sh.)	27	2.2
MM	53	2.5
LLL	53	2.5
Ant.	60	2.5
Tmp.	42	2.6
Ham.	81	2.7

Mac. (Mid.)	0	0.0
Per. 1-2	3	0.4
H8 (Fl.)	12	1.7
H8 (?)	8	2.0
TNK (Fl.)	12	0.9
"Shall I die"	0	0.0

lected from the last seven plays. These redundancies are not so commonly found in Renaissance literature as is often supposed, and are quite rare even in Shakespeare's work prior to 1600. From the beginning of his career through *As You Like It,* there are twenty such instances in the combined plays and poems; from *Hamlet* on, there are forty-three.[32] The Memorial Verse 1570–1630 contains work by more than two hundred poets. Of these, only seven employ redundant *-er* or *-est:* Browne's "worser," Churchyard's "most clearest," Drummond's "more sweeter," Ford's "more primer," Heywood's "perfectest," Whetston's "more better," and Taylor's "worser"—three of the seven involving the use of "perfectest" or "worser," which words appear to have enjoyed a certain measure of respectability. Of the seven poets who use redundant *-er* or *-est,* only Drummond is a university graduate.

Turning to the verbs, we find "have strove" (142), as in *Henry VIII* (2.4.30), not the more orthodox *have strived* or *striven* (as, for example, in the Authorized Version of the Bible, 1611). Though not extraordinary, "strook" (491), rather than the Jacobean alternatives *strake, stroke,* or *struck,* is the most frequent Shakespearean preterit for *strike;* and if, in line 386, "set" is an irregular participle for *seat* (rather than the usual *seated*), it, too, is exampled elsewhere in Shakespeare, as in *Venus and Adonis,* "being set, I'll smother thee with kisses" (*Ven.* 18).

Worth notice also is the poet's use of *hath* and *doth* in third person singular present indicative, for both notional and auxiliary use, when many poets in 1612 preferred *has* and *does.* David Lake, in his monumental survey of Elizabethan and Jacobean dramatic literature, finds that all four auxiliaries were used, at least desultorily, by most of Shakespeare's contemporaries, many of whom preferred either *hath* to *has,* or *doth* to *does.* But fewer than half of the writers surveyed by Lake are like Shakespeare and W. S. in preferring both *hath* and *doth.*[33] In the *Elegy, doth* and *hath* are used throughout. The only exceptions are "Do's thinke" (453) and "ha's none other" (566), to avoid a lisping "Doth think" or "hath other," as is commensurate with Shakespeare's practice elsewhere (as in *Ham.* 1.1.21 and 2.1.49). Then, too, W. S.'s apparent spellings, "ha's" and "do's," are worth note. Lake examines 120 plays by 36 playwrights and 12 anonymous plays, including many that were printed by George Eld (who also printed the *Elegy*). Lake, in a sample that covers more than two million words, locates numerous examples of "ha's" and "do's" (for *has* and *does*)—yet he finds no author but Shakespeare who prefers both these spellings. Nor do I find, in my own samples, any poet who prefers both these spellings, or anyone with the initials W. S. who prefers these spellings, whether in verse or prose, except William Shakespeare and the author of the Peter elegy.

A. C. Partridge is wrong in asserting that "Shakespeare seems to have been the first to use *wert*."[34] Although the dramatist coined many new words, he did not go about inventing auxiliary verbs. For earlier examples we need turn no further than to Sidney or Marlowe or Daniel. Partridge is a victim here of depending too heavily on the *OED*, wherein no examples of *wert* are given prior to *The Winter's Tale*. Yet Shakespeare is indeed numbered among the earliest users of *wert* in our literature. *Wert* appears in *Venus and Adonis*, the *Sonnets*, and in twenty-eight of his plays. Many of his contemporaries never use *wert* at all, preferring instead the alternative *were* for second person singular subjunctive. But what makes Shakespeare's practice especially worth notice is that he (like Daniel and Jonson) uses *wert* for the indicative, when it was to be used only for the subjunctive mood, as is illustrated, for example, in the Authorized Version of the Bible. *Wert* eventually prevailed over *wast*, even for the indicative, but only a distinct minority of Jacobean poets would write, as Shakespeare does,

> I grant thou *wert* not married to my Muse,
> And therefore mayest without attaint o'erlook
> The dedicated words which writers use . . . /
> Thou, truly fair, *wert* truly sympathiz'd
> In true plain words by thy true-telling friend; . . .
>
> (Son. 82.1–3, 11–12)

W. S., however, does not hesitate to do so:

> Although I could not learn, whiles yet thou *wert*,
> To speak the language of a servile breath
>
> · · · · · · · · · · · · · ·
>   I took this task upon me . . . /
> [To] limn thee to the world but as thou *wert*— . . .
>
> (*Elegy* 209–10, 224–28)

Another noteworthy use of a verb in the *Elegy* appears in lines 241–44:

> Here, then, I offer up to memory
> The value of my talent, precious man,
> Whereby if thou live to posterity,
> Though it be not as I would, 'tis as I *can:* . . .

This elliptical use of *can,* in which the verb is to be supplied from the context, appears at least once in Edmund Spenser, John Davies, and Thomas Heywood, and three times in the poetry of Ben Jonson; yet there are few Renaissance poets who use *can* in this fashion so often as Shakespeare.[35] A few characteristic examples:

Let the priest in surplice white,
That defunctive music *can,*
Be the death-divining swan,
Lest the requiem lack his right.

(PhT 13–15)

Pardon me, Proteus, all I *can* is nothing
To her, whose worth makes other worthies nothing: . . .

(*TGV* 2.4.165–66)

I have seen myself, and serv'd against, the French,
And they *can* well on horseback, . . .

(*Ham.* 4.7.83–84)

Now my spirit is going,
I *can* no more.

(*Ant.* 4.15.58–59)

. . . the strong'st suggestion
Our worser genius *can,* shall never melt
Mine honor. . . .

(*Tmp.* 4.1.26–28)

Embalm me,
Then lay me forth. Although unqueen'd, yet like
A queen, and daughter to a king, inter me.
I *can* no more.

(*H8* 4.2.170–73)

Additional examples can be multiplied.

Among the pronouns, W. S.'s use of *his* and *its* is especially noteworthy. The latter, in 1612, was fairly new to the language (for example, "its" appears only once in the Authorized Version of the Bible of 1611). In the sixteenth century, most Englishmen used *his* where we would say *its*. By 1600 Shakespeare could write, "It lifted up *it* [*sic*] head" (*Ham.* 1.2.216; cf. *Ham.* 5.1.221, *Lr.* 1.4.216, et al.), but he shows a marked preference for *his* even in the last years of his career. The modern form appears in Shakespeare only twelve times, and one of these (*2H6* 3.2.393, F1) is a later corruption. A second instance (*MM* 1.2.4) is possibly a corruption as well. The remaining ten examples are confined to the last four plays (*WT, Tmp.,* and Shakespeare's portion of *H8* and *TNK*), all written within two years of the Peter elegy. Moreover, if we may judge from the evidence of the First Folio texts, Shakespeare spelled the word with an apostrophe ("it's"). The modern spelling, though frequent elsewhere in Jacobean texts, appears in the First Folio only in *Measure for Measure*. In the *Elegy, its* (which appears only once, in line 446) is spelled as Shakespeare appears to have spelled it, with the apostrophe. Elsewhere in the poem (1, 173, 178, 255, 423, 522), W. S., like Shakespeare, prefers *his* for the singular neuter possessive, even though many younger poets by 1612 were using *its* everywhere except with personified nouns.

The remaining pronouns are relatively unimportant as a measure of style. Turning, then, to the adverbial forms, we find that Shakespeare and W. S. are alike in preferring *like* to *likely,* and both prefer *afterwards* to *afterward,* but the same is often true of other Jacobean poets. Shakespeare's frequency of adverbial *like* is worth note, however. In the last five works prior to W. S.'s *Elegy* (*Ant.* through *Tmp.*), Shakespeare's substitution of *like* for *likely* falls within the very narrow range of 0.12–0.30/1000 words, with an average of 0.22/1000; its frequency in the *Elegy* is 0.23/1000. Adverbial use of *like,* though not unusual, occurs in only seven of the forty items in the Cross-Sample—and in only one poet, John Davies, does its frequency fall within the range of Shakespeare's last works. Finally, Shakespeare is the only major poet since Chaucer who prefers *sometime* to *sometimes,* as does W. S.[36] All such evidence must remain inconclusive except, perhaps, where clearly distinctive of Shakespeare's hand. It is nevertheless worth noting that W. S.'s grammatical accidence is exactly as we should expect to find in a poem of this date by William Shakespeare and, at least in this particular combination, quite different from that of any identifiable contemporary, no matter what the initials.[37]

Syntax

A. C. Partridge, in his *Substantive Grammar of Shakespeare's Non-dramatic Texts,* has concluded that "The inventiveness of Shakespeare did not often extend to syntactical novelties; by imitation he acquired from contemporaries the basic principles of style, rhythm, and emphasis."[38] Nevertheless, Partridge finds a number of syntactical features that are characteristic of Shakespeare's verse, one of which is Shakespeare's frequent substitution of one relative pronoun for another; thus in the *Elegy,* where we find *who* for *which* when used with animals or with personified nouns: *truth who* (dedication), *death who* (490), *time who* (497), *dove who* (455). But a survey of Renaissance verse shows these examples in fact to be quite ordinary. What makes Shakespeare's practice unique is that he frequently substitutes *who* for *which* when there is no apparent justification for it—as in the *Elegy,* where we find "embracements . . . who" (516–17), "hopes . . . who" (561–63), "designs, on whom" (414), "orbs in whom" (520). Excepting Shakespeare, the use of *who* for inanimate and unpersonified antecedents such as these is rare indeed. The phenomenon never occurs in the poetry of Sidney or Jonson, and never in the poems or plays of Christopher Marlowe except perhaps in those "breathing stars" in *Hero and Leander* "who . . . / Frighted the melancholy earth" (which is probably just another instance of personification). These three are the only poets for whom a detailed concordance is available at present. The only non-Shakespearean example offered in the *OED* prior to Oliver Goldsmith (1774) is by Archbishop George Abbot (1600), who writes in his *Exposition of Jonah* of "The snow and rain, who come down from above . . . water the earth, and procure a fruit out of it"—and even here it seems likely that Abbot is personifying both snow and rain as husbandmen. Charles Barber finds only one non-Shakespearean example in the literature of the sixteenth and seventeenth centuries, and that, some three generations after Shakespeare, in Locke's *Essay concerning Human Understanding* (1690).[39] Turning to the Memorial Verse, I find only one such substitution in eighty-two thousand lines. It occurs in David Murray's epitaph for his cousin of the same name:

And well the greatness of thy *mind* did merit
Even that the greatest spirits should thee cherish,
Who of itself, did from itself inherit
That which in great men does but greatness perish.
    True worth is not discern'd by outward show:
    Virtue's idea by the mind we know.

(31–36)

In the last plays of Shakespeare we find such examples as *vessel who, thing who, smile who, darkness who, anchors who, belly who, knees who, elements on whom, fame which . . . in whom, famine whom, leaf whom*. Such substitution is still more frequent in his nondramatic verse: In *Venus and Adonis* we find *eyelids who, hairs who, brain who, heart who* (twice), *passions who, sun who, sun and wind who, brambles and bushes through whom;* in *Lucrece, flood who, air who, suns who, body who, eye who, eyes who, tongue who, day to whom, black lust, dishonor, shame, misgoverning who* (plus many instances in both poems of unusual personification as in *dial who, pillow who*); and in the *Sonnets, books who, beauty and youth who, heart who* (twice), *night who, chips o'er whom*. Of 108 occurrences in the Shakespeare poems of *who* and *whom*, 25, or 23.1 percent, appear with incongruent antecedents, as against 19.0 percent in the *Elegy* (see table 1.8). Shakespeare's startling use of *who* and *whom* where virtually all of his contemporaries used *which*, if not explicable as a peculiarity of Stratford vernacular retained from his childhood, may result from simple confusion, as it is certainly not mandated by any artistic necessity; and though isolated instances of this phenomenon may be found elsewhere in Renaissance literature, so far as I can ascertain there is no other known

TABLE 1.8 / WHO, WHOM				
Title	who/ whom	incongruent antecedent	incongruent who, whom/ 100 lines	%
Ven.	26	9	.75	34.6
Luc.	36	9	.49	25.0
PhT	0	—	—	—
Son.	4?	6	.28	14.6
LC	5	1	.30	20.0
Total	108	25	.45	23.1
Elegy	21	4	.69	19.0

poet (including David Murray) who makes a habit of doing so—unless, of course, W. S. is someone other than William Shakespeare.

In similar fashion (though it is somewhat less extraordinary), Shakespeare, like W. S., habitually uses *what* with an unemphatic antecedent, or as a substitute for *that which:*

> *what* he spake, though it lack'd form a little,
> Was not like madness.
>
> (*Ham.* 3.1.163–64)

> *what* he spake
> Seem'd rather answers which the wise embrace
> Than busy questions such as talkers make.
>
> (*Elegy* 102–4)

> Who would not wish to be from wealth exempt,
> Since riches point to misery and contempt?
> Who would be so mock'd with glory, or to live
> But in a dream of friendship,
> To have his pomp, and all *what* state compounds,
> But only painted, like his varnish'd friends?
>
> (*Tim.* 4.2.31–36)

> Now men who in a lower region live
> Exempt from danger of authority
> Have fittest times in reason's rules to thrive
>
> . . . .
> Respective titles or a gracious style,
> With all *what* men in eminence possess,
> Are, without ornaments to praise them, vile: . . .
>
> (*Elegy* 457–69)

Still another peculiarity of Shakespearean syntax is his use of an adjectival phrase ("of time," "of day," "of year") in certain expressions denoting temporality, which, if not quite superfluous, is at least irregular syntax, as in Dionyza's epitaph for Marina—

The fairest, sweetest, and best lies here
Who withered in her *spring of year.*

(Per. 4.4.34–35)

Turning to the Henry IV trilogy, we find the following examples:

Well, bear you well in this new *spring of time,* . . .

(R2 5.2.50)

        he is flint,
As humorous as winter, and as sudden
As flaws congealed in the *spring of day.*

(2H4 4.4.33–35)

Shakespeare does not use such phrasing with any temporal noun but *spring;* hence it may be that he has in mind a pun on "spring" as both *season* and as *fountain, dawn,* or *beginning,* but the editors of the *OED* do not find the like outside Shakespeare; nor do I, except for one instance in Robert Greene ("spring of youth") and another in this *Elegy* by W. S. (wherein the poet speaks of William Peter as one who shunned "the glad sleights of ensnaring vice / To spend his *spring of days* in sacred schools" [73–74]).

Shakespeare affects a similar manner, adding a superflous *of,* in certain superlative constructions, as in King Richard's "short'st of day" (for "shortest day," *R2* 5.1.80), or Duke Vincentio's "the best of rest is sleep" (rather than "the best rest is sleep," *MM* 3.1.17), or the poet's own "best of love" (rather than "best love") in Sonnet 110.8, or Gloucester's "best of our times" (rather than "our best times"), in *King Lear* 1.2.47—to which may be compared W. S.'s description of William Peter as one who never wasted his "best of time" (64); but this construction is idiomatic, and may be found in many contemporaneous texts.

One construction that Shakespeare in the last years of his career uses with some regularity is the linking of *so . . . as,* especially on the pattern of "so [verb or adjective] as [adverbial modifier]." He writes, for example, in *The Winter's Tale* of "Thoughts so qualified as your charities / Shall best instruct you" (2.1.113–14); and in *Timon of Athens,* "I might so have rated my expense / As I had leave of means" (2.2.126–27) (cf. *Cym.* 1.4.28–30, 40, 67–68; 2.4.62; 3.2.60; 5.3.17, 4.2). When using these "so . . . as" constructions in his verse, especially in rhymed verse, Shakespeare usually places the "As" at the beginning of a line. The same is true of W. S.:

Ilion . . . /
Which the conceited painter drew so proud
As heaven (it seemed) to kiss the turrets bow'd.

(*Luc.* 1370–72)

embracements . . . /
Are so impatient of a strange remove
As meager death itself seems to lament,
And weep upon those cheeks. . . .

(*Elegy* 515–19)

Poor Lucrece' cheeks unto her maid seem so
As winter meads when sun doth melt their snow.

(*Luc.* 1217–18)

conclude the matter so,
As they will all go weeping to their beds.

(*Elegy* 169–70)

love . . . / . . . not so bright
As those gold candles fix'd in heaven's air: . . .

(Son. 21.10–12)

love . . . so unfeign'd
As he was both an husband and a father— . . .

(*Elegy* 525–26)

O, therefore, love, be of thyself so wary
As I, not for myself, but for thee will,
Bearing thy heart, which I will keep so chary
As tender nurse her babe from faring ill.

(Son. 22.9–12)

he was so constant to his friends
As he would no occasion overpass
Which might make known his unaffected care,
In all respects of trial, to unlock
His bosom and his store, . . .

(*Elegy* 315–19)

So oft have I invok'd thee for my Muse . . . /
As every alien pen hath got my use,
And under thee their poesy disperse.

(Son. 78.1–4)

Hence conster they . . . /
The text of malice, which so often varies
As 'tis by seeming reason underpropp'd.

(*Elegy* 265–69)

not so deep a maim
As to be cast forth in the common air, . . .

(*R2* 1.3.156–57)

Learning my days of youth so to prevent
As not to be cast down by them again. . . .

(*Elegy* 559–60)

Shakespearean examples can be multiplied (e.g., *Luc.* 400–406, 1000–1001, 1041–43, 1811–12; cf. *Elegy* 95–96, 343–44, 376–78). Shakespeare appears to have been influenced in this respect by Samuel Daniel, who is (I believe) the only major Jacobean poet who exceeds Shakespeare in his use of comparable "so . . . as" constructions. The usual formulation during this period is either "such [noun] . . . as," "so [adj. or adv.] . . . that," "as [adj. or adv.] as . . .", or "so [adj.] a [noun]." Turning to the Memorial Verse 1570–1630, I find during these six decades many comparable, although scattered, examples; but among the poets listed, few if any approach Shakespeare and W. S. in their marked predilection for constructions of the "so . . . as" variety. Nor do I find, among the remaining "W. S.'s" indexed in appendix A, any plausible candidate. There are at least a dozen comparable formulations in the collected works of William Strode, but at the time the *Elegy* was written, Strode was only eleven years old.

Perhaps more important than any particular construction is Partridge's observation that "a common source of syntactical difficulty in Shakespeare is his capacity for compression."[40] This is especially true of the later plays, and it is partly this, no doubt, that gives W. S.'s verse a Shakespearean ring. Ellipses are frequent, and sometimes drastic; participial phrases and relative clauses frequently go begging for an antecedent; relative pronouns are sometimes missing; and nearly every sentence in the poem contains parenthetical elements. It is doubtless the extraordinarily complex syntax of this poem, in fact, that caused Eld's compositor such headaches in trying to punctuate it correctly. In the words of S. S. Hussey,

The final plays seem to be characterized by a looser, almost experimental syntax. . . . Shakespeare, while retaining the overall structure of a speech, was now able to convey the impression of a character thinking as he spoke, often under pressure. . . . In thinking aloud we make qualifications and objections, go off at a tangent and partially obscure straightforward communication of ideas. In Shakespeare's final plays, the increase in parentheses attempts to indicate something of this turmoil.[41]

To illustrate Hussey's point, we may turn to *Henry VIII:*

He was most princely: ever witness for him
Those twins of learning that he rais'd in you,
Ipswich and Oxford! one of which fell with him,

Unwilling to outlive the good that did it;
The other (though unfinish'd) yet so famous,
So excellent in art, and still so rising,
That Christendom shall ever speak his virtue.

(H8 4.2.57–63)

—to which may be compared these lines from the *Elegy,* in the like
parenthetical style (to say nothing of its specific verbal echoes):

Those noble twins of heaven-infused races,
Learning and wit, refined in their kind
Did jointly both, in their peculiar graces,
Enrich the curious temple of his mind;
Indeed a temple, in whose precious white
Sat reason by religion oversway'd,
Teaching his other senses, with delight,
How piety and zeal should be obey'd— . . .

(Elegy 55–62)

The frequent parenthetical comments, whether marked by commas,
dashes, or parentheses, the appositives, digressions, asides, participial
phrases, all work together in the *Elegy* to capture the essential rhythms of
speech. Few Jacobean poets are able to approach Shakespeare in this
respect. At the same time, a looser syntax results often in double grammar,
a feature of Shakespeare's plays and poems discussed by Empson in *Seven
Types of Ambiguity.* W. S. has the same predilection for double grammar.
When he writes,

A rock of friendship figured in his name,
Foreshowing what he was, and what should be,

(321–22)

the last phrase, "what should be," denotes future teleology (had Peter
lived) as well as the ideal.

Here, then, I offer up to memory
The value of my talent, precious man,
Whereby if thou live to posterity,
Though it be not as I would, 'tis as I can: . . .

(241–44)

If "it" refers to "the value of my talent," the last line may be taken to
mean, "though my elegy is not as I would have it, 'tis the best that I can
do." But if "it" denotes a manner of "living to posterity," the line becomes
self-reflexive: "You will live to posterity only insofar as *I* am able to do so,
though I would it were otherwise."

Yet ere I take my longest last farewell
From thee, fair mark of sorrow, let me frame
Some ampler work of thank, . . .

(247–49)

Here the parenthetical "fair mark of sorrow" may describe "thee" (248), the deceased friend, as a "fair scar of grief," or again as the "target and aim" of the poet's emotion; but the phrase may likewise refer loosely (as an appositive, not as a term of address) to the poet's own "last farewell" (247), to the poem itself as the visible trace of his sorrow.

The ambiguities thus achieved in the *Elegy* are sometimes quite striking, as in the following passage, beginning at line 213:

And I confess my love was too remiss,
That had not made thee know how much I priz'd thee,
But that mine error was, as yet it is,
To think love best in silence: . . .

(213–16)

In the phrase "as yet it is," there is contained not only a continued affirmation but a poignant recognition of the text's nonaudition. Before his friend's death, the poet could not speak of his love (209–12, 223), and now words are penned in silence that his friend can never hear.

. . . for I siz'd thee
By what I would have been, not only ready
In telling I was thine, but being so,
By some effect to show it.

(216–19)

The primary sense here is still one of apologetic self-justification, but the entire sentence takes on a radically altered meaning if the stress is moved from "what *I* would have been" to "what I *would* have been" (had I a second chance). This second meaning is initially suppressed by the past tense of the verb it modifies ("I *siz'd* thee"), then reasserted by the iambic meter—so that the line struggles with itself, as it were, to contain an overwhelming sense of regret, and moves unsteadily toward finding some measure of compensation in the poet's sincerity of feeling:

. . . He is steady
Who seems less than he is, in open show.

(219–20)

On a lesser note, we find here Shakespeare's tendency to make even individual words do him double service. If this poet is not quite content to

lose the world for a pun, as Johnson said of Shakespeare, neither is he
averse to including wordplay in a funeral elegy for a lost friend. In line 246
there may be a quibble on the poet's own name (as in the *Sonnets*), where
we read "A ready will is taken for the deed." There is another pun, as we
have seen, on the biblical precedent of Peter's name ("a rock of friendship," 321), and a glance at Edward Drew, Peter's killer, in the phrase
"untimely drew / Destruction" (341–42); in the Quarto, *Drew* is capitalized
and italicized, the only verb in the entire poem so printed, which suggests
that it appeared so in the author's manuscript. Finally, in line 41 there may
be a punning, and antagonistic, reference to William Peter's puritanical
cousin, Sir Thomas Ridgway—in the 1612 Quarto, *Ridg-way*, like *Drew*, is
capitalized and italicized—though the line may refer only to the causeway
on which Peter was slain. Multiple meanings are conveyed also by such
words as *limb* (14; cf. *limn*, 228), *curious* (58), *temple* (59), *habit* (95, 208),
rehearse (151), *exercise* (259), *rare* (286, 287), *unsound* (406), *content* (557),
heart (562), and *range* (571). The identical puns in every case appear in
Shakespeare, some of them repeatedly.

Even words omitted from the text cast their shadow over the pages of
the *Elegy*. Appositives and relative clauses that seem to refer to the
deceased friend frequently lack an antecedent; and when the poet speaks
of death, he frequently elides the verb of being, as when he looks ahead to
that day

> When all shall turn to dust from whence we came,
> And we low-level'd in a narrow grave, . . .
>
> (193–94)

W. S.'s wordplay is never heavy-handed, and is sometimes so deft as
almost to escape notice. A splendid example occurs in lines 431–34. I
quote from the 1612 Quarto (with emphasis added):

> His beeing but a priuate man in ranke
> (And yet not rank't beneath a Gentleman)
> Shall not *abridge* the commendable *thanke,*
> Which wise posterity shall give him *than:* . . .

The optimistic assertion that Peter's "thank" shall never be "abridged" is
ironically contradicted, first in the poet's use of *thank* (which is itself an
abridgment of "thanks" or "thankfulness"), and secondly in the phrase
"wise posterity shall give him *than*"—as if to suggest, if only visually, an
inevitable and relentless diminishment of thanksgiving. W. S. experiments
with the same idea in the opening lines, wherein we read that Peter's

> predestinated *end*
> *Abridg'd* the circuit of his hopeful days

Whiles both his youth and virtue did intend
The good *endeavors* of deserving praise, . . .

—so that Peter's "end" comes to stand visually for his own abridged "endeavors." I might well be accused here of overreading if either of these instances appeared alone, but the appearance of two words in the same text being "abridged" in this way seems to confirm that the play on words was not fortuitous.[42]

A slightly more elaborate version of the same flourish appears in Shakespeare's portion of *Henry VIII*, as Cardinal Wolsey seeks to justify himself before the King: "My *endeavors*," he says, "have *ever* come too short of my desires, / Yet . . . Mine own *ends* / Have been mine . . ." (3.2.169–72); which is to say, his "end(eavor)s," lacking "ever," are reduced to selfish "ends." If we may suppose for a moment that both texts were written by Shakespeare, and that I am not guilty of reading into them what is not actually there, one may almost see the poet's brain at work, first experimenting in a private text with a play on words, then reshaping it for use in his next stage-play; though it is of course possible that Shakespeare borrowed the idea from W. S., or thought of it on his own, coincidentally. A similar example is found in the final scene of *King Lear* when Edward— whose name should now be "*Gloster*" [Q1]—remarks, "Know, my name is *lost,* / By treason's tooth bare–gnawn and canker-bit, . . ." (5.3.121–22).

Still another matter for consideration in a study such as this is a poet's longest independent clause, since few writers ever exceed one hundred words. Shakespeare's early works are marked by frequent parallelisms, most of them more or less symmetrical, unlike the complex, parenthetical syntax of the late plays, yet all his works contain at least a few sentences of quite extraordinary length (the syntactical equivalent of Costard's single mouth-filling word, *honorificabilitudinitatibus*). We may define a "sentence" in this case, not as the distance between capital letter and period, since this depends often on editorial preference, but more narrowly as a single independent clause, inclusive of all parenthetical and subordinate elements, but excluding other independent clauses attached to it with a conjunction or semicolon. Shakespeare in his major nondramatic works, and in all of his last plays, has sentences (so defined) of more than ninety words, thereby demanding a great deal of the playgoer in particular, since it is often difficult to follow the thought even in the quiet of one's own study. The longest sentence in *Venus and Adonis* is 122 words, and in *Lucrece,* 162. In the *Sonnets* (where sentence length is limited to the number of words possible in fourteen lines), the longest sentence is 111 words, comprising the whole of Sonnet 15 (cf. Sonnet 18, 118 words, in which the final couplet may nevertheless be considered as a separate independent clause). Less than a third of the poets represented in the

Cross-Sample have any sentence longer than one hundred words, and only five have a maximum sentence-length falling between 111 and 162 words, as in Shakespeare's major nondramatic works. The two longest sentences in the *Elegy* are 111 words (lines 55–70) and 141 words (lines 301–20).

Nor is the reader the only one who may become lost in the branching syntax of Shakespeare's late plays. The speaker often succumbs as well. A. C. Partridge has pointed out that Shakespeare tends in his last plays "to lose track of his relative clauses, especially if used continuatively and in proximity to participial phrases (or adverbial clauses) of time."[43] Partridge gives numerous examples from the Shakespearean portions of *Henry VIII,* for which parallel examples may be found in the *Elegy* in lines 137–44, 230–34, 273–300, 399–414, 451–56, and 553–68.

We find also throughout the *Elegy* Shakespeare's characteristic turn of phrase, as in the frequent use of redundant modifiers. There are many such redundancies in the Peter elegy, all of which find Shakespearean parallels. For example:

> By fair demeanor he had won repute
> Amongst the all of all that lived there, . . .
>
> (*Elegy* 153–54)

> Their images I lov'd I view in thee,
> And thou (all they) hast all the all of me.
>
> (Son. 31.13–14)

There is a kind of triple redundancy in W. S.'s phrase, "superlative above the rest / Of many men in steady faith" (23–24), to which may be compared such Shakespearean oddities as Juliana's reply to Lucetta in *The Two Gentlemen of Verona:*

> *Luc.* Then thus: of many good I think him best. . . . /
> *Jul.* Why he, of all the rest, hath never mov'd me.
>
> (*TGV* 1.2.21, 27)

(He has never moved me more than all other good men have never moved me). The same syntax appears again in *A Midsummer Night's Dream* as Duke Theseus observes, upon the entrance of Moonshine, that

> This is the greatest error of all the rest.
>
> (*MND* 5.1.246)

Shakespeare speaks of "shifting change," W. S. of "unsteady change." W. S. writes of "fond [which is to say, *foolish*] dotage," Shakespeare of those who are "fond mad" and "foolish fond." Shakespeare writes of "mortal murders," W. S. of "love innated from his birth"; W. S. of "mutual harmony," Shakespeare of a "mutual pair," "mutual act of all," "mutual conference." W. S. coins the word "fore-promis'd," and Shakespeare, "fore-vouch'd," both words having, in context, a redundant prefix. W. S. writes of "false pretenses," Shakespeare of "false hypocrisy," "false dissembling guile," "false perjury," and "most false imposition." W. S. speaks of "empty air," Shakespeare of "empty air" and "empty hollowness" (though the redundant use of *false* and *empty* is far less extraordinary than the preceding examples). There are, lastly, a few such redundancies appearing in the *Elegy* ("from whence," "best perfections," et al.) that are quite commonly found elsewhere in Renaissance literature and are therefore of little interest.

One of the most distinctive features of Shakespeare's verse is his habitual use of paired nouns coupled by *and*. As noted by William Empson, "Shakespeare's fondness for such pairs of words is fundamental to his method."[44] The pattern is everywhere evident in the poems and plays, as here again in the *Elegy,* where there are forty-two such phrases in less than six hundred lines, beginning with the first sentence. To these we may add all the noun-pronoun pairs ("for whom and whose sake," "such, and of such condition"), paired verbs ("deserve and hast," "lean and rest," "range and court"), paired adjectives ("sad and sudden," "beloved and lamented"), nouns paired with an *or* ("eminent courts or places great," "respective titles or a gracious style"), and other typically Shakespearean parallelisms ("in use most fast, in tongue most plain," "his taintless goodness, his desertful merit"). We have in the *Elegy* only a handful of double adjectives without the *and,* and even these have a Shakespearean ring: "fair lovely branch too soon cut off," "little ordered commonwealth," "fatal timeless ruin," "uncivil loose opinions," "the sour-bitter scourge," "flourishing and fair long-liv'd deserts," "time's strict flinty hand." W. S. does not share the predilection of John Donne and many others for three items in a series. He thinks rather, like Shakespeare, in paired nouns, paired phrases, paired clauses. Nor are there many of the multiple-item lists so often found, say, in the work of Ben Jonson. W. S. has only four: "birth, life, death, and seat"; "our grace and strength, youth, memory and shape"; "blood, pomp, state, honor, glory and command"; and the remarkable series beginning in line 116, in which W. S. outdoes even Jonson with an inventory seventeen virtues long, a catalog that, as already noted, is itself very like the list of seventeen social goods in Shakespeare's *Timon of Athens* (4.1.15–20). Shakespeare and W. S. nevertheless have (relative to their contemporaries) a much lower than average frequency of *and,* since both poets generally avoid polysyndeton ("This, and that, and that, and that").

One may find in the Peter elegy many of Shakespeare's preferred flourishes, such as *prosonomasia*. When we read,

Hence sprung the deadly fuel that reviv'd
The rage which wrought his end,

(333–34)

it is hardly possible not to notice the poet's substitution of *fuel* for the
expected *duel*, especially since the language of dueling is picked up again
only a few lines after, in line 346. We are reminded, by this simple twist,
that it was in fact *not* a duel that led to Peter's death: he was struck down in
a malicious back-stabbing attack.

Another interesting device, and a favorite with W. S., as with Shakespeare, is *antanaclasis*. Puttenham cites three instances, all three of which
appear afterward in Shakespeare, as for example "The maide that soon
married is, soon marred is"; Shakespeare writes, "a young man married is
a man that's marr'd" (*AWW* 2.3.298). A striking example from the *Elegy* is
W. S.'s assertion that time may "lay *ope* malice" (146), in order to "right
the *hopes* of my endangered youth" (147). The poet's sentence must
"ope," in time, to make room for partially obscured "hopes." A similar
example appears in line 386, when W. S. writes that his friend was "*Sent
innocent* to be in heaven *set*."[45] (Cf. Lysander in *MND:* "O, take the
sense, sweet, of my *innocence!*" [2.2.45].)

We find also among the frequent doublets in the *Elegy* a number of
characteristic Shakespearean devices of style, such as *zeugma* ("to unlock
his bosom and his store"; "liv'd fellow to his counsels and his bed") and
chiastic inversion ("trim behavior, gestures mild"; "active grace, persuasion sweet" "right old griefs, and former joys retain")—but similar examples, especially of the latter, may be found fairly often in Renaissance
verse. Far more important for distinguishing Shakespeare's work from that
of his less inventive contemporaries is a figure called *hendiadys*, a peculiar
rhetorical device in which two parallel words (usually nouns) are linked by
and, but express a single complex notion that would usually be expressed
by an adjective (or adjectival phrase) and a substantive. The usual example is from Vergil, "We poured our libations in cups and gold" (rather than
"in golden cups" or "in cups of gold"). Puttenham calls this figure "*En-
diadis*, or the Figure of Twinnes." He cites four examples, all four on the
Vergilian model, three of them from the classics. His sole example from
contemporaneous English verse is taken from "one of our ordinary
rimers": "Of fortune nor her frowning face, / I am nothing aghast" (rather
than "fortune's frowning face").[46]

The examples found in Shakespeare are usually more complex than this.
He frequently links two opposite or slightly discordant words with an-

other word that seems to qualify both of them, as in that "fantasy and trick of fame" for which the Norwegian soldiers in *Hamlet* march to their death—a characteristic example of Shakespearean hendiadys in which the entire phrase comes to mean something like "a deceitful illusion of fame," with the doublet ("fantasy and trick") serving in effect as a single word combining two disparate notions; to which may be compared, from *Henry VIII,* the king's complaint, "I abhor / This dilatory sloth and tricks of Rome" (2.4.237–38). Or, to select the first of many such examples in *Henry VIII,* when the Prologue says, "Think you see them . . . follow'd with the throng and sweat of thousand friends," the doublet is a typically Shakespearean periphrasis for "the sweating throng of thousand friends." In "The Phoenix and the Turtle," Shakespeare's shortest poetic work, there are three examples of hendiadys in just sixty-seven lines. When he writes,

> Let the bird of loudest lay
> On the sole Arabian tree
> Herald sad and trumpet be,

it is clear that this bird is to be a "sadly trumpeting herald," not a herald first, and a trumpet second. The phoenix and the dove, described later in the same poem as "Co-supremes and stars of love," are "co-supremely stars of love," and the singular verb in line 22 ("Love and constancy is dead") forces "love and constancy" into an hendiadys for "loving constancy," "constant love," or both.

Hendiadys is one of those "syntactical novelties" in Shakespeare that A. C. Partridge overlooks. His extraordinary use of this figure has, however, been noted by William Empson and M. M. Reese—neither of whom actually identifies the phenomenon as "hendiadys"—and it has since been discussed more fully in a landmark study by George T. Wright.[47] Reese finds the figure not entirely to his liking, but he concludes nevertheless that "It was the only technical trick to which Shakespeare returned again and again, and it was his alone."[48]

Empson—offering just one example from Kyd, and two dubious examples from Marlowe, all three of the "(noun) and (noun) of (noun)" pattern—notes the rarity of hendiadys prior to Shakespeare. Wright, on the other hand, notes its rarity after Shakespeare, excepting Sir Thomas Browne and Milton, and concludes that "the only poet since Milton to use it even occasionally is Dylan Thomas." Sir Thomas Browne (1605–82) makes use of the device repeatedly (as if by design, and not by accident). There are a dozen hendiadys in his *Religio Medici,* all of them on the principal Shakespearean model, as in his description of children as "our issue and picture of posterity."[49] But given Browne's confessed zeal for stage plays and his occasional use of Shakespearean texts to illustrate a point, it seems likely that he simply borrowed Shakespeare's manner, for similar examples elsewhere are scarcely to be found. In Milton's collected verse there are seven certain hendiadys, and seven other likely instances, all fourteen on the Vergilian model, as for example "Thy frailty and infirmer sex" for "The frailty of thy infirmer sex" (*PL* 10.956).[50] I have also found several hendiadys in the work of William Rowley (ca. 1585–ca. 1642), a minor poet and playwright who looked to Shakespeare as his principal mentor, but I cannot discover any other writers in the seventeenth century who use the device more than once or twice.

On account of its rarity, hendiadys is perhaps the closest thing we have to a stylistic thumbprint for Shakespeare. Here is a poet who, in the words of George T. Wright, "appears to have taken this odd figure to his bosom and to have made it entirely his own," fashioning in his plays and poems examples that "are dazzlingly various." He in fact uses it so often, writes Empson, that "it has been drummed . . . into the ears of his readers till they take it for granted."[51] There are more than four hundred hendiadys in Shakespeare. Examples may be found in all the poetic works, and in all the plays written after 1594, excepting only *Merry Wives of Windsor*. *Hamlet*, as noted by both Empson and Wright, is the play in which the device makes its most frequent appearance. Wright counts sixty-six certain examples in *Hamlet* (for a frequency of one hendiadys every sixty lines), and twenty-three others that, if not hendiadys, are close. Counting only the best examples, hendiadys in the plays after *Hamlet* range from a low of two (in *Tmp.*) to a high of twenty-eight (in *Oth.*). In *Henry VIII* and *The Two Noble Kinsmen* there are ten examples, all ten in Shakespeare's supposed portion. If it was he who wrote the Peter elegy, we should therefore expect to find therein at least one or two examples akin to those found elsewhere in his work.

We may begin with a doubtful instance in the opening lines:

Since time, and his predestinated end,
Abridg'd the circuit of his hopeful days, . . .

At first glance, "time" and "his predestinated end" appear to express two distinct notions, and there is surely a sense in which William Peter may serve as the missing antecedent for "his"—but "his" refers as well to "time," since possessive "its" had not yet found its way into standard usage and since the opening phrase is echoed in the "predestinated time" of line 497, so that Peter's life is abridged by "the predestinated end of time," with time in its possessiveness absorbing what might have been "his." This figure is followed in turn by another possible instance of hendiadys, in which "his" certainly refers to the poet's deceased friend:

Whiles both his youth and virtue did intend
The good endeavors of deserving praise, . . .

Here "his youth and virtue," not strictly parallel, may mean something like "his youthful virtue," even though the "both" suggests two separate qualities. This "youth and ————" formula, as noted by Wright, is among the most frequent of Shakespearean hendiadys, appearing three times in *Hamlet* alone (1.5.101, 2.1.24, 2.2.12). But then, too, it may be the most frequent formula found outside Shakespeare, as in John Ford's tribute to Sir Thomas Overbury, wherein he speaks of those

> whose hands, imbrued in blood,
> Cropp'd off thy youth and flower in the bud.

(25–26)

"Youth and flower" is here a Vergilian hendiadys for "flowering youth" or "youthful flourish."

But if the phrase concerning Peter's "youth and virtue" in line three of the *Elegy* cannot be considered distinctive, there are other examples in the poem that may: Peter's "short-liv'd deserts" find their preservation in "the hearts and memories of men" (13), another false parallel, in which "hearts" has the force of an adjective, as in "the loving memories of men." In what is perhaps the cleverest example of hendiadys to be found in the *Elegy* we read in lines 33–34 of "the spleenful sense / And spite of malice." Here "sense" may be taken as *sensation* or as *insinuation,* as act or experience. Either way we arrive at something like "the sense of malicious resentment." There are more such: "to unlock / His bosom and his store" was cited above as an example of *zeugma,* but if *bosom* is to be associated with generosity rather than with confidentiality, the line denotes one who "gave heartily of his abundance" (318–19). Consider also "true proof and knowledge of a friend" (for "proven knowledge of a true friend," 354); "the home of his condition and estate" (in which all three nouns converge, 306); and the "scourge / Of torture and affliction" (for "the afflicting scourge of torture," 396). All these have parallels in Shakespeare. To the last of these, for example, we may compare Hamlet's "whips and scorns of time" (3.1.69) or, for a similar coupling of active and passive modifiers, "th'inaudible and noiseless foot of time" in *All's Well That Ends Well* (5.3.41).

I find in the *Elegy* ten certain hendiadys (all ten involving nouns), and seven others (five with nouns, two with adjectives) that at least verge on hendiadys and have a similar effect. The two dubious adjectival examples are, first, "the base / And sensual aptness of disunion'd vices" (where "base" seems to modify "sensual" more directly than "aptness," hence "the basely sensual tendency of disunion'd vices," 277–78), and second, "a hand in vengeance rude and hot" (the two adjectives may modify either "hand" or "vengeance" as "hot with violence," 385); both phrases find parallels in Shakespeare. To the dubious hendiadys in line one may be added at least five additional noun doublets that verge on hendiadys: "his fate and heaven" (83), "hardest fate and time" (222), and "nature and his therein happy fate" (435), are all three phrases that in context seem to denote a single notion, meaning, respectively, something like "his heaven-ordained fate," "time's hardest fate," and "his blessed destiny in nature"; to which may be added "education and new being," a weaker example, which can possibly be taken to mean "new being *through* education" (152).

Shakespeare seems even to think in hendiadys. The term literally translated means "one through two," and in Shakespeare, as noted by Empson, the whole unit often takes a singular verb.[52] This is a peculiarity, as far as I can ascertain, exampled nowhere except in Shakespeare (and in W. S.). Having adopted this unusual and logically discordant rhetorical device as his own, Shakespeare applies to it a singular verb as the final stamp of his own singularity. Of the ten certain examples of hendiadys in the *Elegy,* only three take a verb in which a distinction of number can be made; in all three instances, the verb is singular: *"the bypath and the ridgway,"* or deviant course (with "bypath" having the force of an adjective to describe what kind of ridgway it is), *"leads* to ruin"; the eye, as *"the candle and the body's light"* (which is to say, the body's light-giving candle) *"darkens"* the mind; *"the world and heat of sin"* (a figure that resists analysis) *"entices"* men to purchase commendation by disgrace (41–42, 261–62, 279–80). In each case, the apparent parallel absorbs the "and" into a single, more complex, relation.

Turning to the Cross-Sample, I find only one dubious instance of hendiadys. In Richard Johnson's elegy for the earl of Salisbury we read:

Fair heaven, some supreme wit inspire.
Afford him grace and gift of pen
To light a lamp at honor's fire
And memorize world's worthy men.

(17–20)

Here "grace and gift of pen" suggests, perhaps, "a gift of graceful writing," and so might qualify as an example of hendiadys. In context, it appears more likely that Johnson has in mind two distinct notions, (1) the heavenly *grace* necessary "to light a lamp at honor's fire," and (2) the requisite talent "to memor[ial]ize [the] world's worthy men." Double parallel structure of this sort (A[1] and B[1] to or for A[2] and B[2]) is a Renaissance commonplace first popularized by John Lyly and by various imitators of Petrarch. Nevertheless, hendiadys is so rare outside Shakespeare that one has to take such examples as one can find. I have therefore counted this phrase, in the statistical tabulations to follow, as a valid example, and (above) have punctuated it accordingly.

I find also in the larger bibliography of the Memorial Verse 1570–1630 one instance by John Ford (already quoted) and a third, though dubious, candidate in Richard Mulcaster's "Comforting Complaint" upon the death of Queen Elizabeth:

How tried he her with change and choice of chance,
Not only in her first, but after, years.

(33–34)

"He/her" refers to God and Elizabeth, though I can make little sense of the next phrase, "change and choice of chance." The poet is clearly more interested in alliteration than in a subtle rhetorical flourish, but he may mean something like "the willful vicissitudes of Lady Fortune," rather than two distinct notions. In either case, Mulcaster never again hits upon anything resembling hendiadys. But if we count all three of these instances, we arrive at a *maximum* relative frequency of 0.04 hendiadys/1000 lines for the entire bibliography, versus a *minimum* frequency of 17.3/1000 lines in the Peter elegy, or about a 400-to-1 ratio, 400 by W. S. (by way of extrapolation) for one occurrence by all other poets but William Shakespeare.

Statistical Indices

One of the earliest quantifiable measures of literary style was originated by T. C. Mendenhall a century ago and developed more recently by C. B. Williams.[53] Mendenhall found that Shakespeare has a consistently higher frequency of four-letter words than of two- or three-letter words. Many of his contemporaries—Francis Bacon, for example,—have a peak of three-letter words, as do most modern authors. A few English authors (though not, I believe, in Shakespeare's day) have a peak of two-letter words (Mendenhall cites John Stuart Mill as an example).

C. B. Williams, elaborating upon Mendenhall, has shown that all authors have an individual curve that remains more or less constant throughout their careers. And though a particular sample may vary by as much as a third from the mean for each category (depending on such factors as the size of the sample and its date of composition), no two

TABLE 1.9 / SHAKESPEARE'S WORD-LENGTH: THE POEMS						
1-Letter	**2-Letter**	**3-Letter**	**4-Letter**	**5-Letter**	**6+**	**Total**
1208	6944	9362	11231	6538	9787	45070
26.8	154.1	207.7	249.2	145.1	217.2	1000

authors follow precisely the same curve. The figures for Shakespeare's nondramatic works are shown in table 1.9 (the top figure in each square represents his absolute frequency, and the bottom figure, his frequency per one thousand words, as registered in *Venus and Adonis, The Rape of Lucrece,* "The Phoenix and the Turtle," the *Sonnets,* and "A Lover's Complaint").[54]

To arrive at an expected frequency for each word-length in a presumed poem by William Shakespeare, we may set our parameters, quite narrowly, at 20 percent above and below the Shakespearean mean for each category, while recognizing that a poem actually written by him may deviate by more than 20 percent (short poems, for example, necessarily show less regularity than do longer works by the same poet). Let us turn, then, for our cross-sample, to the works of Francis Bacon and Christopher Marlowe; to the 1611 "Funeral Elegy" by John Donne; and to the elegies for Prince Henry by Cyril Tourneur and John Webster. Mendenhall, unfortunately, does not provide the raw data for Bacon. For these others, I have conducted my own hand count (see table 1.10).[55] It will be seen that W. S. follows Shakespeare's characteristic curve for all six categories, unlike these other writers. Of the authors checked by Mendenhall, he found no author closer to Shakespeare's characteristic curve than Christopher Marlowe. He did not, of course, check the *Funeral Elegy* by W. S. I lack the fortitude to compile a similar word-count for all the poems in the 1610–13 Cross-Sample, but having done a test-count of randomly selected passages, I find no poem that matches Shakespeare's nondramatic curve in all six categories.

We may next turn to W. S.'s vocabulary, and test whether it is in fact distinctive of Shakespeare's hand. This, however, requires an extraordinarily large cross-sample. Given the diversity of Shakespeare's manifest vocabulary and the unusually large size of his canon, almost any poem might show a higher correlation with Shakespeare's vocabulary than with that, say, of Spenser, Marlowe, Jonson, or Donne. Our cross-sample must therefore include the work of several authors, in both verse and prose, and

TABLE 1.10 / WORD-LENGTH PER 1000 WORDS OF TEXT

	Expected range, Shakespeare		Francis Bacon Sample	Christopher Marlowe, Works	John Donne, "Elegy"	Cyril Tourneur, "Grief"	John Webster, "Column"	W.S. Elegy
Sample Size	45070		200,000	133,495	864	1,221	2,624	4,460
1-Letter	Hi	32.2		4745	11	22	52	96
(Sh = 26.8)	Lo	21.4	25	35.5	12.7	18.0	19.8	21.5
2-Letter	Hi	184.9		24034	145	226	385	801
(Sh = 154.1)	Lo	123.3	198	180.0	167.8	185.1	146.7	179.6
3-Letter	Hi	249.3		31464	227	292	601	905
(Sh = 207.7)	Lo	166.2	223	235.6	262.7	239.1	229.0	202.9
4-Letter	Hi	299.0		33994	190	281	591	914
(Sh = 249.2)	Lo	199.4	175	254.6	219.9	230.1	225.2	204.9
5-Letter	Hi	174.1		17016	127	159	407	616
(Sh = 145.1)	Lo	116.1	100	127.5	147.0	130.2	155.1	138.1
6+	Hi	260.6		22242	164	241	588	1128
(Sh = 217.1)	Lo	173.8	279	166.6	189.8	197.4	224.1	252.9

must include works from both the Elizabethan and Jacobean eras. For a cross-sample I have turned to the only concordances available to me at present: These catalogue the poems of Edmund Spenser and Ben Jonson; the plays and poems of Christopher Marlowe; the sonnet sequences of Samuel Daniel, Michael Drayton, and Sir Philip Sidney; and the complete writings of George Herbert. I have manually added the complete poems of William Strachey and the nondramatic verse of William Strode (since their initials are appropriate to the *Elegy*). We thereby arrive at a combined cross-sample that is nearly identical in size to that of the Shakespeare canon. Throughout, the elements of compounds have been counted separately, and titles (which appear in some concordances and not in others) have been disregarded (e.g., "Exeter" appears once in the title of the Peter elegy and twenty-six times in Shakespeare, but not in the cross-sample; this has been excluded from consideration, as has the appearance of the word "Dotage" in the title of a poem by George Herbert). I have excluded from the Shakespeare sample *Pericles* 1-2, the *Macbeth* interpolations, *The Passionate Pilgrim,* and the presumed non-Shakespearean portions of both *Henry VIII* and *The Two Noble Kinsmen.* I have also excluded Hand D of *Sir Thomas More,* "A Lover's Complaint," and "The Phoenix and the Turtle," reserving these three texts for use as a control sample. The difference in size between the Shakespeare and non-Shakespeare samples is less than 1 percent (see table).[56]

We may next isolate all those words found in W. S.'s *Elegy* that fail to appear in the non-Shakespeare sample, but that nevertheless appear in the Shakespeare sample. Such words may be described as Shakespeare "badges": these words, as they appear, are presumably more characteristic of Shakespeare than of his contemporaries at large. We may isolate, too, all those words in the *Elegy* that fail to appear in the Shakespeare canon, but that nevertheless occur in the non-Shakespeare sample. These may be described as "flukes": one should expect to find relatively few of these in any poem actually written by Shakespeare.

As for my methodology in defining what constitutes a distinct word, I have followed the pioneering work of Alfred Hart and Eliot Slater, with only minor refinements.[57] The same configuration of letters, appearing twice, is counted as the same word only when serving as the same part of speech. Thus *float* (n.), for example, has been counted as distinct from the verb. A similar distinction has been made between adjectival and adverbial use even where the forms are identical (as in Shakespeare's use of *faulty* as an adverb). I have counted as identical the inflected forms of a single verb, except where used as a substantive or as an adjective directly linked to a noun (Hart in this respect is confessedly inconsistent). Comparative and superlative forms of the same adjective are counted together (e.g., *dark, darker, darkest*), as are singular and plural forms of the same noun. Homographs with radically different meanings have been counted as distinct even when serving as the same part of speech (e.g., the *bark* of a dog, as in *Venus and Adonis;* the *bark* of a tree, as in *Lucrece;* and a sailing *bark,* as in the *Sonnets*).[58] Lastly, I have segregated compound words as a distinct category (regardless of grammatical function) and have counted

Sample Size	No. of Words
I. W.S.	4,460
II. Shakespeare	847,502
III. Non-Shakespeare	
Daniel	6,920
Drayton	12,907
Herbert	115,258
Jonson	69,078
Marlowe	148,337
Sidney	12,791
Spenser	468,390
Strachey	1,417
Strode	20,359
Non-Sh. Tot.	855,457

each hyphenated compound as a single word. If a particular compound used by W. S. fails to appear in either sample (as is often the case), I have turned by default to the elements that comprise it, isolating any first or second element of a W. S. compound that appears again, in the same position, in either the Shakespeare or non-Shakespeare sample (irrespective of its appearance elsewhere as an independent word). It can be demonstrated that this procedure substantially improves accuracy in measuring any writer's distinctive vocabulary. For example, when this method is followed, each of Shakespeare's known works shows a slightly higher statistical correlation with the rest of the canon than that obtained by Hart, and each shows a somewhat lower affinity with non-Shakespearean texts.

Let us turn, then, to the *Elegy* and identify those words used by W. S. that appear in either the Shakespeare or non-Shakespeare sample, but not in both. A complete breakdown is provided in table 1.11. It will be seen that W. S.'s *Elegy* contains 45 different Shakespeare "badges." Between W. S. and Shakespeare, we find 197 tokens of these 45 words (55 in the *Elegy,* 142 in the Shakespeare canon). Conversely, the *Elegy* contains nine Shakespeare "flukes" (that is, nine words appearing in the non-Shakespeare sample that are foreign to the Shakespeare canon). Between W. S. and the non-Shakespeare sample, we find twenty-three tokens of these nine words (nine tokens in the *Elegy,* fourteen in the non-Shakespeare sample). The ratio of badges to flukes is 9/1. We cannot yet be sure, however, that this figure is statistically significant. If the Shakespeare canon, for example, has a markedly higher number of "different" words than the non-Shakespeare sample, virtually any poem of the same era will show a correlation with Shakespeare greater than 1/1, and perhaps as high as 9/1, as is the case with W. S.

Regrettably, the actual number of "different" words found in the Shakespeare canon and in the non-Shakespeare sample is unavailable to me. In the absence of such data, we must turn to other poems, to check whether we do not, in fact, arrive at similar results for virtually any poem as those obtained for the *Elegy.* I have chosen as my control group two poems by Shakespeare ("The Phoenix and the Turtle" and "A Lover's Complaint"), Hand *D* of *Sir Thomas More* (more recently ascribed to Shakespeare), and "Shall I die" (ascribed to Shakespeare in Bodleian MS. Rawl. Poet. 160); also included in the control group are three poems from the 1610–13 Cross-Sample of English Memorial Verse: John Donne's "Funeral Elegy," Cyril Tourneur's "Grief on the Death of Prince Henry," and John Webster's "Monumental Column." The procedure of compiling data for each poem is a long and arduous process, one that has rendered impracticable a more various sampling. I leave to others the task of expanding the list.

TABLE 1.11 / DISTINCTIVE VOCABULARY

TYPES (Gram.) WORD	WS	Shakespeare	Spenser	Marlowe	Jonson	Daniel	Drayton	Sidney	Herbert	Strachey	Strode
vb. to addict	3	4	—	—	—	—	—	—	—	—	—
adj. affected	1	2	—	—	—	—	—	—	—	—	—
adj. becoming	1	6	—	—	—	—	—	—	—	—	—
adj. besotted	1	1	—	—	—	—	—	—	—	—	—
adj. blemished	1	4	—	—	—	—	—	—	—	—	—
adj. brittle	1	6	—	—	—	—	—	—	—	—	—
cpd. clean-(word)	1	1	—	—	—	—	—	—	—	—	—
adj. complemental	1	—	—	—	—	—	—	—	1	—	—
n. concourse	1	—	—	—	—	—	—	—	1	—	—
n. consummation	1	3	—	—	—	—	—	—	—	—	—
vb. to detract	1	2	—	—	—	—	—	—	—	—	—
adj. disgraceful	1	1	—	—	—	—	—	—	—	—	—
adj. earthy	1	9	—	—	—	—	—	—	—	—	—
cpd. (word)-employed	1	1	—	—	—	—	—	—	—	—	—
n. float	1	1	—	—	—	—	—	—	—	—	—
vb. to foreshow	1	2	—	—	—	—	—	—	—	—	—
adv. fruitlessly	1	—	—	—	—	—	—	—	1	—	—
adj. gainful	1	—	—	—	—	—	—	—	3	—	—
cpd. heaven-(word)	2	4	—	—	—	—	—	—	—	—	—
adj. helpful	1	4	—	—	—	—	—	—	—	—	—
cpd. (word)-honored	1	2	—	—	—	—	—	—	—	—	—
n. lapse	1	3	—	—	—	—	—	—	—	—	—
adj. long-lived	1	1	—	—	—	—	—	—	—	—	—
cpd. (word)-lurking	1	1	—	—	—	—	—	—	—	—	—
n. minority	1	8	—	—	—	—	—	—	—	—	—
n. misconstruction	1	1	—	—	—	—	—	—	—	—	—
adj. offenseless	1	1	—	—	—	—	—	—	—	—	—
vb. to oversway	5	1	—	—	—	—	—	—	—	—	—
n. pawn	1	11	—	—	—	—	—	—	—	—	—
n. priority	1	2	—	—	—	—	—	—	—	—	—
adj. prompt	1	5	—	—	—	—	—	—	—	—	—
adj. questionable	1	1	—	—	—	—	—	—	—	—	—
adj. remiss	1	5	—	—	—	—	—	—	—	—	—
n. repute	2	3	—	—	—	—	—	—	—	—	—
adv. scantly	1	1	—	—	—	—	—	—	—	—	—
n. self-conceit	1	—	—	1	—	—	—	—	1	—	—
n. separation	1	5	—	—	—	—	—	—	—	—	—
adv. sincerely	1	3	—	—	—	—	—	—	—	—	—
n. singleness	3	2	—	—	—	—	—	—	—	—	—
vb. to size	1	1	—	—	—	—	—	—	—	—	—
cpd. (word)-speaking	1	2	—	—	—	—	—	—	—	—	—
adj. spleenful	1	2	—	—	—	—	—	—	—	—	—
adj. subject's, s'	1	11	—	—	—	—	—	—	—	—	—
n. supposition	1	6	—	—	—	—	—	—	—	—	—
adj. surrounding	1	—	—	1	—	—	—	—	—	—	—
adj. taintless	1	—	—	1	—	—	—	—	—	—	—
n. talker	1	3	—	—	—	—	—	—	—	—	—
cpd. (word)-tempered	1	5	—	—	—	—	—	—	—	—	—
adj. unaffected	1	—	—	—	—	1	—	—	—	—	—
adj. unburthened	1	1	—	—	—	—	—	—	—	—	—
adj. unprevailing	1	1	—	—	—	—	—	—	—	—	—
adj. unrespected	1	2	—	—	—	—	—	—	—	—	—
adj. unsteady	1	—	1	—	—	—	—	—	—	1	—
adj. wintered	1	1	—	—	—	—	—	—	—	—	—
Total WS/Shakespeare	55	142	—	—	—	—	—	—	—	—	—
Total WS/Non-Shakespeare	9	—	1	3	0	1	0	1	7	1	0

Taking, then, these seven texts as our control sample, we must find an operational index by which to measure the relative kinship of Shakespeare's distinctive vocabulary with that of our selected poems—an index that is independent of the length of each work. We may therefore add the badge-tokens as they appear both in the poem being tested and in Shakespeare; add the fluke-tokens as they appear in each poem and in the non-Shakespeare sample; and subtract the difference of the two sums. Those poems with more Shakespeare "badges" than "flukes" will have a positive measure, all others a negative measure. We may then prorate our results per one thousand words of source-text. Presumably, any poem by Shakespeare will produce a markedly positive index, and any poem not by Shakespeare a negative, or weakly positive index. Table 1.12 provides the data for W. S.'s *Elegy* and for the seven items in my control sample (compound elements are appropriately counted as separate words).[59] The higher correlative for Hand *D* than for either "A Lover's Complaint" or "The Phoenix and the Turtle" may be partly attributable to the fact that it is a dramatic text: its Shakespeare badges include such words as *alevenpence, half-penny, loaf, luggage, mutine,* and *pumpion,* none of which is likely to appear in nondramatic verse; nevertheless, the remarkably high Shakespeare-correlative may be taken as favoring Shakespearean authorship. The same may be said of W. S.'s *Elegy.*

As for those words in W. S.'s lexicon that are found in *both* the Shakespeare and non-Shakespeare samples, the imbalance is equally striking. Much of W. S.'s diction consists of words that appear frequently in Shakespeare, and no more than once in the non-Shakespeare sample. Examples are *commendable* (9/1 Shakespeare/non-Shakespeare), *commendation* (23/1), *embracement* (12/1), *flinty* (12/1), *-brained* (8/1), *dotage* (10/1); and so for many others.

We may turn next to a test developed by Alfred Hart and Eliot Slater.[60] These scholars discovered that Shakespeare's works may be dated by isolating, in any supposed Shakespearean text, those words that appear only rarely in the canon. During Shakespeare's career, words drifted in and out of his active lexicon, to be replaced by others. In that the *Elegy* is a nondramatic text, if Shakespeare wrote it we should expect to find a higher correlation with his poems than with his plays (as is true of all his nondramatic works). But given the date of the poem, February 1612, we should also expect to find a close affinity with the secondary vocabulary of the late plays (even as *Ven.* and *Luc.* show a high correlation with the early plays). To test whether this is indeed the case, we may take all those words used by W. S. that appear in the Shakespeare canon ten times or less (using the same criteria as before to determine what constitutes a "word"). The results of the Hart/Slater test, as applied to the *Elegy,* are shown in table 1.13.[61] A simple line graph helps to illustrate the relationship between

TABLE 1.12 / SHAKESPEAREAN VOCABULARY						
Title		**Number of words**	**Badges**	**Flukes**	**Difference**	**Index/ 1000/w**
Hand *D* of *Sir*	Types	1389	16	2	14	
Thomas More	Sample-tokens		46	2	34	
	Source-tokens		16	2	14	
	Net Tokens		62	4	58	+41.8
Funeral	Types	4460	45	9	36	
Elegy	Sample-tokens		146	13	129	
by W.S.	Source-tokens		51	9	42	
	Net Tokens		197	24	173	+38.8
"The Phoenix	Types	355	6	2	4	
and the Turtle"	Sample-tokens		9	4	5	
	Source-tokens		6	2	4	
	Net Tokens		15	6	9	+25.4
"A Lover's	Types	2578	30	9	21	
Complaint"	Sample-tokens		68	26	42	
	Source-tokens		30	9	21	
	Net Tokens		98	35	63	+24.4
Tourneur's	Types	1224	0	2	< 2 >	
"Grief"	Sample-tokens		0	3	< 3 >	
	Source-tokens		0	2	< 2 >	
	Net Tokens		0	5	< 5 >	-4.1
Webster's	Types	2638	9	10	< 1 >	
"Column"	Sample-tokens		22	55	< 31 >	
	Source-tokens		9	10	0	
	Net Tokens		34	65	< 31 >	-11.8
Donne's	Types	864	2	5	< 3 >	
"Funeral Elegy"	Sample-tokens		3	13	< 10 >	
	Source-tokens		2	5	< 3 >	
	Net Tokens		5	18	< 13 >	-15.1
"Shall I die"	Types	430	0	3	< 3 >	
	Sample-tokens		0	3	< 3 >	
	Source-tokens		0	7	< 7 >	
	Net Tokens		0	10	< 10 >	-23.3

TABLE 1.13 / SHAKESPEARE'S OCCASIONAL VOCABULARY				
		Total Words	"Rare" Words, *Elegy*	Overlap /100k Words
THE POEMS:				
	Ven.	9730	18	
	Luc.	14548	47	
	PhT	352	0	
	Son.	17520	30	
	LC	2563	6	
		44,713	101	225.9
THE PLAYS:				
I	Err.	14369	14	
	Shr.	20411	9	
	2H6	24450	27	
	3H6	23295	22	
	1H6	20515	23	
	Tit.	19790	18	
	TGV	16833	18	
	LLL	21033	34	
	R3	28309	29	
	Rom.	23913	17	
		212,918	211	99.1
II	MND	16087	19	
	R2	21809	35	
	Jn.	20386	26	
	MV	20921	20	
	1H4	23955	20	
	2H4	25706	24	
	Wiv.	21119	11	
	Ado	20768	16	
	H5	25577	29	
	JC	19110	16	
		215,438	218	101.2
III	TN	19401	20	
	AYL	21305	12	
	Ham.	29551	35	
	Tro.	25516	33	
	Oth.	25887	27	
	MM	21269	22	
	Lr	25221	28	
	AWW	22550	21	
		190,700	198	103.8
IV	Mac.	16197	26	
	Tim.	17748	13	
	Per. 3-5	9868	14	
	Ant.	23742	25	
	Cor.	26579	27	
	Cym.	26778	38	
	WT	24543	21	
	Tmp.	16036	18	
	Sh's H8	12358	19	
	Sh's TNK	9884	11	
		183,733	212	114.3

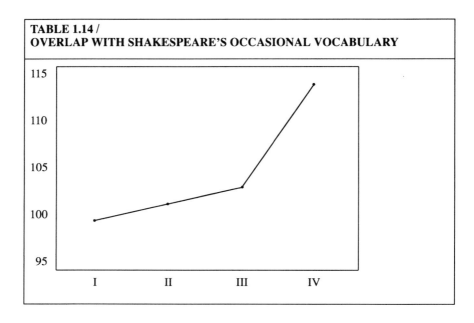

TABLE 1.14 /
OVERLAP WITH SHAKESPEARE'S OCCASIONAL VOCABULARY

TABLE 1.15 / "UNIQUE" WORDS IN SHAKESPEARE				
Title	Lines / Words	Unique Words	/100 Lines	/1000 Words
Ven.	1194 9730	101	8.5	10.4
Luc.	1855 14548	149	8.0	10.2
PhT	67 352	10	14.9	28.4
Son., LC	2483 20083	191	7.7	9.5
Total	5599 44713	451	8.1	10.1

W. S.'s *Elegy* and the late works of Shakespeare (table 1.14). After remaining more or less constant, the correlation between Shakespeare's occasional vocabulary and the Peter elegy registers a sudden jump as we move to the last plays. Nearly identical results are obtained if we limit our sample to those words of W. S. that appear just five times or less in the Shakespeare canon. And it will be seen that W. S.'s diction has a still higher correlation with Shakespeare's nondramatic verse, as should be expected.

But are there enough words in the *Elegy* "new" to Shakespeare to suggest a continuing expansion of his vocabulary? It has often been noted that all of Shakespeare's works include "unique" words, words that appear nowhere else in the canon. We should expect the same to be true here, and in roughly the same proportions as elsewhere. Alfred Hart, using slightly different criteria than those outlined above, finds in Shakespeare's nondramatic verse a frequency of unique words as shown in table 1.15. To these figures we may compare W. S.'s *Elegy* (using Hart's criteria):

Funeral Elegy by W.S.	578			
	4318	50	8.7	11.6

W. S. deviates from Shakespeare's mean in this respect by less than two words per thousand.

In past attributional studies, canonical scholars have often dwelt upon particular words, phrases, or images supposed to be characteristic of this or that poet, while neglecting those words in any English writer's vocabulary that are used most often. This failure may be ascribed in part to the lack of a detailed concordance for most authors, but one can have little confidence in the conjectures of any scholar who neglects to discuss the frequency of such basic structuring devices as a poet's choice and frequency of subordinating conjunctions, his frequency of comparative language, negative assertions, relative pronouns, and the like. Such elementary building blocks of style must be given a careful scrutiny before making even the most tenuous attribution.

Of nearly 30,000 different words (including inflections) in Shakespeare's collected vocabulary, there are nine, and only nine—*and, but, by, in, not, so, that, to, with*—that never deviate in the plays by more than a third from their respective mean frequencies. The four prepositions *(by, in, to, with)* have, unfortunately, little if any value as indices of style: the practice of Shakespeare and W. S., though much the same, is not remarkably different from that of other English poets of the same era. However, the remaining five words *(and, but, not, so, that)* may serve as a kind of stylistic Geiger counter. An index of these words, whether in W. S.'s *Elegy* or in the work of some other poet, reflects those largely unconscious (and inimitable) syntactical habits peculiar to the individual writer. No two poets have the same ratio of coordinate to subordinate structures, or the same manner of expressing negative assertions. One author will use *but that* where another writes *only* or *except*. One will use *that* chiefly as a demonstrative pronoun, while another reserves it to introduce a relative clause. One will often place an *and* between every member of a series, while others habitually omit the *and* altogether, and so on. This, of course, in no way guarantees that all five indices will be as consistent for other poets as for Shakespeare. It does mean, however, that we can use them to help us in distinguishing his hand from that of another, if we keep in mind that no such index is perfectly constant even in Shakespeare's work. Each varies somewhat from year to year, or from verse to prose. Shakespeare's use of *and*, for example, gradually decreases following an early high in *Titus Andronicus* of 38.5, while his use of *not* peaks in midcareer, drops somewhat after *The Winter's Tale,* and appears in the poems less frequently than in the plays.

There are various means of arriving at an expected frequency for each of these words in a supposed nondramatic work of William Shakespeare written in 1612, and all come to roughly the same figures, within a point or two of one another for both the expected high and expected low. The simplest method to arrive at an "expected range" for a Shakespeare poem is to note for each word Shakespeare's career high, and career low, in the drama, and to multiply these figures by a ratio of the respective means for the poems and plays. Then, to arrive at the "most probable frequency" within this broader spectrum, we may take as our strictest possible control group the four plays that immediately precede the *Elegy* (*Cor., Cym., WT,* and *Tmp.*), and again multiply the high and low in each case by the Poetry/ Drama ratio for each word. We thereby arrive at the figures in tables 1.16 and 1.17. In table 1.16, the first two columns provide the mean frequency for each word as it appears in the poems and plays; while column three gives the "P/D" ratio of the mean frequencies. The first two columns of table 1.17 give the high and low for Shakespeare's collected plays, columns 3 and 4 the probable range for any poem by Shakespeare (the high and low in the drama, multiplied by the P/D ratio). Columns 5 through 8 provide the same information for the more narrowly restricted control group, and column 9 provides the frequency for each word as it appears in the *Elegy.* It will be seen that the indices for the *Elegy* by W. S. consistently fall not only within the "probable range" for a poem by William Shakespeare, but with uncanny predictability fall in every case within the more narrowly circumscribed range of the "most probable frequency" within the broader spectrum, for a poem written late in his career.

	mean frequency:		P/D ratio
TABLE 1.16 / **SINGLE-WORD INDICES**			
	POEMS	PLAYS	
	1	2	3
AND	1322	24070	
	29.57	29.98	.99
BUT	370	6073	
	8.27	7.56	1.09
NOT	362	8393	
	8.10	10.45	.78
SO	342	4905	
	7.65	6.11	1.25
THAT	719	10648	
	16.08	13.26	1.21

Of the one hundred words most often used by Shakespeare (as given in Spevack, from "the" [#1] through "king" [#100]), few other individual words will serve as reliable measures of Shakespeare's style. The articles and prepositions are of no help, for neither Shakespeare's nor W. S.'s usage is remarkably different from that of other writers. Nor can any of the personal pronouns serve to distinguish W. S.'s practice from that of other poets, except in a very general way (e.g., many Jacobeans, unlike either Shakespeare or W. S., reserve *thou* and *thee* for addressing God). As for the auxiliary verbs, Shakespeare has, overall, a higher relative frequency for verbs in the present tense than do many of his contemporaries, but that says simply that the writer of stage plays requires the present tense more frequently than the author of works written in the past tense, as, say, a prose romance or a historical narrative—though once again, for what it's worth, of Shakespeare's most often-used auxiliaries (in order of frequency, *is, be, have, do, shall, are*), *be* has the smallest standard deviation, as well as the smallest differential between the poems and plays. The frequency

TABLE 1.17 / SINGLE-WORD INDICES								
	combined works		probable range		control group		most probable frequency	
	LOW	HIGH	LOW	HIGH	LOW	HIGH	LOW	HIGH	*Elegy*
	1	2	3	4	5	6	7	8	9
AND	*TGV*	*Tit.*			*Cym.*	*Tmp.*			109
	24.1	38.4	23.6	37.6	24.5	29.6	24.3	29.3	25.2
BUT	*Lr.*	*MM*			*Tmp.*	*WT*			37
	5.1	9.3	5.6	10.1	7.0	9.1	7.6	9.9	8.6
NOT	*H5*	*JC*			*Tmp.*	*WT*			41
	7.9	13.4	6.2	10.5	9.7	12.4	7.6	9.7	9.5
SO	*Wiv.*	*WT*			*Cor.*	*WT*			28
	4.7	7.9	5.9	9.9	5.1	7.9	6.4	9.9	6.5
THAT	*Wiv.*	*TGV*			*Tmp.*	*Cym.*			62
	9.8	16.9	11.9	20.4	11.8	13.6	14.3	16.5	14.4

for *be* in the *Elegy* is 8.8 per 1000 words, as opposed to 8.4 in *The Tempest,* 9.7 in *Cymbeline,* 10.3 in *The Winter's Tale,* and 8.1 in the *Sonnets.*

We may, however, add *like* as a useful index of style if we exclude its use as a verb. Since no two writers express comparative language in quite the same fashion, an index for *like* (including its appearance in compounds such as "harvest-like") may often serve to distinguish the hand of this or that poet. Shakespeare makes only moderate use of the word relative to his contemporaries, and with five exceptions is remarkably consistent throughout his career. His frequency for *like,* excluding only *Venus and Adonis, The Rape of Lucrece,* "The Phoenix and the Turtle," *Othello,* and *Richard III,* never deviates by more than one-third from his mean frequency of 2.09 per 1000 words—as in the *Elegy,* where the frequency is 2.08.

The five indices of table 1.17 (*and, but, not, so, that*), together with *most* and *like* are probably the seven most reliable single-word measures of Shakespeare's style, in that Shakespeare's frequency for all seven is so remarkably consistent. Of the forty items in the 1610–13 Cross-Sample, none passes more than four of the seven tests. The distribution of the items in the Sample is provided in table 1.18. If these poems provide a representative sample—and it would be difficult to conceive a more accurate cross-sample than that employed here—then the chances are quite negligible that any non-Shakespearean poem from this period will match Shake-

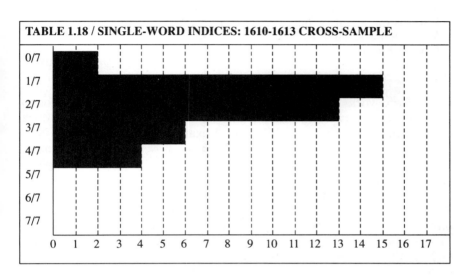

TABLE 1.18 / SINGLE-WORD INDICES: 1610-1613 CROSS-SAMPLE

speare's probable frequency for all seven words (no matter what the poet's initials). The *Funeral Elegy,* by W. S., matches the frequency for all seven.

Nor is it the frequency alone for these several words which suggests that Shakespeare may have written the Peter elegy, but the particular manner in which they are used. Some distinctive uses in Shakespeare for *and, like,* and *that* have already been discussed, to which we may add here his idiosyncratic use of *not.* A basic element of syntax in any writer's work is his manner of expressing negative assertions. One noteworthy feature of Shakespeare's late work in this respect is his tendency to place *not* before a verb without adding an auxiliary, as in the following examples from *The Tempest:*

I not doubt / He came alive to land.

(*Tmp.* 2.1.122–23)

> . . . you demi-puppets that
By moonshine do the green sour ringlets make,
Whereof the ewe not bites; . . .

(*Tmp.* 5.1.36–38)

> Whe'er thou beest he or no,
Of some enchanted trifle to abuse me
(As late I have been), I not know.

(*Tmp.* 5.1.111–13)

Sir, I invite your Highness and your train
To my poor cell, where you shall take your rest
For this one night; which, part of it, I'll waste
With such discourse as, I not doubt, shall make it
Go quick away— . . .

(*Tmp.* 5.1.301–5)

Of the forty works in the Cross-Sample, this irregular use of *not* is found only four times, twice in William Basse's elegy for Prince Henry, once each in Richard Niccols's and William Alexander's elegies for the Prince. Of the more than two hundred authors whose work is represented in the larger sample of the Memorial Verse 1570–1630, irregular *not* appears seven times more, in the work of five poets.

In Shakespeare there are just four instances of irregular *not* prior to *King Lear* (two in *1H4*, one each in *Ado* and *MM*); but from *King Lear* onward there are twenty-four, with examples to be found in every play but *Pericles*. In the last four plays (*WT, Tmp.,* and Shakespeare's portion of *H8* and *TNK*), the word *not* appears 651 times, for a relative frequency of 10.5/1000 words, twelve of which are irregular, or 1.8 percent, from a low in *The Winter's Tale* of 1.3 percent to a high of 2.6 percent in *The Tempest*. If written by Shakespeare, one should expect to find in the Peter elegy 29–42 occurrences of *not,* one of which is irregular. We find in fact 41 instances of *not* in the *Elegy*—and in lines 79–80 we read, "But that I *not intend* in full discourse / To progress out his life." To put it another way, W. S. has one irregular *not* in 578 lines. William Shakespeare in the two works immediately preceding the *Elegy* (*The Winter's Tale* and *The Tempest*) has on the average one such instance every 632 lines, and in his supposed portion of *Henry VIII* and *The Two Noble Kinsmen*—the two plays immediately following—he has one instance every 668 lines. All other English elegiac verse from 1570 to 1630 has on the average one irregular *not* every 6,200 lines, and from 1610 through 1613, one instance every 3,300 lines. The vast majority of Jacobean writers never use *not* before a verb without the auxiliary. Those few who do, do so repeatedly.

Table 1.19 provides statistical data for the forty elegiac works listed in the Cross-Sample, including the relative frequencies for these seven key words, along with relevant data for certain other stylistic features as discussed earlier. The table is, I think, fairly self-explanatory, though a few words of clarification are in order. The top line (marked "Shakespeare"), provides for each variable the most probable frequency for a Shakespearean poem written late in his career. In lines 1–42, where applicable, the top figure in each square gives the absolute frequency, and the bottom figure the relative frequency, for each index. Shaded squares indicate figures that fall within the expected parameters for Shakespeare.

Reading vertically, the figures in column one give the maximum percentage of "open" or unstopped lines, if lightly pointed, though the number of open lines in these texts as originally printed is in most cases much lower than the figures given here. The frequencies for *like* in column 5 include its appearance in compound words, since these are a form of comparative language, but omit its use as a verb, while those given in column 7 for *most* exclude its (very infrequent) use as a noun. Column 15, which provides an index of hyphenation, excludes those words that are not genuine compounds (*mis-take, a-weeping,* etc.), while column 16 gives the frequency of compounds that have a participle as their second element. Lastly, column 17 gives the number of words in the longest independent clause for each work, inclusive of all subordinate or parenthetical elements but excluding any independent clause linked to it by means of conjunction or semicolon. Specific titles may be identified by finding the *STC* number given below each author's name, and by turning to the bibliography of the "Memorial Verse, 1570–1630," in appendix C of this text.

Table 1.20 provides the same information for Shakespeare as for the items in the Cross-Sample, excepting only those indices that have already been presented in tables 1.1–1.18. All word-counts are based on Spevack. Line-counts are taken directly from *The Riverside Shakespeare,* upon which the Spevack concordance is based.[62] Relevant data are provided at the bottom of table 1.20 for both Hand *D* of *Sir Thomas More,* and the presumed non-Shakespearean portions of *Macbeth, Pericles, The Two Noble Kinsmen,* and *Henry VIII.*[63]

It will be seen that the Peter elegy passes all seventeen tests. To these seventeen we might add many others—the ratio of *because* to *since,* or the appearance of *for that* as a substitute for *because;* the appearance of *whiles* and *sith,* or of *wert* for the second person singular; the frequency of participles, or of nonce-contractions, or of proper nouns, or of words in *un-, -less,* and *-full;* congruency with W. S.'s preferred auxiliaries and accidentals; and so on—each of which seems to point toward Shakespearean authorship of the Peter elegy. But I leave to others the multiplying of such tests on the Cross-Sample. In the absence of quantifiable internal evidence *against* Shakespearean authorship, further tests of this sort can accomplish little except to nudge the statistical probability of non-Shakespearean authorship closer to absolute zero (disregarding, even, the problem of finding a poet with the appropriate initials). In the interests of objectivity, I have therefore made a concerted effort to find a statistically significant test of Shakespearean style that the *Elegy* does not pass. I have not been able to find one. The poem does have a higher frequency of *as* and *which* than might be expected given Shakespeare's practice elsewhere, but the discrepancy is too small to be of mathematical importance.[64]

TABLE 1.19 / CROSS-SAMPLE: ELEGIAC VERSE, 1610-1613

Author STC#	# lines # words	1 % lines runon	2 % feminine endings	3 *and* / 1000 w	4 *but* / 1000 w	5 *like* / 1000 w	6 (word)-*like* / 1000 w	7 adv., adj. *most* / 1000 w	8 redundant *-er*, *-est*, 1000 w	9 *not* / 1000 w	10 [do] *not* / 1000 w	11 *so* / 1000 w	12 *that* / 1000 w	13 incongruent *who* / 100 l	14 hendiadys 100 l	15 hyphenated compounds / 1000 w	16 participial compounds / 1000 w	17 longest ISU
Shakespeare		52.2 43.8	13.5 7.5	29.0 24.0	9.9 7.6	2.8 1.4	.26 .20	2.6 1.7	.25 .06	9.7 7.6	.37 .04	9.9 6.4	16.5 14.3	.75 .28	4.48 .14	6.7 3.6	5.9 2.2	162 111
Anon. 13158	302 2334	80 26.5	2 0.7	86 36.8	25 10.7	4 1.7	2 .86	0 .00	0 .00	11 4.7	0 .00	15 6.4	45 19.3	0 .00	0 .00	4 1.7	1 0.4	113
Anon. 13142	288 2286	75 26.0	50 17.4	37 16.2	14 6.1	9 3.9	2 .87	5 2.2	0 .00	16 7.0	0 .00	12 5.2	43 18.8	0 .00	0 .00	8 3.5	2 0.9	114
Alexander 339	126 1343	15 11.9	0 0.0	22 16.4	13 9.7	2 1.5	0 .00	3 2.2	0 .00	19 14.1	1 .74	11 8.2	24 17.9	0 .00	0 .00	2 1.5	1 0.7	46
Allyn 384	368 3103	109 28.5	33 9.0	75 24.2	29 9.3	2 0.6	0 .00	6 1.9	0 .00	14 4.5	0 .00	8 2.6	43 13.9	0 .00	0 .00	0 0.0	0 0.0	131
Basse 1546	170 1426	57 33.5	23 13.5	38 26.6	7 4.9	17 11.9	8 5.61	4 2.8	0 .00	8 5.6	2 1.39	12 8.4	23 16.1	0 .00	0 .00	10 7.0	2 1.4	68
Beaumont 18911/B1602	180 1506	78 43.3	0 0.0	37 24.6	17 11.3	3 2.0	0 .00	1 0.7	0 .00	13 8.6	0 .00	11 7.3	20 13.3	0 .00	0 .00	3 2.0	0 0.0	65
Brooke 3831	400 3080	108 27.0	20 5.0	118 38.3	22 7.1	12 3.9	3 .97	2 0.6	0 .00	19 6.2	0 .00	21 6.8	35 11.4	0 .00	0 .00	12 3.9	4 1.3	68
Browne 3831	144 1027	42 29.2	10 6.9	22 21.4	9 8.8	2 1.9	0 .00	0 0.0	1 .97	6 5.8	0 .00	7 6.8	14 13.6	0 .00	0 .00	3 2.9	2 2.0	82
Burton 23578	194 1604	50 25.8	20 10.3	28 17.5	19 11.8	0 0.0	0 .00	0 0.0	0 .00	10 6.2	0 .00	8 5.0	26 16.2	0 .00	0 .00	9 5.6	2 1.3	43
Campion 4546	196 1492	79 40.3	28 14.3	52 34.9	7 4.7	5 3.4	0 .00	2 1.3	0 .00	9 6.0	0 .00	9 6.0	25 16.8	0 .00	0 .00	4 2.7	2 1.3	64
Chapman 4974	656 5252	240 36.6	41 6.3	198 39.8	33 6.3	24 4.6	7 1.33	10 1.9	0 .00	29 5.5	0 .00	35 6.7	69 13.1	0 .00	0 .00	38 7.2	13 2.5	135
Cornwallis 23578	188 1473	57 30.3	10 5.3	58 39.4	14 9.5	7 4.8	2 1.36	1 0.7	0 .00	22 14.9	0 .00	6 4.1	16 10.9	0 .00	0 .00	8 5.4	4 2.7	51

Author STC#	# words / # lines	1 runon lines %	2 feminine endings %	3 and / 1000 w	4 but / 1000 w	5 like / 1000 w	6 (word)-like / 1000 w	7 adv, adj. most / 1000 w	8 redundant -er, -est / 1000 w	9 not / 1000 w	10 [op] not / 1000 w	11 so / 1000 w	12 that / 1000 w	13 hendiadys 100 I	14 hyphenated compounds / 1000 w	15 participial compounds / 1000 w	16 longest ISU	17 who / incongruent 100 I
Cozen 4481	53 / 419	10 / 18.9	4 / 7.5	10 / 23.9	4 / 9.5	0 / 0.0	0 / .00	0 / 0.0	0 / .00	2 / 4.8	0 / .00	8 / 19.1	5 / 11.9	0 / .00	0 / .00	1 / 2.4	1 / 2.4	31
Davies 1612 6338	592 / 4860	193 / 32.6	4 / 0.7	131 / 27.0	73 / 15.0	17 / 3.5	3 / .62	9 / 1.9	0 / .00	28 / 5.8	0 / .00	59 / 12.1	98 / 20.2	0 / .00	0 / .00	27 / 5.6	5 / 1.0	80
Davies 1613 6339	1080 / 8835	395 / 34.7	0 / 0.0	238 / 26.9	138 / 15.6	35 / 4.0	2 / .23	29 / 3.3	0 / .00	53 / 6.0	0 / .00	116 / 13.1	174 / 19.7	0 / .00	0 / .00	24 / 2.7	7 / 0.8	64
Donne 1611 7022	580 / 4655	190 / 32.8	2 / 0.3	195 / 41.9	57 / 12.2	4 / 0.9	0 / .00	3 / 0.6	0 / .00	51 / 11.0	0 / .00	41 / 8.8	91 / 19.5	0 / .00	0 / .00	16 / 3.4	7 / 1.5	172
Donne 1612 7023	570 / 4595	187 / 32.8	0 / 0.0	174 / 37.9	51 / 11.1	5 / 1.1	0 / .00	3 / 0.7	0 / .00	43 / 9.4	0 / .00	45 / 9.8	91 / 19.8	0 / .00	0 / .00	7 / 1.5	3 / 0.7	239
Donne 1613 23578	98 / 781	32 / 32.7	0 / 0.0	21 / 26.9	6 / 7.7	0 / 0.0	0 / .00	0 / 0.0	0 / .00	10 / 12.8	0 / .00	14 / 17.9	17 / 21.8	0 / .00	0 / .00	4 / 5.1	0 / 0.0	106
Drummond 7257	237 / 1832	58 / 24.5	0 / 0.0	53 / 28.9	5 / 2.7	6 / 3.3	1 / .55	1 / 0.5	1 / .55	9 / 4.9	0 / .00	12 / 6.6	31 / 16.9	0 / .00	0 / .00	9 / 4.9	4 / 2.2	77
G. Fletcher 4481	84 / 680	14 / 16.7	0 / 0.0	16 / 23.5	4 / 5.9	0 / 0.0	0 / .00	0 / 0.0	0 / .00	6 / 8.8	0 / .00	4 / 5.9	9 / 13.2	0 / .00	0 / .00	3 / 4.4	1 / 1.5	106
Goodyer 23578	74 / 587	27 / 36.5	15 / 17.9	20 / 34.1	5 / 8.5	1 / 1.7	0 / .00	0 / 0.0	0 / .00	6 / 10.2	0 / .00	10 / 17.0	14 / 23.9	0 / .00	0 / .00	4 / 6.8	3 / 5.1	47
Gorges NL/STC	1222 / 9588	334 / 27.3	21 / 1.7	283 / 29.5	95 / 9.9	25 / 2.6	3 / .31	14 / 1.5	0 / .00	47 / 4.9	0 / .00	71 / 7.4	228 / 23.8	0 / .00	0 / .00	102 / 10.6	77 / 8.0	92
Herbert 23578	66 / 550	48 / 72.7	0 / 0.0	18 / 32.7	4 / 7.3	1 / 1.8	0 / .00	0 / 0.0	0 / .00	12 / 21.8	0 / .00	8 / 14.5	13 / 23.6	0 / .00	0 / .00	0 / 0.0	0 / 0.0	66
Heywood 13323	376 / 3054	90 / 23.9	73 / 19.4	77 / 25.2	24 / 7.9	4 / 1.3	0 / .00	5 / 1.6	1 / .32	26 / 8.5	0 / .00	48 / 15.7	48 / 15.7	0 / .00	0 / .00	2 / 0.7	2 / 0.7	90
Holland 23578	162 / 1394	21 / 13.0	114 / 70.4	51 / 36.6	15 / 10.8	4 / 2.9	0 / .00	1 / 0.7	0 / .00	4 / 2.9	0 / .00	15 / 10.8	26 / 18.7	0 / .00	0 / .00	2 / 1.4	0 / 0.0	39
Johnson 14691	188 / 1201	41 / 21.8	0 / 0.0	44 / 36.6	5 / 4.2	4 / 3.3	1 / .83	3 / 2.5	0 / .00	5 / 4.2	0 / .00	4 / 3.3	5 / 4.2	0 / .00	1 / .83	8 / 6.7	4 / 3.3	98
Maxwell 17701	294 / 2260	56 / 19.0	14 / 4.8	80 / 35.4	10 / 4.4	9 / 4.0	3 / 1.32	4 / 1.8	0 / .00	5 / 2.2	0 / .00	13 / 5.8	22 / 9.7	0 / .00	0 / .00	16 / 7.1	5 / 2.2	51

Author STC#	# words / # lines	1 run-on lines %	2 feminine endings %	3 and / 1000 w	4 but / 1000 w	5 like / 1000 w	6 (word)-like / 1000 w	7 adv., adj. most / 1000 w	8 redundant -er, -est / 1000 w	9 not / 1000 w	10 [do] not / 1000 w	11 so / 1000 w	12 that / 1000 w	13 hendiadys 100 l	14 hyphenated compounds / 1000 w	15 participial compounds / 1000 w	16 longest ISU	17 who / incongruent 100 l
Murray 18296	100 / 785	14 / 14.0	8 / 8.0	16 / 20.4	9 / 11.5	0 / 0.0	0 / .00	3 / 3.8	0 / .00	9 / 11.5	0 / .00	4 / 5.1	12 / 15.3	1 / 1.00	0 / .00	5 / 6.4	5 / 6.4	49
Niccols 18525	614 / 5057	218 / 35.5	20 / 3.3	144 / 28.5	27 / 5.3	21 / 4.2	4 / .79	5 / 1.0	0 / .00	31 / 6.1	1 / .20	33 / 6.5	94 / 18.6	0 / .00	0 / .00	21 / 4.2	8 / 1.6	64
Peacham 19513	480 / 3310	113 / 23.5	0 / 0.0	121 / 36.6	24 / 7.3	8 / 2.4	2 / .60	0 / 0.0	0 / .00	11 / 3.3	0 / .00	8 / 2.4	54 / 16.3	0 / .00	0 / .00	7 / 2.1	1 / 0.3	87
Primrose 20393	120 / 916	28 / 23.3	1 / 0.8	34 / 37.1	5 / 5.5	6 / 6.6	1 / 1.10	0 / 0.0	0 / .00	3 / 3.3	0 / .00	2 / 2.2	15 / 16.4	0 / .00	0 / .00	8 / 8.7	4 / 4.4	121
Rogers 21241.5	180 / 1451	32 / 17.8	0 / 0.0	41 / 28.3	6 / 4.1	3 / 2.1	2 / 1.38	3 / 2.1	0 / .00	3 / 3.8	0 / .00	13 / 9.0	16 / 11.0	0 / .00	0 / .00	5 / 3.4	0 / 0.0	49
Rowley 23760.5	88 / 732	15 / 17.0	2 / 2.3	15 / 20.5	9 / 12.3	1 / 1.4	0 / .00	0 / 0.0	0 / .00	3 / 4.1	0 / .00	7 / 9.6	12 / 16.4	0 / .00	0 / .00	1 / 1.4	0 / 0.0	44
Sylvester 23578	370 / 2146	60 / 16.2	10 / 2.7	86 / 40.1	22 / 10.3	8 / 3.7	1 / .47	2 / 0.9	0 / .00	13 / 6.1	0 / .00	20 / 9.3	25 / 11.6	0 / .00	0 / .00	34 / 15.8	4 / 1.9	125
Sylvester, tr 17661	642 / 4930	88 / 13.7	12 / 1.9	134 / 27.2	34 / 6.9	10 / 2.0	5 / 1.01	5 / 1.0	0 / .00	36 / 7.3	0 / .00	31 / 6.3	62 / 12.6	0 / .00	0 / .00	35 / 7.1	9 / 1.8	61
Taylor 23760.5	212 / 1641	48 / 22.6	22 / 10.4	75 / 45.7	14 / 8.5	4 / 2.4	1 / .61	1 / 0.6	1 / .61	7 / 4.3	0 / .00	17 / 10.4	33 / 20.1	0 / .00	0 / .00	17 / 10.4	6 / 3.7	66
Tourneur 24148.3	156 / 1221	66 / 42.3	2 / 1.6	27 / 22.1	11 / 9.0	1 / 0.8	0 / .00	0 / 0.0	0 / .00	13 / 10.6	0 / .00	8 / 6.6	36 / 29.5	0 / .00	0 / .00	0 / 0.0	0 / 0.0	63
Walkington 4481	62 / 479	18 / 29.0	8 / 12.9	6 / 12.5	4 / 8.4	1 / 2.1	1 / 2.10	0 / 0.0	0 / .00	3 / 6.3	0 / .00	4 / 8.4	10 / 20.9	0 / .00	0 / .00	3 / 6.3	1 / 2.1	39
Webster 25174	328 / 2624	138 / 42.1	20 / 7.6	92 / 35.1	14 / 5.3	15 / 5.7	0 / .00	2 / 0.8	0 / .00	22 / 8.4	0 / .00	21 / 8.0	52 / 19.8	0 / .00	0 / .00	14 / 5.3	8 / 3.1	234
Wither 25915	960 / 7551	149 / 25.9	124 / 12.9	232 / 30.7	87 / 11.5	10 / 1.3	2 / .26	12 / 1.6	0 / .00	77 / 10.2	0 / .00	51 / 6.8	106 / 14.0	0 / .00	0 / .00	36 / 4.8	15 / 2.0	60
Combined Poems	13200 / 104060	3673 / 27.8	713 / 5.4	3205 / 30.8	972 / 9.3	290 / 2.8	56 / .54	139 / 1.3	4 / .04	719 / 6.9	4 / .04	842 / 8.1	1782 / 17.1	1 / .01	1 / .01	512 / 4.9	213 / 2.0	avg 85
Elegy by W.S.	578 / 4318	266 / 46.0	67 / 11.6	109 / 25.2	37 / 8.6	9 / 2.1	1 / .23	11 / 2.6	4 / .23	42 / 9.5	1 / .23	28 / 6.5	62 / 14.4	4 / .69	10 / 1.73	22 / 5.1	16 / 3.7	141

TABLE 1.20 / WILLIAM SHAKESPEARE

	# lines / # words	% lines runon	and / a, and't and / 1000 w	but / 1000 w	like / 1000 w	(word) -like / 1000 w	adv., adj., most / 1000 w	redundant -er, -est / 1000 w	not / 1000 w	[do] not / 1000 w	so / 1000 w	that / 1000 w
Ven.	1194	136	324	78	53	4	5	0	79	0	68	107
	9730	11.4	33.30	8.02	5.55	.41	.51	.00	8.12	.00	6.98	11.00
Luc.	1855	322	404	107	44	3	6	3	89	0	109	240
	14548	17.4	27.77	7.35	3.02	.21	.41	.21	6.12	.00	7.49	16.50
PhT	67	11	12	5	0	0	0	0	5	0	5	6
	352	16.4	34.09	14.20	.00	.00	.00	.00	14.20	.00	14.20	17.05
Son.	2154	374	489	163	34	2	25	3	167	0	145	321
	17520	17.4	27.91	9.30	1.94	.11	1.43	.17	9.53	.00	8.28	18.32
LC	329	69	93	17	5	0	2	0	22	0	15	45
	2563	21.0	36.29	6.63	1.95	.00	.78	.00	8.58	.00	5.85	17.56
Err.	1764		437	111	21	1	13	1	167	0	73	217
	14369	9.0	30.41	7.72	1.46	.07	.90	.07	11.62	.00	5.08	15.10
Shr.	2625		722	145	34	0	7	0	231	0	149	233
	20411	10.5	35.37	7.10	1.67	.00	.34	.00	11.32	.00	7.30	11.42
2H6	3111		877	175	51	3	14	0	204	0	132	285
	24450	13.1	35.87	7.16	2.09	.12	.57	.00	8.34	.00	5.40	11.66
3H6	2904		871	193	54	2	5	0	198	0	115	336
	23295	11.6	37.39	8.29	2.32	.09	.21	.00	8.50	.00	4.94	14.42
Tit.	2517		761	117	44	1	9	0	172	0	101	273
	19790	14.3	38.45	5.91	2.22	.05	.45	.00	8.69	.00	5.10	13.79
1H6	2675		680	151	51	2	15	1	177	0	128	253
	20515	13.8	33.15	7.36	2.49	.10	.73	.05	8.63	.00	6.24	12.33
TGV	2242		405	148	27	4	9	1	201	0	111	285
	16833	15.2	24.06	8.79	1.60	.24	.53	.06	11.94	.00	6.59	16.93
LLL	2748		565	162	44	1	53	0	216	1	148	286
	21033	13.9	26.86	7.70	2.09	.05	2.52	.00	10.27	.05	7.04	13.60
R3	3602		867	192	36	2	31	1	261	0	173	435
	28309	15.8	30.63	6.78	1.27	.07	1.10	.04	9.22	.00	6.11	15.37
MND	2152		540	120	28	2	20	2	170	0	115	185
	16087	15.1	33.57	7.46	1.74	.12	1.24	.12	10.56	.00	7.15	11.50
Rom.	2994		681	180	38	2	16	2	259	0	147	345
	23913	15.6	28.48	7.53	1.59	.08	.67	.08	10.83	.00	6.15	14.43

	# lines / # words	% lines runon	and'a.and't and / 1000 w	but / 1000 w	like / 1000 w	(word) -like / 1000 w	adv., adj., most / 1000 w	redundant -er, -est / 1000 w	not / 1000 w	[do] not / 1000 w	so / 1000 w	that / 1000 w
R2	2755		692	150	44	1	17	0	204	0	127	284
	21809	20.7	31.73	6.88	2.02	.05	.78	.00	9.35	.00	5.82	13.02
Jn.	2569		682	150	38	1	14	0	190	0	130	308
	20386	17.7	33.45	7.36	1.86	.05	.69	.00	9.32	.00	6.38	15.11
MV	2620		579	181	30	1	18	1	219	0	118	255
	20921	24.7	27.68	8.65	1.43	.05	.86	.05	10.47	.00	5.64	12.19
1H4	2870		837	178	57	0	12	0	258	0	156	255
	23955	27.7	34.94	7.43	2.38	.00	.50	.00	10.77	.00	6.51	10.64
2H4	3285		875	168	64	2	40	3	234	2	169	297
	25706	26.8	34.04	6.54	2.49	.08	1.56	.12	9.10	.08	6.57	11.55
Wiv.	2881		569	124	44	4	9	0	205	0	99	207
	21119	18.9	26.94	5.87	2.08	.19	.43	.00	9.71	.00	4.69	9.80
Ado	2765		601	172	44	2	24	2	250	1	138	292
	20768	19.8	28.94	8.28	2.12	.10	1.16	.10	12.04	.05	6.64	14.06
H5	3266		960	162	59	2	42	0	201	0	149	312
	25577	26.0	37.53	6.33	2.31	.08	1.64	.00	7.86	.00	5.83	12.20
JC	2457		594	141	37	0	28	2	256	0	139	285
	19110	20.3	31.08	7.38	1.94	.00	1.47	.10	13.40	.00	7.27	14.91
TN	2542		499	166	41	0	32	0	229	0	128	276
	19401	24.6	25.72	8.56	2.11	.00	1.65	.00	11.80	.00	6.60	14.23
AYL	2772		657	192	48	2	36	1	253	0	136	343
	21305	22.0	30.84	9.01	2.25	.09	1.69	.05	11.88	.00	6.38	16.10
Ham.	3832		902	260	79	4	81	4	315	0	193	389
	29551	24.2	30.52	8.80	2.67	.14	2.74	.14	10.66	.00	6.53	13.16
Tro.	3396		746	200	60	3	34	3	314	0	143	304
	25516	26.9	29.24	7.84	2.35	.12	1.33	.12	12.31	.00	5.60	11.91
Oth.	3271		746	219	24	1	56	5	320	0	161	372
	25887	24.3	28.82	8.46	.93	.04	2.16	.19	12.36	.00	6.22	14.37
MM	2742		538	197	32	0	53	2	236	1	118	303
	21269	28.2	25.30	9.26	1.50	.00	2.49	.09	11.10	.05	5.55	14.25
Lr.	3245		683	128	43	5	51	7	280	2	137	342
	25221	29.6	27.08	5.08	1.70	.20	2.02	.28	11.10	.08	5.43	13.56
AWW	2845		591	187	30	2	41	1	251	0	152	326
	22550	33.8	26.21	8.29	1.33	.09	1.82	.04	11.13	.00	6.74	14.46
Mac.	2038		498	117	43	3	24	1	163	0	95	226
	16197	31.2	30.75	7.22	2.65	.19	1.48	.06	10.06	.00	5.86	13.95
Tim.	2312		500	134	44	3	36	1	194	2	112	227
	17748	27.9	28.17	7.55	2.48	.17	2.03	.06	10.93	.11	6.31	12.79

	# lines / # words	% lines runon	and, a, and't and / 1000 w	but / 1000 w	like / 1000 w	(word) -like / 1000 w	adv, adj, most / 1000 w	redundant -er, -est / 1000 w	not / 1000 w	[do] not / 1000 w	so / 1000 w	that / 1000 w
Per. 3-5	1430		251	87	27	3	20	0	83	0	47	108
	9868	31.8	25.44	8.82	2.74	.30	2.03	.00	8.41	.00	4.76	10.94
Ant.	3021		599	180	52	4	60	2	260	5	140	292
	23742	40.8	25.23	7.58	2.19	.17	2.53	.08	10.95	.21	5.90	12.30
Cor.	3338		681	190	67	7	50	2	283	1	136	319
	26579	43.8	25.62	7.15	2.52	.26	1.88	.08	10.65	.04	5.12	12.00
Cym.	3291		657	227	55	7	46	3	288	2	210	364
	26778	45.9	24.54	8.48	2.05	.26	1.72	.11	10.76	.07	7.84	13.59
WT	3002		630	224	48	5	50	2	305	4	194	320
	24543	46.5	25.67	9.13	1.96	.20	2.04	.08	12.43	.16	7.90	13.04
Tmp.	2054		475	113	39	3	42	4	155	4	85	190
	16036	45.5	29.62	7.05	2.43	.19	2.62	.25	9.67	.25	5.30	11.85
H8	1492		368	65	21	3	27	1	106	1	55	175
	12358	52.2	29.78	5.26	1.70	.24	2.18	.08	8.58	.08	4.45	14.16
TNK	1178		254	67	19	2	17	1	85	3	46	144
	9884	60.6	25.70	6.78	1.92	.20	1.72	.10	8.60	.30	4.65	14.57
Elegy	578	266	109	37	9	1	11	1	41	1	28	62
	4318	46.0	25.24	8.57	2.08	.23	2.55	.23	9.50	.23	6.48	14.36
THE POEMS	5599		1322	370	136	9	38	6	362	0	342	719
	44713		29.57	8.27	3.04	.20	.85	.13	8.10	.00	7.65	16.08
THE PLAYS	102603		24070	6073	1577	90	1152	56	8393	29	4905	10648
	802789		29.98	7.56	1.96	.11	1.43	.07	10.45	.04	6.11	13.26
STM (Sh.?)	166		38	12	5	0	0	0	15	0	2	23
	1387	41.1	27.39	8.65	3.60	.00	.00	.00	10.81	.00	1.44	16.58
Mac. Midd'n	49		19	3	1	0	0	0	2	0	1	3
	239	26.5	79.50	12.55	4.18	.00	.00	.00	8.37	.00	4.18	12.55
Per. 1-2 anon.	1613		235	61	35	1	3	0	72	0	48	95
	7855	19.4	29.92	7.77	4.46	.13	.38	.00	9.17	.00	6.11	12.09
H8 ? Fl/Sh	474		116	23	7	0	8	0	35	1	26	63
	3926	37.4	29.55	5.86	1.78	.00	2.04	.00	8.91	.25	6.62	16.05
H8 Fletch	850		186	45	19	1	12	0	51	0	47	86
	7041	33.3	26.42	6.39	2.70	.14	1.70	.00	7.24	.00	6.68	12.21
TNK Fletch	1617		511	100	39	2	12	0	113	1	80	166
	13519	27.6	37.80	7.40	2.88	.15	0.89	.00	8.36	.07	5.92	12.28

It cannot, of course, be proven that my Sample is perfectly representative of all non-Shakespearean verse of the period. Nor can it be demonstrated that the tests I have chosen are perfectly representative of Shakespeare. One must therefore be cautious and not draw too hasty a conclusion from statistics such as these. The chances are quite remote, by any method of calculation, that a non-Shakespearean poem, by an author of any initials, should have so close an affinity with Shakespeare as that found in this elegy by W. S.; still, the mathematical significance of the various tests discussed here begs a more detailed analysis than I am able to provide. I have therefore submitted the raw data to various statisticians who have prior expertise in the statistical analysis of literary texts, and who have expressed interest in studying, independently, the significance of the data presented here.[65] As this book goes to press, their research has not yet been completed.

Thematic and Verbal Affinities

The appearance in an anonymous work of phrasing that appears elsewhere in a work of known authorship is rarely convincing as a basis of attribution. Barring instances of wholesale plagiarism, verbal echoes generally dwell in the ear of the beholder. What one scholar calls an "echo" of this or that author may in fact be nothing more than a commonplace expression or sentiment, and even when two or more texts contain obvious similarities of diction or phraseology, no firm conclusion may be drawn from it, for there is nothing easier than for one writer simply to borrow the words of another. Then, too, the Shakespeare canon is so large and various that we may extract "Shakespearean parallels" from the work of virtually any contemporaneous poet. Yet the parallels of phrasing between William Shakespeare and W. S. are so pervasive that the poem, if not written by Shakespeare, was at least written under Shakespeare's influence. One finds also in the *Elegy* many of Shakespeare's insistent thematic concerns. The elegist writes of loving in silence, of blind men who think they see, of virtuous men falsely accused by slanderous tongues. He shares Shakespeare's nearly obsessive concern with man's relation to time (e.g., *Elegy* 1, 63–64, 85, 132, 145, 157, 160, 198, 341, 344, 358, 496) and borrows Shakespeare's vision of each human life as a textual structure, to be read and interpreted. The Shakespearean thematic and verbal parallels are, indeed, so numerous that our discussion of the poem's authorship will not be complete without looking at some of them.

The *Elegy* recalls the *Sonnets* more often than any other canonical work, followed by *Henry VIII, Cymbeline, Richard II,* and *The Winter's Tale;* but most of Shakespeare's works contain at least a few notable parallels with this *Elegy* by W. S. One may almost proceed through the poem line by line, finding for each sentence a Shakespearean counterpart. Compare, for example, the following brief passage from the *Elegy* (51–62) with related phrasing from the poems and plays, interlineated, in italics. (It should be noted, however, before proceeding, that I submit this interlineated passage as a single unit of evidence—as is true also of each grouped sample that follows. I do not wish to dignify any particular phrase as evidence that Shakespeare wrote the *Elegy*):

His younger years gave comfortable hope
> *hope, which elder years / May happily bring forth*
>> (*R2* 5.3.21–22)

To hope for comfort in his riper youth,
> *Which elder days shall ripen and confirm*
>> (*R2* 2.3.43)

Which, harvest-like, did yield again the crop
> *valor / That . . . yields a crop*
>> (*Cym.* 4.2.179–80)

> *when wit and youth is come to harvest*
>> (*TN* 3.1.132)

Of education, better'd in his truth.
> *better'd with his own learning*
>> (*MV* 4.1.158)

> *Puts to him all the learnings*
> . . . .
> *And in's spring became a harvest*
>> (*Cym.* 1.1.43–46)

Those noble twins of heaven-infused races,
> *Those twins of learning*
>> (*H8* 4.2.58

> *a race of heaven*
>> (*Ant.* 1.3.37)

> *infused with a fortitude from heaven*
>> (*Tmp.* 1.2.154)

> *heaven hath infus'd them with these spirits*
>> (*JC* 1.3.69)

> *Those best affections that the heavens infuse*
>> (*TNK* 1.3.9)

Learning and wit, refined in their kind,
> *jewels often in their silent kind*
>
> (*TGV* 3.1.90)

> *distemper in this kind*
>
> (*Wiv.* 3.3.216)

[Plus many other such, but this syntax is commonplace.]

Did jointly both, in their peculiar graces,
> *Jointly list'ning, but with several graces*
>
> (*Luc.* 1410)

Enrich the curious temple of his mind;
> *his valor did enrich his wit*
>
> (*R3* 3.1.85)

> *That temple, thy fair mind*
>
> (*Cym.* 2.1.64)

Indeed a temple, in whose precious white
> *hand . . . whose perfect white*
>
> (*Luc.* 393–94)

> *flank, whose wonted lily white*
>
> (*Ven.* 1053)

Sat reason by religion oversway'd,
> *The will of man is by his reason sway'd*
>
> (*MND* 2.2.115)

Teaching his other senses, with delight,
> *Mine eyes are made the fools o' th' other senses*
>
> (*Mac.* 2.1.44)

How piety and zeal should be obey'd.
> (*Elegy* 51–62)

> *Which my love makes religion to obey*
>
> (*Ant.* 5.2.199)

W. S.'s possible borrowings from Shakespeare are not the sort that may be described as plagiarism, nor even as deliberate imitation. Most appear to be instances of unconscious repetition, sometimes involving no more than the linking of a noun with a particular adjective, as in "fair conditions" (appearing also in *H5*), "true friendship" (as in *Tim.*), "deep unrest" (as in *Luc.*; *Elegy*, "deep'st unrest"), and many other such, some of which appear repeatedly in Shakespeare. For instance, where W. S. writes of "fittest times in reason's rules to thrive" (rather than "best time"), Shakespeare writes of "fittest time and safest way / To hide" (*AYL* 1.3.135–36), of "fitt'st time / For best solicitation" (*TNK* 1.1.169–70), and even of the "fittest time to corrupt a man's wife" (*Cor.* 4.3.32). Most such adjective-noun links in the *Elegy* that have identical counterparts in Shakespeare involve a displaced epithet (e.g., "unadvised wounds," "curious eye," or "servile breath"), only a few of which are likely to be found also in non-Shakespearean texts (e.g., "sick desires"). We find as well many instances of shared imagery, as when W. S. says that his former joys "are leapt into thy tomb," which recalls the image of Laertes and Hamlet leaping into the grave of Ophelia, or of young Hotspur, who "led his powers to death, / And winking, leapt into destruction" (*2H4* 1.3.32–33). In addition, W. S. frequently duplicates Shakespeare's most distinctive syntactical habits. To the many examples that have already been provided from the *Elegy,* one may cite numerous other, less habitual, mannerisms, as when W. S. describes his friend as "noble in the mind," evincing a peculiar spatialization and localization of nobility, as in Hamlet's phrase, "nobler in the mind."

A noteworthy feature of Shakespeare's figurative language is that he has a higher tolerance than many of his contemporaries for mixed metaphors, some of which are habitual. One such is his continual linking of "taste" with another figure of speech that cannot be tasted, as in the *Sonnets:* "I *taste* / At first the very worst of *fortune's might*" (Son. 90.11–12); as also in the *Elegy,* wherein W. S. writes of saints who "*tasted* of the sour-bitter *scourge* / Of torture" (*Elegy* 395–96). Many Renaissance poets speak of "tasting" such emotions as cowardice, sorrow, or wrath, but few speak of tasting such nouns as "obedience," "correction," or "affliction" (much less "horse," "legs," or "book") after Shakespeare's manner. It is also noteworthy that in Shakespeare such figurative use of the verb, "to taste," sometimes appears in a context in which one or more words are logically discordant with tasting. A characteristic example is Leonato's remark in *Much Ado about Nothing* that men

Can counsel and speak comfort to that grief
Which they themselves not *feel*—but *tasting* it,
Their counsel turns to passion, . . .

(*Ado* 5.1.20–23)

The second clause should logically read, "but *feeling* it, / Their counsel turns to passion." Shakespeare prefers discord to repetition, as does W. S.:

Though I, rewarded with some sadder *taste*
Of knowing shame, by *feeling* it have prov'd
My country's thankless misconstruction. . . .

(*Elegy* 137–39)

Nor may all of the verbal affinities between W. S. and Shakespeare be written off as simple coincidence. Consider, for example, the following quatrain:

> such as do recount that tale of woe,
> Told by remembrance of the wisest heads,
> Will in the end conclude the matter so,
> As they will all go weeping to their beds.
>
> *(Elegy* 167–70)

W. S., with his "wisest heads," makes a peculiar link between "wisest" persons and a sad remembrance, as is habitual with Shakespeare: in *A Midsummer Night's Dream* we hear of "The wisest aunt telling the saddest tale" (*MND* 2.1.51). In *Hamlet,* Claudius slyly professes to honor his dead brother "with wisest sorrow, / Together with remembrance of ourselves," and later, after the death of Polonius, consoles Gertrude, saying, "we'll call up our wisest friends / And let them know" (*Ham.* 1.2.6–7, 4.1.38–39). In *The Winter's Tale,* a gentleman having witnessed Perdita's reunion with her father reports that "The wisest beholder, that knew no more but seeing, could not say if th'importance were joy or sorrow" (*WT* 5.2.16–18). More noteworthy is that the lines quoted above from the *Elegy* are a resounding echo of King Richard's parting speech to Queen Anne:

> let them tell thee tales
> Of woeful ages long ago betid;
> And ere thou bid good night, to quite their griefs,
> Tell thou the lamentable tale of me,
> And send the hearers weeping to their beds.
>
> *(R2* 5.1.41–45)

This is just one of more than thirty such echoes in the *Elegy* which suggest that the poet, whoever the author, knew Shakespeare's *Richard II.* For example, Queen Anne in the same scene likens Richard to a beautiful inn, and Bolingbroke to a common alehouse. That metaphor appears again in W. S.'s *Elegy,* where it is expressed in much the same language, with abstract qualities serving in both instances as lodgers:

> his mind and body made an inn,
> The one to lodge the other, both like fram'd
> For fair conditions, guests that soonest win
> Applause; . . .
>
> *(Elegy* 113–16)

> thou most beauteous inn,
> Why should hard-favor'd grief be lodg'd in thee
> When triumph is become an alehouse guest?
>
> *(R2* 5.1.13–15)

It is impossible to say with conviction that this particular speech provided the inspiration for W. S., for the like may be found elsewhere—the elegist's notion of the mind as a lodger in the inn of flesh, for instance, finds a specific precedent in *The Rape of Lucrece,* and may possibly be found in non-Shakespearean texts as well—yet when considered in the context of other such correspondences of phrasing and imagery, a relationship between *Richard II* and the *Elegy* is, I think, indisputable. The following examples collectively indicate that W. S. was well-familiar with Shakespeare's play:

Oblivion . . . /
Cannot rase out the lamentable tomb
Of his short-liv'd deserts

(*Elegy* 9–12)

     . . . 'tis not my meaning
     To rase one title of your honor out

(*R2* 2.3.74–75)

As nature never built in better kind

(*Elegy* 108)

     . . .built by Nature for herself

(*R2* 2.1.43)

Of true perfection, in a perfect breast

(*Elegy* 112)

     Truth hath a quiet breast

(*R2* 1.3.96)

When the proud height of much affected sin
Shall ripen to a head

(*Elegy* 175–76)

     . . . foul sin gathering head
     Shall break into corruption

(*R2* 5.1.58–59)

Then in a book where every work is writ

(*Elegy* 179)

     When I do see the very book indeed
     Where all my sins are writ

(*R2* 4.1.274–75)

And we low-level'd in a narrow grave,
. . . .
And buried in that hollow vault of woe

(*Elegy* 194, 550)

> *. . . lie full low, grav'd in the hollow ground.*
>
>   (*R2* 3.2.140)

> . . . in a narrow grave,
> What can we leave behind us but a name,
> Which, by a life well led, may honor have?
>
>   (*Elegy* 194–96)

> *Convey me . . . to my grave;*
> *Love they to live that love and honor have.*
>
>   (*R2* 2.1.136–37)

> Although I could not learn, whiles yet thou wert,
> To speak the language of a servile breath,
> My truth stole from my tongue into my heart,
> Which shall not thence be sund'red, but in death.
> And I confess my love was too remiss
>
>   (*Elegy* 209–13)

> *. . . we are too remiss,*
> *Whilst Bullingbrook, through our security,*
> *Grows strong and great in substance and in power.*
> . . . .
> [To] *fight and die is death destroying death,*
> *Where fearing dying pays death servile breath.*
>
>   (*R2* 3.2.33–35, 184–85)
>
> *What my tongue dares not, that my heart shall say.*
>
>   (*R2* 5.5.97)

> Fair lovely branch too soon cut off
>
>   (*Elegy* 234)

> *. . . branches by the Destinies cut;*
> . . . .
> *One flourishing branch . . . / Is hack'd down*
>
>   (*R2* 1.2.15–20)

> Ruling the little ordered commonwealth
> Of his own self,
> . . . .
> Which ever he maintain'd in sweet content
> And pleasurable rest, wherein he joy'd
> A monarchy of comfort's government
>
>   (*Elegy* 294–99)

> *Cut off the heads of too fast growing sprays,*
> *That look too lofty in our commonwealth:*
> *All must be even in our government.*
>
>   (*R2* 3.4.34–36)

The grave, that in his ever-empty womb
For ever closes up the unrespected

(Elegy 423–24)

a grave,
Whose hollow womb inherits nought but bones

(R2 2.1.82–83)

Feeds on the bread of rest

(Elegy 444)

Eating the bitter bread of banishment

(R2 3.1.21)

"He died in life, yet in his death he lives."

(Elegy 536)

In that I live, and in that will I die.

(R2 1.1.185)

Expecting yet a more severer doom

(Elegy 551)

. . . for thee remains a heavier doom

(R2 1.3.148)

. . . in despite of fearful change

(Elegy 569)

. . . prophets whisper fearful change

(R2 2.4.11)

Although solitary or unrelated verbal parallels cannot constitute evidence for authorship, the grouped sample provided here removes any doubt that W. S. knew *Richard II*. Moreover, the kind of borrowing that is evident in the *Elegy*—involving always an incremental change—is characteristic of the way in which Shakespeare usually borrows from himself, as in the many echoes of *Richard II* that appear in *Macbeth*. For example, John of Gaunt remarks to his son, "Let thy blows, doubly redoubled, / Fall like amazing thunder"; and in the latter play a wounded Sergeant reports of Macbeth and Banquo, "As cannons overcharg'd with double cracks, so they / Doubly redoubled strokes upon the foe" (*R2* 1.3.80–81; *Mac.* 1.2.37–38). There are some two dozen such correspondences between *Richard II* and *Macbeth*. It may even be that Richard's remark about murdered kings, "some sleeping kill'd," helped to inspire Macbeth's horror after killing King Duncan: "Sleep no more! / Macbeth doth murther sleep" (*R2* 3.2.159, *Mac.* 2.2.32–33).

Although a list of parallels with W. S. may be produced for virtually any of Shakespeare's works, the correspondences between the *Funeral Elegy* and *Richard II* are somewhat more frequent, and more explicit, than is the case with most other plays in the canon. This is surprising, even assuming Shakespearean authorship, for *Richard II* was written ca. 1595, much earlier than the *Elegy*. More surprising still is that the parallels with W. S. are not randomly distributed in *Richard II,* as appears to be the case with Shakespeare's other works. All of the most obvious, and most of the less striking, parallels appear in speeches by King Richard (e.g., 1.3.148, 4.1.274–75; 5.1.41–45, 58–59) or in Richard's cue lines (e.g., 1.1.185; 1.3.96; 2.1.82–83, 135–38; 3.2.33–35; 5.1.13–15). Of the few remaining examples cited above, three are spoken to Richard, though not as cue-lines (3.2.138–40, 184–85, 5.5.97), and two are from bit parts that may been played by the same actor who played Richard (Berkeley, 2.3.74–75; Welsh captain, 2.4.11; Richard does not appear in 2.4–3.1).

This evidence is not unequivocal. W. S. presumably wrote his *Elegy* between 25 January 1612 (the date of Peter's death) and 19 February (the date on which the poem was registered to be printed). The King's Men generally played at court quite often during the winter months, but no original documents have survived for the winter of 1611/12, so there is no record that the King's Men during this period performed or rehearsed *Richard II.* Nor do we know who usually played the title role. It is widely believed that Shakespeare played only minor roles in his own plays (such as Adam in *As You Like It* and the ghost in *Hamlet*), and that Richard II may have been played by Richard Burbage. Nor is there proof that Shakespeare acted at all after about 1603. Nevertheless, W. S. clearly had *Richard II* on his mind at the time he wrote the *Elegy*, and it appears quite likely that he had recently reviewed or acted King Richard's part. This is at least an interesting coincidence.

Nor is all the borrowing between W. S. and William Shakespeare one-directional. W. S. seems to recall at least a line or two, as well as habitual mannerisms, from the four major nondramatic works and from all of Shakespeare's plays, many of which had not yet been printed in 1612. Shakespeare, in turn, appears to have been influenced by W. S. when writing *Henry VIII* and *The Two Noble Kinsmen.* I have found no other literary work, apart from Shakespeare's *Sonnets,* having a greater overlap with W. S.'s vocabulary, imagery, and thematic material than Shakespeare's presumed portion of *Henry VIII.* Though this play was a collaborative effort with John Fletcher, most of the ensuing examples appear in passages that are indisputably Shakespeare's. A few are doubtful, appearing in scenes thought to be of joint authorship (these few examples are flagged with a question mark). None, however, is taken from a passage that is certainly or even probably by Fletcher. Indeed, in a careful search I have been able to find among the Fletcher scenes only one clear echo of the Peter elegy: W. S. writes of "being but a private man in rank" (*Elegy* 431), while Secretary Gardiner in *Henry VIII* speaks of "being but a private man again" (*H8* 5.2.90)—and even here Shakespeare could have had a hand in the phrasing, since act 5, scene 2, is among those few scenes that appear to have been written (or rewritten) partly by one poet, and partly by the other.

Unlike Fletcher, Shakespeare in his portion of *Henry VIII* repeatedly expresses himself after the manner of W. S. Perhaps the most striking instance is the dramatist's playful abridgment of "endeavors" (as noted earlier), following W. S.'s example, but one finds many other phrases and particular images in *Henry VIII* with antecedents in the *Elegy*. If Shakespeare wrote both works, the affinities between them are hardly surprising: the *Elegy* was written in February 1612; *Henry VIII* was first acted no later than June 1613; and Shakespeare is not known to have written any poems or plays in between.

There is, first, a great overlap of diction between W. S.'s *Elegy* and William Shakespeare's portion of *Henry VIII*. Where the elegist writes of "trim behavior" and "blushless vanities," Shakespeare speaks of "rude behavior," "empty vanities," "fierce vanities," and "blushing honors." Cranmer says, "Let *heaven / Witness* how dear I hold this confirmation," to which the King replies, "*The common voice,* I see is verified / Of thee" (*H8* 5.2.207–9 [?]); W. S. avers that he could easily "force / *The common voice* to warrant" what he says, and likewise calls heaven to witness (*Elegy* 81–82). The King must take care that he "be not found a talker" (*H8* 2.2.78 [?]), while Peter never gave himself to "busy questions such as talkers make" (*Elegy* 104). Peter is one who "Strove to win love" (*Elegy* 508); Katherine asks the King, "Which of your friends / Have I not strove to love?" (*H8* 2.4.29–30). Both men write of "embracements," not "embraces," of "plenteous safety" (Shakespeare) and "plenteous skill" (W. S.), rather than "plentiful," "bountiful," "great" or "much." Peter is a man of "fair conditions," King Henry's subjects men "of true condition." Shakespeare's Wolsey is "prone to mischief" (*H8* 1.1.160), while W. S.'s world, accurs'd in its "mischiefs," has a "proneness . . . to error" (*Elegy* 255, 505). Norfolk warns Buckingham, "let your reason with your choler question" (*H8* 1.1.130); W. S. wishes that "reason [were] set above / Most unjust choler" (*Elegy* 340–41). When the King divorces Queen Katherine, the tidings are heard "everywhere; every tongue speaks 'em, / And every true heart weeps for't" (*H8* 2.2.38–39) [?]). After Peter's death, his fame "lives ever whole, / In every heart seal'd up, in every tongue / Fit matter to discourse" (*Elegy* 200–202).

Queen Katherine advises the Duke of Buckingham's Surveyor to

> Take good heed
> You charge not in your spleen a noble person
> And spoil your nobler soul; . . .
>
> (*H8* 1.2.173–75)

And the elegist addresses William Peter, wishing, he says, to

> free thee from the scandal of such senses
> As in the rancor of unhappy spleen
> Measure thy course of life, with false pretenses. . . .
>
> (*Elegy* 251–53)

King Henry asks

> At what ease
> Might corrupt minds procure knaves as corrupt, . . .
>
> (*H8* 5.1.131–32)

while Peter's adversaries conster

> with corrupt commentaries,
> Proceeding from a nature as corrupt, . . .
>
> (*Elegy* 265–66)

When W. S. speaks in the *Elegy* of "both fortunes," he appears to mean good fortune and bad, prosperity and hardship, as in Shakespeare's *Henry VIII.* Katherine remarks that her women

> Have follow'd *both* my *fortunes* faithfully,
> Of which there is not one, I dare avow
> (And now I should not lie), but will deserve,
> For virtue and true beauty of the soul,
> For honesty and decent carriage,
> A right good husband (let him be a noble),
> And sure those men are happy that shall have 'em.
>
> (*H8* 4.2.140–47)

Here "both my fortunes" surely denotes "both my earlier good luck and present ill luck," though the phrase, both here and in the *Elegy,* may also suggest "heavenly and earthly fortunes," as when Macbeth speaks enigmatically of letting "both the worlds suffer" (*Mac.* 3.2.16). It is also worth note, with respect to the above passage, that where Shakespeare writes of "beauty of the soul," of "honest and decent carriage" which well deserve "A right good husband," W. S. writes of "beauty of the mind," of "honesty and worth," "carriage just, / Offenseless resolution," which "well deserve / Just commendation."

The two texts likewise share a great number of particular images. W. S., in the *Elegy,* writes,

> But whether doth the stream of my mischance
> Drive me beyond myself, fast friend, . . .
>
> (*Elegy* 573–74)

This image, derived from hunting, appears elsewhere in *Hamlet* (2.1.112), and again in *Henry VIII:*

> We may outrun
> By violent swiftness that which we run at,
> And lose by overrunning. . . .

(H8 1.1.141–43)

W. S. compares the man of high honors to a "seeled dove" (that is, one with its eyes stitched shut by falconers), who

> seeks to be secure by mounting high,
> Whence, when he falls, who did erewhile aspire,
> Falls deeper down, for that he climbed higher.

(Elegy 454–56)

Wolsey, in *Henry VIII*, discovers that

> There is, betwixt that smile we would aspire to,
> That sweet aspect of princes, and their ruin,
> More pangs and fears than wars or women have;
> And when he falls, he falls like Lucifer,
> Never to hope again. . . .

(H8 3.2.368–72)

King Henry, in eulogizing Buckingham, describes him as one "enroll'd 'mongst wonders," who "into monstrous habits put the graces / That once were his" (*H8* 1.2.119–23); Peter is "enrolled" by W. S. as a man of "perfect graces" and "peculiar graces" who suited "so his habit and desire / As that his virtue was his best attire" (555, 57, 95–96); and so on.

   In a more general way, one may note the many thematic concerns shared by the *Elegy* and *Henry VIII*, as in the attempt of both texts to define genuine "nobility" within a context of malice. The very words "noble" and "malice" appear in *Henry VIII* more frequently than in any other work by Shakespeare. More importantly, the attitude of his best characters toward "nobleness" is indistinguishable from that of W. S., and he frequently uses identical language with which to express himself, as when he speaks of those who live "exempt" from the fear of authority (*Elegy* 458; *H8* 1.2.88–92). Anne Bullen's sentiment, were it not for the absence of rhyme, might have been lifted directly from the *Elegy:*

> 'tis better to be lowly born,
> And range with humble livers in content,
> Than to be perk'd up in a glist'ring grief
> And wear a golden sorrow. . . .

(H8 2.3.19–22)

This theme of living contentedly in a "lower region" is central to W. S.'s *Elegy,* where it is expressed in similar language (e.g., 129–36, 293–300, 439–50).

W. S. writes that Peter was "to a lower blessedness confin'd" (*Elegy* 438), and Shakespeare of Wolsey as one who at last "found the blessedness of being little" (*H8* 4.2.66). Wolsey, whose heart, like Anne Bullen's, has "Affected eminence," is, however, "not propp'd by ancestry," "neither allied / To eminent assistants, . . . / The force of his own merit makes his way" (*H8* 2.3.29, 1.1.58–64). W. S., lacking "Birth, blood, and ancestors," "With all what men in eminence possess," finds that his heart has "none other prop" but hope "Whereon to lean and rest itself" (*Elegy* 463–68, 566–67). W. S. speaks of those who "ever sweat" for "power's commission" (449–50), Shakespeare of men who act "by commission and main power," follow'd by "the general throng and sweat / Of thousand friends" (*H8* 2.2.6, pro.28–29).

One especially striking thematic parallel between the *Elegy* and Shakespeare's portion of *Henry VIII* is a shared notion, first, of human life as a textual structure, and second, of "malice" as a text to be read and interpreted. Peter is described as a virtuous man, slandered by the ignorant tongues of those who would construct a false text of his life, a theme recollected in *Henry VIII* by Cardinal Wolsey:

> If I am
> Traduc'd by ignorant tongues, which neither know
> My faculties nor person, yet will be
> The chronicles of my doing, let me say
> 'Tis but the fate of place, . . .
>
> (*H8* 1.2.71–75)

Peter's detractors, with the help of "corrupt commentaries," are said to read and conster "The text of malice" (*Elegy* 265–67).

> So in his mischiefs is the world accurs'd:
> It picks out matter to inform the worst. . . .
>
> (*Elegy* 255–56)

In *Henry VIII,* Norfolk warns Buckingham,

> I advise you
> ·   ·   ·   ·   ·
>   that you read
> The Cardinal's malice and his potency
> Together; . . .
>
> (*H8* 1.1.102–6)

—and Wolsey himself complains,

> What we oft do best,
> By sick interpreters (once weak ones) is
> Not ours, or not allow'd; what worst, as oft,
> Hitting a grosser quality, is cried up
> For our best act. . . .

(H8 1.2.81–85)

In this case, however, even if Shakespeare and W. S. are presumed to be separate individuals, the dramatist cannot be accused of borrowing from the *Elegy,* for the peculiar notion of malice as a text to be read or translated is habitual with Shakespeare, appearing in plays that antedate the *Elegy* by as much as twenty years:

> I fear we should have seen decipher'd there
> More rancorous spite, . . .

(1H6 4.1.184–85)

> Wherefore do you so ill translate yourself
> Out of the speech of peace that bears such grace,
> Into the harsh and boist'rous tongue of war?
> Turning your books to graves, your ink to blood,
> Your pens to lances, and your tongue divine
> To a loud trumpet and a point of war?

(2H4 4.1.47–52)

> his unbookish jealousy must conster
> Poor Cassio's smiles, gestures, and light behaviors
> Quite in the wrong.

(Oth. 4.1.101–3; cf. 5.2.341–43)

> no levell'd malice
> Infects one comma in the course I hold, . . .

(Tim. 1.1.47–48)

> Translate his malice towards you into love, . . .

(Cor. 2.3.189)

It is instructive also to take a look at Shakespeare's particular habits with respect to eulogistic verse, for though he is not often thought of as an elegiac poet, his plays do contain some eulogistic verse, much of which may be recalled in the Peter elegy, as when the King of France eulogizes Helena in *All's Well That Ends Well* (cf. selected passages from the *Elegy,* interlineated, in italics):

From lowest place when virtuous things proceed,
The place is dignified by th' doer's deed.

> *In minds from whence endeavor doth proceed,*
> *A ready will is taken for the deed.*
>
> . . . .
> *. . . virtues and perfections in our powers*
> *Proceed most truly from us, if we do them.*
>   (*Elegy* 245–46, 465–66)

Where great additions swell's, and virtue none,
It is a dropsied honor. Good alone
Is good, without a name; vileness is so:
The property by what it is should go,
Not by the title. . . .

> *Respective titles or a gracious style,*
> *With all what men in eminence possess,*
> *Are, without ornaments to praise them, vile.*
>
> . . . .
> *. . . the sum of all that can be said*
> *Can be but said that "He was good" (which wholly*
> *Includes all excellence can be display'd)*
>   (*Elegy* 467–69, 531–33)

          Honors thrive,
When rather from our acts we them derive
Than our foregoers. The mere word's a slave
Debosh'd on every tomb, on every grave
A lying trophy, and as oft is dumb
Where dust and damn'd oblivion is the tomb
Of honor'd bones indeed. What should be said?

> *Oblivion in the darkest day to come,*
> *When sin shall tread on merit in the dust,*
> *Cannot rase out the lamentable tomb*
> *Of his short-liv'd deserts*
>   (*Elegy* 9–12)

          Virtue and she
Is her own dower
                                   (*AWW* 2.3.125–44)

> *. . . his virtue was his best attire*
>   (*Elegy* 96)

Certain images appear habitually in Shakespeare's eulogistic verse. One such is a repeated reference to everlasting characters, with an occasional pun on "characters" as written delineations of individual traits (a popular Renaissance genre) and on "characters" as individual letters in printed texts or sepulchral inscriptions. Duke Vincentio, for example, exclaims (ironically) to Lord Angelo that his desert

> deserves with characters of brass
> A forted residence 'gainst the tooth of time
> And razure of oblivion.
>
> (*MM* 5.1.9–13)

Gloucester, in *2 Henry VI,* warns the English peers that the proposed league with France will have the result of

> cancelling your fame,
> Blotting your name from books of memory,
> Rasing the characters of your renown, . . .
>
> (*2H6* 1.1.99–101)

Dionyza, in telling Cleon of Marina's monument, says that

> Her monument
> Is almost finished, and her epitaphs
> In glitt'ring golden characters express
> A general praise to her, . . .
>
> (*Per.* 4.3.42–45)

W. S., in a similar vein, writes of deserts that oblivion cannot rase out (9–12), and of men who, like William Peter,

> well deserve
> Eternal characters, that after death
> Remembrance of their worth we may preserve,
> So that their glory die not with their breath.
>
> (*Elegy* 471–74)

Another characteristic Shakespearean device is to find the sum of all that can be said, as in the *Elegy,* lines 531–32, and to reduce it to a sentence, as in *3 Henry VI:*

Write in dust this sentence with thy blood:
"Wind-changing Warwick now can change no more."

> (*3H6* 5.1.56–57)

The phrasing is characteristic of Shakespeare, even in other contexts:

And art thou chang'd? Pronounce this sentence then:
"Women may fall, when there's no strength in men."

> (*Rom.* 2.3.79–80)

With that she sighed as she stood,
  And gave this sentence then:
"Among nine bad if one be good,
Among nine bad if one be good,
  There's yet one good in ten."

$$(AWW\ 1.3.75-79)$$

W. S. writes,

His due deserts, this sentence on him gives,
"He died in life, yet in his death he lives."

$$(Elegy\ 535-36)$$

One finds also in Shakespeare a continuing fascination with the potential symmetry of life and death. The Duchess of York tells Richard III, "Bloody thou art, bloody will be thy end; / Shame serves thy life and doth thy death attend" (*R3* 4.4.195–96). John of Gaunt curses Richard II, saying, "Live in thy shame, but die not shame with thee!" (*R2* 2.1.135); while King Henry, later in the same play, retires his enemy Carlisle with the benediction, "So as thou liv'st in peace, die free from strife" (*R2* 5.6.27). It is interesting to note also the epitaph for the London brewer Elias James, alleged to have been written by William Shakespeare after James's death in 1610:

When God was pleas'd, the world unwilling yet,
Elias James to nature paid his debt
And here reposeth; as he liv'd he died,
The saying in him strongly verified,
"Such life, such death." Then, the known truth to tell,
He liv'd a godly life and died as well.[66]

Perhaps the most interesting example with respect to the Peter elegy appears in *2 Henry VI*.[67] Upon witnessing the death of Cardinal Beaufort, the Earl of Warwick passes judgment, saying, "So bad a death argues a monstrous life" (*2H6* 3.3.30). King Henry responds, piously, "Forbear to judge, for we are sinners all" (3.3.31), but he was not above making precisely the same assumption only moments earlier: "Ah, what a sign it is of evil life, / Where death's approach is seen so terrible!" (*2H6* 3.3.5–6).
  This belief that one may read a man's life by means of his death is, of course, the assumption of Peter's detractors as presented in the *Elegy:*

. . . the life that purity adorn'd
With real merit, by this sudden end
Is in the mouth of some in manners scorn'd,
Made questionable, for they do intend,

According to the tenor of the saw
Mistook, if not observ'd (writ long ago
When men were only led by reason's law),
That "Such as is the end, the life proves so."

(Elegy 359–66)

W. S.'s defense of William Peter against the proverbial formula, "Such life, such death," is his organizing principle for the *Elegy*. He argues that a bad death does not, in fact, intimate the story of a monstrous life, and he offers several examples to the contrary, turning to Jesus, Abel, and the saints as cases in point (though not without some irony). Should William Shakespeare have undertaken, at any point in his career, to write a funeral elegy, we could hardly ask to find as its central theme a more distinctively Shakespearean notion than this concern of W. S. with the faulty parallel structure of his friend's life and death.

As a final example of Shakespeare's elegiac verse, we may turn to Claudio's epitaph for Hero in *Much Ado about Nothing:*

EPITAPH

Done to death by slanderous tongues
Was the Hero that here lies.
Death, in guerdon of her wrongs,
Gives her fame which never dies.
So the life that died with shame
Lives in death with glorious fame.

(Ado 5.3.3–8)

Here again, as in the *Elegy,* we find a concern with the damage done by slanderous tongues; an interest in the symmetry (or, again in this case, the asymmetry) of an individual life and death; and a focus on fame, rather than eternal life in heaven, as the principal compensation for a virtuous life. Also remarkable, in the second line, is "the *Hero* that *here* lies," Hero having been abridged by death.

Internal Biographical Evidence

In the act of chronicling the life and virtues of William Peter, W. S. (unlike many elegists of the period) is rather tight-lipped about himself, providing us little in the way of concrete facts by which to identify him. From the dedication we learn that elegiac verse is a form for which he had little affection, and rarely practiced, yet, as he says, "There must be a miracle in that labor which, to witness my remembrance to this departed gentleman, I would not willingly undergo." The dedication is forthcoming with nothing else but the poet's initials. If, as appears likely, there is a pun on "will" in line 246, we may conclude that his first name was William, but as there were relatively few Englishmen with the first initial *W,* in 1612, who were not named William, the observation does not get us very far. We do learn that Peter was a "fast friend," that W. S. had once promised, with a "constant and irrefragable vow," to immortalize him in verse, and that neither he nor Peter were of the nobility ("Birth, blood, and ancestors are none of ours"). When the poet describes his friend as "but a private man in rank / (And yet not rank'd beneath a gentleman)," one may hear, perhaps, the sound of a writer who took some pride in his own right to sign himself as "Gentleman," but this is mere conjecture; and though W. S. seems duly impressed with Peter's great learning, he says nothing on that score that could not have been said by one of Peter's former schoolmates. None of this is the stuff of which convincing attributions are made.

W. S. pulls back the curtain on his own history only once or twice, to present us with a brief glimpse of a public disgrace suffered by him some years earlier when he was "rewarded with some sadder taste / Of knowing shame" (137–38)—the result, he says, of

My country's thankless misconstruction cast
Upon my name and credit, both unlov'd
By some whose fortunes, sunk into the wane
Of plenty and desert, have strove to win
Justice by wrong, and sifted to embane
My reputation with a witless sin; . . .

(Elegy 139–44)

The poet does not elaborate. He does not explain what "witless sin" he was said to have committed, or when the scandal took place, or how it was resolved, if at all (though it appears from the phrasing—they "sifted to embane" my name and credit—that the incident did not lead to a legal conviction, only to a tarnished reputation). Nor does the elegist name his accusers unless "the ridgway" that leads to ruin (41–42) is meant to point the finger at Peter's kinsmen of that name, and there is no external evidence to support such a conjecture. The only thing we can say with any certainty is that the alleged sin took place in Oxford, "Even in which place" William Peter acquired "education and new being" (149–52)— though the poet's disgrace appears to have been a public scandal of some sort, not linked to the university. It seems quite unlikely, if the said disgrace refers, say, to the poet having been "sent down" as a former student, that he would use such language to describe the business as "My country's thankless misconstruction." At the time of his disgrace, W. S. appears to have been already a man of some prominence—at least in the

Midlands and perhaps nationally—and in a position to be envied by those whose fortunes were sunk "into the wane / Of plenty and desert."

We know very little of the personal life of William Shakespeare. We have only four documents in which he expresses himself in the first person: the two dedications to Southampton of the early narrative poems (1592–94); the *Sonnets* (of uncertain date); and his last will and testament (1616). In neither of the early dedications to Southampton, nor in his will, is there any mention of his having suffered a public disgrace. Yet we need not suppose any connection whatever between the Peters of Bowhay and the young man of the *Sonnets* to see at least the possibility of a connection between W. S.'s unnamed scandal and that infamous (and equally myste-rious) disgrace suffered by William Shakespeare as intimated in the *Son-nets*. That the poet endured some kind of public humiliation is suggested by Sonnets 33–38, 71–72, 111–12, 121, and perhaps also by Sonnets 88–90. In Sonnet 112, for example, Shakespeare writes to the fair youth, saying,

> Your love and pity doth th'impression fill
> Which vulgar scandal stamp'd upon by brow,
> For what care I who calls me well or ill,
> So you o'er-green my bad, my good allow?
> You are my all the world, and I must strive
> To know my shames and praises from your tongue;
> None else to me, nor I to none alive,
> That my steel'd sense or changes right or wrong.
> In so profound abysm I throw all care
> Of others' voices, that my adder's sense
> To critic and to flatterer stopped are.
> Mark how with my neglect I do dispense:
>   You are so strongly in my purpose bred
>   That all the world besides methinks are dead.

Much paper and ink has been expended on the "vulgar scandal" stamp'd on Shakespeare's brow. Some have supposed the disgrace had something to do with the Earl of Southampton, the patron of Shakespeare's early narrative poems, perhaps in connection with the Essex rebellion. Others have supposed that Shakespeare had a scandalous affair with the wife of the Oxford innkeeper John Davenant, since his son William later claimed to be Shakespeare's illegitimate offspring. John Forbes in *The Shake-spearean Enigma and an Elizabethan Mania* (1924) details Shakespeare's struggle with a shameful addiction to demon rum. Still others believe that the sonnets are chiefly fictional or that the poet's insistent talk of shame is only figurative. More recent (and far more plausible, I think) than these other theories is Joseph Pequigney's suggestion, based on a close reading of the sonnets themselves, that Shakespeare ca. 1600 was denounced for homosexual conduct of some sort.[68] I do not wish, however, to endorse here any particular hypothesis; nor is speculation of this sort important to a consideration of authorship. I mention the sonnets here only to point out that W. S.'s professed disgrace has at least the possibility of a referent in the life of William Shakespeare, and to note that it was not customary in Jacobean elegiac verse (or, for that matter, in a sonnet-sequence) to complain of a tarnished reputation.

W. S. wishes, he says, to "Immure those imputations I sustain, / Learning my days of youth so to prevent / As not to be cast down by them again" (558–60). And he expresses a wish that "time, the father of unblushing truth, / May one day lay ope malice which hath cross'd it, / And right the hopes of my endangered youth, . . ." (145–47). Twice, then, the poet speaks of his "youth" in connection with that unnamed and undated scandal that led others "to embane / [his] reputation with a witless sin" (143–44); and these lines raise a possible objection—perhaps a major objection—to a hypothesis of Shakespearean authorship, for Shakespeare in February 1612, at age forty-seven, had long ago bid farewell to his youth.

Let us consider these lines first as a literal statement of personal chronology. John Peter arrived in Oxford in 1596. His younger brother William arrived three years later. That the poem is addressed to John Peter suggests that he, at least, knew something of the poet's sullied reputation, and we are invited, I think, to understand that the scandal took place during William's years at Oxford. In other words, it seems improbable that the poet's "days of youth" can be dated earlier than July 1599, at which time Shakespeare was thirty-five years old. This fact alone does not pose a major problem. It is not remarkable that an aging poet in 1612 should speak of his thirties as youthful, for Shakespeare's contemporaries tended to think of masculine youth as lasting potentially well into middle age. Examples can be afforded from Shakespeare's own drama. Henry V, for example (presumably at age twenty-seven), is said to be in "the very May-morn of his youth" (*H5* 1.2.120; cf. 1.2.250; 2.4.28, 130); in *Richard II*, Bolingbroke and King Richard are repeatedly spoken of as youths, presumably at age thirty-three (*R2* 1.3.305; 2.1.2, 20, 69); and Hotspur in *1 Henry IV*, presumably at age thirty-seven, is likewise described, repeatedly, as a youth (*1H4* 1.1.99; 3.2.145; 5.2.17, 62; 5.4.77). Perhaps Shakespeare was thinking of his fictional Henries and Richard and (more probably) Hotspur as somewhat younger than their historical counterparts; but the principal actors for the Lord Chamberlain's Men from 1595 to 1598 were mostly in their late twenties to late thirties, and Shakespeare cannot have conceived these characters as markedly younger than the actors who were to play them. Then, too, Prince Hamlet is addressed by his father's ghost as a "noble youth"; he is again described by Ophelia as a rose in the full bloom of "youth" (*Ham.* 1.5.38, 3.1.159). Hamlet himself speaks of his "consonancy of . . . youth" with Rosencrantz and Guildenstern (2.2.285). Hamlet's affection for Ophelia is described by Laertes as "A violet in the youth of primy nature," flourishing "in the morn and liquid dew of youth" (1.3.7, 41, 44). Yet Hamlet is reported to be thirty years old (5.1.162; cf. 3.2.155). Shakespeare in this respect is not at all remarkable. Renaissance authors generally thought of masculine youth as lasting from adolescence until as late as age forty, provided good health and continued vigor. Nor do I find evidence that Shakespeare himself revised downward his estimate of *youth* as he approached the end of his career.

W. S., whoever he is, speaks repeatedly of William Peter as a youth. Peter's "youth" was "abridg'd" at only twenty-nine years (*Elegy* 3), while he was yet in his "riper youth" (52). Peter at the time of his death "Had all that youth and happy days could give him" (488). If Peter can be described by W. S. as "a youth untimely lost" at twenty-nine years old (197), it is not incredible that the same poet, in the same poem, should recall himself as a youth while still in his thirties, during Peter's years at Oxford. So there is not a major conflict here with Shakespeare's biography even if we take "youth" in a strictly literal sense—and I am not at all sure that this is the poet's primary thought when he considers, with some "taste / Of knowing shame," those days of "youth" that caused him to be slandered by his "country's thankless misconstruction" (137–47).

The figurative use of "youth" is commonplace in Renaissance literature, as is frequently illustrated by Shakespeare. "Youth" in Shakespeare is often used as a synonym for impulsiveness, lust, or lack of discernment. Leontes, for example, approaching fifty years old, covets Perdita's beauty, and is scolded by Paulina for having an eye that "hath too much youth in't" (*WT* 5.1.225). Examples can be multiplied. So unless W. S. asks us to think that his "days of youth" are still upon him in a literal sense, such phrasing cannot offer much of an obstacle to a hypothesis of Shakespearean authorship. W. S. professes to have been "cast down," not *in* his days of youth, but *by* them, which lends itself to a figurative reading (*Elegy* 560)— and it is usually older, not younger, poets who are inclined to speak wistfully about the hopes of their youth (147). Nor is it obvious how a poet of any age can learn to "*prevent*" "days of youth" (558) unless youth is taken figuratively to mean something like sexual desire.

Having said all that, there yet remains a possibility that W. S. is himself a young man in February 1612. If we take "prevent" to mean, not *to ward off* or *to thwart* (as, say, in Son. 18 or *Tim.* 5.1.203), but "to anticipate chronologically," and if we take "Learning" as a transitive verb meaning "to teach" (an accepted usage in 1612) and "youth" to denote the poet's literal age, we arrive at a possible reading that would dictate an author who is himself still quite young (i.e., "Thereby teaching what remains of my youthful days so as to anticipate the possibility of such imputations in the future"). The poet expresses a wish that time will one day right the hopes of his "endangered youth" (147), and the participial adjective surely lends itself to a reading that would view the poet as having some youth still left in him in 1612. If this is the poet's meaning, the *Elegy* can hardly have been written by Shakespeare, who in February of 1612 was nearly forty-eight years old. Of the many possible ways to read these lines about the poet's "youth," I find this last reading to be the least likely, quite apart from other evidence of the poet's advanced age (as in his use of *sith, whiles, hath, doth, his* for *its, that* as a conjunctional affix, and so on—none of which taken by itself is archaic, but which, taken together, may point to a poet born as early as 1550). Still, it is certainly possible in the phrase "the hopes of my endangered youth" to envision a poet who is speaking as a young man, perhaps a man even younger than Peter himself. Indeed, those readers who are disinclined to accept Shakespearean authorship of the poem may find here an insurmountable objection, one that counterbalances all evidence that Shakespeare may have written the poem.

There is, finally, one additional clause in connection with the poet's mysterious disgrace which invites comment. The poet believes that

> time, the father of unblushing truth,
> May one day lay ope malice which hath cross'd it,
> And right the hopes of my endangered youth,
> Purchasing credit in the place I lost it— . . .
>
> (*Elegy* 145–48)

"Credit," as used here, has perhaps the dual valence of "esteem" and "believability," but it is at first difficult to see how "time" by itself should vindicate the poet, and still less clear why Oxford should be named as a place where he may yet regain some of his lost credit. This redemptive process is to be the work of time itself, not of the poet, and so seems to preclude a plan by W. S. to redeem his own reputation on the basis of good behavior (say, as a student at Oxford University). Quite possibly, the poet (whether Shakespeare or another W. S.) has some hope that his *Elegy* will be preserved in the Bodleian Library (together, perhaps, with additional works), thereby to obtain for him in after-ages, at Oxford, the esteem that he lost there while living. The Bodleian Library was the first secular institution that could extend to English poets a hope of immortality. With its founding in 1602, authors could hope that their verse would, in fact, last so long as men can breathe or eyes can see. W. S. has presented himself as one whose success has been, already, a source of envy in the hearts of others. It may be, then, that a hope of lasting fame, even at Oxford, was not altogether unfounded.

The External Evidence

If Shakespeare's authorship of the *Elegy* had to be proven in a court of law solely on the basis of surviving external evidence, the case would be dismissed in short order. Such evidence is slight indeed, consisting of little more than a set of appropriate initials, and a publisher, Thomas Thorp, who is known to have arranged the printing of *Shake-speares Sonnets* in 1609. If William Shakespeare's full name were printed on the title page of the *Elegy,* there could remain no doubt who wrote it. We have instead only a set of rather ordinary initials. In the early seventeenth century *William* was second only to *John* as a Christian name for English males, and surnames beginning with *S* were common as well. The elegist was presumably an adult, literate male, not of the nobility, perhaps an untitled gentleman. In 1612 there may have been several dozen individuals fitting that description in the capital alone, and countless others who dwelt in the provinces, many of whom doubtless took pleasure in poetry. Thanks to such institutions as the Bodleian and British libraries, there has been preserved at least a sample or two from most persons known to have written in verse during Shakespeare's lifetime, yet there may be many others whose verse perished without notice. We cannot, therefore, be certain that every living poet with the initials W. S. has been accounted for.

That the *Elegy* was printed for Thomas Thorp is inconclusive evidence. If we may believe that Shakespeare wrote the sonnets credited to him in the 1609 Quarto, we may be fairly sure that he was acquainted with Thorp by 1612. Yet we know virtually nothing of their relationship. Thorp received the repeated business of several men in Shakespeare's circle and was closely associated with Shakespeare's dramatic company after the turn of the century. Some scholars, however, still believe that the original issue of the *Sonnets* was published by Thorp without Shakespeare's permission. If that theory is correct, one might suppose Thomas Thorp to be the last stationer to whom the poet would go to have his elegy printed. The most that can be said in this respect is that Thorp remained on cordial terms with Marston, Chapman, and Jonson even when these three fiery-tempered dramatists could not be cordial to one another; that he had close and lasting ties with Shakespeare's dramatic company; and that his track record during his forty years with the Stationers' Company—including twenty-five years as an active, independent publisher—was remarkably free of any kind of blemish, unless he indeed purloined the Sonnets. But Shakespeare is, after all, just one of three W. S.'s published by Thorp together with William Strachey (who has a commendatory sonnet in Jonson's *Volpone,* published by Thorp in 1605) and W. Shute (*Holy Meditations,* 1612). There might easily have been a fourth—if indeed the *Elegy* was not written by Strachey or Shute.

Having made a fairly exhaustive search, I think it safe to say that the *Elegy* is not ascribed to Shakespeare (or to another poet) in any surviving document. Nor do we have surviving testimony, even by way of hearsay, linking his name directly to that of William Peter. The absence of a contemporaneous attribution is disappointing though not, of course, surprising. Such documentation is generally lacking for anonymous and initialed publications of the sixteenth and seventeenth centuries. Yet one could wish to find at least some unequivocal record of a friendship between Shakespeare and Peter. Lacking such documentation, much of what follows can hardly be called "evidence" at all, for it simply establishes a possibility that the two men were acquainted. I have therefore thought it best to present this material last, in the interest of maintaining a healthy skepticism. In the minds of many readers, the general absence of external evidence may finally outweigh any amount of internal evidence for Shakespearean authorship.

Although I have not found the Peter elegy directly mentioned, either in manuscript or in print, in any volume save the Stationers' Register, the poem was not entirely unknown in the seventeenth century, nor its merits altogether unrecognized, for it was twice recollected by John Ford, and boldly plagiarized a decade later by Simon Wastell. Ford, not long after Peter's untimely death, was smitten with an uncharacteristic fit of repentance. Hoping (in his own words) to "undoe the many follies" of his youth, he composed *Christes Bloodie Sweat,* a narrative poem of nearly 2,000 lines that is annotated throughout with cross-references to Scripture.[69] The poem was registered on 8 April 1613 to stationer Ralph Blower and subsequently published under Ford's initials.

I have not investigated the extrabiblical sources for *Christes Bloodie Sweat*—the poem owes no obvious debt to Shakespeare—but it is clear, at least, that Ford had read W. S.'s *Funeral Elegy.* A few examples will suffice to illustrate W. S.'s influence (orthography has been normalized):

Even in which place the subject of the verse
(Unhappy matter of a mourning style
Which now that subject's merits doth rehearse)
Had education and new being

(Elegy 148–52)

    Which bloody sweat, for that it is a theme
    (The happy matter of a moving style),
    That now I challenge from thy sacred dream

(C. B. S. 79–81)

Who when they die, die all, . . .
Comparing by thy death what thou hast been. . . .

That "Such as is the end, the life proves so. . . ."
"He died in life, yet in his death he lives. . . ."

(Elegy 425, 254, 366, 536)

> And here they die, and dying once die all,
> Die all as they unworthily have liv'd,
> No part of them survives but feels the thrall
> Of life in death. . . .

(C. B. S. 1213–16)

The curious eye of a quick-brain'd survey
Could scantly find a mote amidst the sun
Of his too-short'ned days, or make a prey
Of any faulty errors he had done—

(Elegy 29–32)

> . . . the most curious eye
> That saw him lead his solitary life
> Whiles he was man on earth, could not espy
> One blemish in his actions, prone to strife.

(C. B. S. 1543–46)

And now if I [have] level'd mine account
And reckoned up in a true measured score

(Elegy 553–54)

> And now, my God, if I discharged have
> This imposition of thine heavenly task

(C. B. S. 1837–38)

A few years later, Ford published his "Memoriall, Offered to That Man of Virtue, Sir Thomas Overburie." The poem appears in Overbury's *Wife*, beginning with the seventh edition of 1616 (orthography has again been normalized):

> Once dead and twice alive: death could not frame
> A death whose sting could kill him in his fame.
> He might have liv'd, had not the life which gave
> Life to his life betray'd him to his grave.
> 5   If greatness could consist in being good,
> His goodness did add titles to his blood—
> Only unhappy in his live's last fate
> In that he liv'd so soon, to die so late.
> Alas, whereto shall men oppressed trust
> 10 When innocence cannot protect the just?
> His error was his fault, his truth his end,
> No enemy his ruin, but his friend—
> Cold friendship, where hot vows are but a breath,
> To guerdon poor simplicity with death.

15   Was never man, that felt the sense of grief,
        So Over-bury'd in a safe belief?
        Belief? O cruel slaughter! Times unbred
        Will say, "Who dies, that is untimely dead
        By treachery of lust, or by disgrace
20   In friendship, 'twas but Overbury's case"—
        Which shall not more commend his truth, than prove
        Their guilt, who were his opposites in love.
        Rest, happy man, and in thy sphere of awe
        Behold how justice sways the sword of law
25   To weed out those whose hands, imbrued in blood,
        Cropp'd off thy youth and flower in the bud.
            Sleep in thy peace. Thus happy hast thou prov'd,
            Thou mightst have died more known, not more belov'd.

                                                        Jo. Fo.

Ford in this poem, as in all his later works, registers the influence of
Shakespeare. Though indebtedness is perhaps not so obvious here as in
Ford's dramatic verse, the poem may recall Sonnet 104, the epitaph for
Hero in *Much Ado about Nothing,* and such favorite Shakespearean
themes as ruinous friendship and the notion that "vows are but breath"
(*LLL* 4.3.66). Ford's principal source, however, is the Peter elegy. The first
five lines of Ford's poem recall lines 490–95 of the *Elegy,* while his next
seven recall lines 345–58. He borrows also a number of scattered phrases,
thoughts, and images. His familiarity with the *Elegy* is especially obvious
in the last two lines, a paraphrase of W. S.'s final couplet. W. S. addresses
his young friend as one

    Who herein hast forever happy prov'd:
    In life thou liv'dst, in death thou died'st belov'd.

Ford's dependence on W. S. is suggestive, for if Ben Jonson loved Shakespeare "this side idolatry," Ford loved him just this side of grand theft. His
habitual forages into Shakespeare are well-documented, and need not be
detailed here. T. S. Eliot was surely too severe in giving Shakespeare the
credit for anything worthwhile to be found in John Ford, but one may
hardly question Shakespeare's importance as Ford's chief mentor.[70] His
borrowings are frequent and direct, so that a majority of his critics and
biographers have felt compelled to comment upon his debt to the elder
dramatist. There is no other author on whom Ford depends so heavily, and
none whom he paraphrases so unabashedly, as William Shakespeare.
    The *Elegy* was plundered more directly in 1627, by the Reverend Simon
Wastell. Robert, Baron Spencer of Wormleighton, died on 25 October of
that year. Wastell at the time was Vicar of Daventry and the Master of the

Free School of Northampton, under Spencer's patronage. Wastell's memorial tribute to Spencer, entitled *The Muses Thankfulnesse,* was published anonymously shortly after Spencer's death. Wastell's authorship of the poem has not been previously noted, but it is clear, both from external evidence and from the epistle dedicatory, that Wastell is indeed the responsible party. The attribution is all but certain.

The Muses Thankfulnesse ranks among the boldest acts of plagiarism of the seventeenth century. In 614 lines of verse, there is scarcely a single original line. This was not Wastell's first excercise in plagiarism (he had already stolen in a previous publication from Robert Southwell and Francis Quarles), but in this case, Wastell merely produced a cut-and-paste collage of earlier funeral poems.

Two passages from the Peter elegy appear in Wastell's poem, rearranged into awkward couplets (original orthography has again been normalized):

> He was descended from illustrious blood,
> And by his nature he was truly good.
> His enemies (if enemies he had)
> Cannot reprove him of ought that was bad.
>
> (619–22)

Baron Spencer is said to have possessed many virtues:

> All which, if that they can to glory raise
> And, being knit to one, can merit praise
> In after times, then justly may I say,
> No name is like to live a longer day.
> The many hours till the day of doom
> Will not his dateless memory consume.
>
> (631–36)

These ten lines are taken from the Peter elegy, lines 133–36, 125–29, and 157–58.

The other poems from which Wastell steals in the same fashion are Michael Drayton's elegy "Upon the Death of the Lady Olive Stanhope" (1627), Samuel Daniel's *Funerall Poeme* for the earl of Devonshire (1606), Cyril Tourneur's *Funerall Poeme* for Lord Oxford (1609), and John Webster's *Monumentall Column* for Prince Henry (1613).[71] In other words, Wastell's poem is comprised chiefly of passages stolen almost verbatim from little-known nondramatic works by at least four of England's principal playwrights—together with the *Funeral Elegy* by W. S. The pattern of borrowing suggests that Wastell knew, or at least assumed, that "W. S." stood for William Shakespeare; and this implied attribution may be as close as we will ever come to a seventeenth-century ascription for the *Elegy*. Unfortunately, Wastell provides us with no additional clues to W. S.'s identity. (Given the fact that Wastell, like W. S., borrows from Daniel's *Funerall Poeme,* and that Wastell's initials are simply the reverse of "W.S.," one might suppose that it was Wastell who wrote the Peter elegy fifteen years earlier. But it will be clear, I think, to anyone familiar with Wastell's career and with his capabilities as a poet that he cannot possibly have written W. S.'s *Elegy*. Wastell's borrowings from W. S. are clearly no more than that.)

In the absence of an unambiguous ascription of the *Elegy* to William Shakespeare, either on the title page or elsewhere, our only recourse in pursuing additional external evidence of Shakespearean authorship is to turn to the largely obscured tracks of his biography, a search that in this case yields small prey indeed. To begin, it does not appear that Shakespeare and William Peter were related by either blood or marriage. Somewhat more likely, perhaps, is a shared friendship with John and Francis Beaumont. Their father, Sir Francis Beaumont of Gracedieu, Leicestershire, was a longtime friend of Edward Drew, senior (father to Peter's killer and brother-in-law to Thomas Southcott, Peter's maternal uncle, by Southcott's third marriage to Elizabeth Fitzwilliam). The elder Drew and elder Beaumont were close personal friends for at least thirty years. They worked together, conducted business together, and, in April 1598, died together, while touring the Northern Circuit of Assize. But it seems unlikely that there could have been more than a casual acquaintance between William's friend, Edward Drew, Jr. (n. 1589) and Francis Beaumont, Jr. (n. 1584), who were more than four years apart—and less likely still that Shakespeare could thereby have come to know either John or William Peter.

There is, of course, a remote possibility that the Peters came to know the Beaumonts directly, without the intervention of the Drew family, since John Peter was in residence concurrently with the Beaumont brothers at Oxford in 1596–98 and at the Inns of Court after 1600. Both John and Francis Beaumont by 1602 were spending time reveling with Jonson and Drayton, and perhaps with Shakespeare as well, but we have no record of their having been joined by either son of Otho Peter.

Sergeant Drew was likewise a friend and relation of Henry Wriothesley, third earl of Southampton, Shakespeare's patron of the early 1590s. In fact, it was from Southampton that Drew purchased the manor of Broadhembury, his greatest estate.[72] The acquisition was made in part with funds borrowed from Thomas Southcott, William Peter's maternal uncle. It is perhaps worth note, too, that Southampton, like the Peters, was allied by marriage to the Arundell family; nevertheless, I think it quite improbable that there was any direct link between Southampton and William Peter, much less a three-way connection with William Shakespeare.

A third acquaintance possibly shared by William Shakespeare and William Peter, at least after 1602, is that of the poet John Ford. On 26 October 1599, shortly before his seventeenth birthday, Peter matriculated at Exeter College, Oxford, having begun boarding there in July. He was followed a year later, in September 1600, by John and William Ford, both of Ilsington, Devon. William Ford was the youngest son of John Ford of Ashburton. His father died in January 1587, when he was just six years old, leaving him to the care of his uncle Thomas Ford of Ilsington, father of the dramatist. Both branches of the family dwelt at Ilsington, and were extraordinarily close, as is apparent from their surviving wills and other records.

William Ford is the only person who we can say with some assurance was a friend of Peter during his college years. He and Peter had probably known one another since childhood. As they were only a year apart in age, it is likely that they attended the Latin high school together in Exeter, and their families were allied on their mothers' side—Ford's maternal grandmother, Barbara Pomeroy (n. Southcott) was paternal aunt to William Peter's mother, Frances. Following Ford's admission to the university in 1600, he and Peter were much in one another's company, at least until April 1607 (when Ford graduated M.A.) and perhaps until the summer of 1608 (when he departed for Constantinople). Peter and Ford studied together for several terms under the tutelage of Simon Baskerville, and on more than one occasion had concurrent absences, as is indicated in the surviving Buttery Books of Exeter College.[73] They cannot have seen one another again after September 1608, but their friendship did not end entirely even with Peter's untimely death. After his return from Constantinople in 1613, Ford completed his B.D. from Exeter College (graduating on 12 December 1615), and in 1618 was appointed vicar of East Coker, Somerset, with the assistance of Peter's widow, Margaret (who had since married Edward Cotton). The tithing garb and tithing hay of the rectory of East Coker, which had belonged to William Peter as part of his marriage settlement, was retained by his widow after his death in 1612.[74]

The John Ford with whom this William Ford first entered Exeter College has not been positively identified, though he is thought to be the poet John Ford, who was the son of Thomas and Elizabeth Ford of Ilsington, Devon, and first cousin to William. The single bit of contrary evidence is not much of an obstacle: John Ford the poet was christened at Ilsington on 17 April 1586, while the John Ford who matriculated from Exeter College on 26 March 1601 is reported then to have been sixteen years old. This would place his birth sometime between 27 March 1584 and 25 March 1585. But the ages given in the Register are frequently inaccurate by a year or two, especially for those students who, like Ford, professed to be sixteen when registering. Matriculating students were required to subscribe to the Thirty-Nine Articles if they were sixteen years or older. If a seventeen- or eighteen-year-old student had been slow to matriculate, it was more convenient for him to give his age as "recently turned sixteen" than to raise suspicion of recusancy, wherefore a great number of students (perhaps even a majority who found themselves in this situation) did just that; they were not asked their age upon oath. Conversely, if a student was under age at matriculation, he could give his age as sixteen and thereby avoid an extra trip to subscribe to the Articles at a later date. John Ford, though still a few weeks shy of his fifteenth birthday when he matriculated in March 1601, may well belong to the latter group.

The evidence in favor of the identification is, on the other hand, fairly convincing. Throughout the college records, William and John Ford are described, respectively, as "Ford, se." and Ford, ju." These notations are used throughout to denote elder and younger family members, usually brothers, sometimes cousins. This John Ford was certainly not William's brother of that name, for that John Ford (1568–1638) was thirteen years older than William, and there is not known to have been a second child named John—or, for that matter, any children—born to John Ford of Ashburton following the birth of William. Moreover, though William continued at Oxford to receive his B.A., M.A., and B.D., John Ford left the university in April 1602 (as is indicated in the Buttery Books of Exeter College), which fits well enough with the poet's admission to the Middle Temple in November of that year. Lastly, the poet John Ford is the only individual of this name listed in the *International Genealogical Index* (1984) who was christened in Devonshire between 16 March 1584 and 3 December 1586.[75] In the absence of any other known John Ford with whom this William might have been closely associated, it seems reasonable to conclude that his companion was, indeed, the poet of that name.

Otherwise, our first certain record of the poet John Ford's schooling is on 16 November 1602, when, at the age of sixteen, he entered the Middle Temple. Several of his relations were already there, including his elder brother Henry, and William's elder brother Thomas Ford, both of whom had entered the Temple two years earlier. In the Hilary term of 1605/6, however, John Ford was expelled for his failure to pay his buttery bills. He was not reinstated until 10 June 1608. In the interim he published his first poem, a funeral elegy on Charles Blount, Lord Mountjoy, entitled, *Fames Memoriall* (1606). Included in the volume is a dedicatory sonnet to the earl's infamous widow, Lady Penelope, along with commendatory verses by Barnaby Barnes and one "T. P.," who may possibly be identified with Thomas Petre of Essex (a fellow Middle Templar who was second cousin to William Peter). Ford began writing for the stage as early as 1613, at least if his comedy, *An Ill Beginning Has a Good End* (not extant), may be identified with a play, acted at court that year by the King's Men, called *A*

Bad Beginning Makes a Good Ending. Two years later he wrote a poem or prose tract (not extant) entitled *Sir Thomas Overburyes Ghost*. The volume was entered in the Stationers' Register on 25 November 1615. By this date he appears already to have come into that circle of friends who only a few months later paid their respects to Overbury in the seventh edition of Overbury's *Wife*, a volume that contains poems thought to have been written by John Donne, John Marston, Francis Beaumont, John Fletcher, and other principal writers of the age. It is not altogether unlikely that he knew Shakespeare as well.

Even if it could be proven that the usual identification made between John Ford the poet and John Ford of Exeter College is erroneous, we should still have cause to believe that John Ford (the poet) and William Peter were known to one another. The poet and Peter's friend, William Ford, grew up together at Ilsington, were in fact virtual stepbrothers. The Fords of Ilsington and Peters of Bowhay shared numerous friends and relations among the prominent families of Devon, and Peter's elder brother John attended the Middle Temple with John, Thomas, and Henry Ford. Moreover, at the time of Henry Ford's death in 1616, his younger brother John (the poet) possessed an estate nearly surrounded by lands owned by the Peter clan. Located between Ipplepen and Torbrian, the poet's property neighbored, on the west, an estate owned first by Otho Peter, then by William himself until his death in 1612, and on the east, a much larger estate owned by Peter's cousins of Torbrian. It is also worth note, given his "Memorial" to Overbury in 1616, that Ford found access to a copy of the *Elegy* despite what appears to have been a private printing of limited circulation. Yet none of this can do more than to provide the merest possibility of a link between William Peter and the London playwrights.

If indeed William Peter ever met Shakespeare, it was probably during his nine years at the university. Oxford is the only place outside London and the county of Warwick known to have been frequently visited by the dramatist. The university was hostile to "common players," and influential enough in local affairs to prohibit public performances within the city limits, but an exception was made for the King's Men, who played there with some regularity. Though records were kept in a rather haphazard and desultory fashion, it is known that the King's Men played at Oxford in 1603/4, October 1605, July 1606, September 1607, August 1610, and again in 1613. It seems likely, too, that Shakespeare's company (as the Lord Chamberlain's Men) was one of the unidentified companies allowed to play at Oxford in 1600 and again in 1601.[76] Any Oxford student during these years with a fascination for the drama and a bit of initiative could hardly have been prevented from meeting London's most popular playwright. There have been many students since who have flattered themselves to think that, had they been alive in the years 1590–1616, they would surely have sought the friendship of William Shakespeare. If young William Peter was of that inclination, he had at least numerous opportunities.

Then, too, there is the much-publicized friendship between Shakespeare and the Oxford vintner John Davenant. It is impossible to say how or when the two men were first brought together, though it was probably at the Davenants' wineshop between 1601 (when Davenant first came to Oxford) and 1606 (the year of William Davenant's birth). If Shakespeare and he were acquainted before 1601, it cannot have been at Oxford, for despite the firm conviction of Arthur Acheson that Davenant came to the city no later than 1592, there is preserved in the University Archives the vintner's own sworn testimony of 1611, naming 1601 as the year of his arrival (as is borne out also by the register of St. Martin's parish, and by other surviving evidence).[77]

There can be little doubt that Shakespeare was on friendly terms with the Davenants for at least a portion of the years 1601–9. John Aubrey, an acquaintance of the Davenant family, reports that when Shakespeare traveled to Stratford, he "did commonly in his journey lye at this house in Oxon: where he was exceedingly well respected."[78] Davenant's eldest son, Robert, told Aubrey that the dramatist "here gave him a hundred kisses"—and though we need not believe the rumors that his mother, Jane Davenant, received as many kisses, and more, from Shakespeare, the evidence remains that Shakespeare found a warm reception in the Davenant household during his visits to Oxford.[79]

Another possible Oxford connection between William Shakespeare and William Peter is through Leonard and Dudley Digges, who from 1600 (and legally from 1603) were the stepsons of Shakespeare's close friend and executor, Thomas Russell (by Russell's second marriage, to their mother Anne Digges). Leonard is remembered today for having eulogized Shakespeare in the First Folio of 1623 and again in the 1640 *Poems*. Both he and his brother were at Oxford concurrently with William Peter. Dudley Digges, who was only a few months younger than Peter, matriculated on 18 July 1600 as a student of University College. At the time of his matriculation he had already been in residence for several terms. Leonard, also of University College, matriculated on 1 July 1603 and graduated B.A. on 31 October 1606 (but was probably in residence from July 1600, or earlier).[80] William Digges (son of Richard Digges of Wiltshire, and kin to Dudley and Leonard) was at the same time a fellow student of William Peter at Exeter College. William Digges matriculated on 23 March 1604, but the college records indicate that he entered the hall in December 1602. He remained until at least 8 September 1605, except during the Hilary term, 1603/4, when he appears to have been absent.[81] It is probable that Shakespeare knew two of the Diggeses, and quite possible that Peter knew all three.

A more likely Shakespeare/Peter connection than any of these may be a shared acquaintance with the family and friends of Henry Willoughby of Knoll Odiern in West Knoyle, Wiltshire. In 1594 stationer John Windet published a book called *Willobie his Avisa*. According to the editor "Hadrian" Dorrell, *Avisa* was penned by his good friend Henry Willoughby, before he left school to enter the queen's service. On account of its interest for Shakespeare studies, this volume of doggerel verse has engaged a great deal of attention, more than it perhaps deserves. A dedicatory verse signed "Vigilantius : Dormitanus" contains the first mention of William Shakespeare, by name, in English literature—

Though Collatine has dearly bought
(To high renown) a lasting life,
And found (that most in vain have sought)
To have a fair and constant wife,
   Yet Tarquin pluck'd his glistering grape,
   And Shakespeare paints poor Lucrece' rape.

(7–12)

The narrative that follows is very much a student production, which in some respects may be viewed as a lampoon on the disputations required of university students.

Willoughby's "Avisa," the heroine of this *poème à clef,* is a beautiful woman, thirty years old, who during her ten years of marriage has refused the advances of countless suitors—"Ruffians, Roysters, young Gentlemen, and lustie Captains, which all shee quickly cuts off." Willoughby tells the history of five such wooers, the first "a Noble man," the second a "Caveleiro." Third is "D. B.," fourth "Didymus Harco.," fifth "Henrico Willobego" (also called "Harry" and "H. W."). Each suitor attempts to seduce the virtuous Avisa, but to no avail, for she is able to counter every rhetorical strategy. The lamentable case of Henrico Willobego (a thinly-disguised pseudonym for Willoughby himself) comprises the final third of the volume. Upon visiting the place where Avisa dwells, Willobego is "suddenly infected with the contagion of a fantastical fit, at the first sight of *A.*" Finding himself smitten by the woman's good looks and inaccessibility, he seeks the counsel of "his familiar friend W. S., who not long before had tried the courtesy of the like passion, and was now newly recovered." This friend, described as a "player," is hinted to be William Shakespeare.

W. S. proves a "miserable comforter," who, either because he desires "secretly [to] laugh at his friend's folly ([he] that had given occasion not long before unto others to laugh at his own) or because he would see whether another could play his part better than himself," encourages young Henrico to pursue Avisa's affection (Canto 44). With W. S. standing by as a bemused counselor, Willobego makes renewed attempts on Avisa's virtue, but without success. Avisa's tongue and chastity prevail, leaving poor Henrico, in the end, with a broken heart.

Henry Willoughby, the son of Henry Willoughby, esquire, of West Knoyle, Wiltshire, entered Exeter College in the Easter term of 1590, on or about the same day that three other students were admitted to the same college, as indicated by the surviving Buttery Books. Their order of admission is as follows:

> [Nicholas] Lowes
> [George] Petre
> [Henry] Willowbye
> [John] Hartgill

The two students (Egerton and Philpot) immediately preceding these four entered the College several weeks earlier, the two immediately following (Parvish and Bridges) some weeks later. Since the record of their actual admission has not survived, it remains unclear whether or not the foursome in between arrived in one another's company, but it is likely that at least three of them—Petre, Willoughby, and Hartgill—were acquainted before coming to Oxford.

George Petre, of Hayes, Devonshire, was the son of William Petre (first cousin to Otho Peter) and of Cecily Southcott, his wife (sister to Otho's wife, Frances). George was thus first cousin on his mother's side, and second cousin on his father's side, to William Peter of Bowhay (though "Petre" was the preferred spelling of Otho's wealthier kin). The Hayes estate at which he grew up was situated to the west of Exeter, a few miles north of Bowhay.

George matriculated at the age of fifteen on 28 May 1590, shortly after his arrival, together with his eight-year-old Essex cousin, John Petre. Since students were not required to subscribe to the Articles until reaching age sixteen, Willoughby waited until after his next birthday, matriculating finally on 10 December 1591, together with John Hartgill, Thomas Dorrell, and William Marvin (a Wiltshire neighbor), all three of whom appear to have been numbered among his closest friends while at the university. Willoughby and Hartgill, however, were erroneously recorded as students of St. John's College, an error everywhere repeated in discussions of *Avisa*. Mistakes of this kind are enormously frequent in the University Register, for reasons that are explained by Andrew Clark.[82] It is quite certain, however, that Hartgill, Petre, and Willoughby were present continuously at Exeter College beginning with the Easter term of 1590, as recorded in the surviving Bursar's Accounts and Buttery Books. None of the three, prior to 1598, was associated with any college other than Exeter (nor was

William Marvin). Only Dorrell, a student at Brasenose, belonged to another college.

In the spring of 1592, Willoughby and Petre were joined at Exeter College by Richard Petre, gent., also of Devon, whose parentage is uncertain, though he was certainly a close relation of the other Devon Petres. He was possibly a grandson of Otho Peter's uncle, Richard Petre, canon and precentor of Exeter. None of these three students thereafter was absent from Oxford for any appreciable length of time until the Hilary term of 1592/3, when Willoughby was gone from the hall for three weeks in the month of January, during which time both Petres remained in school. Willoughby's second absence lasted much longer. In July 1593, he, John Hartgill, Richard Bennet, and the two Petres stopped boarding within a few days of one another (Richard "Dick" Bennet is possibly, though doubtfully, Avisa's third alleged suitor, whom Willoughby refers to as "D. B."). All five were absent for at least eight months. Hartgill never returned, but continued thereafter to be associated with the Willoughby family in real estate transactions and by his subsequent marriage to Willoughby's sister. George Petre (who had already graduated B.A. in 1592) proceeded a year later with Richard Bennet to the Inns of Court. In May 1594, Petre entered the Inner Temple, and Bennet the Middle Temple.[83] Willoughby and Richard Petre returned to Oxford in the Hilary term of 1593/4. Petre resumed boarding in the first week of February, Willoughby in the first week of March.

Following the Trinity term of 1594, Willoughby left the university. The last day on which he was certainly present at Oxford is September fifth. His whereabouts in the autumn of that year is not known, though editor Dorrell, in an epistle dated October first, testifies that his friend had "departed voluntarily to her Majesties seruice."[84] After an absence of five months, Willoughby returned for a brief visit, at which time he requested, and was granted, a dispensation of two terms (from the sixteen terms normally required for graduation) so that he could depart for his tour overseas as a B.A. The Act Books of the Congregation and Convocation for the month of February 1595 have three entries concerning Willoughby's grace for B.A., one of which is as follows:

> Henry Willoughby may count two extra creations as general sophister instead of his Lenten responsions. Reason: he is going abroad.[85]

G. B. Harrison supposes that Henry Willoughby had nothing to do with *Willobie his Avisa*. Rather, the book is a satire by Matthew Roydon on his supposed adversaries, William Shakespeare and the Earl of Southampton. Roydon, as Harrison tells it, adopted the pseudonym "Henry Willobie" for himself while attacking Southampton as the lustful "Henrico Willobego."

Harrison based this extraordinary theory on a number of ill-advised suppositions, one of which is that "if the real Willoughby took his degree in the ordinary way in February 1595, it is not likely that he would have 'departed voluntarily on [sic] her Maiesties seruice' in 1594."[86] It should come as no surprise that the university records confirm Dorrell's version rather than Harrison's. There is no factual statement made in the original edition of Willoughby's Avisa, either by the author or by his friend Dorrell, which appears in any respect to be erroneous or deliberately misleading, except for Dorrell's dubious assertion that Avisa was published without the author's knowledge or consent.

With the help of new information that turned up while I was researching the Elegy (which, regrettably, must await later publication), I have located the inn at which Henrico Willobego is alleged to have wooed the chaste Avisa, and have found also nearly every landmark mentioned in the book. The action takes place just north of Bristol, not far from the Almondsbury manor house of Thomas Chester. We may also date the episode, for if these events were based on the actual experience of Henry Willoughby, as he asks us to believe, they can have taken place only during his eight-month-long absence from Exeter College (13 July 1593–1 March 1594). The London theaters during this period were closed because of the severity of the plague, forcing players to take to the road until the theaters reopened in December. There were few, however, who made it to Bristol. Apart from the local productions of "Mr Wood the scoolemaster" (who was paid two pounds by the corporation of Bristol "in regarde of his charges in makeinge of plaies"), we have record of only two troupes visiting the city in 1593, these being the Queen's Men and the Lord Strange's Men (Shakespeare's company).[87] It has not yet been proven that Shakespeare belonged to the Lord Strange's Men before December 1594 (by which time he was a principal actor and shareholder), but it is widely believed that he joined the company much earlier, perhaps as an original member together with Kemp, Bryan, and Pope after the breakup of the old Leicester company in 1588. He was writing plays no later than 1592. When he began his acting career no one knows, but it is at least possible to place Shakespeare at the right place at the right time for the Avisa episode—in Bristol, on a provincial tour with his dramatic company, along with one or more Oxford students who went along for the ride.

That Shakespeare is Willoughby's friend, the player "W. S.," is directly suggested in the text. Much of Willoughby's verse betrays his admiration for the elder poet, as seems true also of Willoughby's friend, "Dormitanus," who in the front matter of Avisa gives Shakespeare his earliest surviving advertisement. The influence of Venus and Adonis (and, to a lesser degree, The Rape of Lucrece), is apparent throughout Avisa. There is a third link in a miscellany of verse called Sonnets to Sundry Notes of

Music (part two of *The Passionate Pilgrim* [1599]). One selection bears obvious affinities to Willoughby's *Avisa*, and may well be an extract from the book, originally intended to be spoken by Willobego's friend, W. S. ("When as thine eye hath chose the dame . . ."). There is, moreover, no actor with the initials W. S., besides William Shakespeare, known to have been associated with either the Queen's Men or Lord Strange's Men prior to 1 June 1595. On that date a William Smith ("Smyght") is mentioned as one of Henslowe's players (who was probably, though not certainly, with the Queen's Men).[88] No William Smith is known to have had any connection with the Willoughbies of Wiltshire.

Shakespeare's association with the Willoughby family, through Thomas Russell, has been well established (despite some rather excessive claims) by Leslie Hotson. The salient points are these: Russell, one of Shakespeare's closest friends and the executor of his will, married Katherine Bampfield, the daughter of Hugh Bampfield, in the same month that Henry Willoughby's brother William married Eleanor, her sister. In 1591 Russell joined with his friend Henry Willoughby, Sr., in a bond dated 17 May of that year, for a debt of £980 from Russell's stepfather, Sir Henry Berkeley. The elder Willoughby had also various other business dealings with the Berkeleys and Russells, which are detailed by Hotson.[89]

To trace the Peter-Willoughby connection, we must go back as far as 1567–75, for it was apparently during these years that a circle of friendship was established that lasted for several decades. Willoughby's father studied at the Inns of Court, beginning in 1567, with various of Petre's kinsmen (including Otho Peter in the years 1571–74). Both Otho Peter and Henry Willoughby the elder belonged thereafter, if not before, to a shared circle of friends that included William Petre of Hayes, Matthew Ewens, Edward Hext, John Dackomb, Henry Keymer, and the elder Willoughby's several brothers.[90]

This circle remained close for many years, and many of their children intermarried. William Peter's own sister, Elizabeth, married first, James Daubeney of Pendomer, Somerset, and second, William Keymer of Chelborough, Dorset, both of whom belonged to the Willoughby circle. James Daubeney, her first husband, died without issue in 1614. In his will he leaves forty shillings each to his brother-in-law John Peter and to his former sister-in-law Margaret (William's widow), to buy themselves rings. He leaves also five pounds to his "cousin Willoughby" (whom I have not positively identified).

Elizabeth's second husband, William Keymer, had an aunt Elizabeth who married Matthew Ewens's paternal uncle, John Ewens of Wincanton. Ursula Bampfield married Giles Daubeney of Wayford, Somerset (a cousin of Elizabeth Peter's first husband), while Margaret, their daughter, married Ellis Keymer (brother to Elizabeth's second husband). Still another

Bampfield, Mary, daughter of Robert, married a Giles Keymer in the same period. William Peter's sister by her second marriage was thereby related in various ways to Henry Willoughby (who had since died) and to Thomas Russell, both of whom are associated with Shakespeare, and the latter of whom appears to have been Shakespeare's closest friend outside London. There are various other links between the Willoughbies and Peters, but none as significant as the direct connection between William Peter's sister and the Willoughby-Russell clan, or between Henry Willoughby and Peter's cousin George.

The last article of external evidence may be entirely coincidental, and so cannot count for much, but it requires comment nonetheless. William Peter took five extended leaves during his years as a student at Oxford, and a sixth during his regency. On at least three of these six occasions his absence coincides with provincial tours by the King's Men that began or ended in Oxford.[91]

We have, unfortunately, no daily record of Peter's attendance during his first two years at the university (the Buttery Books of Exeter College are lacking for the years 1599–1601). He cannot, however, have been absent for more than a few weeks. Peter's first extended leave began in the autumn of 1600, and extended through March (as is indicated in the surviving Bursar's Accounts of Exeter College).[92] Since he was only eighteen years old at the time, it is likely that Peter spent this period either at home in Exeter or with his elder brother in London. Shakespeare was presumably kept busy in the capital during the same period, but he cannot be linked to William Peter. In 1599, probably about 20 July, Shakespeare and his colleagues—now the Lord Chamberlain's Men—began performances at the newly erected Globe Theatre. Once situated, Shakespeare's company had little cause to venture outside London. Apart from court performances at nearby Richmond and their annual visits to Oxford (usually in October), there is no record of the Lord Chamberlain's Men having played outside the capital in the years 1599–1602.

The Buttery Books for Exeter College recommence on 23 October 1601, with the sixth week of the autumn term. From that date until 30 July 1602, William Peter left school only once, for ten days in December 1601. In that month the Lord Chamberlain's Men performed two plays at court (on 26 and 27 December), both during Peter's absence from school. But it seems quite likely that Peter simply went home for Christmas (or to celebrate his birthday on 31 December).

Much of 1603, a plague year, was spent touring the provinces. The Lord Chamberlain's Men were at Bath when James's accession to the throne was proclaimed by the local authorities, probably in the last week of March. Two months later, by letters patent dated 19 May, King James extended his patronage to Shakespeare and his fellows, to make them the

King's Men. William Peter, meanwhile, received his grace for B.A. on 10 May, and was formally admitted B.A. on 23 May.[93] Though the Buttery Books do not survive for the spring of 1603, there is no reason to suppose that he was absent from the hall for his final term as an undergraduate.

In the last week of May or first week of June, when plague deaths in the city first reached thirty per week, the London theaters were shut down. The toll was later to soar as high as three thousand per week for London and the outlying parishes, forcing the theaters to remain closed for the rest of the year. The King's Men, like most other London companies, again took to the road. In the summer and fall of 1603 they performed at Shrewsbury, Coventry, Maldon, and (probably) Ipswich. Their last public performance of 1603 appears to have been in November, at Oxford.[94] On 2 December they were summoned from Mortlake for a court performance at Wilton, the Wiltshire estate of William Herbert, Earl of Pembroke. Then, after a few weeks' respite (probably spent in rehearsal), they provided their usual holiday entertainment at Hampton Court, performing at least six times, beginning on 26 December and closing with two performances on New Year's Day. (Later that winter they performed at least twice more before the king, on 2 and 18 February.)

If, as seems most likely, Shakespeare performed (or at least traveled) with his fellows in 1603, this was perhaps his longest absence from London in ten years—since the tour of 1593, when he is thought to have been joined by Henry Willoughby. We have no evidence that Oxford students accompanied the Lord Chamberlain's Men either on their long tour of 1597 or on their visit to Bath in the spring of 1603, and no hint that students were present for their lengthier tour (as the King's Men) in the summer and fall of 1603. It may yet be worth noting, however, that William Peter left school at about the same time that the King's Men left London, and that he remained absent until at least mid-November.[95] Perhaps he left the hall only to escape the threat of the plague, which was severe in Oxford that summer, causing many students to stay away from July through September. Peter's home city of Exeter was among the other locales most severely struck with the epidemic; whether he found in this a reason to go home or a reason to go elsewhere is impossible to say. There is of course no record that he accompanied the King's Men, nor any proof that Shakespeare himself did so. The chronological coincidence of his absence from school during this period is suggestive only because it happens, as we shall see, on at least two subsequent occasions.

In midsummer Peter left the hall and once again stayed away for the entire autumn term. He returned to Oxford in the eighth week of the winter term, arriving at the hall on 24 January 1605 after another absence of at least six months. It appears that he returned in the company of William Ford, who arrived on the same day, having been gone for the same period except for the month of October, when Ford was present in the hall, and William Peter absent. The King's Men during this interval may have remained in London, except from 9 to 27 August, when they were assigned to attend at Somerset House upon Juan Fernandez de Velasco. Whether they played at Oxford in October 1604, as in other years, is unclear. It is theoretically possible that Ford and Peter, who were probably together, associated with Shakespeare's company during all or part of their leave, that they visited Oxford with the players in October, and that Ford during their visit boarded in the hall while Peter stayed away; but the conjecture will not get us very far, and has little or no value as evidence.

From 25 January until 12 July 1605, William Peter was continuously present in Oxford; but in mid-July he and his cousin, George Peter of Bristol, were absent from the hall for five days.[96] Then, on 29 July, less than two weeks after his return, William left school for another extended leave, his fourth long absence since his arrival at Exeter College six years earlier. His cousin George this time remained in school. Meanwhile, on 24 July in Stratford, Shakespeare purchased a half-interest in tithes in Old Stratford, Wedgcombe, and Bishopston.[97] It is thereby possible to imagine that the playwright in mid-July stopped over in Oxford on his way to Stratford, that he spent a few days in the company of William and George Peter, returned at the end of the month, and invited William to accompany him on the western tour of 1605. I do not place any weight on this as evidence, but it is interesting that Peter's movements should coincide so closely, once again, with the known and presumed movements of Shakespeare.

Following his departure from the hall on 29 July 1605 Peter remained absent throughout the autumn term. That he went home to Devon is more than I can say with certainty; it is certain, however, that the King's Men went to Devon. This was (apparently) their first trip, as a company, so far west. Sometime before Michaelmas, they played at Barnstaple. It seems likely enough that Shakespeare went along and that his use of the West Country dialect in *King Lear* (4.6) owes something to this western tour. By autumn, the King's Men had returned to Oxford, where they played on 9 October. Here, then, is at least one instance in which Peter remained absent from the hall while Shakespeare is likely to have been visiting Oxford; if Peter was traveling with the players, one might guess that he would eat in hall during his brief sojourn in Oxford. Since it is apparent from the Buttery Books that he did not, he may simply have been elsewhere, miles away from Shakespeare and the King's Men; but his leave does correspond with the dates of their 1605 tour.

During the winter holidays, the King's Men performed ten times at court, most of the performances occurring, probably, in late December and early January, as in other years; and Peter finally returned to school in the last week of January, seven weeks into the winter term (as he did the year before). He remained in hall until September, without interruption but for an absence of five days in mid-April.[98] He was, by now, almost finished with his master's degree, despite his frequent lapses. On 22 May 1606, William Peter received his grace for M.A., and was numbered among the seventy-two students who incepted on 14 July, the Day of Comitia. The King's Men in the same month (ca. 17–25 July) entertained Christian IV, king of Denmark, at Greenwich. The London theaters at the time were recently closed (about 10 July) and remained so till the year's end; so after closing at Greenwich, the King's Men took to the road. They went first to Oxford, where they performed in the last week of July. In August they moved on to Leicester (and perhaps to Wiltshire, for they played at Marlborough sometime that year; it is not known when). With the plague still raging in London, they extended their tour, traveling southward to Kent. In September they played at Dover, and at Maidstone sometime before 2 November. One of the plays performed was undoubtedly *King Lear*. It is again possible to suppose that William Peter joined the King's Men on this trip, for he left school during the first week of August, on or about the same day that the players left Oxford; and he was gone for all or most of the two terms following. This was his fifth extended absence from school, and one that again coincides with a tour by Shakespeare's dramatic company.

During the 1606/7 academic year, Peter was expected to serve the first half of his required regency—all graduated M.A.'s owed the university two years' service as a regent-master—but he was absent for much of the year, perhaps playing truant in London. No Buttery Books survive for the 1606/7 academic year; it is clear, however, from the Bursar's Books and Tutorial Books of Exeter College, that Peter was absent for the entire spring and summer terms. It is doubtful that he was at home in Exeter: when his father, Otho Peter, died in June of that year, William was apparently elsewhere. He was not present at the inquest with his mother Frances and brother John.[99] One may assume that he returned to Exeter for the funeral, and it may be that he spent the summer at home. In September, however, he returned to Oxford to finish his regency. Shakespeare's company, in the meantime, paid their second visit to Devon. That summer they played at Barnstaple and Dunwich, then returned to Oxford, where they played on 7 September. That William Peter returned to Oxford at about the same time is indicated in the Tutorial Book for 1606/7, where it is noted that he resumed study, under Simon Baskerville, in the Michaelmas term.

The autumn term of 1608 was William Peter's last as a registered student. He is listed in the Tutorial Book as a student of John Prideaux, but the surviving Buttery Books (which recommence on 9 September 1608) show that he was absent for the entire term. He was probably gone home to Exeter. It must have been in the autumn of 1608 that he arranged with Mrs. Elizabeth Brewton to wed her daughter Margaret, whom he married on 9 January 1609, at Exminster.[100] On 3 February following, Peter's name was dropped from the Buttery Books of Exeter College.

William Peter's last recorded visit to the university came in the spring of 1609. He returned to Oxford without his bride, arriving at the hall on 13 or 14 April. On 24 April he departed. Shakespeare's whereabouts at the time is not known, though I seriously doubt that he was having a birthday celebration in Oxford with William Peter. Only two weeks later the King's Men departed on another tour (performing on 9 May at Ipswich and on 17 May at New Romney). It seems likely enough that Shakespeare went with them—and virtually certain that William Peter did not.

Little else can be known of Shakespeare's and Peter's whereabouts from 1599 to 1609. If Peter again visited his alma mater, we have no record of it, for the Buttery Books have not survived. There seems little reason to doubt that he dwelt at Whipton, near Exeter, until his death three years later at the hands of Edward Drew. Nor is there any indication that the King's Men, much less Shakespeare himself, returned to Devon during Peter's lifetime.

This, then, is the sum of the external evidence for Shakespeare's authorship of the *Funeral Elegy:* the poem was written during the latter part of Shakespeare's career by someone with the initials W. S. It was registered for copyright by Thomas Thorp, the same stationer who registered Shakespeare's *Sonnets,* and printed by George Eld, the same printer. Shakespeare is thought to have been a visitor to Oxford during the years in which William Peter was a student there, and he may have known several persons within Peter's circle. Lastly, Peter's movements from 1599 to 1609 coincide largely with those of Shakespeare's dramatic company and, in at least one instance, with Shakespeare himself (in July 1605); it is therefore theoretically possible that William Shakespeare and William Peter spent some time together. But evidence of this sort will not convince anyone that William Shakespeare wrote the *Elegy.*

Since it cannot finally be proven that Shakespeare and Peter even knew one another, the case for Shakespearean authorship must rest primarily on the strength of the internal evidence. That the poem was written either by Shakespeare *or* by an imitator can hardly be questioned—W. S. knows his Shakespeare, including plays not yet printed—but, then again, Shakespeare had many imitators, including a few men of remarkable talent. Barring the discovery of additional documents linking Shakespeare's name to that of William Peter, there will always remain a possibility that the *Funeral Elegy* was the work of a clever mimic.

Contrary Evidence

Though the *Elegy* was clearly written under Shakespeare's influence, it cannot be said that every familiar phrase or image finds its original in Shakespeare. The notion that time is the father of truth was proverbial (*Elegy* 145). Even so dull a wit as King James had got hold of it for use in his *Basilicon Doron*. The more striking figure of the seeled dove (451–56) appears in Sidney's *Arcadia:* "Now she brought them to see a seeled Dove, who, the blinder she was, the higher she strave" (*Arc.* 1.15). More importantly, W. S. has clearly used as his model Samuel Daniel's *Funerall Poeme uppon the Late Noble Earle of Devonshire.* Like Daniel, W. S. writes his elegy in continuous quatrains, with couplets interspersed. Like Daniel, he includes apostrophes to the deceased. W. S.'s borrowing from Daniel extends even to the theft of particular thoughts and phrases; in fact, the echoes appear frequently enough for us to identify the particular edition in W. S.'s possession: he used the privately printed Quarto of 1606 (on which the ensuing quotations are based, though with modernized orthography). There is no clear sign that W. S. consulted Daniel's published version, substantially revised, of 1607 and 1611.

It is begging the question to suppose that W. S. borrowed unabashedly from Samuel Daniel, but could not have borrowed as much and more from William Shakespeare. Daniel's tribute to Devonshire begins,

> Now that the hand of death hath laid thee there
> Where all must lie, and level'd thee with earth
> . . . .
> Now thou hast nothing left thee, but a name.
>
> (*Funerall Poeme* 1–5)

W. S. asks,

> When all shall turn to dust from whence we came
> And we low-level'd in a narrow grave,
> What can we leave behind us, but a name?
>
> (*Elegy* 193–95)

Daniel describes the Earl as one who

> was so nobly fram'd, so well compos'd,
> As virtue never had a fairer seat,
> Nor could be better lodg'd nor more repos'd
> Than in that goodly frame where all thing[s] sweet
> And all things quiet held a peaceful rest;
> . . . .

Though thou hadst made a general surview
Of all the best of men's best knowledges,
And knew as much as ever learning knew,
Yet did it make thee trust thyself the less,
And less presume.

(Funerall Poeme 57–75)

William Peter was one whose qualities

        might well deserve
Just commendation, yet his furnish'd mind
Such harmony of goodness did preserve
As nature never built in better kind;
Knowing the best, and therefore not presuming
In knowing, but for that it was the best,
Ever within himself free choice resuming
Of true perfection, in a perfect breast;
So that his mind and body made an inn,
The one to lodge the other, both like fram'd
For fair conditions.

(Elegy 105–15)

Daniel addresses the Earl, saying,

The Belgique war first tried thy martial spirit
And what thou wert, and what thou wouldst be found.

(Funerall Poeme 115–16)

W. S. says of William Peter that

A rock of friendship figured in his name,
Foreshowing what he was, and what should be,
Most true presage.

(Elegy 321–23)

Daniel writes,

But in what noble fashion he did suit
This action, with what wit and industry,
There is no room to place it in this strait.

(Funerall Poeme 213–15)

and W. S.,

For that his actions did so wholly suit
With worthiness, still memorable here.

(Elegy 153–56)

W. S. expresses many of the same sentiments as Daniel, sometimes in similar language. "And let me say," writes Daniel,

> that herein there amounts
> Something unto thy fortune, that thou hast
> This monument of thee, perhaps may last,
> Which doth not t'every mighty man befall:
> For lo, how many when they die, die all.
> And this doth argue, too, thy great deserts,
> For honor never brought unworthiness
> Further than to the grave, and there it parts,
> And leaves men's greatness to forgetfulness.
>
> (*Funerall Poeme* 374–82)

W. S. follows suit:

> The grave, that in his ever-empty womb
> For ever closes up the unrespected,
> Who, when they die, die all, shall not entomb
> His pleading best perfections as neglected.
>
> (*Elegy* 423–26)

Daniel concludes by addressing his deceased subject:

> And thus, great patron of my muse, have I
> Paid thee my vows, and fairly clear'd th'accounts
> Which in my love I owe thy memory.
>
> (*Funerall Poeme* 371–73)

as does W. S.:

> And now if I [have] level'd mine account
> And reckon'd up in a true measured score
> Those perfect graces which were ever wont
> To wait on thee alive, I ask no more . . . .
>
> (*Elegy* 553–56)

The mere fact that W. S. has borrowed from Daniel's poem is not in itself a problem. Indeed, this is precisely the sort of theft that Shakespeare is noted for, even in the last plays. He was often brasher in borrowing from other writers than from himself, and the same pattern obtains here. W. S.'s borrowings from Shakespeare are generally diffuse and indirect, yet he appears to have written his *Funeral Elegy* with Daniel's *Funerall Poeme* lying open on his desktop. In this, the *Elegy* seems characteristically Shakespearean. Moreover, W. S., like Shakespeare, offers always an augmentation of the image or phrase in question, even when borrowing most directly—as when "*measured* score" takes the "borrowing" from Daniel and compounds the interest of the mercantile metaphor with a metrical one (while qualifying the entire thought, Shakespeare-like, with a circumspect "If"). It should be noted, however, that Shakespeare's boldest thefts elsewhere are generally restricted to the drama. One does not find in any of Shakespeare's nondramatic works the same close study of a particular source that is evident here. We might provide excuses for Shakespeare— that he wrote the *Elegy* in obvious haste, that he had little affection for "exercise in this kind," that he borrows as heavily from Daniel in other works. Still, I suspect that many readers will find W. S.'s use of Daniel's poem a major obstacle to a hypothesis of Shakespearean authorship.

Nor is everything in the Peter elegy especially worthy of William Shakespeare. The poem contains a few embarrassments over and beyond the author's thefts from Samuel Daniel. W. S. may doubtless be forgiven line eight—"Sith as [that] ever he maintain'd the same"—as it contains a crux and may be wrong, even with my emendation of "that" for "it"; and the latter half of the line was standard Jacobean syntax, as in *Cymbeline:* "Thou dost approve thyself the very same" (*Cym.* 4.2.380). This archaic construction appears more than forty times in Shakespeare, as also in virtually any Renaissance text of more than a few thousand words, whether in verse or prose (it appears, for example, twice in Daniel's 388-line *Funerall Poeme*). The phrasing would not have sounded odd to a Jacobean audience.

Certain other lines of W. S., however, I find less easy to defend. Take, for example, the first rhymed couplet:

Now therein liv'd he happy, if to be
Free from detraction happiness it be.

(49–50)

The syntax here is convoluted, the phrasing repetitive, the thought unnecessary, and the rhyme "pushed over" into the line succeeding, so that the second line rhymes with itself ("Free . . . be"). This may, I suppose, be described as a bold experiment. It is not, in my judgment, a very successful experiment.

But even apart from such particulars, there arises a more general question as to whether the *Elegy,* as a whole, is "good enough" to have been written by William Shakespeare. It is not, for one thing, an especially quotable poem. In some parts, W. S. does little more than to catalogue his friend's virtues after the manner of other Jacobean elegists. As a result, the *Elegy* has a number of flat spots. It might well be hoped that a memorial poem by Shakespeare could be ranked beside Donne's two Anniversaries and Milton's "Lycidas," or still better, that his hypothetical elegy should stand as a peerless triumph of English poetry. The Peter elegy is superior to most other memorial verse of the age, but as a candidate for admission to the Shakespeare canon, I find the poetry itself rather disappointing—no better, if no worse, than what may be found in *Henry VIII* or *The Two Noble Kinsmen*. Perhaps this is another indication of Shakespeare's declining engagement during the last years of his career. But it may be, too, that the *Elegy* was simply written by some other W. S., one who admired William Shakespeare enough to imitate him.

A still greater obstacle in ascribing the *Elegy* to Shakespeare may be that the poem suggests some measure of intimacy with young Master Peter, as in lines 183–88, 205–46, 313–24, 507–14, 537–78, and in the prefatory epistle. W. S. professes, for example, to have uttered an "irrefragable vow," while his friend was yet living, to immortalize him in verse (235). The poet's mysterious statement that his expressions of affection were "hindered" during Peter's lifetime is not enough to explain away the obvious difficulty (223). It is difficult to see how a friendship could have existed between an Oxford student and a largely untutored playwright, nearly twenty years his senior, who lived much of the time in London, fifty-five miles away.

Nor is this the sole obstacle to belief. Perhaps the strongest evidence against Shakespeare's authorship of the Peter elegy appears in the burial register of Stratford-upon-Avon. On 3 February 1612, just nine days after Peter was slain, and sixteen days before the *Elegy* was registered in London, there was buried at Stratford one "Gilbertus Shakespeare, adolescens." It seems likely that this was Shakespeare's brother Gilbert. The poet's brother, born in 1566, was neither an "adolescent" in 1612, nor a Gilbert, "junior," but the *"adolescens"* is probably the result of a country parson's small Latin, who took the word to mean "unmarried."[101] If, then, as seems likely, Shakespeare's brother (who is thought to have been a London haberdasher) was buried in Stratford in the same week that William Peter was buried at Exminster, one may well ask what the chances are of Shakespeare's finding either the time or the inclination to write a funeral elegy for a young man with whom he can no longer have had a close association. Indeed, even assuming that Shakespeare performed at court with the King's Men during the winter of 1611/12, one may ask what the chances are that he would hear of William Peter's death in time to write a major poem on the subject, and to have it completed within three weeks of his friend's burial. Add to this the fact that Shakespeare cannot with certainty be placed in Oxford for any length of time, nor William Peter in London; the fact that Shakespeare was old enough to be Peter's father; the fact that no seventeenth-century writer makes mention of

Shakespeare having written a funeral elegy; and that the *Elegy* was omitted from John Benson's *Poems* in 1640 (while many items not written by Shakespeare were included)—and the case for Shakespeare's authorship of the Peter elegy becomes clouded. We shall do well to consider such problems before adding this *Funeral Elegy* to the canon of William Shakespeare.

THE CASE FOR WILLIAM
STRACHEY

Given the weight of the evidence for Shakespeare's authorship of the *Funeral Elegy,* some readers will perhaps think it superfluous to consider the possibility of its having been written by William Strachey, a poet of far less repute. In fact, Strachey's candidacy must be given serious consideration. Among known writers with the initials, W. S., he is certainly the likeliest candidate after Shakespeare. Strachey's circle of friends included Ben Jonson, Richard Martin, and John Marston, all three of whom were published by Thomas Thorp, and he was perhaps acquainted with other of Thorp's clients, including Shakespeare and Chapman. Strachey, in addition, contributed a commendatory sonnet to Thorp's 1605 edition of Jonson's *Sejanus.* It is therefore quite plausible that he knew the publisher of the *Elegy.* The fact that Strachey took his single independent publication (the *Lawes,* 1612) to stationer Walter Burre does not rule out the possibility of his having been published by Thorp in the same year. Writers often did business with more than one shop, and Burre was himself a close associate of Thomas Thorp.

Strachey knew also, through the Inns of Court, men who may have known John Peter. More noteworthy is that he dedicated a copy of *The Historie of Travell* to Sir Allen Apsley in 1612. Forty years later, Apsley's son, Sir Allen, Jr., married John Peter's daughter, Frances, which is potentially a more direct link than any between Shakespeare and the Peters. The internal evidence for Strachey is admittedly weak, yet we find in him a poet of far more talent than most contemporaries, one who might easily have written a major poem of unusual merit. It would therefore be foolish to reject his candidacy without having first marshaled every scrap of available evidence in his behalf.[1]

Prosody

The appearance in W. S.'s *Elegy* of continuous quatrains, with couplets interspersed, is fairly consonant with Strachey's known poetry; of his ten surviving poems, five are sonnets; two others are "abbreviated sonnets,"

203

with one or two quatrains omitted. For his single elegiac poem, "Upon the Untimely Death of Sir Thomas Overbury," he uses couplets, according to convention, but that does not preclude his having used a different form for a longer elegy written four years earlier.

Strachey was also capable of enjambing his verse lines. Though his poems are too short to show much consistency, his unstopped lines reach fifty percent by 1615 (see table 2.1). Strachey's frequency of "open" lines prior to 1615 is about average for the period, while his last poem, "Hark" (perhaps dictated from his deathbed), is far below average for late Jacobean verse, as there is a marked increase across the board for English poets in the frequency of unstopped lines beginning about 1615. Yet his sonnet on *Sejanus* and the two poems in the Overbury volume demonstrate that he was indeed able to make effective use of open lines. The high incidence of unstopped lines in the Peter elegy (46.0%) need not be considered a serious obstacle to Strachey's candidacy, as indeed it would be for many of his contemporaries. Apart from Strachey and Shakespeare, no known Jacobean poet with the initials W. S. has a frequency of unstopped lines, in any single poem, greater than 30 percent (the first exception is William Singleton in 1624).

Nor is the high frequency of feminine endings in the Peter elegy (11.8%) especially problematic. Strachey, at 4.4 percent overall, is below the average of 5.4 percent for the combined poems in the Cross-Sample, and far below W. S. Nevertheless, Strachey's two earliest poems, though brief, are both 10 percent or higher. (See table 2.2.) It is not inconceivable that he should make as frequent use of feminine endings once again in a major work such as the Peter elegy. If the high frequency of unstopped lines and

TABLE 2.1 / UNSTOPPED LINES				
Short title	date	lines	"open"	%
"Michell"	1604	10	2	20.0
"Sejanus"	1605	14	6	42.9
"La Warr"	1611	14	5	35.7
"Smith"	1611	14	4	28.6
"Council"	1611	14	5	35.7
"Ecclesiae"	1612	6	1	16.7
"Seneca"	1612	6	2	33.3
"Overbury"	1615	66	33	50.0
"Wife"	1615	14	7	50.0
"Hark"	1621	24	4	16.7
Total		182	69	37.9

TABLE 2.2 / FEMININE ENDINGS				
Short title	**date**	**lines**	**fem.**	**%**
"Michell"	1604	10	1	10.0
"Sejanus"	1605	14	2	14.3
"La Warr"	1611	14	0	0.0
"Smith"	1611	14	1	7.1
"Council"	1611	14	0	0.0
"Ecclesiae"	1612	6	0	0.0
"Seneca"	1612	6	0	0.0
"Overbury"	1615	66	4	6.1
"Wife"	1615	14	0	0.0
"Hark"	1621	24	0	0.0
Total		182	8	4.4

feminine endings in the *Elegy* does not point strongly to Strachey's hand, neither may this be taken as solid evidence against his authorship of the poem.

Diction

W. S.'s vocabulary has a much lower concordance with Strachey's work than with Shakespeare's, but that is to be expected: Strachey's tabulated poetry and prose amount to only 82,050 words, whereas Shakespeare's poems and plays amount to ten times that number, providing a much larger sample.[2] Moreover, Strachey uses three words, "concourse," "generality" (twice), and "disunion" (*Elegy:* "disunion'd"), that appear in W. S. but are not found in Shakespeare (though it should be added that Strachey both times uses "generality" to mean "the masses," a different sense than that found in the *Elegy*). Lastly, W. S.'s frequency of compound words, at 4.6, falls within the expected range for a poem by William Strachey of 2.6–5.0. None of the twenty-two compounds in the *Elegy* has an identical counterpart in Strachey's poetry or prose, yet his practice is not remarkably different from that of W. S. The word most frequently used by Strachey in compounds, as by Shakespeare and W. S., is *well-*. Strachey, in fact, sometimes has more compounds using *well-* than all others combined. In the *Elegy* we find "well-employ'd," "well-abled," "well-profited," and "well-worthy."

Accidence

Strachey's accidence is similar in many respects to that of W. S. He generally writes in correct English, but he employs, five times, a redundant comparative or superlative: "more fuller" and "most inmost" (in the "True Reportory"), "perfectest," "most terriblest," and "most necessariest" (in the *Historie*). He might therefore have written "more severer," as in the *Elegy*. Strachey has, moreover, a high frequency of superlatives in both his poetry and prose, and an unusually high incidence of "most" (3.5 in his poetry and 1.5 in his prose, versus 2.6 in the *Elegy*). Turning to the auxiliary verbs, Strachey, like the elegist, prefers "hath" and "doth" to "has" and "does." He never uses *wert,* but never does he have recourse to the use, with the pronoun *thou,* of a verb of being in either the past indicative or past subjunctive. We cannot, therefore, say what form he might have preferred.

Syntax

Sentence structure in Strachey's surviving poetry and prose is considerably simpler than that of W. S., but the compressed and irregular syntax of the Peter elegy might be explained as a stylistic choice. One may, at least, find in Strachey's verse a few examples of elision. And though his verse is generally lacking in the double entendre found throughout the *Elegy,* he does not entirely abjure wordplay: His poetry contains one obvious pun, "As we are *Angli,* make us *angels,* too" ("Ecclesiae," 5); and there is perhaps an additional quibble in the phrase, "make us angels," since an "angel" was a gold coin worth ten shillings.

More importantly, Strachey's introduction to the *Lawes* contains a phrase that may be taken as a hendiadys. He writes of those

> in Magnuza who have restored (as I may say), after *so great a floud and rage of abused goodnesse,* all Lawes, literature, and Vertue againe, which had well nigh perished. . . . [Emphasis added][3]

Though I find no additional examples in Strachey's poetry or prose, I think we may paraphrase the italicized figure as "a raging flood of abused goodness," and count it as a hendiadys. If so, Strachey and Shakespeare stand alone in their use of this figure. Among other W. S.'s known to be living in 1612, none appears to have used hendiadys even once.

Themes, Imagery, and Verbal Echoes

Strachey in his poetry employs a number of thoughts or images that appear also in the *Elegy:*

What memorable monument can last
Whereon to build his never-blemish'd name
(Elegy, 5–6)

> *Nor any other honor build upon*
> *Than only this: since 'tis for Christ's dear Word*
("La Warr," 12–13)

Whose very virtues are, not to detract
Whiles hope remains of gain (base fee of slaves)
(Elegy, 45–46)

> *though 'tis the fashion now*
> *Noblest to mix with basest, for their gain*
("Council," 1–2)

The willful blindness that hoodwinks the eyes
(Elegy, 257)

> *Swift lightning blinds his eyes*
("Sejanus," 10)

Those saints before the everlasting throne
Who sit with crowns of glory on their heads,
Wash'd white in blood, from earth hence have not gone
All to their joys in quiet on their beds
(Elegy, 391–94)

> *And where white Christians turn, in manners, Moors,*
> *You wash Moors white with sacred Christian blood.*
("Council," 11–12)

> *O but dear Christ, I humbly sue*
> *Thy blood may wash my red soul white*
("Hark," 14–15)

[others] ever sweat
For popular applause and power's commission.
(Elegy, 447–50)

> *Sale and profane applause mere fools affect*
("Michell," 10)

There may be another echo of the *Elegy* when Strachey speaks in the *Historie* of "the most false (yet eye-pleasing objects) of our carnal senses":

O our dull Ignorance, depraved wills, or Imperfection of Reason, or all three, how doe yee transport vs? . . . that we neglect all good things, and *(like english Lords)* pursue these on *the Streame of delight,* in swift Bardges? [Emphasis added][4]

W. S. writes of those who, "Only like Lords, [are] subjects to their will" (290), and he later speaks of "the stream of my mischance" (573).

I do not pretend that these verbal affinities with the Peter elegy are as striking as those found in Shakespeare, but it must be kept in mind that Strachey's collected works amount to only a tenth of Shakespeare's. The relatively smaller sample must be taken into consideration. Had Strachey written additional verse or prose, we might well find echoes of W. S. as striking as those found in the poems and plays of William Shakespeare.

Internal Biographical Evidence

W. S., though an able poet, is no aristocrat. The poet freely confesses, in speaking of himself and William Peter, that "Birth, blood, and ancestors are none of ours." Strachey, a second generation gentleman, fits that description as well as William Shakespeare. The statement of W. S. that he has little affection for "exercise in this kind" might, again, describe Strachey as aptly as Shakespeare. Most of his poetry is of a eulogistic nature, but his surviving verse includes only one poem that can be described as a memorial verse (for Sir Thomas Overbury), and it was not yet written in 1612. Moreover, if we take "exercise in this kind" to mean, not elagiac verse, but poetry in general, Strachey is surely the stronger candidate, for his poetic output is negligible compared to that of Shakespeare. The assertion is, after all, ambiguous. And though Strachey is not known to have had any connection with Oxfordshire, it cannot be proven that he never visited Oxford, to suffer some manner of disgrace there.

The External Evidence

There are three possible points of contact between William Strachey and William Peter. The first is through the Inns of Court. Though no record survives of his admission, Strachey at some point studied at Gray's Inn, almost certainly in the interval following his studies at Cambridge in 1588 and before his marriage to Frances Forster in 1595. It was apparently as a member of Gray's Inn that he became friends with John Donne (of Lincoln's Inn, 1591–94), Thomas Campion (Gray's Inn, 1586–ca. 1595), Francis Michell (Gray's Inn, 1590–94), and Richard Martin (Middle Temple, 1587–1618). Martin, writing to Strachey in 1610, speaks of "our auncient acquaintance & good intentions."[5] Though Strachey is not known ever to have set foot in Oxford, William Peter's brother John spent several years in London at the Middle Temple, and it may be that Strachey came to know John Peter through the auspices of Martin or another templar.

Then, too, there is a possible connection through the Fords of Devonshire. Both William Strachey and Peter's friend, William Ford, spent time in the service of Sir Thomas Glover in Constantinople, Strachey as the ambassador's secretary, and Ford as preacher to the English community there. Strachey had returned home by the time Ford arrived in Turkey in November of 1608, yet the two men undoubtedly shared some of the same acquaintance in later years, if not before. More importantly, both John Ford ("Io:Fo:") and William Strachey ("W. S.," "W:Stra:") contributed poems to the seventh edition of *Sir Thomas Overbury His Wife* (1616). This is the occasion on which Ford imitated W. S.'s *Elegy*. It seems likely enough that Strachey knew Ford by 1615. If they were friends, Ford might well have mimicked the *Elegy* with Strachey's approval.

Lastly, Strachey addressed his *Historie of Travell* in 1612 to Sir Allen Apsley, whose son, Allen, Jr., later married John Peter's daughter, Frances. The poet presented his unfinished manuscript to Apsley, Purveyor of his Majesty's Navy, after having been rebuffed by Henry Percy, earl of Northumberland (and perhaps also by the Council of Virginia). It does not appear from his letter of dedication that he was previously acquainted with Apsley, but if we suppose that Strachey knew John Peter and that Peter knew Apsley, then Strachey might have appealed to Apsley for assistance upon his friend's recommendation. In his letter of dedication the poet asks

> your honour to pardoun me the appealing of you from your more serious affaires to the perusall of these infirme and scatter'd collections, since yf I have offended, the noblenes & Bountie of your faire Disposicioun (expressed evenn in my knowledge to manie of my best Freindes) makes me presume that I cannot (in any actioun, which hath relish of virtue and goodnes) too much challenge or provoak your patience. . . .[6]

However great Apsley's interest in Virginia (and he was later instrumental in the founding of the Plymouth colony), he had, apparently, no money to support aspiring writers. Yet, though he declined to supply Strachey with funds to see his work through to the press, the possibility remains of a three-way connection between Apsley, Strachey, and John Peter.

CONTRARY EVIDENCE

The Text

It is quite apparent from the Quarto of 1612 that George Eld's compositor, in setting forth the *Elegy*, had to work from a manuscript almost entirely lacking in punctuation. The endless punctuative errors (excluding, of course, mere peculiarities of Jacobean practice) appear to stem from someone's sincere but misguided attempts to sort out the complexities of the poet's unpointed text. Yet all the surviving manuscript materials in Strachey's hand, whether intended for publication or otherwise, are meticulously punctuated, according to the best standards of the age. Few writers took such evident pains with their work as William Strachey. Each time that his manuscripts were copied by a scribe, and again after they were printed, Strachey proofread the text and corrected the errors in his own hand. It seems unlikely that in just one instance he should abandon his usual care in preparing and proofreading his work.

It is, however, interesting to note that Shakespeare is known to have pointed his manuscripts lightly, or not at all, as is evident from the frequent and egregious errors made by those compositors who set up type from the dramatist's own papers (as, for example, in the First Folio text of *Cor.*). Indeed, among the strongest evidence of Shakespeare's hand in the manuscript of *Sir Thomas More* is that Hand *D* is distinguished by a general lack of punctuation. Perhaps, as an actor, Shakespeare conceived punctuation to be primarily the speaker's, not the writer's, responsibility. But whatever his reason, relatively few Renaissance poets show a greater disregard than he for punctuation. That the manuscript copy of the *Elegy* appears likewise to have been lightly punctuated does not, of course, prove that Shakespeare wrote it (for there were countless other authors who paid little mind to pointing and proofreading), but it does speak against Strachey's authorship of the poem.

Title Page and Dedication

William Strachey in 1611 penned verse dedications addressed to the Lord De La Warr, Sir Thomas Smith, and to the Council of Virginia, and wrote prose dedications to Thomas Lawson, William Crashaw, Sir Anthony Aucher, Sir William Wade, Henry Percy, earl of Northumberland, and Sir Allen Apsley. In 1618, he wrote his last dedication, addressed to Sir Francis Bacon. All the prose pieces are much after the same manner, some longer, others shorter. None bears any notable affinity with that by W. S., nor is it apparent why Strachey, in just one dedication, should choose to imitate Shakespeare's earlier epistle to Southampton. The title given to the poem—*A Funeral Elegy*—must remain a problem too, given W. S.'s departure from convention, for Strachey labored to present himself as a classicist. It seems improbable that he should become suddenly forgetful of form. Nor do we have reason to believe that the poem's title was supplied by anyone but the author, W. S. The title as given in the Stationers' Register is identical to that found in the printed Quarto, with the exception of variant spellings.

Prosody

Strachey's one poem with a percentage of "open" lines comparable to that of the Peter elegy is his sonnet on *Sejanus,* in which four of fourteen lines are enjambed, and two others unstopped. But if we had just two poets from whom to choose, Shakespeare in this respect is the stronger candidate. In each of Shakespeare's last seven plays the frequency of open lines is greater than forty percent; this is far more significant, statistically, than the freak occurrence of six unstopped lines in a single sonnet.

W. S.'s use of feminine endings likewise speaks more strongly for Shakespeare than for Strachey. One may take on faith that Strachey might have written a major poem having a frequency of feminine endings within five percentage points of W. S.'s 11.6 percent. Yet with a frequency in his combined verse of 4.4 percent he is a less likely candidate than half the poets living in 1612—and far less likely than Shakespeare, whose use of feminine endings never varies in his nondramatic works by more than four points from that found in the *Elegy.*

Also worth note is a formal characteristic of Strachey's verse: when writing in quatrains, Strachey appears always to have indented the alternating rhymed lines (*bb, dd,* etc.), unlike either Shakespeare or W. S. It seems unlikely that Strachey would have altered his usual practice in just one poem, or that Eld would have altered the poet's alignment. Eld had previously printed quatrains by Strachey (in the "Sejanus" sonnet) and by Shakespeare (in the 1609 Quarto) and on both occasions he preserved what appears to have been each poet's preferred alignment of the quatrains.

Spelling

As already noted, past discussions of Jacobean orthography have often proved misleading. No Renaissance author may be identified solely on the basis of spelling, no matter how irregular his habits may be. Yet when one has to choose from a limited number of candidates, orthography can be a helpful indicator, if the evidence is treated responsibly, and with some familiarity with contemporaneous practice in both manuscript and printed texts. It is therefore worth noting that W. S.'s orthography (though quite consistent with that of Shakespeare) is out of keeping with Strachey's practice, at least insofar as we may judge from the printed text of the *Funeral Elegy.*

Strachey, for example, prefers the French spelling for words ending in *-ic,* thus *catholique, frantique, politique, pragmatique, publique, traffique, Atlantique,* and so on, most of these appearing more than once. Never in

Strachey does the modern -*ic* spelling appear. With very few exceptions, -*ick* appears only in *zodiack* and *heroicke* (also *heroyicke*) and in such monosyllables as *sick* or *trick*. The rare exceptions appear only in printed or scribal copies of his work, not in his own manuscripts; usually, though, Strachey's -*ique* spelling is preserved even in the printed texts. Compositors in this case had no reason to alter his orthography, as the -*ique* spelling was a widely accepted alternative among London stationers (as in the printed text of Daniel's *Funerall Poeme,* W. S.'s principal source). Shakespeare, however, prefers to spell all such words -*ick,* as is true also of the *Elegy* Quarto, in which we find *publick* (twice) and *fantastick.*

Many spellings in the *Elegy* that may seem odd to the modern reader (*bee, goe, wast[e], sunck, shortned,* and so on) appear in the best texts of both Strachey and Shakespeare. Yet there remain consistent differences in a great number of words, and of those distinctive spellings that appear in the *Elegy,* all (without exception) agree with Shakespeare's, rather than with Strachey's customary orthography. Table 2.3 shows, for example, the spellings used habitually by Strachey, versus the preferred form in both the *Elegy* Quarto and in the best Shakespearean texts. The "preferred" spellings given here for Shakespeare are quite reliable, if it be agreed that

TABLE 2.3 / PREFERRED SPELLINGS

Strachey	W.S.	Shakespeare
affourd	affoord, afford	affoord, afford
amongest	amongst	amongst
answear	answer	answer
devine	divine	divine
ells, elles	else	else
falce	false	false
fewell	fuell	fuell
fruict	fruit	fruit
maie	may	may
misciefe	mischief(e)	mischief(e)
somtymes	sometime	sometime
straung(e)	strang(e)	strang(e), straing(e)
tonge, tongue	toung	toung
true	true, trew	trew(e), true
truith, triuth	truth	truth

the cumulative evidence of the best texts can tell us anything at all of Shakespearean orthography. The spellings given for Strachey are based in part on his own manuscripts (including correspondence), and in part on scribal and printed copies of his work (such as his Algonquin/English dictionary, in which the scribe, twice copying the original manuscript, adhered quite closely to the author's own spelling). Strachey is remarkably consistent in his spelling of these words; the occasional exceptions are insignificant.

There are many additional words and phonemes for which Strachey's and Shakespeare's spelling consistently differ. Strachey, for example, never writes "adventer," "venter," or "adventerous" (though all three words make frequent appearances in his work with -*ur*-), and with one exception, he never elides the vowel (i.e., *Q:* "ven'tring" [*sic*] in the "Smith" sonnet). In the *Elegy* we find "adventer" (once), and in Shakespeare, "adventerous" (twice), "venter" four times, "advent'rous" (once), and "vent'ring" (thrice). I can find no instance in which W. S.'s preferred orthography agrees with that of Strachey when differing from that of Shakespeare. This, again, will not prove Shakespeare's authorship of the *Elegy,* but insofar as one may judge from the 1612 Quarto, the orthographic evidence seems at least to speak against William Strachey.

Diction

None of the peculiarities of diction found in the *Elegy* are found in the work of William Strachey. Never, for example, does Strachey use "memorable" to mean "commemorative," or "comfortable" to mean "comforting." The use of "timeless" to mean "untimely," though not unique to W. S. and Shakespeare, is not found in Strachey. W. S. (like Shakespeare) makes frequent use of "whiles" and occasional use of "sith"; Strachey, in eighty-two thousand words, never uses either, preferring instead "whilst" (which never appears in the *Elegy*) and "since." And unlike either W. S. or late Shakespearean texts, Strachey generally prefers "because" to "since" for logical distinctions, reserving the latter for temporal usage.

Though Strachey's poetry has an incidence of compound words similar to that of W. S., both his poetry and prose lack the high frequency of participial compounds found in the *Elegy,* as shown in table 2.4. Shakespeare is again the stronger candidate.[7]

As in most contemporaneous verse, proper nouns and adjectives are frequent in the verse of William Strachey: 21 in 182 lines, for an incidence per 100 lines of 11.5, versus less than 0.2 in the *Elegy,* a ratio of 68:1. Shakespeare has a frequency of 0.6 in "A Lover's Complaint," 0.7 in the sonnets, 1.6 in "The Phoenix and the Turtle." *Venus and Adonis* has a

	number of words	hyphenated words	percent diff.	participial compounds	percent diff.
TABLE 2.4 / **COMPOUNDS IN STRACHEY, SHAKESPEARE, AND W. S.**					
Shakespeare's verse	44713	241 5.39	5.9	152 3.40	8.3
Strachey's verse	1417	6 4.23	17.0	3 2.12	42.9
Strachey's prose	80636	120 1.49	70.7	36 0.45	88.0
W.S.	4318	22 5.09	—	16 3.71	—

frequency of 0.9, or 0.3 if we exclude the names of the title characters, which are necessary to the narrative (that the frequency of proper nouns in *Lucrece* is somewhat higher is largely the result of its having a more numerous cast of characters than the other poems).

Strachey, moreover, in both poetry and prose, displays his learning by inserting unnecessary Latin phrases in his text, most of which, as noted by S. G. Culliford, he seems to have picked up indirectly, from grammar-books.[8] None such appears in the *Elegy*. Strachey is fond also of pretentious diction. His readers are given a fairly steady diet of such words as "cautelous," "commutative," "defaulk," "dissite," "docible," "epiphonema," "epitrapezia," "exorbitate," "gynaeceum," "mnemosynon," "peregrination," "plenulune [*sic*]," "surreption." Sir Thomas Overbury's *Wife* is described in Strachey's verse as a "cynosura in neat poesis." Despite the rich and varied vocabulary of the Peter elegy, W. S. demonstrates no interest in arcane loanwords.

Accidence

Strachey, like W. S. and Shakespeare, prefers "hath" and "doth" to "has" and "does" for both notional and auxiliary use. This, however, is among the least distinctive features of W. S.'s grammatical accidence. In other respects, Strachey's practice differs from that of the elegist: "wert" fails to appear anywhere in Strachey's collected works for the simple reason that he, unlike W. S. and Shakespeare, never uses "thou" for the second person singular, except when addressing God. Whether writing to friend or stranger, to a wealthy lord or to an imprisoned debtor, Strachey uses "you" exclusively.

W. S., like Shakespeare, prefers "sometime" where most writers of the age, including William Strachey, add final -*s*. With but two exceptions, Strachey drops the -*s* only when in accordance with modern usage, where "sometimes" would be inappropriate, as in the phrase, "made sometyme of aboad there" (i.e., "some time"), or "wherein our westerne colony was somtyme planted" ("for a time"). Shakespeare and W. S. both prefer "like" to "likely" for adverbial use. Strachey prefers "likely" in all his works but the "True Reportory." Strachey uses "struck" as a preterit for *strike* (and "strucken" as past participle). W. S. and Shakespeare both prefer "strook." Nor does Strachey ever use "can" idiosyncratically after the manner of Shakespeare and W. S.

Syntax

Whatever William Strachey "might" have done, no matter what kind of verse or prose he "might" have written, the fact remains that his syntax, in all his surviving works is much simpler than that found throughout the Peter elegy. Neither in Strachey's verse, nor in the mannered prose of the "True Reportory," nor in his private correspondence, do we find anything comparable to the compressed and sometimes tangled syntax of W. S. Nor are Strachey's sentences any longer than what is commonly found elsewhere in Jacobean literature. His longest clause in the poetry is 85 words (in "Sir Thomas Smith"), compared to 141 words in the *Elegy* and a mean of 86 words in the Cross-Sample.

Nor does Strachey ever vary from standard usage, as does W. S., by employing "not" before the verb without the required auxiliary, in either his poetry or prose. Nor does he ever use "for that" after the manner of W. S. and Shakespeare. Strachey adds the affix to "for" only twice in his collected works, and both times the affix is superfluous. Never in his poetry or prose does Strachey affect the syntax "spring of day," "best of time," or anything similar. Nor does he ever use "who" with an incongruent antecedent, as do W. S. and Shakespeare. Quite the reverse: in his poetry, Strachey never employs "who" at all, but substitutes "that" where most of his contemporaries, including W. S., write "who." For example:

More than the world he gains, *that* gains a soul

("Smith," 12)

Yet doth it fare far otherwise with you
That scorn to turn to chaos so again,

And follow your supreme distinction still,

. . . .

What had you been, had not your ancestors
Begun to you *that* make their nobles good?

("Council," 3–5, 9–10)

Be all *that* gentle are, more high improv'd

("Wife," 13)

Strachey uses "who" fairly often in his prose, but never after the idiosyncratic (and habitual) manner of W. S.

Strachey has also, like any author, a number of syntactical habits peculiar to himself. One of his most characteristic phrases is "how (adjective) soever": "how *prepared* so ever," "how *young* soever," "how [*cruel, desperate, near, unfit*] soever," and so on; or "what [*time, place, means, etc.*] soever." Another of his favorite mannerisms is "so (adjective) and (adjective) a (noun)": "so great and glorious a building," "so beloved and sacred a business," "so remote and barbarous corners of an unknown world." His relatively fewer noun-doublets come linked by "or" far more often than in either Shakespeare or W. S., and then, often, he selects nouns that are approximate synonyms ("heat or zeal," "shame or contrition," "journal or diary books"). And unlike either W. S. or Shakespeare, Strachey frequently links words or phrases three at a time, three verbs, three nouns, three adjectives. To all these may be added at least a dozen more syntactical flourishes characteristic of Strachey. The absence of one or two of these from the Peter elegy would not be especially significant. The absence of them all is more telling.

Statistical Tabulations

In tabulating Strachey's work, I have omitted those items that were not actually written by him (e.g., the main text of *Lawes*) as well as portions that for some other reason might introduce inaccuracies (e.g., his "Algonquin/English Dictionary," and extended quotation of other writers). I have divided his works as follows:

I. Poems, 1604–12
    A. "To. . .Francis Michell"   (1604, 79 words)
    B. "Upon Sejanus"   (1605, 110 wds.)
    C. "To. . .Lord La Warr"   (1611, 113 wds.)
    D. "To. . .Sir Thomas Smith"   (1611, 109 wds.)

	E. "To. . .the Council"	(1611, 108 wds.)
	F. "Ecclesiae"	(1612, 50 wds.)
	G. "Seneca"	(1612, 49 wds.)
II.	Poems, 1613–21	
	A. "Upon. . .Sir Thomas Overbury"	(1615, 529 wds.)
	B. "To the Clean Contrary Wife"	(1615, 109 wds.)
	C. "Hark"	(1621, 161 wds.)
III.	Letters and prose dedications	
	A. to Peter Ferryman	(letter, 1609)
	B. to the Council of Virginia	(*Lawes,* 1612)
	C. to Thomas Lawson	(ibid.)
	D. to William Crashaw	(ibid.)
	E. to Sir Anthony Aucher	(ibid.)
	F. to Sir William Wade	(ibid.)
	G. to Henry Percy, Earl of Northumberland (*Hist.*, 1612)	
	H. to Sir Allen Apsley	(ibid.)
	I. "Praemonition to the Reader"	(ibid.)
	J. to "Sir"	(1613)
	K. to Sir Francis Bacon	(*Historie,* 1618)
IV.	"True Reportory"	(1610)
V.	*Historie,* Book One	(1612)
VI.	*Historie,* Book Two	(1612)

(The texts used for tabulation, and sources, are provided in "A Checklist of Strachey's Works," in appendix B.)

Before applying to William Strachey the various tests that were applied earlier to William Shakespeare, we must obtain for each variable the expected range for a Strachey poem. But because his total output is considerably smaller than Shakespeare's, Strachey's usage is somewhat less predictable. Larger parameters are required: We must settle for the high and low frequencies for Strachey's career as they appear in Groups I–VI above, without trying to determine a "most probable frequency" within this broader spectrum. We thereby arrive at the figures in table 2.5. It will be seen that the Peter elegy, despite its length, has a meager correlation with the expected figures for William Strachey. I have not bothered to search for the longest independent clause in Strachey's several prose works; but of the remaining sixteen tests as applied to the *Elegy*, only four fall within the expected range for Strachey, while all sixteen fall within the expected range for Shakespeare. And yet, of the thirteen variables for which Strachey registers more than a single instance in the course of his career, eleven have broader parameters than those for Shakespeare, by as much as 500 percent.

TABLE 2.5 / STRACHEY'S VERSE: Expected Range

	# of words	1 — % lines runon	2 — % feminine endings	3 — and / 1000 w	4 — but / 1000 w	5 — like / 1000 w	6 — (word)-like / 1000 w	7 — adv. adj. most / 1000 w	8 — redundant -er, -est / 1000 w	9 — not / 1000 w	10 — [do] not / 1000 w	11 — so / 1000 w	12 — that / 1000 w	13 — incongruent who / 100 l	14 — hendiadys / 1000 w	15 — hyphenated compounds / 1000 w	16 — participial compounds / 1000 w
Poems 1604-12	618	25/78, 32.1	4/78, 5.1	17, 27.51	5, 8.09	2, 3.23	0, .00	4, 6.47	0, .00	5, 8.09	0, .00	3, 4.85	8, 12.94	0, .00	0, .00	3, 4.85	2, 3.24
Poems 1613-21	799	44/104, 42.3	4/104, 3.8	35, 43.80	5, 6.26	2, 2.50	0, .00	1, 1.25	0, .00	7, 8.76	0, .00	10, 12.51	8, 10.01	0, .00	0, .00	3, 3.75	1, 1.25
Total/ Poems	1417	69, 37.9	8, 4.4	52, 36.70	10, 7.06	4, 2.82	0, .00	5, 3.53	0, .00	12, 8.47	0, .00	13, 9.17	16, 11.29	0, .00	0, .00	6, 4.23	3, 2.12
Letters	11982	—	—	599, 49.99	50, 4.17	17, 1.42	2, .17	25, 2.09	0, .00	85, 7.09	0, .00	75, 6.26	114, 9.51	0, .00	1, .08	25, 2.09	12, 1.00
"Reportory"	22652	—	—	1142, 50.41	113, 4.99	35, 1.54	0, .00	28, 1.24	2, .09	152, 6.71	0, .00	121, 5.34	162, 7.15	0, .00	0, .00	36, 1.59	10, 0.44
Historie Book I	33228	—	—	1667, 50.17	175, 5.27	110, 3.31	6, .18	50, 1.50	2, .06	175, 5.27	0, .00	182, 5.48	277, 8.34	0, .00	0, .00	36, 1.08	10, 0.30
Historie Book II	12774	—	—	675, 52.84	56, 4.38	15, 1.17	0, .00	15, 1.17	1, .08	60, 4.70	0, .00	69, 5.40	92, 7.20	0, .00	0, .00	23, 1.80	4, 0.31
Total/ prose	80636	—	—	4082, 50.62	394, 4.89	177, 2.20	8, .10	118, 1.46	5, .06	472, 5.85	0, .00	447, 5.54	645, 8.00	0, .00	1, .01	120, 1.49	36, 0.45
Expected range, Strachey		42.3, 32.1	7.1, 0.0	52.8, 27.5	8.1, 4.2	3.3, 1.2	.18, .00	6.5, 1.2	.09, .00	8.8, 4.7	.00, .00	12.5, 4.9	12.9, 7.2	.00, .00	.08, .00	4.9, 1.1	3.2, 0.3
Elegy by W.S.	266	266, 46.0	67, 11.6	109, 25.2	37, 8.6	9, 2.1	1, .23	11, 2.6	1, .23	41, 9.5	1, .23	28, 6.5	62, 14.4	4, .69	10, 2.31	20, 4.6	16, 3.7
Expected range, Shakespeare		52.2, 43.8	13.5, 7.5	29.0, 24.0	9.9, 7.6	2.8, 1.4	.26, .20	2.6, 1.7	.25, .06	9.7, 7.6	.37, .04	9.9, 6.4	16.5, 14.3	.75, .28	4.48, 0.14	6.7, 3.6	5.7, 2.2
Spread, Strachey		10.2	7.1	25.3	3.9	2.1	.18	5.3	.09	4.1	.00	7.6	5.7	.00	.08	3.8	2.9
Spread, Shakespeare		3.8	6.0	5.0	2.3	1.4	.06	0.9	.19	2.1	.33	3.5	2.2	.47	4.34	3.1	3.5

Internal Biographical Evidence

Occasional poets like William Strachey rarely wrote poems longer than two hundred lines. Most of the longer works in the Memorial Verse, for example (about 90%), were composed by well-known poets who made a career of their writing. Strachey's longest known work is his 66-line tribute to Sir Thomas Overbury. It is yet possible to believe him capable of a sustained effort, though not without difficulty, since Thomas Campion praises Strachey in 1619 as a writer of several "elegant little verses." He makes no mention of his friend's greatest work, if indeed Strachey wrote the Peter elegy. But perhaps the most obvious testimony against Strachey's authorship is the elegist's mention of a past disgrace suffered in Oxford. Although Strachey's life is far better documented than Shakespeare's, he is not known ever to have set foot in Oxfordshire. He cannot, in any case, have spent much time there during William Peter's adult life. Nor does it appear that Strachey ever suffered a worse disgrace than falling into debt, unless we count his dismissal from the service of Sir Thomas Glover in Constantinople in 1607 as a serious embarrassment. Yet neither of these difficulties was the result of his "country's thankless misconstruction," neither was connected in any way with Oxford, and neither appears to have had an adverse effect on his reputation as a man of ardent faith and firm morals. John Donne gives the following account of Strachey in a letter to Sir Henry Wotton in 1608:

> to say but truth for me to open my mouth in his commendations were but to play the owle or some other bird in a painted cloath in whose mouth some sentence is put w[ch] most men know: and so of his vertues. . . .[9]

A less obvious, though no less formidable, obstacle to a consideration of Strachey's authorship is that the authorial voice of the *Elegy* in no way conforms with Strachey's earnest evangelicalism. Strachey was a devout and zealous Christian, one who had little patience with those who doubted a life hereafter. To W. S.'s confession of doubt (in the last forty lines of the *Elegy*) may be compared, as a typical example of Strachey's thought, his comments on immortality in the *Historie of Travell*. Strachey rails at great length against those "heathenous" Englishmen who supposed that "the sowle of man, as of bruit beasts, was nothing ells but lief or the vitall power . . . and extinguished togither with the body":

> who would (even out of Scripture) prophanely conclude no ymortality of the sowle to be, . . . wresting that of Solomon who saith, 'The condicion of men and beasts are euen as one,' not acknowledging their impious reasoning by fallacies, . . . [B]ut, (alas) well may these poore

Heathen be pytied and pardoned vntill they shalbe taught better, neither borne vnder grace nor of the Seed of promise, when such as professe themselues in their great places to be our Saviour Christs chief vicars here vpon earth, dare be far more dissolute, as yt is written of Paule the 3. Pope of Rome, when he was breathing out his sowle, and ready to dye, sayd, that now at length he should try and know three things, whereof in his whole tyme he much doubted (viz.) first, whether there was a god, secondly whether Sowles were ymmortall, and lastly whether there was any Hell. . . . I say therefore yt maie well seeme lesse straunge, yf among these Infidells both the knowledg of our Saviour be questioned and the ymmortality of the sowle not rightly vnderstood. . . .[10]

The authorial voice here, as everywhere in William Strachey's works, is so different from that of W. S. that one cannot suppose him to have written the poem without indicting him of the grossest hypocrisy elsewhere. Even in his tribute to Overbury, his most pessimistic work—written at a time when he was in and out of debtor's prison—Strachey seems to affirm the fundamental doctrines of Christian faith. Nor is his last poem, "Hark," the testament of a profligate life. The self-effacing and penitential tone of Strachey's "Hark" is not confined to his last written utterance; the same is evident in much of his earlier work. Like most sincere Christians of his day, Strachey had an exaggerated sense of his own sinfulness. The reverse is true of W. S., who vigorously asserts his innocence.

The External Evidence

The external evidence linking William Strachey to William Peter is far less significant than may at first appear. Strachey may never have come within fifty miles of William Peter. Culliford has traced the poet's steps in some detail from 1595 to 1613. The only major gap in the record of Strachey's adult life is from 1588 to 1595 (during Peter's childhood), and it is thought, upon good evidence, that he was at Gray's Inn during these years. When sixteen-year-old William Peter entered the university in 1599, Strachey was already four years married and living in Surrey. During most of Peter's adult life, Strachey was more than a thousand miles away, either in Turkey, the Bermudas, or Virginia. He returned to England in November 1611, only three months before Peter died, and spent all or most of the interim in the capital, dwelling in the Blackfriars, while Peter spent his last weeks and days in Devon.

At no point in his career does it appear that Strachey could have met William Peter, much less develop an intimate friendship. Even the possible link between Strachey and William Ford withers under close scrutiny. Though Ford was probably a close friend of William Peter, it seems quite unlikely that he knew Strachey. Ford left for Constantinople in the autumn of 1608, to be employed by Glover as a preacher to the English community, some few months after Strachey returned home. Peter's friend remained in Constantinople for the next four years, serving with apparent content the one man whom Strachey despised more than any other. When Ford at last returned to England, Strachey was living in obscurity, largely dependent upon the charity of his in-laws, and struggling with his creditors. William Peter was dead. There is no reason to believe that Strachey and William Ford ever set eyes on one another, much less that the poet came thereby to know William Peter. They at least did not see eye-to-eye on the merits of Sir Thomas Glover. Upon his return to England Ford published a funeral sermon, eulogizing Anne Glover; in it, he lavishes praise as well on her infamously belligerent husband.[11] Strachey only a few months earlier published his verse tribute to Sir Thomas Overbury, in which he subtly compares Glover to Richard Weston, Overbury's killer.[12] Nor is the simile merely capricious: Strachey in 1608 was reprimanded by the Council of the Levant for having accused Glover, publicly, of poisoning his first steward, George Coxden (and he perhaps suspected that Glover had poisoned his own wife to boot); hence the comparison to Weston, who poisoned Overbury.

Nor is it possible, after all, to link Sir Allen Apsley, even indirectly, with both Strachey and William Peter. Strachey addressed his *Historie* to Apsley upon the advice of unnamed friends. It is not, on that score, inconceivable that the poet had a speaking acquaintance with him, for Apsley, too, lived in the Blackfriars district, and was known to be favorably inclined toward the colonial enterprise. But the wording of Strachey's letter and the lack of the wished-for response speak against a Strachey-Apsley connection. Furthermore, the association between Frances Peter and Allen Apsley, Jr., appears to have begun at least thirty years later. In 1612, neither Allen, Jr., nor John Peter's daughter was even born. Frances Peter was born at Bowhay, and baptized on 31 December 1629 at Shillingford, St. George, eighteen years after William Peter died. Allen Apsley, Jr., was baptized at All Hallows, Barking, on 5 September 1616 (as the eldest of nine children by Apsley's third wife, Lucy St. John, whom he married on 23 October 1615). Young Apsley was educated at the Merchant Taylors' School, beginning in 1626, five years after Strachey's death. Three years later he proceeded to the Inner Temple, and then to Trinity College, Oxford. In September 1643, following the capture of Exeter by the king's army, Apsley, a staunch royalist, was made "Governor of the Fort of Exeter," and Lieutenant Governor of the city under Sir John Berkeley. It was doubtless in this capacity that he first met Frances Peter. It is quite unlikely, however, that he ever met the girl's father, since John Peter died in April 1643, before Apsley's first appearance in Exeter.

No record survives of Apsley's wedding, as parish records were poorly kept during the war years and immediately following. His marriage cannot have taken place much earlier than 31 December 1645, when Frances turned sixteen. Most likely, they were married after the war ended, perhaps ca. 1646, though I find no reference to Frances as Lady Apsley prior to 1664. But whatever the date of Apsley's first acquaintance with Frances Peter, there is no reason to believe that he, or his father, or anyone in his family, had dealings with the Peters within thirty years of William Peter's death. Nor is there evidence of an Apsley-Strachey link apart from Strachey's unsuccessful bid to receive the patronage of the elder Apsley in 1612.

There yet remains the possibility of a Strachey-Peter connection through poet John Ford. It seems probable that Strachey and Ford were acquainted, since both men contributed poems to the Overbury volume in 1616, and it is virtually certain that John Ford knew William Peter. Ford's contribution to *Sir Thomas Overbury His Wife* is modeled in part on the *Elegy* by W. S.; one of Strachey's two contributions to the same volume is signed "W. S." This, finally, is far more noteworthy than the Apsley connection, which seems quite improbable. It is tempting to say that no one, including John Ford, would plagiarize a poem when its author was writing for the same volume, lest the theft be detected and ridiculed, but this is to misunderstand Jacobean notions of originality. We may as well suppose that Ford and Strachey were the best of friends, and that Ford viewed his paraphrase as a tribute to the elder poet. If Strachey knew John Ford before 1612, and Ford knew William Peter, Strachey might, then, have met Peter before his own departure for Turkey in 1606, or again a year or two later, before he set out for Virginia.

One cannot, however, make a convincing attribution for any author on the basis of a single conjecture, uncorroborated by other evidence. The fact remains that Strachey has no ties to Oxfordshire, to the university, to Devonshire, or to anyone in William Peter's known circle, with the possible exception of John Ford. He took his single independent publication to another stationer (in the same year, too, that W. S. took his *Elegy* to Thomas Thorp), and he lived abroad during most of William Peter's adult life. This may not rule out a close friendship between them, yet even a casual acquaintance seems, at best, unlikely. One might yet leave open the door to Strachey's candidacy were there convincing internal evidence of his having had a hand in the poem, but the internal evidence speaks still more loudly against his authorship. None of this—if it will bear saying one more time—proves that Shakespeare wrote the *Funeral Elegy* for William Peter. We can, however, be reasonably sure that the poem was not written by William Strachey.

EVIDENCE FOR AUTHORSHIP: SOME CONCLUSIONS

T HE central theoretical issue of canonical studies in recent years has been the continuing dispute over the proper role to be played by "internal" versus "external" evidence in the identification of authorship. Internal evidence is concerned with such matters as diction, accidence, syntax, orthography, imagery, prosody (where applicable), and with verbal parallels to be found elsewhere in works presumed to be by the same author. External evidence deals with attributions made either by the author's contemporaries or in the text itself, and with such matters as date of composition, the circumstances and place of publication, identifiable pseudonyms, and so on. One hears also in canonical studies of "direct external evidence," of "indirect external evidence," even of "internal-external evidence." Such terms in the parlance of canonical investigation are perhaps the equivalent in generic studies of Shakespeare's "pastoral-comical, historical-pastoral, tragical-comical-historical-pastoral." As descriptive labels, they refer more properly to something found not in literary texts, but in our discussion of them. It is pointless to ask how much "internal evidence" there is of Shakespeare's hand in *Richard III*, or *As You Like It,* or in *The Tempest*. Presumably, every sentence of these works is indicative of Shakespeare's manner. "Internal evidence" consists rather of our own (sometimes inept) efforts to identify, in a text of uncertain authorship, those features of style and substance that are peculiar to a particular writer. The same is true of the external data: Pavier's attribution to Shakespeare of *Sir John Oldcastle* has not been submitted by any modern scholar as "evidence" that Shakespeare wrote the play. Except, then, in the context of an attributional study, such terms as "internal" and "external" evidence are of little value.

It is impossible, finally, to say which variety of evidence is more necessary to the formation of authorial canons. That fact has not, however, dissuaded scholars from expressing their convictions on the subject. At one extreme stand certain advocates of stylistic analysis. The "basic premise" of Arthur Sherbo, for example, is that "internal evidence deals with essentials while external evidence deals with accidentals." "Short of an unequivocal acknowledgment by the author himself," writes Sherbo, "the value of internal evidence outweighs any other."[1] Thus any anonymous text may, in time, be correctly paired with an author if only we have a sufficient sample of the author's work elsewhere. (Sherbo may be right concerning the final authority of internal evidence, but since we have no proven or widely accepted system by which to test internal evidence, Sherbo's premise can make little practical difference.) At the opposite extreme, and commanding a far more receptive audience, stands S. Schoenbaum, who takes the position that "External evidence may and often does provide incontestable proof; internal evidence can only support hypotheses or corroborate external evidence."[2]

In his book on *Internal Evidence and Elizabethan Dramatic Authorship* Schoenbaum blasts more than four hundred attributional studies, most of them falling under the rubric of what Schoenbaum terms "the bedlamite antics of the wildmen."[3] No one should venture onto the minefield of authorial attribution without having first consulted this remarkable book. Schoenbaum's sarcasm is more restrained here than in his treatment of aspiring biographers in *Shakespeare's Lives,* though no less justified. The "impressionists," "disintegrationists," "fantastics," and others who fall victim to his withering irony well deserve the punishment they receive.

The presentation of internal evidence, as Schoenbaum amply demonstrates, has been subject to all manner of abuse. Literary scholars have proven themselves too adept at manufacturing internal proofs to support even the most absurd attributions. Thus has *Locrine* been ascribed to Shakespeare, his sonnets to Queen Elizabeth, *Julius Caesar* to Francis Beaumont, and *Henry VIII* to Massinger (to name but a few examples among hundreds). Once a scholar is possessed of an *idée fixe* that so-and-so wrote such-and-such, it is a simple matter to find "internal evidence": he need only track down a few supposed verbal parallels, apply an arcane metrical test, discover a few "unique" spellings, and the job is done. In the words of Ephim Fogel:

> Trifles light as air are, to the zealous, confirmations strong as proofs of holy writ. Among such trifles few are more airy or more exhilarating than isolated parallels—salmons in both, or Coventrys and Albemarles in both, or caudles or amorous ditties in both, or hearts with bending knees in both. Understandably so, for these illusions marshal us the way that we were going.[4]

It is an old proverb that statistics lie. So, too, may internal evidence, whether statistical or otherwise. The possibilities for developing an incorrect thesis are limited only by the author's ingenuity in deceiving himself. As a result of these past failures, the scholarly community has been left with a vague and widespread impression that no author, Jacobean or otherwise, can be identified on the basis of internal evidence alone.

Arthur Sherbo bemoans the prevailing skepticism. He complains that "a bare attribution by an intimate of the author is enough to lend authority to an otherwise dubious addition to the canon. And almost no amount of internal evidence will exercise similar authority in the absence of such an attribution." An argument based primarily on internal evidence, he says, will "hardly be allowed a hearing at the bar of present-day scholarship."[5]

But if Sherbo is partly right, the solution lies elsewhere than in granting him his "basic premise" that internal evidence is paramount. Rather, as Ephim Fogel has said,

> an experienced scholar will surely be intelligently skeptical about both types and will bring to bear upon *all* attributions a stringent analysis. To pit external against internal evidence is to set up a barren and unprofitable dichotomy.[6]

"Evidence" of authorship, of whatever kind, has a life of its own. It exists independently of historical actualities, and may be said to be "good" or "bad," "strong" or "weak," only insofar as it proves convincing to a broader audience than the scholar who proposes to have discovered it. David Erdman, in a carefully reasoned discussion, concludes that "internal evidence *can* be sufficient—provided the indirect testimony is not seriously inclement."[7] Few scholars will find cause to quarrel with him, at least in theory, since our established canons afford us numerous examples of undisputed attributions that depend largely on the internal evidence. The problem arises in the particular instance: the internal evidence and supporting indirect testimony may sometimes be sufficient for Erdman, though not for Schoenbaum; for Schoenbaum, though not for Erdman; for Sherbo, but for neither Schoenbaum nor Erdman. Each scholar can speak, finally, only as an individual. He cannot speak for that larger community of readers that must pronounce the ultimate verdict. Erdman writes:

> [I]f we agree that there need not always be direct external evidence, we may be tempted to ask, in return, whether there always *must* be internal evidence. But the answer is that there must. We are talking of course about *good* evidence. Our actual working limits keep us to debatable instances, in every one of which there is presumably some internal and some external (if only indirect) evidence. *The debate is over what constitutes evidence sufficiently good to persuade us that an admittedly probable attribution can be accepted as certain.* [Emphasis in last sentence is mine.][8]

We shall do well, I think, in forever laying to rest that futile debate. The canon of our best authors has never depended upon a precise ratio of internal to external evidence, or on a certain measure of either. What matters finally is not the ratio but the quality of the evidence, and the manner in which it is presented. When the evidence is sufficiently strong, in whatever proportion, it manages to take care of itself.

Schoenbaum's *Internal Evidence* has exerted a powerful influence over canonical investigation for the past twenty years—though the net effect has not been, as one might have hoped, to stimulate and to improve attributional research, but to curtail it altogether. The book-length attributional studies published in the last twenty years by professional scholars can be counted on one hand. After the deluge, a drought. The principal reason for the change is that a large segment of the scholarly community has taken refuge with Schoenbaum in the "conservative" stance that attributions must indeed be accepted or denied on the strength of the external evidence.

There is, however, small comfort in such a posture: first, because there exists very little direct external evidence for most Renaissance texts; second, because what evidence does exist is often equivocal; and third, because external evidence, so-called, is almost as vulnerable to abuse as the pursuit of tenuous and farfetched verbal echoes. The resulting undependability of external evidence is a problem treated too lightly by Schoenbaum. It may be time now to reconsider his basic premise.

One frequently finds in Renaissance texts that the bibliographical flatly contradicts the internal evidence, as for instance in the attribution to Shakespeare, during the poet's own lifetime, of *The London Prodigal* (1605) and *A Yorkshire Tragedy* (1608). Sometimes the external evidence may be quite formidable. *A Yorkshire Tragedy* was reputedly acted by the King's Men, and is reported on the title page to have been written by "W. Shakspeare." It was entered in the Stationers' Register as a work by "Wylliam Shakespere," and was accepted as authentic throughout most of the seventeenth century, its omission from the First and Second Folios notwithstanding. Nor do we have any indication that Shakespeare ever disavowed the attribution, as in the case of the Heywood poems ascribed to Shakespeare by William Jaggard in 1612. The attribution has therefore received the endorsement of a few modern scholars (e.g., Schlegel, Collier, Ulrici, Fleay), but one may safely say that *A Yorkshire Tragedy* will never be admitted to the Shakespeare canon, for the internal evidence is entirely lacking.

Style and content are often our only checks against such faulty attributions. In addition to those few works that were ascribed fraudulently to Shakespeare and to other popular writers to increase sales, early editors sometimes interlarded their author's works with spurious items, as in *The Passionate Pilgrim;* editors of verse anthologies guessed at the authorship of poems in their collection, and guessed wrongly; and plays in which several men collaborated are ascribed on the title page to only one of them (as again in our own day, when Hollywood screenplays are ascribed sometimes to one writer, though representing the work of three or four different authors).

No unconfirmed testimony—not even a direct acknowledgment or denial by the author himself—may have the final say in establishing authenticity. An author may have countless reasons, aesthetic, political, psychological, religious, for neglecting to acknowledge his authorship of a particular composition. Nor is it altogether uncommon, historically, for an individual to accept the credit for a work in which he had no part. A playwright or poet publishing his own work may neglect to acknowledge his collaborators or joint contributors. Even an indisputable signature may prove untrustworthy as evidence. Ephim Fogel cites as an early nineteenth-century example the sonnet by Charles Lamb to which Coleridge signed his initials. Surely the author's acknowledgment of his work carries more weight than an attribution made to the same writer by a friend or stationer, yet the further we get from the author, the more questionable does external evidence become. And even where the evidence is reliable, it remains lamentably subject to manipulative interpretation.

The impulse to exaggerate or to distort external evidence is especially seductive in Shakespeare studies, where we have little such evidence to begin with. As a result, those who profess to rely principally on "the facts" are frequently no less guilty of mishandling the evidence than their opponents. Schoenbaum himself furnishes us with frequent examples of the ways in which external evidence may be abused. With respect to the *Sonnets,* for example, he insists on a premise (which may or may not be true) that the Thorp/Eld publication of *Shakes-speares Sonnets* in 1609 was completed without the poet's consent—"All the signs," he says, "point to unauthorized publication"—and from this "external evidence" draws a series of doubtful conclusions.[9]

Schoenbaum, to begin, presents two "signs" that point toward unauthorized publication, the first of which is another unsupported hypothesis, that Shakespeare earlier in his career, at the print shop of stationer Richard Field, personally supervised the printing of the narrative poems: "he saw them through the press personally—they were carefully proofread—and furnished them with the prefatory epistles his plays so conspicuously lack."[10] The contrast between Field's relatively clean texts on the one hand, and the poorly proofread text of *Shake-speares Sonnets* on the other, becomes for Schoenbaum the proof of Thorp's surreptitious dealing, since "The numerous misprints [in the *Sonnets*] indicate that the poet who took such pains with *Venus and Adonis* and *The Rape of Lucrece* had no part in supervising the printing of his most important body of non-dramatic verse."[11] The absence of prefatory epistles, either in the good dramatic quartos or in *Shake-speares Sonnets,* does not, in fact, indicate unauthorized publication; nor does careless proofreading. Yet it is from

this "external evidence"—the supposed circumstances of publication—
that Schoenbaum by a circuitous route comes finally to deny "A Lover's
Complaint" its place in the Shakespeare canon, as we shall see in a
moment.

Unfortunately, the notion that Shakespeare himself supervised the
printing of Field's texts is not an established fact, but merely a conjecture
(and a bad one), here disguised as authoritative pronouncement. Moreover, Schoenbaum pulls the rug from under himself when, in the same
volume, he gives the credit to Richard Field for having proofread the
Shakespeare poems—and it seems that he does so with some conviction,
for he again credits Field in his next book (*Shakespeare, the Globe, and
the World,*) wherein the stationer is praised for having "printed *Venus and
Adonis* with unusual care—there are few misprints").[12]

In fact, the honors do go to Richard Field. It has since been established
that the careful orthography of the early narrative poems may be attributed to the printer, and not to Shakespeare. Virtually all of Field's
publications are distinguished by the relative care given to proofreading.
The punctuation, too, of the Shakespeare poems is vintage Field (as for
example in what A. C. Partridge calls "the comma pedantry" of these
texts).[13] Besides, even if Field were the most slovenly printer in London,
that is, everywhere but in *Venus and Adonis* and *Lucrece,* we could draw
no certain conclusion that the poet "saw [these] through the press personally," for Field might have had good cause to show more than ordinary
care in printing the poems of his friend and fellow Stratfordian, William
Shakespeare.

As it happens, there is no single publication of Shakespeare's work that
shows the least sign of having been proofread by the poet—as Schoenbaum himself partly acknowledges in *Shakespeare's Lives:*

> The plays published during his lifetime, even those that were not un-
> authorized, he failed even to proofread; so the gross errors, left uncor-
> rected, tell us.[14]

It appears that Shakespeare was disinclined to read even his own manuscripts. It is generally agreed today, on the basis of those texts thought to
have been set up from the poet's own papers, that his manuscripts were
characterized by very light pointing, frequent mislineation, and numerous
amendable errors of every sort that were nevertheless passed along to the
printer, unamended. Moreover, even if the poet had, in fact, been invited to
take part "in supervising the printing of his most important body of nondramatic verse," it remains doubtful that he would have done so. Renaissance authors assisted in reading the proofs far less often than has usually
been supposed in past criticism. It was the exception, rather than the rule,

for a writer in Shakespeare's London to make a thorough inspection of his proofs, since this was a labor that took at least several days, and sometimes months, to complete. Most authors were content instead to let the printer's own readers do the job, despite the inevitable errors. We need turn no further for a typical example than to the Peter elegy: this was certainly an authorized publication, no matter who the author; yet the uncorrected errors suggest that the poet did not see the printed text until after the presswork was completed.

In short, neither the frequent misprints in the *Sonnets* quarto (some forty in all), nor the gross errors of punctuation, tell us anything of the circumstances of publication, except that George Eld (or his compositor) was a less meticulous proofreader than Richard Field.

From 1597 to 1622, eleven plays were registered and printed with the apparent authorization of Shakespeare's company (the Chamberlain's/ King's men).[15] Of these eleven, eight were published by Thomas Thorp and his senior partners Andrew Wise (1597–1603) and William Aspley (1597–1609); the other three were published by the two stationers with whom Thorp formed an informal syndicate—Edward Blount and Walter Burre (the group also included James Roberts until his retirement in 1608).[16] Neither Thorp nor any of his partners is responsible for a bad quarto. Indeed, of some three hundred Jacobean stationers, none but Thorp's senior partners have better credentials than he as a select agent of Shakespeare's company. If Thorp in the last years of his career did not participate as a principal with Blount and Aspley in the Shakespeare First Folio of 1623, it is only because Thorp, as their junior associate, did not control the copyright to any of the Shakespeare plays; while Jaggard and Smethwick (F1: Smithweeke) were included by necessity, since they had acquired the rights to various Shakespeare plays indirectly, from other stationers.

Thomas Thorp was a devout Christian who maintained a spotless reputation during his forty years with the Stationers' Company—unless, as Schoenbaum insists, he resorted to stealth in a single instance in mid-career. Nor does Schoenbaum take into account that England in 1609 suffered the most relentless plague of Shakespeare's lifetime. Though the total number who perished was larger in both 1593 and 1603, never was the plague more unremitting than in 1609: from 28 July 1608 until 7 December 1609 there were only two weeks in which plague deaths in London dropped below fifty per week. The London theaters were forced to close for eighteen months.[17] This was the first time in twenty-five years that the theaters were closed for so long a period. The last time around, in 1593–94, Shakespeare published two poems—*Venus and Adonis* and *The Rape of Lucrece*.

Schoenbaum's thesis is further contradicted by our earliest surviving references to the Thorp/Eld quarto: first, by William Drummond, who includes Shakespeare in his catalogue of England's most famous authors "on the Subject of Love." The last poets mentioned by Drummond are "Sir *William Alexander* and *Shakespear,* who have lately published their works"—with an obvious reference to Alexander's *Aurora* (1604) and Shakespeare's *Sonnets* (1609).[18] Drummond's remark appears in 1614, the same year that he first became acquainted with Alexander, and he is certainly correct in averring that *Aurora* was an authorized publication. It is not known upon what authority he thinks the same true of Shakespeare's *Sonnets,* though he is not alone in saying so: stationer John Benson in 1640 writes that the "purity" of Thorp's text was "avouched" by "the Authour himself, then living."[19] It is impossible to verify either assertion—Benson's testimony is at best hearsay thirty years after the fact—yet we have no contrary testimony by anyone in the seventeenth century who supposes the *Sonnets* to have been purloined.

According to the ethical standards of the age, it was perfectly acceptable to print a manuscript without the author's permission—but it was never allowed in such cases to use his name, except after his decease. There were inevitable violations (including a few cases in which Shakespeare's name was printed without apparent authorization), but most are unregistered works, surreptitiously printed. An author was entitled to press charges against stationers who printed his name in the front matter without his consent; and though the offending stationers rarely lost their copyright, they were often required to remove the author's name from every printed copy. Thomas Thorp could scarcely have risked that expense.

None of this evidence, even when taken together, proves absolutely that Shakespeare authorized the Thorp/Eld quarto of 1609, yet I find little grounds for an uncritical faith in the contrary hypothesis.

The second (and last) reason given by Schoenbaum for his indictment of Thorp has still less to recommend it: "Few close students," he writes, "believe that the 154 poems of the cycle follow the sequence that their creator intended."[20] "Close students" are those who agree with Schoenbaum that Shakespeare's manuscripts were purloined. The solecism is not "evidence" at all, but merely a patting of oneself on the back with a long-handled speculation. In fact, dissenters have been few, since the sonnets are arranged quite sensibly as is.[21] The first 126 are addressed to a young man; Sonnets 127–44 are addressed to the so-called dark lady, who figures also in part one; and the last ten are a miscellany of sonnets on various subjects, written probably over a period of years. The first of these, Sonnet 145, is widely thought to be a juvenile effort addressed to Anne Hathaway—a consensus in which even Schoenbaum himself concurs.[22] Yet Schoenbaum fails to address the question, raised by E. K. Chambers and others, concerning how Thorp managed to retrieve sonnets from the young man, from the dark lady, from Anne Hathaway, and from perhaps three or four other addressees without Shakespeare's knowledge or consent, and then to have arranged them in their present order. Chambers writes,

> It is impossible, I think, to be dogmatic on the evidence available. But on the whole, it does not seem to me likely, in view of the character of some of the sonnets in the second series, that the whole collection can have been kept together by any one but Shakespeare himself. And if so, it is most likely that the arrangement of 1609 was his. It does not, of course, follow that in putting them together he made no departure from the chronological order of composition.[23]

At least a few sonnets by Shakespeare were circulated among his friends in 1598; perhaps Thorp obtained his copy through a shared acquaintance. Anything is "possible." Yet Schoenbaum's dogmatism in this respect is hardly called for in the light of the available evidence, especially given Chambers's point that the sonnets may have been arranged thus by the author himself, regardless of a surreptitious printing. Schoenbaum has therefore failed to convince many "close readers" that the sonnets are disorganized as originally printed. Yet his insistence that the Thorp/Eld quarto was unauthorized has indeed carried the day. One finds the charge repeated almost everywhere in recent criticism, and in most printed editions of the *Sonnets,* as an established fact.[24]

From the "external evidence" that the sonnets were purloined, Schoenbaum draws the remarkable conclusion that "A Lover's Complaint"—published with the sonnets and clearly attributed to William Shakespeare—was written by someone else (though he shields his conclusion in the armor of an imaginary consensus):

> In Thorpe's 1609 edition of the Sonnets, these are followed by *A Lover's Complaint,* a poem of some three hundred lines, with a clear attribution to Shakespeare; but because of the unauthorized nature of the publication, the ascription would not in general win favor. Some critics, however, would convince themselves of the genuineness of the *Lover's Complaint. . . .*[25]

Schoenbaum's pronouncements concerning "A Lover's Complaint" were long conceded by many of Shakespeare's best critics and editors—though the tide has turned. MacDonald Jackson in 1965 presented a convincing case for Shakespearean authorship of "A Lover's Complaint," despite its flaws; his study was seconded by Kenneth Muir in 1973.[26] Jackson and Muir were followed by Eliot Slater, whose statistical analysis of Shakespeare's vocabulary confirmed the attribution, and by A. C. Partridge, who found that the orthography of Thorp's text points to Shakespeare's hand.[27] In recent years editors have accepted the poem as authentic, even while supposing (with Muir) that its publication was unauthorized.

The question next arises why, if Thorp's alleged theft is sufficient grounds for rejecting "A Lover's Complaint," we should accept any or all of the sonnets as having been written by Shakespeare. The answer, Schoenbaum tells us, lies in *Palladis Tamia* (1598), wherein Francis Meres mentions in passing that Shakespeare had circulated "sugred sonnets among his private friends" (as what poet, in the 1590s, had not?). Schoenbaum concludes that these were the same 154 sonnets published by Thorp eleven years later. To seal the argument, he enlists Meres, in *Shakespeare's Lives,* as an involuntary witness for the prosecution in his indictment of Thomas Thorp and George Eld:

> Although (as Meres affirms) the Sonnets were evidently intended only for manuscript circulation, they appeared in 1609 in an unauthorized edition printed (so the title-page tells us) "By G.Eld for T.T."[28]

Schoenbaum thereby rejects "A Lover's Complaint" for lack of sufficient evidence, while accepting the sonnets, though we have the same external evidence for both. Schoenbaum merely shapes the facts to conform with his own vague impression that Shakespeare's hand is more apparent in one than in the other, while preserving the illusion of having weighed the "external" more heavily than the "internal" evidence. Surely, to play this kind of game, while at the same time demanding that attributions must stand upon the external evidence, is to remove all props whatever from the Shakespeare canon.

We have, in fact, remarkably little external evidence for most of those works ascribed today to William Shakespeare. But rather than confess as much, Schoenbaum simply inflates what little evidence we do have out of all reasonable compass. He lends to the preface of the First Folio the authority of a papal bull, calling it, extravagantly, "the most crucial single document in the annals of authorship attribution."[29] Why? because Hemings and Condell profess to have collected Shakespeare's "writings," both those formerly printed, "and all the rest, absolute in their numbers, as he conceived them."[30] Schoenbaum does not question either the meaning or the accuracy of this statement.

Granted, the testimony of Hemings and Condell is important. This is, after all, the only external evidence we have for many of the dramatic works. Eighteen of the thirty-six plays in the First Folio might never have been known to us, had they not been gathered by these two actors following Shakespeare's death. Four others would be known to us only in bad quartos. We would know of *Titus Andronicus,* but only in anonymous texts, and would have to depend on unconfirmed or questionable attributions for most other plays in the canon. Yet the collection does not carry the authority of Shakespeare's own voice, and even if it did, it would not provide conclusive evidence for any play *omitted* from the Folio text. Ben Jonson, for example, published his *Works,* under his own supervision, in 1616. Yet he omitted *The Case Is Altered* (printed 1609), perhaps for aesthetic reasons, and *Eastward Ho!* (1605), a collaboration with Chapman and Marston that had earned him enough grief already. *Bartholomew Fair* (1614) was likewise left out, though *The Golden Age,* a masque (1615), was included. A fourth play, *A Tale of a Tub* (ca. 1596); revised before 1633), was omitted in the Jonson First Folio of 1616, though included in the Second Folio of 1640. Much early poetry was omitted as well, and of course the Jonson First Folio contains nothing written by him after 1616. Moreover, Jonson in 1619 told Drummond that "the half of his Comedies were not in print," and Meres in 1598 lists Jonson as among the playwrights "best for Tragedie," though his *Sejanus* (1603) and *Catiline* (1611) are the only tragedies extant.[31] If Jonson could be so nonchalant about identifying and preserving his own works, it is mere wishful thinking to suppose that the selection of Hemings and Condell carries anything like absolute authority, at least when taken by itself without respect to the internal evidence.

Schoenbaum nevertheless assumes that their testimony may be taken as oracular, merely on the strength of their friendship with Shakespeare. He scolds E. K. Chambers for suggesting that the judgment of Hemings and Condell is a matter deserving of further study. Chambers has noted, quite sensibly, that the particular selection settled upon for the First Folio "must not be pressed too far":

> Heminges and Condell and their publishers were not attempting a modern "critical" edition, and no doubt their methods were imperfect. . . . alien matter may be present. . . . Contrariwise the possibility that Shakespeare may have had a hand in some uncollected plays cannot be wholly disregarded.[32]

According to Schoenbaum, this is to "undervalue" the First Folio, for it "lets disintegration in again (as it were) through the back door."[33] In fact, Chambers is quite right. No one today supposes that Hemings and Condell were uninformed or disingenuous witnesses, yet their voice, in itself, carries no more weight than many contemporaneous ascriptions to other writers, some of which Schoenbaum himself vigorously rejects; while their omission of other plays, taken by itself, carries hardly any weight at all.

The printing of the Folio was begun by William Jaggard and completed by his son Isaac following the elder Jaggard's death. Jaggard, ironically, is a poor authority with respect to authorial ascriptions. In 1599 he published *The Passionate Pilgrim,* "By W. Shakespeare," containing poems by other authors. In 1619 he joined with his friend Pavier in the surreptitious printing of ten plays—seven of them by Shakespeare, plus three others ascribed to him incorrectly—and he would have printed more, had he not been ordered to desist. Jaggard's participation in the First Folio hardly lends credit to the attributions made therein by the editors. If the Folio selection has nevertheless been accepted as authoritative, it is largely because the testimony of the editors and printer is confirmed by the internal continuity of the plays themselves. Readers for at least the past two centuries have thereby concluded that the editors were, for the most part, correct in their attributions to Shakespeare, as in the omission of other works.

If any plays were omitted from the Folio though written wholly or in part by Shakespeare, or again, if any were included that contain scenes or brief interpolations by other poets, it was surely for some other reason than a wish to deceive and delude. Such "errors" may reflect simply matters of convenience or editorial preference. It is generally agreed today that *Timon of Athens, Macbeth,* and *Henry VIII* include passages not by Shakespeare, and there are several others (e.g., *Shr., 1H6, Tit.*) that contain disputed portions. There is a general consensus also that Shakespeare had a hand in *Edward III, Pericles,* and *The Two Noble Kinsmen.* These three plays, and a lost comedy, *Love's Labor's Won* (ascribed to Shakespeare by Francis Meres in 1598) are omitted by Hemings and Condell. Moreover, the editors did some last-minute shuffling of the Folio collection for reasons that have never been certainly established. *Troilus and Cressida* is omitted from the table of contents. It was later inserted in the text, though with unnumbered foliation, between the Histories and Tragedies, after the printing began—possibly because Walley, the printer of the 1609 quarto, was reluctant to give up his rights in the play. Might the editors have had similar difficulties with other plays? Had they plans originally to print the poems, or to include dramatic texts that were finally omitted? to omit scenes, or perhaps entire plays, that were at last included? No one knows. *Edward III* could not, in any case, have been reprinted in 1623 without risk, for the satire on the Scots is structural, and much more biting than the two jests in *Eastward Ho!* which landed Jonson and Chapman in prison in 1605. Was this the cause of its omission from the Folio, or was *Edward III,* in the editors' judgment, a poor collaboration in which Shakespeare had little part (or none at all)? Again, why was *The Two Noble Kinsmen* excluded from the Folio text (or, for that matter, *Cardenio,* a lost play likewise alleged to have been written by Shakespeare and Fletcher) if, like *Henry VIII,* Hemings and Condell knew *The Two*

Noble Kinsmen to be Shakespeare's, at least in part? And what ever became of *Love's Labor's Won?* Were there other plays by Shakespeare (perhaps even many such?) that were not available to the editors of the Folio, say, unprinted scripts that were lost in the Globe fire of 1613? No one knows the answers to these questions. We know only that the judgment of Hemings and Condell was, for the most part, reliable, and that they were not guided by our own notions of what should constitute a proper scholarly edition.

It must be remembered that Shakespeare, in 1623, had not yet become an international industry. Hemings and Condell, in their epistle to the Herberts, describe his plays as mere "trifles"; not "milke, creame, fruites . . . gummes and incense," but only "a leavened Cake," "the meanest of things," yet made "precious" by the Herberts' patronage. Such trifles in 1623 were not accorded the honor lent them in modern literary scholarship. Hemings and Condell had no reason to suppose their preface to the First Folio to be "the most crucial single document in the annals of authorship attribution." Nor, for that matter, do we. In fact, we do not even know that the dedication and preface to the First Folio were written by Hemings and Condell. Despite the external evidence of their signatures, A. C. Partridge has shown it to be quite likely that both items were actually written for them by Ben Jonson.[34]

The fundamental weakness in Schoenbaum's doctrine was made clear in the recent controversy over "Shall I Die," a poem preserved in the Bodleian Library and ascribed to "William Shakespeare" (MS. Rawl. poet. 160, fol. 108r–109v). Here is a perfectly unambiguous attribution, appearing in a manuscript compiled only twenty-one years after Shakespeare's death. Nothing more was needed for the editors of the Oxford Shakespeare—Schoenbaum, Wells, and Taylor—to announce that the poem was authentic, and to include the lyric with Shakespeare's "Various Poems" in *The Complete Works.*[35] Barring the discovery of new evidence, I doubt that many future editors will follow suit, for the internal evidence argues against the attribution.

The Shakespeare canon, as it now stands, has little to do with the strength of the external evidence. Nor am I aware of any Renaissance text, Shakespearean or otherwise, for which the external evidence alone provides "incontestable proof," as argued by Schoenbaum. This is wishful thinking. Schoenbaum is, nevertheless, instructive when pointing out why speculative attributions, in the absence of such evidence, have failed to alter the established canons of Renaissance playwrights. In his *Internal Evidence* he cites some 430 studies of authorship, more than half of which were written before 1925, and most of which are characterized by special pleading, fallacious reasoning, and by a cavalier disregard of contrary evidence, as Schoenbaum effectively demonstrates. In most cases, however, the fundamental error of these studies was simply that the critic started with an insupportable hypothesis. As a result, Schoenbaum necessarily spends most of his time tilting at straw men. If *Richard II* or *Hamlet* or *The Tempest* were discovered tomorrow for the first time in an anonymous seventeenth-century manuscript, one might present a convincing case for Shakespeare's authorship, strictly on the internal evidence. It is another matter to prove that Shakespeare wrote *The Puritaine* or *Arden of Feversham*.

Schoenbaum is less helpful concerning those works that have, in fact, been *accepted* into the canons of our best Renaissance authors, even without convincing external evidence. For example, he speaks in all his books of "Marlowe's *Tamburlaine*," apparently indifferent, in this case, to the fact that we have virtually no external evidence at all for the attribution. The first clear ascription of *Tamburlaine* to Christopher Marlowe was made by Francis Kirkman in 1671, in a play-list appended to *Nicomede*, some eighty-four years after *Tamburlaine* was written. If this is the stuff of convincing attributions, we must assign to Shakespeare *Fair Em, The Birth of Merlin, A Yorkshire Tragedy, Mucedorus,* and a half-dozen other unlikely plays, along with all the spurious items in John Benson's *Poems: Written by Wil. Shake-speare* (1640). No one today doubts that Marlowe wrote *Tamburlaine,* but the unanimous conviction has little to do with the external evidence.

Granted, there must always be some such evidence, if only indirect. At the very least one has always the knowledge that a particular work was written at a given moment in history, in this or that place, in this or that tongue, bearing the marks of a specific cultural milieu. Were it known that *Tamburlaine* was written after Marlowe's death in 1593, the attribution would of course be impossible. Again, had William Peter died five years later, in January of 1617, William Shakespeare could not have written this or any other funeral elegy for him, for Shakespeare was himself, by that time, dead. It is therefore easier, on the basis of external evidence, to disprove than to prove the authorship of a Renaissance text. Without the confirmation of internal evidence, it can do little more than that.

As it happens, Schoenbaum is quietly willing to accept attributions that have the benefit of a time-honored tradition behind them, with or without direct external evidence. "The Phoenix and the Turtle" is a case in point. In 1601 Ben Jonson, John Marston, George Chapman, and Shakespeare contributed poems to a miscellany of verse on the theme of the Phoenix. This volume, apparently edited by Jonson, was given the title *Turtle and the Phoenix*. It was appended to Robert Chester's *Love's Martyr* in 1601 as a means of lending aid to Chester's literary ambitions. The single piece ascribed to Shakespeare is a fifteen-line "Threnos," subscribed "William Shake-speare." On previous pages, in a different rhyme scheme and stanzaic form, and printed as a separate poem, are some untitled and anonymous verses beginning, "Let the bird of loudest lay. . . ." The two poems (or parts of a poem) are rhetorically linked, but the linking of verses by different authors in a miscellany of this kind is a practice that had such popular precedents as *Astrophel,* and can tell us nothing concerning the authorship of either piece. "Let the bird of loudest lay" and the "Threnos" were first combined and ascribed to Shakespeare in 1640 by John Benson, whose editorial judgment carries no weight whatever. In 1807 the combined poems were given the title "The Phoenix and the Turtle," under which name they have been known ever since.

Schoenbaum, curiously, after rejecting "A Lover's Complaint" (though it is clearly ascribed to Shakespeare in the printed text of a reputable stationer) accepts the so-called "Phoenix and the Turtle" as authentic.[36] Yet the first fifty-two lines must surely be rejected outright by all who demand external evidence, for these have found their way into the canon without a shred of external evidence to support the attribution, not so much as a set of initials. Even the "Threnos," by "conservative" standards, is questionable, for the printer elsewhere in the same miscellany displays obvious uncertainty regarding the authorship of the poems in his possession. I should not like to see "The Phoenix and the Turtle" excluded from the canon—the internal evidence points to Shakespeare's hand—but if, as Schoenbaum has said, "internal evidence can only support hypotheses or corroborate external evidence," the poem has no place in the collected works of William Shakespeare.

If I have been severe on Schoenbaum, it is not without his invitation: he asks, in matters of such consequence as canonical studies, that we speak out boldly, even against erring friends and colleagues.[37] Nor do I wish to undermine the importance of Schoenbaum's *Internal Evidence.* His book has found a powerful and lasting voice in Renaissance studies, while serving as an efficient check on past abuses. It is perhaps regrettable, however, that Schoenbaum so studiously avoids untilled ground. He demonstrates why so many past attributions have failed to stick, and provides some useful caveats. Yet after almost three hundred pages we finally go out by the same door we came in.

In the years ahead we are unlikely to discover much that is new in the way of external evidence for the authorship of anonymous, pseudonymous, or initialed Renaissance texts. We must therefore rest content in our ignorance, or else seek to refine our methods of evaluating style and content. The latter approach is, I think, far preferable. We may start by insisting of all canonical scholars that they follow Ephim Fogel's "Caveats," as well as Schoenbaum's sensible rules for "Avoiding Disaster."[38] A correct attribution, when defended by an irresponsible presentation of the available evidence, may do more harm than good. If at any point I have violated the principles set forth by these two scholars, I have done so unwittingly and shall welcome their censure.

I am nonetheless left with the impression that my methods have been terribly rudimentary in some respects, due to the lack of available tools. For none of the two-hundred-and-some poets represented in the Memorial Verse is there available at present a detailed concordance. Indeed, without Spevack's *Complete and Systematic Concordance to the Works of Shakespeare,* my own book in its present form could not have been completed. The word-counts presented in table 1.19 are the partial product of many tedious weeks devoted to counting *not*s and *but*s and *so*s and *that*s. To these labors were added several tedious days and nights performing the same operation, three times, for the poetry and prose of William Strachey. I would despair at the thought of having to perform the same task, by hand, for the works of William Shakespeare. I discovered a maddening tendency to arrive at a different count for my several variables no matter how many times I tallied a particular poem, and am not certain, even now, that my tables are perfectly accurate. Had there been available funds, it would have been far more practical to put the entire Memorial Verse and all the works of William Strachey on a computer disk, in both the original and modernized texts, thereby to arrive at the correct frequencies for each work with greater speed and reliability. It would have then been possible, too, to conduct far more statistical tests than the few presented here.[39]

Until very recently, the statistical analysis of literary texts has been fallow ground. Literary scholars and statisticians have been slow to learn from one another, and even slower to work in consort. The field has been left instead to amateur Jacks-of-both-trades. The resulting harvest has been a mixed bag of exotic fruit, as is illustrated, for example, in the "stylometrics" craze of the last two decades. The failures of this popular science have been manifold. Thomas Merriam, an outspoken pioneer of stylometrics, has demonstrated, for example (though to no one's satisfaction), that William Shakespeare is responsible, not just for Hand *D* in *Sir Thomas More,* but for the entire play (the various hands in the manuscript may be explained by Shakespeare's need of secretarial assistance).[40] M. W. A. Smith has proven, with the same aplomb, that "A Lover's Complaint" is by George Chapman.[41] Still other enthusiasts have demonstrated that *Hero and Leander* was, and was not, written entirely by Marlowe; that *Pericles* was, and was not, written entirely by Shakespeare; that *Titus Andronicus* and *Julius Caesar* were, and were not, written by the same man; and so for many other, equally contradictory, results.[42]

Statisticians have repeatedly shown as much naiveté in their understanding of language and literature as have literary scholars in their knowledge of mathematics. Nevertheless, statistical analysis continues to hold great promise for canonical studies. We have only just begun to pool our expertise. Recent years have seen a marked increase both in the volume and sophistication of literary-statistical analysis. Mathematicians have focused their attention on a rich variety of literary texts, ancient, medieval, and modern, from Junius to Joyce, from Addison and Aeschylus to Xenophon and Zwingli. In Shakespeare studies, statistical analysis has helped us to date the plays; to demonstrate Shakespeare's hand in *The Two Noble Kinsmen, Henry VIII,* and *Titus Andronicus;* to discredit the eccentric but unkillable rumor that his works were actually written by Marlowe or Bacon or Lord Oxford; to measure the diversity and distinction of his vocabulary; and much more besides. We have been able to establish accurate measures of Shakespeare's vocabulary-pool and median word-length. We have tested his customary frequencies of the various parts of speech, of alliteration, of run-on lines. With the help of an exhaustive, computer-based concordance, we now have exact word frequencies for the entire canon, including those words most often used (*and, but, not,* and so on) which, though of key importance in literary-statistical analysis, are regrettably omitted from the concordances of most other authors for whom such aids are available at all.

In coming years we shall undoubtedly devise more reliable methods of analyzing literary texts than are presently available to us. Progress will be made by fits and starts. In the meantime, as Fogel has said, "the scholar's unaided eye and brain can arrive at very convincing results."[43] There is much ground yet to be covered. Many readers would agree that *Edward III* is a finer play than *1 Henry VI* or *Henry VIII,* and it is certainly more pleasing to modern sensibilities than *Titus Andronicus,* yet no one has made a thorough and convincing case for authorship, whether for Shakespeare or for anyone else.[44] Sundry questions have yet to be answered concerning the *Henry VI* trilogy, *Titus Andronicus, Taming of the Shrew, Timon of Athens, Pericles, Henry VIII, The Two Noble Kinsmen,* and *The Passionate Pilgrim.* Nor has there yet been written a useful study of the many verses, commendatory and sepulchral, ascribed to Shakespeare either in the seventeenth century or in modern scholarship. It would again be worth the effort if we could identify correctly the authors of the various apocryphal plays which (though universally agreed to be by someone other than Shakespeare) have too long malingered on the sidelines of scholarly investigation. That we shall ever arrive at a consensus for all these works is doubtful; that we may come to agree concerning at least some of them is certain.

The task of defining the canon as it exists today, containing all or part of some thirty-seven (or -eight or -nine) plays along with the various non-dramatic works, did not begin till long after the poet's death, nor has the task ever been completed. Perhaps the simplest way to identify the "canonical" poems and plays at any point in time is to peruse the current editions of Shakespeare's collected works, but even here, contradictions and uncertainties abound. *The Passionate Pilgrim* (1599) contains disputed items and others that are almost certainly spurious, yet the entire text is usually reprinted in modern editions of Shakespeare's works. Included also, inexplicably, are those poems in the appended miscellany, *Sonnets to Sundry Notes of Music* that were *not* ascribed to Shakespeare, even in Jaggard's original text.[45] Nor are canonical issues independent of textual problems. It is almost universally agreed that *Macbeth* contains non-Shakespearean interpolations, and that the order of the scenes has been muddled; yet while actors have taken advantage of the information, the changes have never been made in printed texts of the play, but are merely footnoted. This is perhaps as it should be, since the First Folio is our only primary text. There is implicit, however, a contradiction between the "canonical" version of the play and Shakespeare's presumed version. To these may be added a dozen other points at which the Shakespeare canon resists precise definition.

The day may yet come when we shall resolve all such problems simply by tracing the poet's stylistic fingerprints with the help of carefully controlled statistical analysis. If so, that day is a long way off. In the meantime, we must weigh the evidence for authorship of this text, or that, as we have always done—according to our best collective judgment. If, for example, a consensus develops concerning the authorship of W. S.'s *Funeral Elegy* for William Peter, it will come irrespective of the precise measure of internal or external evidence. In the words of Samuel Taylor Coleridge,

> Any work, which claims to be held authentic, must have had witnesses, and competent witnesses; this is external evidence. Or it may be its own competent witness; this is called the internal evidence. Or its authenticity may be deduced from indirect testimony, such as the absence of all contradiction; or from the *absurdity* of supposing it to be a forgery, as in the case of the works of Virgil, Cicero, &c. which the Jesuit Hardouin contended to have been forged by Monks, in the dark ages.[46]

This is surely a more tempered appraisal than either Sherbo's or Schoenbaum's position. Yet let us amend Coleridge's remarks somewhat, to read: ". . . or from any combination of these, but only on the condition that the attribution receives the approbation of time and expert opinion"—for it is not, finally, the evidence itself (no matter how powerful), nor the fiat of any particular scholar, but a community of readers, that defines a literary canon. For most of those authors who continue to be read long after their death, a shared opinion is forged over a period of years concerning which works are authentically his or hers, and which are spurious. It is a process in which every thoughtful reader participates. No one can add to the canon of William Shakespeare a single word, even by way of emendation, without the consent of other informed readers.

Such a consensus may sometimes take shape almost imperceptibly, without respect to any particular expression of the available evidence. Marlowe's *Tamburlaine* is an example. Other works may cling to the outer fringes of an author's canon while a debate concerning their authenticity lingers on for centuries. Such has been the fate of *The Two Noble Kinsmen* and *Edward III*. But whatever the final verdict may be concerning either these two plays or the Peter elegy, we shall do well to keep in mind that literary canons are fictional constructs having no essential relation to the actualities of authorship. Whether consciously or not, we are speaking always of presumed likelihoods, never of certain "truths." The earlier the author, the more likely is his canon to include works (or at least portions thereof) that he did not write, or to exclude works that he did write, including even the omission of extant works. No one living today saw Shakespeare write *Hamlet*. Nor did Shakespeare himself, in any surviving document, profess to have written this or any other play. We say that *Hamlet* belongs to Shakespeare because the majority of readers and playgoers for nearly four centuries have found small cause to think otherwise.

The historical "truth" concerning authorial canons is, in a sense, almost irrelevant. The *man* Shakespeare is dead and buried and turned to dust. *Shakespeare* today exists as a body of texts that have a strong affinity with one another. These are presumed to have derived chiefly from the brain and pen of a single individual, and are widely deemed, by virtue of their historical and aesthetic merit, to be worthy of continued study. Yet the man Shakespeare did not invent the Shakespeare "canon," and barring the discovery of some unknown document in his own hand, he can have no further say in its formation.

It is apparent that all authorial canons are, in some measure, concessions to a collective pretense, while having at the same time an imprecise, though positive, correlation with historical fact. They have value for us only insofar as they accommodate the study of literature. We speak thus of Homer's *Iliad* and *Odyssey,* not knowing for certain whether Homer is chiefly an historical personage, a legend, or a committee. All but the most scrupulous pedants speak of the Theocritan *Idylls,* though it is universally agreed that several of these were written by someone other than Theocritus. Could it be proven that the *Iliad* and *Odyssey* were composed by five anonymous bards over a period of years, and edited by a sixth, none of whom was named Homer, little could be gained by banishing his name from literary studies. Homer is a useful concept even if he never existed.

At times, the existence of an authorial canon may work to our detriment—as will be apparent to anyone who has tried to buy a copy of *Edward III*, only to find that it is out of print. *Titus Andronicus, 1 Henry VI*, and *Henry VIII*, though inferior in some respects to *Edward III*, have not been out of print at any time in the past hundred years. Inevitably, those works that are excluded from a canon—whether by commission or omission—generally go unread, regardless of merit. We may agree that the Peter elegy, whoever its author, is an unusually fine example of Jacobean poetry, yet its absence from an authorial canon has in the past left it upon the dust heap of literary studies.

The longer the tradition, and the more valued the author, the more resistant is a canon to any kind of change, even in the light of fresh evidence. It took well over a hundred years, following George Steevens's resurrection of the Thorp Quarto in the latter eighteenth century, before the sonnets were fully welcomed into the canon. If, finally, they triumphed over all obstacles, including the Victorians' moral revulsion, it was not without a lengthy battle. According to many, the great bard could never have written such stuff. According to many others, he shouldn't have.

Yet canons do change. The Shakespeare canon has not had precisely the same shape for two successive generations. Plays such as *The Puritaine* and *Locrine*, once accepted as authentic, are today universally disclaimed. Plays such as *Titus Andronicus, Pericles*, and *Henry VIII*, omitted from the nineteenth-century canon, have since been readmitted, albeit with an acknowledgment that the latter two have dual authorship. Since Shakespeare was sometimes given to collaborative efforts, his canon will always remain blurry about the edges. The focus meanwhile will remain on his ten or twelve most popular works—for each generation likewise renders its verdict as to which of the unquestioned works are most successful, thereby forming an "inner" canon of those plays and poems that are thought to represent Shakespeare at his best.

If we have learned anything at all from the recent controversy over "Shall I die, shall I fly," it is that scholars ought not to let their enthusiasm triumph over a reasoned and reasonable skepticism. Today's great discoveries too often become tomorrow's embarrassments. Under no circumstances should the *Elegy* be admitted to the Shakespeare canon, or be included in forthcoming editions of his collected works, without having first been subjected to the most rigorous cross-examination. Many talented scholars will find it quite preposterous that Shakespeare should be credited with such a poem. Their voice needs to be heard. I do not think that I have blinded myself to any scrap of contrary evidence, yet it may be that there yet lurks in the *Elegy* itself, or elsewhere, some weighty evidence that Shakespeare could have had no part in writing this poem. One must allow also for a time of probation, to permit the scholarly community to digest such contrary evidence as the nearly simultaneous death and burial of William Peter and Shakespeare's brother, and to find where my own discussion of the evidence may be objectionable, my methodology defective, or my figures inaccurate. It may be that the *Funeral Elegy* for William Peter will one day be admitted to the canon, despite its shortcomings; or perhaps it will be firmly rejected. I confess that the *Elegy* looks to me like the work of William Shakespeare. But it is a worldwide community of readers, not I, nor even W. S. himself, who will have the final word.

NOTES TO THE COMMENTARY

Introduction

1. Exeter City Muniments, Letter 145, Devon Record Office. It is from this inquest that I have taken the account of Peter's murder as presented above in "A Killing at Exeter."

2. Arber, 3.477. Entering a title in the Register served two functions: it gave the Wardens an opportunity to inspect, and sometimes to censor, printed books and pamphlets, though this prerogative appears to have been exercised only desultorily in nonreligious publications, usually in response to a complaint. More importantly, registered works were protected from a surreptitious printing by another stationer.

3. The memorial poems that appear to have been privately printed are indicated as such in appendix C, A Checklist of English Memorial Verse, 1570–1630.

Authorship

1. Horden *(D.A.P.)* lists fewer than two hundred initialed works in the period 1475–1640 for which the author's initials, as given, are known or suspected to be incorrect. The vast majority of these are religious polemics, 116 of them tracts by Roman Catholics. The list includes also four instances in which "G." or "Guil." stands for *Guilielmus* (the Latinized form of William, which in each case is the author's Christian name); twelve obvious misprints; and twelve sets of pseudonymous initials by a single author, Nicholas Breton, who is the only writer who made a regular habit of using pseudonymous initials for no apparent reason. Apart from these exceptions, there are fewer than two dozen initialed works printed in the years 1475–1640 for which the author's initials are possibly transposed or otherwise in error—a very small number, considering the many thousands of books and tracts printed during these years.

The Case for William Shakespeare

1. *The First Part of the Return from Parnassus* 992–1001, in *The Three Parnassus Plays*, ed. J. B. Leishman (London: Nicholson, 1949), 184.

2. Puttenham, 55, 39.

3. Marco Mincoff, "*Henry VIII* and Fletcher," *SQ* 12 (1961): 239–60. D. L. Chambers, *The Metre of "Macbeth": its Relation to Shakespeare's Earlier and Later Work* (Princeton: Princeton University Press, 1903), 65; cf. E. K. Chambers, "Overflows," table IV, *W. S.*, 2.401, and Goswin König, *Der Vers in Shakespeares Dramen* (Strasbourg, 1888), 133. The index of "open" or "unstopped" lines that I

244

have used here is far more consistent for most authors than that of syntactic enjambent, as may be seen, for example, in the erratic figures, supplied by Mincoff, for enjambment in Fletcher's plays (Mincoff, 241).

4. In my breakdown of authorship for *H8* and *TNK* I fully endorse the conclusions of Cyrus Hoy, with only a few exceptions. I have assigned 5.2b of *H8*, and 4.3b of *TNK*, to Shakespeare (where the frequency and usage of "and," "so," "thus," "which," "you," etc., and the frequency of unstopped lines, seem to indicate Shakespeare's hand); I have classed 1.4b of *H8* as "doubtful" (Hoy assigns it to Fletcher); and I have given 1.5 of *TNK* to Fletcher (a brief scene that has a higher correlation with Fletcher's than with Shakespeare's vocabulary). Of those scenes in *H8* that Hoy assigns jointly to "Fletcher and Shakespeare" (2.1–2.2, 3.2b–c, and 4.1–4.2), 3.2b and 4.2b may be ascribed to Fletcher, 3.2c, 4.2a, and 4.2c to Shakespeare, with some confidence. But in *H8* 1.4b–2.2 and 4.1, one of these two poets appears to have revised the work of the other. I have therefore excluded *H8* 1.4b–2.2 and 4.1 from my ensuing statistical tabulations for Shakespeare and Fletcher. The respective assignments for *H8* and *TNK* are noted hereafter as "(Sh.)," "(Fl.)," and "(?)." I believe that this breakdown has a high degree of reliability. Nevertheless, in weighing the evidence of Shakespeare's hand in the *Elegy,* I have tried to avoid any statement or statistical test that might depend upon the accuracy of the particular division given here, and have excluded both *H8* and *TNK* from the plays in the "Control Group" by which the *Elegy* has been measured. Scene and line numbering is keyed to *The Riverside Shakespeare,* ed. G. Blakemore Evans (Boston: Houghton Mifflin, 1974):

Henry VIII		Two Noble Kinsmen	
Prologue	Shakespeare	Prologue	Fletcher
1.1–1.2	Shakespeare	1.1–1.4	Shakespeare
1.3–1.4.64	Fletcher	1.5	Fletcher
1.4.64–108	(Fletcher and Shakespeare)	2.1	Shakespeare
2.1–2.2	(Fletcher and Shakespeare)	2.2–2.6	Fletcher
2.3–2.4	Shakespeare	3.1–3.2	Shakespeare
3.1	Fletcher	3.3–3.6	Fletcher
3.2.1–203	Shakespeare	4.1–4.2	Fletcher
3.2.203–349	Fletcher	4.3.1–57	Fletcher
3.2.350–459	Shakespeare	4.3.58–101	Shakespeare
4.1	(Fletcher and Shakespeare)	5.1.1–33	Fletcher
4.2.1–82	Shakespeare	5.1.34–173	Shakespeare
4.2.83–108	Fletcher	5.2	Fletcher
4.2.108–73	Shakespeare	5.3–5.4	Shakespeare
5.1	Shakespeare	Epilogue	Fletcher
5.2.1–182	Fletcher		
5.2.182–215	Shakespeare		
5.3–5.4	Fletcher		
Epilogue	Fletcher		

5. One nondramatic poet who consistently exceeds Shakespeare in the use of unstopped lines is Edward, Lord Herbert, but most of his surviving poetry was written later than 1612.

6. For this count I have again used *The Riverside Shakespeare,* which forms the basis also for Spevack's *Concordance.* Someone else's count may vary by a point or two, depending first on the edition used, and second on the number of tetrameter, hexameter, or unfilled lines included in the count. Excluded from my tabulations for Shakespeare here (as elsewhere) are *Mac.* 3.5, 4.1.39–43 and 125–32, *Per.* 1–2, and the non-Shakespearean portions of *H8* and *TNK* (see n. 4 above). I have made no effort to sort out the problems of such plays as 1–3 *H6, Tit., Shr.,* and *Tim.*

7. In *Tmp.* (1611), 11 of 130 rhymed lines have feminine endings, or 8.5%. Or, if we include the trochaic song of Juno and Ceres in 4.1.106–17, the figures are 23 of 142 lines, or 16.2%. The percentage of feminine endings in Shakespeare's blank verse in the same play is, of course, much higher.

8. This figure includes one rhyme-pair, *apprehension:dissension,* appearing in lines of different length (270, 272), so that the first *-sion* is disyllabic; only the second *-sion* may be considered a feminine ending (though one may scan line 272, alternatively, as a hexameter, without a feminine ending).

9. Unless otherwise stated, all subsequent quotations from Shakespeare are cited from G. Blakemore Evans, ed., *The Riverside Shakespeare* (Boston: Houghton Mifflin, 1974).

10. Dorothy Sipe, *Shakespeare's Metrics* (New Haven: Yale University Press, 1968).

11. Puttenham, 67.

12. John Davies, "The Muses Teares" (498), in *The Muses-Teares for the Losse of . . . Henry Prince of Wales* (London, 1613). Unless otherwise noted, all quotations from the Memorial Verse (appendix C) are taken from the original printed texts, but are reprinted here in normalized orthography (in the interests of a more objective comparison with W. S.'s *Funeral Elegy* than would otherwise be possible).

13. Fausto Cercignani, *Shakespeare's Works and Elizabethan Pronunciation* (Oxford: Clarendon, 1981), 256.

14. Cercignani, *Elizabethan Pronunciation,* 344.

15. Of the 270 different rhymes in the *Elegy,* 115 are found in Shakespeare. The identical rhymes, in order of appearance in the *Elegy,* are as follows (the first figure within each parenthesis is the number of occurrences in W. S., and the second, the number of occurrences in Shakespeare's canonical works): *end:intend* (2, 1), *days:praise* (1, 12), *name:same* (3, 8), *come:tomb* (1, 2), *dust:must* (1, 4), *men:then* (1, 7), *him:limb* (1, 1), *are:care* (1, 7), *love:reprove* (1, 2), *leave:receive* (1, 3), *done:sun* (1, 13), *bad:had* (1, 1), *be:be* (1, 1), *truth:youth* (2, 7), *kind:mind* (3, 11), *delight:white* (1, 6), *obey'd:oversway'd* (1, 1), *age:rage* (1, 5), *ill:will* (2, 14), *fools:schools* (1, 1), *me:see* (1, 16), *affords:words* (2, 4), *dote:float* (1, 1), *best:breast* (1, 3), *discreet:sweet* (1, 1), *birth:mirth* (1, 1), *just:trust* (1, 1), *gone:one* (1, 7), *day:say* (1, 10), *great:seat* (1, 2), *blood:good* (2, 17), *come:home* (1, 1), *sin:win* (1, 1), *rehearse:verse* (1, 4), *here:there* (1, 4), *heart:impart* (1, 1), *so:woe* (1, 26), *beds:heads* (2, 2), *forms:storms* (1, 1), *begin:sin* (2, 5), *pride:tide* (1, 1), *wit:writ* (1, 4), *owe:show* (1, 3), *change:strange* (1, 7), *length:strength* (1, 1), *grave:have* (1, 13), *coast:lost* (1, 2), *tongue:wrong* (1, 6), *forth:worth* (1, 8), *breath:death* (2, 28), *show:so* (1, 8), *first:worst* (1, 2), *men:pen* (1, 6), *control:soul* (1, 4), *now:vow* (1, 2), *me:thee* (1, 65), *mine:thine* (1, 13), *can:man* (3,

8), *deed:proceed* (1, 3), *farewell:tell* (1, 1), *light:night* (1, 26), *blind:mind* (1, 3), *light:spite* (1, 2), *fashion:passion* (1, 4), *base:disgrace* (1, 1), *praise:raise* (1, 1), *care:rare* (1, 2), *awe:law* (1, 2), *love:strove* (1, 1), *comprehends:friends* (1, 1), *ever:persever* (1, 1), *found:sound* (1, 1), *been:sin* (1, 1), *above:love* (1, 1), *trust:unjust* (1, 1), *begin:sin* (1, 5), *end:friend* (1, 12), *law:saw* (1, 1), *ago:so* (1, 1), *blood:stood* (1, 4), *guilt:spilt* (1, 1), *curse:worse* (1, 6), *make:take* (1, 5), *destiny:he* (1, 1), *gone:throne* (1, 1), *froward:untoward* (1, 1), *air:despair* (1, 1), *hope:scope* (1, 3), *merit:spirit* (1, 1), *fate:state* (1, 4), *content:spent* (1, 6), *delight:night* (1, 10), *great:sweat* (1, 2), *above:dove* (1, 4), *aspire:higher* (1, 2), *live:thrive* (1, 2), *life:strife* (1, 15), *contend:end* (1, 1), *about:out* (1, 8), *deserts:parts* (1, 1), *had:sad* (1, 1), *love:remove* (1, 6), *father:rather* (1, 1), *another:other* (1, 1), *love:strove* (1, 1), *gives:lives* (1, 2), *belong:song* (1, 1), *how:now* (1, 5), *should:would* (1, 1), *know:woe* (1, 4), *more:score* (1, 3), *again:sustain* (1, 1), *heart:part* (1, 32), *breast:unrest* (1, 1), *lost:most* (1, 2). I have excluded from the list of identical rhymes any that do not appear in Shakespeare precisely as in the Peter elegy, as for instance the same word-pair but in a different inflection; and I have excluded from consideration any identical counterpart that appears in *PP,* in *Per.* 1–2, or in the presumed non-Shakespeare portions of *Mac., H8,* and *TNK.* My source is Cercignani, *Elizabethan Pronounciation.*

16. Cf. Shakespeare's *straight:conceit* (*Err.* 4.2.63–65) and, in blank verse, *gate:height* (*Tit.* 4.2.34–35), *right:exploit* (1H6 2.3.4–5), and *seat:straight* (2H6 1.1.169–70 Q).

17.:The "un-Shakespearean" rhymes are as follows. *Ven.:* *voice:juice, should:cool'd, imprinted:contented, temp'ring:vent'ring, sentinel:kill, wretch:scratch, adder:shudder, hallow:follow, unlikely:quickly. Luc.: singular:publisher, conspirator:ravisher, theft:shift, imparteth:vanisheth, troth:oath:growth,* and *replenish:blemish. Son.: field:held, fleet'st:sweets,* and *dead:o'erread* (*o'erread* in present tense). *LC:unto:vow* (The last of these, like *command:prophane* in the *Elegy,* may be the result of a misprint; many editors have mended "vow" to "woo"). In figuring the percentages of "unlikely" rhymes, I have considered triplets as a single unit, and have counted off-rhymes only once even when they occur in a triplet. This provides a more accurate standard by which to measure the *Elegy.*

18. The unlikely Shakespearean rhymes in the Hecate scenes of *Mac.* are *stanch:wench* and *turrets:spirits;* in *PP, fickle:brittle, flameth:framing, overburneth:a-turning, abhor thee:adore thee, suddenly:presently, refresh:redress, ditty:pretty,* and *soon:hour* (the last of which is probably a misprint for *soon:moon*); and in "Shall I die," *breeding:deceiving, meadows:shadows, plenty:scanty, shew:rue, tresses:senses, retire:despair, banner:upon her, moan:frown.*

19. Eliot Slater, "Shakespeare: Word Links between the Poems and Plays," *NQ,* n.s., 22 (1975): 157–64; Alfred Hart, "Vocabularies of Shakespeare's Plays" and "The Growth of Shakespeare's Vocabulary," *RES* 19 (1943): 128–40, 242–54. The following principles are used by Hart and Slater in defining "unique" words: no proper nouns or adjectives are included; different parts of speech are taken to be different words even when spelt identically; different inflections of a word are not taken to constitute a difference; words hyphenated in Bartlett's *Concordance* (or in the case of the *Elegy,* words hyphenated in my edited text) are taken as one word; and homonyms with radically different meanings are taken to be different words. The count in table 1.3 of unique words in the Shakespeare poems is borrowed from Slater (160).

20. See for example, G. L. Brook, *The Language of Shakespeare* (London: André Deutsch, 1976), 132; Dolores Burton, *Shakespeare's Grammatical Style* (Austin: University of Texas Press, 1973), 64–65; Wilhelm Franz, *Shakespeare Grammatik* (Heidelberg: Carl Winter, 1909), 95–96; Bernard Groom, *The Diction of Poetry from Spenser to Bridges* (Toronto: University of Toronto Press, 1955), 42–45; Alfred Hart, *Shakespeare and the Homilies* (1934; New York: Octagon, 1970), 226–28; S. S. Hussey, *The Literary Language of Shakespeare* (New York: Longman, 1982), 55, 125; Josephine Roberts, "*King Lear* and the Prefixes of Inversion," *Neuphilologische Mitteilungen* 79 (1978): 384–90; and Sipe, *Shakespeare's Metrics*, 191–92 +.

21. Hart, *Homilies*, 253.

22. See, for example, G. L. Brook (1976), Burton (1973), Groom (1955), works cited in n. 20 above; Edwin A. Abbot, *A Shakespeare Grammar* (London: Macmillan, 1881); N. F. Blake, *Shakespeare's Language* (London: Macmillan, 1983); A. C. Partridge, *A Substantive Grammar of Shakespeare's Nondramatic Texts* (Charlottesville: Univ. Press of Virginia, 1976).

23. "God, the great All," in Thomas Bastard, *Chrestoleros* (London, 1598), B2v.

24. Hart, *Homilies*, 250.

25. Ibid., 251–52.

26. Ibid., 252–53.

27. Ibid., 253.

28. Among the more than two hundred poets represented in the Memorial Verse, the substitution of *for that* for *because* occurs only in George Wither (a native of Hampshire), Joseph Hall (of Leicestershire), and Thomas Churchyard (of Shropshire). But see also Holinshed's *Chronicles*, in which this usage appears rather frequently.

29. Dover Wilson, "Bibliographical Links between the Three Pages and the Good Quartos," in *Shakespeare's Hand in the Play of "Sir Thomas More"* (Cambridge: Cambridge University Press, 1923), 113–41.

30. Partridge, *A Substantive Grammar*, 120, 156, 203, and passim.

31. By way of comparison, the Authorized Version of the Bible (1611) has an incidence of only 131/773,746 words, or 0.2/1000 wds., despite the frequent repetition of the phrases, "most high" and "most holy." The average for English elegiac verse from 1610 through 1613 is 1.3/1000 words.

32. These figures include "perfectest" in *Ado* and "perfect'st" in *Mac.*, but not logical redundancies such as "most complete," "most omnipotent," "most absolute," "most infallible," "most infinitely," "most equal," and so on. The same distinction is made in the figures given for other poets.

33. David Lake, *The Canon of Thomas Middleton's Plays* (Cambridge: Cambridge University Press), 252–53, band 1(e)–4(e). In Shakespeare's nondramatic works *has* and *does* fail to appear, against more than one hundred uses of *hath*, and more than two hundred of *doth*, in the same poems. The modern forms appear somewhat more frequently in the dramatic verse (especially after 1602), and more often still in his dramatic prose, but only in the *TNK* and *H8* are they the preferred forms, and even there it seems that Fletcher, or possibly a compositor or scribe, has systematically modernized Shakespeare's text, as is surely the case in the F1 text of *Shr.*, in which we find an anomalous frequency of the more modern forms.

34. Partridge, *A Substantive Grammar*, 51.

35. Spenser, *FQ* 2.3.16.8. Jonson, "To Sir William Uvedale" 2, "To Mr. Arthur Squib" 20, and "Horace, *Of the Art of Poetrie*" 553 (H & S 8.79, 229, 331).

Heywood, *The Golden Age* 2.1.1–2 (London, 1611). Davies, "The Muses Teares," 78–80.

36. In the five plays preceding the *Elegy, sometime* ranges from 0.08–0.31, with an average of 0.14. Turning to the Cross-Sample, only three of the thirty-six poets use *sometime,* and for none of the three does its frequency fall within the expected range for a late work by Shakespeare. *Sometime* in the *Elegy* has a frequency of 0.23.

37. In addition, the "*alway* sound" in line 332 of the *Elegy* may be compared with "*alway* shed" in *3H6* (5.6.64); among all the poets represented in the Memorial Verse, only John Davies drops the final letter of *always* when followed by initial *s*. But it must be conceded in all three instances that the omitted *s* may be owing to the compositor rather than to the author.

38. Partridge, *A Substantive Grammar,* 201.

39. Charles Barber, *Early Modern English* (London: Deutsch, 1976), 218–19.

40. Partridge, *A Substantive Grammar,* 201.

41. Hussey, *The Literary Language,* 97.

42. I am nevertheless open here to a charge of overreading, for in the Quarto, "endeavors," in line 4, is spelled "indeuor's," which of course obliterates the visual, and possibly even the phonetic, link with *end* in line 1. But Eld's compositors habitually altered initial *en-* and *em-* to *in-* and *im-,* as first noted by Partridge, *A Substantive Grammar,* 207. This practice, everywhere evident in Eld's texts (as for example in *Shake-speares Sonnets*), is one of the principal distinguishing marks of his shop and may have been expressly articulated as a house rule. Yet the preservation in the *Elegy* Quarto of "endeavor" in line 245, along with such spellings as "enough" (35, 237), "enrole" (239), "ennoble" (437), and "envie" (409, 460), despite Eld's usual practice of altering these to *in-,* makes it a virtual certainty that *en-* spellings were frequent in the author's manuscript. Furthermore, the compositor's haphazard addition of apostrophes for elided participles and for possessive nouns suggests that apostrophes rarely appeared in W. S.'s manuscript. On both counts, it seems likely that "indeuor's" is a compositor, not a copy, spelling.

43. A. C. Partridge, *Orthography in Shakespeare and Elizabethan Drama* (Lincoln: University of Nebraska Press, 1964), 158.

44. William Empson, *Seven Types of Ambiguity* (New York: New Directions, 1947), 90.

45. *Antanaclasis* (or the "rebound," as Puttenham calls it), because frequent in Shakespeare, has inspired much critical cleverness, as is possible here: One might say that Peter was *sent* to heaven, but with the *inn* of his body, line 113, *not-sent:* "sent," with "inn not sent" (or with the letter *n* not sent), leaves him to be "set" ("inn" and "n" were pronounced the same). Whether such labored exegesis is convincing or contemptible is, for the point I wish to make here, quite irrelevant. Obviously, such ingenious readings cannot with confidence be attributed to the poet's intention. It is sufficient, however, to note that *antanaclasis* is an habitual feature of Shakespeare's style. A familiar example is Sonnet 64.11–12: "*Ruin* hath taught me thus to *ruminate,* / That time will come and take my love away" (*ruminate – mate = ruin*).

46. Puttenham, 188.

47. Empson, *Ambiguity,* 90; George T. Wright, "Hendiadys and *Hamlet,*" *PMLA* 96 (1981): 168–93; and M. M. Reese, *Shakespeare: His World and His Work* (London: Arnold, 1953), 517–19.

48. Reese, *Shakespeare,* 518–19.

49. Sir Thomas Browne, *Religio Medici* (London, 1643), 184. These constructions in Browne are often obscured by a comma, as in his description of avarice as "that subterraneous Idol, and God of the earth" (188).

50. As noted by Wright, *PL* 1.233–34, 771, 786; 2.80; 3.417; 4.562; 5.349; 10.345–46, 956; *PR* 1.457, 2.29, 4.439; *Samson Agonistes* 34, 1654; and three doubtful instances at *PL* 2.67, 69, or 346.

51. Empson, *Ambiguity*, 94–95; Wright, "Hendiadys," 169–71.

52. Empson, *Ambiguity*, 90.

53. T. C. Mendenhall, "The Characteristic Curve of Composition," *Science* 11 (1887): 237–49, and "A Mechanical Solution of a Literary Problem," *Popular Science Monthly* 60 (1901): 97–105; C. B. Williams, *Style and Vocabulary: Numerical Studies* (London: Griffin, 1970). It should be noted, however, that their labor is fruitless in comparing Shakespeare to writers of other periods (e.g., J. S. Mill, Charles Dickens, William Thackeray). Such comparisons have little or no diagnostic value. The frequent use in Shakespeare's day, for instance, of *thee, thou,* and *hath,* and the absence of contractions in *n't,* renders pointless any comparison of particular writers from different generations.

54. These figures are taken directly from Spevack, with the following exceptions: (1) genuine compounds are counted as two words (or, where three-element compounds occur, as three words); and (2) I have supplied elided letters. Thus *lik'd* has been counted as a five-letter word, *short-liv'd* as two five-letter words, *he's* as two two-letter words, *th'* as a three-letter word, *I'll* as a one- and a four-letter word. *Love's* as a contraction for "love is" (4, 1) has been differentiated from *love's,* possessive, and so for related instances. *'Tis* and *'gan,* however, have been counted as three-letter words, *'twas* and *'gins* as four-letter, *'twere* as a five-letter, and *'gainst* as a six-letter word; this, in order to conform with the apparent practice of Mendenhall and Williams, though both are somewhat vague about their procedure. The same rules have been applied to W. S., Marlowe, and Donne. In each instance, all proper nouns have been included in the count.

55. For the broadest available sample of W. S.'s median word-length, I have tallied both the *Elegy* (but not the title) and the dedication (but not the address to John Peter or the initialed signature). My source for Bacon's work is C. B. Williams, whose figures are derived from Mendenhall's useful, though imprecise, graphs (Williams, 38). The figures for Marlowe are based on Louis Ule, ed., *A Concordance to the Works of Christopher Marlowe* (Hildesheim: Georg Olms, 1979). Ule provides word-length graphs, but these are inaccurate. The totaled percentages vary from 74 to 107. I have therefore conducted an exact count, using the catalogue of Words by Order of Frequency (Ule, 517–43), and have tallied all words that appear in the Marlowe canon at least five times; the resulting sample comprises 90.0% of the Marlowe canon. I have used the same measures for determining "word-length" as those applied to Shakespeare (n. 54 above).

56. These figures are derived from Steven L. Bates and Sidney D. Orr, eds., *A Concordance to the Poems of Ben Jonson* (Athens: Ohio University Press, 1978); Mario di Cesare and Rigo Mignani, eds., *A Concordance to the Complete Writings of George Herbert* (Ithaca: Cornell University Press, 1977); Herbert S. Donow, ed., *A Concordance to the Sonnet Sequences of Daniel, Drayton, Shakespeare, Sidney, and Spenser* (Carbondale: Southern Illinois University Press, 1969); Charles G. Osgood, ed., *A Concordance to the Poems of Edmund Spenser* (Carnegie Institution of Washington, 1915); and Ule, *A Concordance to . . . Marlowe.* The word counts given for Jonson, Herbert, Spenser, and Marlowe are as accurate as I am able to estimate from the information provided in my respective sources;

for a count of the most frequent words (*and, the, but,* etc.) I have had to extrapolate. Actual sample sizes for these four poets may therefore differ slightly from the figures I have provided. The figures for Strachey and Strode are based on a handcount: the count for Strachey is taken directly from the original texts, and for Strode's nondramatic poetry, from the *Poetical Works,* ed. Bertram Dobell (London, 1907), 1–136. The figures for Sidney, Daniel, and Drayton are supplied by Donow, and the figure for Shakespeare is based on Spevack (but with non-Shakespearean passages subtracted).

57. Slater, "Shakespeare: Word Links" (1975); Hart, "Vocabularies of Shakespeare's Plays" (1943), 128–40, and "The Growth of Shakespeare's Vocabulary" (1943), 242–54. The modified guidelines as set forth have been followed with meticulous care, so as to avoid introducing a bias that might favor Shakespeare. For example, W. S. uses *predestinated,* and Shakespeare, *predestinate,* as an adjective. Neither form appears in the non-Shakespeare sample, but since the two words are not identical, *predestinate* (adj.) has been listed as a word unique to W. S., appearing in neither cross-sample.

58. This occurs in only one relevant instance: "fillet" as *ribbon* (in LC) is distinguished from "fillet" as *slice* (in *Mac.*).

59. The badges and flukes for the sample texts are as follows: The first element of each set is the absolute frequency in the source poem, and the second, its frequency either in the Shakespeare canon (badges) or non-Shakespeare sample (flukes). Hand *D,* badges: v. *to adhere* (1,6), n. *alevenpence* (1,1), adj. *clement* (1,1), adj. *dexter* (1,1), adj. *half-penny* (1,3), n. *hurly* (1,3), n. *loaf* (1,2), n. *luggage* (1,5), n. *mediation* (1,2), n. *mutine* (1,2), v. *to physic* (1,4), n. *pumpion* (1.1), v. *to shark* (1,1), n. *stillness* (1,5), n. *supposition* (1,5), n. *undoing* (1,4); Hand *D,* flukes: adj. *appropriate* (1,1), n. *inhumanity* (1,1). *PhT* badges: n. *supreme* (1,1), cpd. *-divining* (1,1), n. *gender* (1,4), n. *surplice* (1,1), cpd. *treble-* (1,1), cpd. *-dated* (1,1); *PhT* flukes: adj. *turtle's* (1,1), v. *to interdict* (1,3). *LC* badges: adv. *a-twain* (1,1), cpd. *-betrayed* (1,1), n. *cautel* (1,1), adj. *credent* (1,3), v. *to daff* (1,6), n. *defiling* (1,1), n. *dialect* (1,2), v. *to dialogue* (1,1), n. *falseness* (1,2), adj. *filial* (1,3), v. *to glaze* (1,3), adj. *glowing* (1,1), adj. *gouty* (1,2), adj. *grained* (1,3), cpd. *heaven-* (1,3), cpd. *-hued* (1,1), adj. *leveled* (1,1), adj. *orbed* (1,2), n. *origin* (1,4), n. *outwards* (1,1), adj. *potential* (1,2), adj. *prompt* (1,4), n. *replication* (1,3), v. *to reword* (1,1), n. *schedule* (1,6), adv. *slackly* (1,1), adj. *sleided* (1,1), adj. *spungy* (1,4), n. *tempter* (1,3), adj. *threaden* (1,1); *LC* flukes: n. *fillet* (= ribbon) (1,1), adj. *unshorn* (1.1), adj. *termless* (1,1), adj. *pallid* (1,10), n. *supplicant* (1,1), n. *stole* (1,9), cpd. *well-doing* (1,1), adj. *religion's* (1,1), adj. *authorized* (1,1). Donne's Shakespeare-badges: n. *commissioner* (1,1), adj. *sundered* (1,2); Donne's Shakespeare-flukes: n. *material* (1,2); adv. *piecemeal* (1,5), n. *porphiry* (1,2), n. *tabernacle* (1,2), cpd. *through-* (1,2). Tourneur's Shakespeare-badges: none; Tourneur's Shakespeare-flukes: adj. *unguilty* (1,2), adv. *fluently* (1,1). Webster's Shakespeare-badges: n. *accountant* (1,1), adj. *haggish* (1,1), n. *impostor* (1,2), cpd. *jewel-* (1,1), n. *ostentation* (1.8), (adj.) *provident* (1,2), n. *quietus* (1,2), cpd. *wax-* (1,1), n. *acquittance* (1,4); Webster's Shakespeare-flukes: n. *academy* (1,1); n. *column* (1,2), n. *curiousness* (1,1), adj. *complemental* (1,1), adv. *jestingly* (1,1), n. *prease* (1,19), n. *screw* (1,1), n. *solitariness* (1,1), cpd. *-spent* (1,3), adv. *sternly* (1,25). "Shall I die" Shakespeare-badges: none; "Shall I die" Shakespeare-flukes: n. *desiring* (1,2), v. *to explain* (1,4), n. *speck* (1,1). All those words in "Shall I die" that are presented by Gary Taylor as distinctive of Shakespeare (n. *bare,* n. *annoy,* cpd. *star-like,* etc.) appear in the non-Shakespeare sample as well. Taylor, "Shakespeare's New Poem," *New York Times Book Review,* 15 December 1985, 11–14.

60. Slater, "Shakespeare: Word Links" (1975); Hart, "Vocabularies of Shakespeare's Plays" (1943), 128–40, and "The Growth of Shakespeare's Vocabulary" (1943), 242–54.

61. The raw data for table 1.13, which extends to many pages, may be obtained by writing to me.

62. Marvin Spevack, *A Complete and Systematic Concordance to the Works of Shakespeare,* 9 vols. (Hildesheim: Georg Olms, 1968). Though Spevack's word-counts and line numbering are keyed to *The Riverside Shakespeare,* he takes his line-counts from F1, counting half-lines as whole lines, a procedure that is unsuitable for my purposes here.

63. For a detailed breakdown of which scenes have been omitted as "non-Shakespearean," see n. 4 above.

64. The relatively high incidence of *as* and *which* in the *Elegy,* no matter who the author, may only reflect the influence of Daniel's *Funerall Poeme,* which W. S. used as a source—a high frequency of both words is a distinctive feature of Daniel's syntax, in the *Funerall Poeme* as elsewhere—but Shakespeare's use of both *as* and *which* increases in the last years of his career.

65. Ronald Efron, Department of Statistics, University of Chicago; Joseph Gani and Gordon Smyth, Statistics and Applied Probability Program, University of California, Santa Barbara.

66. Bodleian Library MS. Rawl. poet. 160, fol. 4lr. Spelling and punctuation have been normalized. The attribution to Shakespeare, though plausible, is uncertain. The same scribe, 135 pages later, ascribes "Shall I die, shall I fly" to Shakespeare (fol. 109v); the attribution is almost certainly wrong.

67. This example from *2H6* was brought to my attention by Garrett Stewart, in *Death Sentences* (Cambridge: Harvard University Press, 1984), 364.

68. Joseph Pequigney, *Such Is My Love* (Chicago: University of Chicago Press, 1985).

69. John Ford, *Christes Bloodie Sweat* (London, 1613), 1882. For a discussion of Ford's authorship of this poem, see M. Joan Sargeaunt, "Writings Ascribed to John Ford by Joseph Hunter in *Chorus Vatum, RES* 10 (1934): 165–76, and *John Ford* (Oxford: Oxford University Press, 1935), 8–11; also Clifford Leech, *John Ford and the Drama of His Time* (London: Chatto and Windus, 1957), 22–24; and G. D. Monsarrat, "John Ford's Authorship of *Christes Bloodie Sweat,*" *English Language Notes* 9 (1971–72): 20–25.

70. T. S. Eliot, "John Ford," *Selected Essays* (New York: Harcourt, Brace, 1950), 170–80. For a fair appraisal of Ford's debt to Shakespeare, see M. Joan Sargeaunt, *John Ford,* 117–27.

71. Compare, for example, Wastell 1–6 with Drayton 1–6; Wastell 7–18 with Tourneur 13–24; Wastell 19–80 and 81–96 with Daniel 1–66 and 283–98; Wastell 107–8 with Webster 277–78; and so throughout.

72. On 17 May 1595 Sergeant Drew purchased the manor of Broadhembury from the young earl of Southampton, together with the manor of Woolston from Thomas Arundell (Wriothesley's brother-in-law), by a deed enrolled in the Court of Common Pleas, the combined acquisition comprising 5,950 acres, virtually all of Broadhembury parish. The property neighbored, on the southwest, the Pehembury estate of the Devonshire Willoughbies and, on the southeast, the Gittisham estate of the Devon Beaumonts.

73. November 1604–January 1605, August 1605, mid-April 1606, winter 1606/7.

74. Peter's marriage settlement is detailed in the will of his mother-in-law, Mrs.

Elizabeth Brewton (4 July 1609, London PRO P.C.C. 26 Wood). In 1620 William Ford became vicar of West Coker, where he remained for many years. He was still living in 1640, when he was mentioned in the will of his nephew Thomas Ford.

75. The *International Genealogical Index* is a microfiche transcript of the parish registers of England and of other nations for which such records survive (Salt Lake City, Utah: Church of Jesus Christ of Latter Day Saints, 1984).

76. Murray, *E.D.C.,* 2.378–79; Chambers, *W.S.,* 3.323, 327.

77. Bodleian Library, Oxford. Chancellor's Court, Deposition Books (1604), fols. 28, 60r, and (1611), D 180v; cf. the St. Martin's parish register (Oxford Record Office), in which the first entry for the Davenant family is dated 11 February 1601. These records disprove Acheson's thesis in *Mistress Davenant: The Dark Lady of Shakespeare's Sonnets* (London: Quaritch, 1913).

78. John Aubrey, *Aubrey's Brief Lives,* ed. Oliver Lawson Dick (London: Secker and Warburg, 1949), 85.

79. The rumor that Shakespeare fathered William Davenant has never been widely credited. According to Aubrey, the story was encouraged, if not actually initiated, by Davenant himself, who in every respect wished to be known as Shakespeare's successor.

80. Even if granted the customary dispensation of four terms as the eldest son of an esquire, Leonard Digges must have entered the university no later than July 1598, for he graduated B.A. on 1 July 1601. Because the Buttery Books of University College for this period do not survive, the Digges brothers' residence at Oxford cannot be traced in detail.

81. The Buttery Books of Exeter College reveal that William Digges had, in addition, a few brief periods of absence in between, the longest of which extended to five weeks.

82. Andrew Clark, ed. *Register of the University of Oxford,* 2 vols. (Oxford: Clarendon, 1887), 2.1.vi–xxv.

83. Petre returned to Oxford in April 1598. On 3 May he was granted a dispensation of eighteen terms toward his M.A., in consideration of his studies at the Inner Temple.

84. Hadrian [Thomas] Dorrell, "To the Gentle and Courteous Reader," in Henry Willoughby, *Willobie his Avisa,* ed. G. B. Harrison (1922; New York: Barnes and Noble, 1966), 5. Willoughby may have enlisted before his return to Oxford in February 1594, but he did not begin active duty till September. In the six months intervening he remained at school, without a single day's absence, at least through the tenth week of the summer term. Unfortunately, the Buttery Book for the 1593/94 academic year is in mutilated condition, with the last three weeks (beginning 6 September) torn away. By 21 September, the first day of the fall term, Willoughby had withdrawn from school. But *Avisa* was registered in London on 3 September, which seems to belie Dorrell's testimony that he published the volume without his friend's knowledge, unless Dorrell found the manuscript during Willoughby's earlier extended absence, which concluded on 1 March—in which case it would be difficult to explain why the book was not registered until six months afterward, shortly before Willoughby's departure from Oxford. The evidence suggests that Willoughby conspired with Dorrell in the publication of his book. There are many similar examples in the 1590s of authors falsely, if modestly, pretending that a manuscript was printed without authorization.

85. Act Books of the Congregation and Convocation, (Univ. Oxon. Arch. L10: 1582–94), fol. 205v.

86. Harrison, *Willobie his Avisa,* 225.

87. Murray, *E.D.C.*, 1.89, 2.216–17.
88. Walter W. Greg, ed., *Henslowe's Diary*, 2 vols. (London: Bullen, 1908), 2:312.
89. Leslie Hotson, *I, William Shakespeare* (London: Jonathan Cape, 1937), 53–70+. There are, in addition, a number of relevant marriages that Hotson has overlooked: John Dackomb married Elizabeth, daughter of William Hartgill of Calmington, Somerset; Dackomb's sister Joan married Thomas Chafin of Meere, Wiltshire, who died childless, after which Chafin married Jane Bampfield, Thomas Russell's eldest sister-in-law; and Dackomb's son John married Elizabeth Willoughby, young Henry's elder sister, while another sister, Margaret, married John Hartgill. Lastly, Chafin's brother William married young Willoughby's first cousin, the daughter of Christopher Willoughby of Knoyle.
90. One cannot pick up this thread at any point without finding a connection to others in the same group. For example, Matthew Ewens, a clerk of the Exchequer, was possibly the closest friend of Henry Willoughby the elder. Ewens married Francis Willoughby (n. Rogers), the widow of Henry Willoughby's cousin John Willoughby of Silton, Dorset (grandson of Richard Willoughby). In 1584 Ewens served as overseer of the will of William Chaldecott together with James Dackomb of Ewern Stapleton, Dorest, whose first cousin, John Dackomb of Funtmill, Dorset, later married young Willoughby's sister, Elizabeth. Ewens in his own will (1598) names as his best friends not only Henry Willoughby the elder, but also Edward Hext and John Strode, both of whom are associated in various ways with the Peter family.
91. Except where noted otherwise, the ensuing record of court performances and provincial tours by Shakespeare's dramatic company is based on Murray, *E.D.C.*, 1.97–109 (Lord Chamberlain's), and 1.145–55, 173–84 (King's Men).
92. I wish to thank Dr. J. R. Maddicott, Librarian of Exeter College, for giving me generous access to the college archives. In tracing Peter's movements, I have drawn on the College Register (1540–1619); the Bursar's Quarterly Accounts, A.IV.15 (1600–1603), 16 (1604–10), 17 (1603–12); the Tutorial Books, L.II.1 (1605–30); and the Buttery Books (1592–1611).
93. Act Books of the Congregation and Convocation (Univ. Oxon. Arch. L11), fol. 155r.
94. Murray, *E.D.C.*, 2.147, 183. The King's Men played at Oxford sometime after 3 November 1603 and probably before the theaters reopened in London the following April. Since the King's Men rarely performed in the winter or early spring (except at court), their Oxford visit was probably in November, before their engagement of 2 December at Wilton.
95. Peter left the hall sometime in midsummer and did not return until sometime during the winter (lacking the Buttery Books for these two terms, one can only guess at the precise dates). Exeter College, Bursar's Quarterly Account (1600–1603), A.IV.15.
96. This George Peter is the son of John Peter of Compton, and should not be confused with George Petre, son of William Petre of Hayes, the friend of Henry Willoughby.
97. Chambers, *W. S.*, 2.118–22.
98. On 8 April 1606, Peter was granted a dispensation to "deliver his solemn lectures on any day this week and at any hour without giving the usual notice. Reason: he has to go away on business and cannot wait for another term." His responsion of 10 April counted in quodlibets pro forma. Such dispensations were fairly routine. Bodleian Library, Oxford: Act Books of the Congregation and Convocation (1606), fol. 212v.

99. PRO, London: Inq. p. m. C142.296.106 (1607).
100. Devon Record Office, Exeter: Exminster Parish Register.
101. Chambers, *W. S.,* 2.7.

The Case for William Strachey

1. Strachey's verse has never, heretofore, been gathered and reprinted. As a result, he remains a virtual unknown in literary studies. I have found it necessary, therefore, to provide a brief summary of his life and works in appendix B.
2. For a complete list of works tabulated, see appendix B. "A Checklist of William Strachey's Works." The figure given for Shakespeare omits here, as elsewhere, *PP* and the non-Shakespearean portions of *Mac., Per., H8,* and *TNK* (see "The Case for William Shakespeare," n. 4 above).
3. Strachey, *Lawes* (London, 1612), [vii]. Cf. *TN* 4.3.11, "this accident and flood of fortune."
4. William Strachey, *The Historie of Travell into Virginia Britania* [Princeton MS], ed. Louis B. Wright and Virginia Freund (1953; Nendeln, Liechtenstein: Kraus, 1967), 23.
5. In a manuscript letter quoted in full by Culliford, *Strachey,* 125.
6. Bodleian Library MS Ashmole 1758. The dedication only is printed in *The Genesis of the United States,* ed. Alexander Brown (New York: Houghton Mifflin [1890]), 2.562–65.
7. Strachey's *mis-won* and *over-looks,* appearing in "Overbury," are not included in the count of compound words, as is consonant with the statistics given for Shakespeare and W. S.
8. Culliford, *Strachey,* 160–62.
9. Evelyn M. Simpson, *A Study of the Prose Works of John Donne* (Oxford: Clarendon, 1924), 317.
10. Strachey, *Historie of Travell* (1967), 100–101.
11. William Ford, *A Sermon Preached at Constantinople* (London, 1616).
12. See "Upon the Untimely Death of . . . Sir Thomas Overbury," 53–55, in appendix B.

Evidence for Authorship: Some Conclusions

1. Arthur Sherbo, "The Uses and Abuses of Internal Evidence," in *Evidence for Authorship: Essays on Problems of Attribution,* ed. David V. Erdman and Ephim G. Fogel (Ithaca: Cornell University Press, 1966), 7.
2. S. Schoenbaum, *Internal Evidence and Elizabethan Dramatic Authorship* (Evanston, Ill.: Northwestern University Press, 1966), 150.
3. Ibid., 107.
4. Ephim G. Fogel, "Salmons in Both, or Some Caveats for Canonical Scholars," in Erdman and Fogel, *Evidence for Authorship,* 100.
5. Arthur Sherbo, "Can *Mother Midnight's Comical Pocket-Book* Be Attributed to Christopher Smart?" in Erdman and Fogel, *Evidence for Authorship,* 283–84.
6. Fogel, "Salmons," 71.
7. David V. Erdman, "The Signature of Style," *Bulletin of the New York Public Library* 63 (1959): 46.
8. Ibid., 45.

9. S. Schoenbaum, *William Shakespeare: A Documentary Life* (New York: Oxford University Press, 1975), 218.

10. S. Schoenbaum, *Shakespeare's Lives* (New York: Oxford University Press 1970), 64.

11. Schoenbaum, *William Shakespeare*, 218.

12. Schoenbaum, *William Shakespeare*, 132, and *Shakespeare: The Globe and the World* (New York: Oxford University Press, 1979), 83.

13. A. C. Partridge, *Orthography*, 136–38.

14. Schoenbaum, *Shakespeare's Lives*, 60.

15. The plays that were apparently authorized for publication by the Chamberlain's/King's Men are as follows: (1) Shakespeare, *R2* (Wise, [Aspley, and Thorp], 1597). (2) Shakespeare, *R3* (Wise, [Aspley, and Thorp], 1597). (The hypothesis, once widely accepted, that *R3* was printed without authorization from a corrupt manuscript has been discredited by Stephen Urkowitz ["Reconsidering the Relationship of the Quarto and Folio Texts of *Richard III*," *ELR* 16 (1986): 442–66]; Q represents an earlier version of the play than that found in F1, but— excepting obvious misprints—we have every reason to believe the Q1 text to be authoritative.) (3) Anon., *A Warning for Fair Women* (Aspley [and Thorp], 1599). (4) *Ado* (Aspley, Wise [and Thorp], 1600). (5) Shakespeare, *2H4* (Aspley, Wise [and Thorp], 1600). (6) Ben Jonson, *Every Man in His Humour* (Burre and Burby, 1600). (7) John Marston, *The Malcontent* (Aspley and Thorp, 1604). (8) Jonson, *Sejanus* (Thorp [and Aspley], 1605, by assignment of Blount). (9) Jonson, *Volpone* (Thorp [and Aspley], 1607; assigned by Thorp to Burre on 3 October 1610). (10) Jonson, *The Alchemist* (Burre, 1612). (11) *Catiline* (Burre, 1611). Shakespeare's *MND* (T. Fisher, 1600), although a good quarto, was probably printed without the authorization of the Chamberlain's Men; see Leo Kirschbaum, *Shakespeare and the Stationers* (Columbus: Ohio State University Press, 1955), 172–73 + .

A few plays belonging to the Chamberlain's/King's Men were apparently sold to stationers by the author (a practice condemned by Thomas Heywood in his preface to *The Rape of Lucrece* (1608). These include George Wilkins, *The Miseries of Inforst Marriage* (G. Vincent, 1607); Barnabe Barnes, *The Divils Charter* (J. Wright, 1607); and Thomas Dekker, *Satiromastix* (J. Barnes and E. White, 1602). *The Revenger's Tragedy* (1607, printed and published by George Eld) may likewise have been sold by the author; otherwise, this is the only remaining play that may have been released by the King's Men to someone other than Thorp and his associates. Ten additional plays of the Chamberlain's/King's Men were entered in the Stationers' Register as blocking entries (five to James Roberts from 1598 to 1603, and five to Edward Blount from 1607 to 1618); half of these were eventually published by other stationers, either because the blocking entry failed to forestall publication of an unauthorized text or because Roberts or Blount, with the subsequent permission of the players, assigned the copyright to another stationer.

Thorp was chosen to publish the plays of other companies as well. His authorized dramatic quartos include Thomas Dekker, *Old Fortunatus* (Aspley [and Thorp], 1600); George Chapman, *Al Fooles* (Thorp [and Aspley], 1605), *The Gentleman Usher* (Thorp [and Aspley], 1606), *Bussy D'Ambois* (Aspley [and Thorp], 1607), and both parts of *Charles Duke of Byron* (Thorp [and Aspley], 1608); Chapman, Marston, and Jonson, *Eastward Hoe* (Aspley and Thorp, 1605); John Marston, *What You Will* (Thorp [and Aspley], 1607) and *Histrio-Mastix* (Thorp, 1610); he also published three of Jonson's masques with the poet's consent. Thorp cannot be linked to the bad quarto of any play or to any good quarto that was published without authorization.

16. Both Burre and Thorp served their apprenticeship under Roberts at the "Love and Death" bookshop; and although they worked at different shops after receiving their freedom, Thorp and Aspley, Burre and Blount, formed an informal syndicate that lasted from 1600 until at least 1618. They shared in many joint ventures and frequently exchanged copyrights.

17. See Murray, "The Relation of the Plague to the Closing of the Theatres," in *E.D.C.*, 2.171–91.

18. From notes appended to an abstract of Drummond's conversations with Jonson, in *Works* (London, 1711), 226; repr. Chambers, *W. S.*, 2.220–21.

19. John Benson, "To the Reader," *Poems: Written by Wil. Shake-speare. Gent.* (London, 1640), sig. A2r.

20. Schoenbaum, *William Shakespeare*, 218. Schoenbaum nevertheless remarks, from time to time, on which sonnets were addressed by the poet to whom. Sonnet 55, for instance, was addressed by the poet "to his adored Fair Youth." Such an identification rests entirely on the context of Sonnet 55, since it contains no other means by which to identify an addressee.

21. No one supposes that Shakespeare arranged the Sonnets in precise chronological order. To recover that order (an obvious impossibility) might be of some biographical interest, though of dubious aesthetic merit. In the New Variorum edition of the *Sonnets* (2 vols. [Philadelphia: Lippincott, 1944], 2:74–116), Hyder Rollins discusses the theories of nineteen rearrangers from John Benson (1640) to Tucker Brooke (1936). To these may be added Brents Sterling, *The Shakespeare Sonnet Order: Poems and Groups* (Berkeley: University of California Press, 1968) and S. C. Campbell, *Shakespeare's Sonnets Edited as a Continuous Sequence* (London: Bell and Hyman, 1978). Although Rollins's perspective is colored by his belief that the *Sonnets* quarto was printed without Shakespeare's permission, his essay is no less instructive on that account. Few of the sonnet rearrangers can be called "close readers." Most make their emendations in the interest of some extravagant private hypothesis. Campbell, for instance, the most recent, is convinced that the dark lady "was never a real lady at all," but a metaphor for homosexual lust, "a Spenserian witch who masqueraded as the fair friend in order to lead the poet into vice[;] she was Plato's dark horse or emblem of carnal love masquerading as the white horse of spiritual love" (p. x).

22. Schoenbaum, *William Shakespeare*, 73–74.

23. Chambers, *W. S.*, 1.562.

24. But see Katherine Duncan-Jones, "Was the 1609 *Shake-speares Sonnets* Really Unauthorized?" *RES* n.s. 34 (1983): 151–71.

25. Schoenbaum, *Shakespeare's Lives*, 70.

26. MacD. P. Jackson, *Shakespeare's "A Lover Complaint": Its Date and Authenticity* (University of Auckland Bulletin 72, English Series 13, 1965); and Kenneth Muir, " 'A Lover's Complaint': A Reconsideration," in *Shakespeare the Professional, and Related Studies* (Totowa, N.J.: Rowman and Littlefield, 1973), 204–19.

27. Eliot Slater, *NQ* n.s., 22 (1975): 157–63; and Partridge, *A Substantive Grammar*, 158–213. If, as Slater's statistics seem to suggest, "A Lover's Complaint" was written shortly before publication in 1609, it would appear that the poem was written expressly to be published, to follow the model of such poets as Samuel Daniel, whose sonnet sequence, *Delia* (1592), ends with the "Complaint of Rosamond," and Thomas Lodge, whose *Phillis* (1593) ends with the "Complaint of Elstred." Shakespeare's title is apparently borrowed from "The Lover's Complaint," a ballad mentioned in *Oth.*

28. Schoenbaum, *Shakespeare's Lives,* 66.

29. Schoenbaum, *Internal Evidence,* 167.

30. John Hemings and Henry Condell, "To the Great Variety of Readers," F1, sig. A3a.

31. *Ben Jonson's Conversations with William Drummond of Hawthornden,* ed. R. F. Patterson (London: Blackie, 1924), 34. Francis Meres, *Palladis Tamia, Wits Treasury* (London, 1598), 283.

32. Chambers, *W. S.,* 1.207.

33. Schoenbaum, *Internal Evidence,* 167.

34. Partridge, *Orthography,* 136–38.

35. See, for example, Otto Friedrich, "Shall I Die? Shall I Fly . . .?" *Time,* 9 December 1985, 76; Joseph Lelyveld, "A Scholar's Find: Shakespearean Lyric," *New York Times,* 24 November 1985, sec. A, p. 1+; Herbert Mitgang, "Two American Experts [Robert Giroux and S. Schoenbaum] Excited by Find," *New York Times,* 24 November 1985, sec. A, p. 40; Gary Taylor, "Shakespeare's New Poem," *New York Times Book Review,* 15 December 1985, 11–14; Jo Thomas, "Critics Say Newly Found Poem Isn't Shakespeare," *New York Times,* 6 December 1985 sec. C, p. 36; and Stanley Wells, "Shall I Die?" *TLS,* 10 January 1986, 37. "Shall I Die" is included with Shakespeare's "Various Poems" in William Shakespeare, *The Complete Works,* ed. Stanley Wells and Gary Taylor (Oxford: Oxford University Press, 1986), 883.

36. Schoenbaum, *Shakespeare's Lives,* 71.

37. Ibid., viii–ix.

38. Schoenbaum, "Avoiding Disaster," in *Internal Evidence,* 145–219; and Fogel, "Salmons in Both," in Erdman and Fogel, *Evidence for Authorship,* 69–101.

39. A "computerized library" of Renaissance texts in a machine-readable format would prove invaluable to literary scholarship. I suspect that the day is coming when virtually all surviving Renaissance texts will be available on computer banks as they are today on microfilm, so that any scholar with a terminal and modem may consult them. When that day comes, I hope it will be found that my margin of error has been negligible. In the meantime, nothing could persuade me to undertake another study that would require the same manual labors as were performed for this study.

40. Thomas Merriam, "Computer Finds 'New' Play by Shakespeare," *Observer,* 6 July 1980; and "The Authorship of *Sir Thomas More,*" *Bulletin of the Association for Literary and Linguistic Computing* 10 (1982): 1–7.

41. M. W. A. Smith, "Stylometry: The Authorship of *A Lover's Complaint,*" *Shakespeare Newsletter* 34 (1984): 27–37.

42. For a report of these and other computer-assisted studies (some more successful than others), see the annual index of the *Shakespeare Newsletter.* Editor Lewis Marder for the past twenty years has carefully tracked the development of computers in literary studies. His useful abstracts and bibliographies are too numerous for a detailed listing here.

43. Fogel, "Salmons," 99.

44. But see Karl P. Wentersdorf, "The Authorship of *Edward III*" (Ph.D. diss., University of Cincinnati, 1960; Ann Arbor: University Microfilms Int.); with bibliography. Also Hart, "The Vocabulary of *Edward III,*" in *Shakespeare and the Homilies,* 219–41.

45. Only the first fourteen poems are ascribed by Jaggard to William Shakespeare. The appended *Sonnets to Sundry Notes of Music* is unambiguously presented as a miscellany of poems by sundry other poets. The continuous numbers 1–20 are the misleading addition of later editors.

46. S. T. Coleridge, "Intercepted Correspondence," *Morning Post,* 3 February 1800; reprinted in *The Collected Works of Samuel Taylor Coleridge,* eds. Lewis Patton and Peter Mann (London: Routledge and Kegan Paul, 1978), 3.1.147. Coleridge's comments were brought to my attention by David Erdman in "The Signature of Style," *Evidence for Authorship,* 45.

Appendixes and Bibliographies

Appendix A
W. S., 1570–1630

THE ensuing bibliography lists all works of poetry and prose by writers with the initials W. S., printed in the years 1570–1630 (excluding only William Shakespeare, for whom a similar list is readily available in the *STC*, and William Strachey, whose works are listed in Appendix B). It includes also, for the same sixty-year period, various manuscript verses in the Huntington, Bodleian, and British Libraries which are ascribed to persons with the initials "W. S." (excluding William Strode, whose poetry has been collected and edited by Bertram Dobell, q.v.). The resulting bibliography is comprised mostly of sermons, devotional tracts, and religious polemics; it includes also two almanacs, four plays, a few newssheets and historical pamphlets, very little poetry. There were, during these years, surprisingly few English poets with the initials "W. S."— these being Shakespeare, Strachey, Slatyer, William Segar, Wentworth Smith, and the W. Smith (possibly Wentworth) who in 1613 wrote a play called *The Hector of Germany;* William Smith, a pastoral poet last heard of in 1596; the Reverend William Swaddon, who in 1619 composed a Latin epitaph for Queen Anne; and the authors of a few scattered prefatory verses, most of which are in Latin.

Swaddon is of little interest here. He was born in Wiltshire in 1562, entered Oxford prior to William Peter's birth, and was already canon of Lincoln by the time Peter was admitted to Exeter College in 1599. When Peter died in 1612, Swaddon was archdeacon of Worcester. In 1619 he wrote a Latin epitaph for Queen Anne (his only known poetry), since he was chaplain to the queen at the time of her death. He cannot be linked to the Peter elegy.

Sir William Segar deserves note, at least in passing. *The Blazon of Papistes* (1587), his only volume of poetry, consists of eleven single-stanza poems. The volume begins with "A Poem Aenigmaticall vppon the Letter *P*":

The letter *P* is most accurst, I trow,	P (the Pope)
Of all the letters in the Christ-cross row,	the Christ-cross
For that it setteth (as it plain appears)	row (Christendom);

The Christ-cross row together by the ears: the letters (particular
The reason is, this most proud letter, *P*, signatories, estates,
Could be above both *A, B, C*, and *D*, and degrees);
And would proceed before *E, F*, and *G*, Q (the Queen);
H, J, K, L, M, N, O, worthy *Q*, R (religion); S (state)
Seeking the spoil of *R, S, T*, and U. T (truth); U (your majesty)

Six years following, in a popular verse-anthology called *The Phoenix Nest* (1593), there appeared a fifteen-line poem, in two stanzas of uneven meter, by one who signs himself "W. S. gent.":

"A Notable Description of the World"

Of thick and thin, light, heavy, dark and clear,   Mixtures
White, black, and blue, red, green, and purple dye,   Colours
Gold, silver, brass, lead, iron, tin, and copper,   Metals
Moist air, hot fire, cold water, earth full dry,   Elements
Blood, choler, phlegm, and melancholy by,   Complexions
A mixed mass, a chaos all confus'd: Chaos
Such was the world, till God division us'd.

In framing heaven and earth, God did divide
The first day's light, and dark'th to night and day.   1
The second, he a firmament applied.   2
Third, fruitful earth appear'd, seas took their way.   3
Fourth, sun and moon, with stars in skies he fix'd.   4
Fift, fish and foul, the sea and land possess'd   5
And God made man, like to himself, the sixt.   6
The seventh day, when all things he had blest,   7
He hallow'd that, and therein took his rest.

W. S. gent.

It is not known who wrote this poem. It has been ascribed by some to William Smith for no apparent reason but that the initials fit (it is not even known that Smith was a "gent." as is indicated here). If we had to choose, it seems far more likely that "A Notable Description" was written by Segar. In addition to the unusual marginal notations for both poems, nine of the eleven stanzas in Segar's *Blazon of Papistes* are in rime royal, as is the first stanza here. The *A, B, C, D, E, F*, and *G* syntax is characteristic of Segar, as is the emphasis on order and degree. Though Segar was knighted in 1616, he was only a "gent." in 1593, and he is likely to have known several others who contributed to *The Phoenix Nest,* including Raleigh, Roydon, and Sir Edward Dyer. But whether or not Segar wrote this poem, none of his few surviving verses suggests that he may have written the

Funeral Elegy; nor is it possible to establish any link between Segar and the Peter family.

In 1596 there appeared a volume of pastoral poetry by William Smith, entitled *Chloris, or the Complaint of the Passionate Despised Shepheard.* Though we know virtually nothing of Smith, some scant information can be gleaned from his two surviving volumes of poetry. From *Chloris,* we learn that Smith considered Edmund Spenser a "deere and most entire beloved" mentor; that he was a fairly young man hoping to embark on a career as a writer; and that *Chloris* was an early step toward that end. Smith's other volume is a collection of nine brief poems totaling sixty-four lines. *A Newyeares Guifte: Made upon Certen Flowers* (British Museum MS. Additional 35,186) was never published, but was presented in manuscript to Mary, countess of Pembroke, the sister of Sir Philip Sidney. Smith styles himself her dutiful, zealous, and devoted servant. He mentions in passing that he owns no land, and is therefore not likely to have been a man of rank. After 1596, nothing more is heard of him. If we suppose that he was still alive in 1612, and that his muse underwent a great transformation in the intervening years, it is possible to nominate him as a remote candidate for authorship of the Peter elegy, but such a conclusion would have to rest entirely upon conjecture, as there is little evidence of any kind to support it.

In 1597, in the prefatory matter to Nicholas Breton's *The Will of Wit,* there appeared a poem signed "W. S.," but the signature is suspect since this eulogy by "W. S." is written in Breton's usual manner. Breton is known to have used pseudonymous initials more often than any other English writer of the age, and he was not above praising himself and his work in print. Unless these commendatory verses are the work of a mimic, it seems likely that they were composed, disingenuously, by Breton himself.[1]

In 1598 Robert Barret published his *Theorike and Practike of Modern Warres,* a volume dedicated to the earl of Pembroke. Barret was a retired soldier who had spent much of his life on the continent in the service of the French, Dutch, Italians, and Spanish. In the front matter of his book is a commendatory poem of twelve lines, written by a friend who signs himself "William Sa., gentleman." Also in 1598 (though erroneously dated 1589), in Edinburgh, the Reverend James Melville published his *Spirituall Propine of a Pastour to His People.* The volume contains poems by various Scotsmen, all of whom, as it appears, were members of Melville's congregation. Among them are two poems in Scots dialect by a certain "M. W. S." (i.e., Master W. S.). Yet neither "William Sa., gent." nor "M. W. S." has any apparent links with the W. S. who wrote the *Funeral Elegy* for William Peter fourteen years later, nor does their verse have much in common with that of Peter's elegist.

Two entire plays were originally published as having been written "by
W. S.," and a third supposed to have been either written or edited by a
"W. S.," for which the authors have not been positively identified. *The
Lamentable Tragedy of Locrine* is an Elizabethan academic tragedy of the
sort then in vogue at the Inns of Court. It was published in 1595, "Newly
set foorth, ouerseene and corrected, By W. S." We are apparently meant
to credit W. S., not with original authorship, but only with the editing of
the text: "to set forth" was reserved, in Elizabethan parlance, for the act of
editing and publication. The text of *Locrine* as it has come down to us is
thought by many to be the work of at least two writers (often identified as
George Peele and Robert Greene); and there are substantial borrowings,
especially in the first half of the play, from Spenser and Lodge. It has not
yet been demonstrated, however, that the initials W. S. for editor or author
are incorrect. There is, at least, no reason to suppose that "W. S." was
intended, or in fact taken by anyone, to refer to William Shakespeare,
whose name and initials were omitted even from his own dramatic works
until 1598. One possibility not yet explored is that *Locrine* was revised and
edited by William Smith, as there are peculiarities of style shared by this
play and *Chloris*. It is of interest also (though one can hardly draw any firm
conclusion), that there was an actor named William Smith (or "Smyght"),
mentioned in Philip Henslowe's account book for the year 1595–96 (after
which nothing more is heard of him). Smith was apparently connected
with the Queen's Men, the company that acted *Locrine* until breaking up
in May of 1594, and he is the only person with these initials, apart from
Shakespeare, known to have been connected with any theatrical company
during these years. We have, however, no external evidence to link this
actor with the William Smith who wrote *Chloris*.[2]

Seven years later William Jones published *The True Chronicle Historie
of the Whole Life and Death of Thomas Lord Cromwell* (printed by
Richard Read, 1602); and in 1607 George Eld published *The Puritaine, or
the Widdow of Watling-Streete*. Both plays were reputedly "Written by
W. S.," though neither can be Shakespeare's. It has been proven to the
satisfaction of many scholars that *The Puritaine* is principally, if not
entirely, the work of Thomas Middleton.[3] How the Quarto came then to
bear the initials "W. S." must remain a mystery. As noted by David Lake,
it seems quite unlikely that George Eld, whose attributions are depend-
able elsewhere, would deliberately falsify the authorship of this particular
play.[4] One possibility is that William Strachey sold the manuscript to Eld,
representing it as his own work. Though a devout Christian, Strachey's
moral scruples did not extend so far as to guard the rights of other authors;
in 1604 he knowingly supported Francis Michell in the purloining of
Francis Dallington's *View of Fraunce*. It was in the summer of 1607 that
Strachey returned to London in dire financial straits from his sojourn in

Constantinople; and since *The Puritaine* was acted by the Children of St. Paul's, in which Strachey was a principal shareholder, he must have had access to the script. It is possible, too, though perhaps less likely, that Strachey brought *Cromwell* to the press as the work of W. S. in 1602.

About the authorship of *Cromwell* and *Locrine* there is little agreement. For neither has there been published a detailed and convincing attributional study, nor have I studied the problems of either text. But whoever the respective authors, no one familiar either with these two plays or with *The Puritaine* would suggest that they were written by William Shakespeare (as was supposed in the latter seventeenth century), or by the same W. S. who composed the *Elegy* for William Peter.[5]

We may turn next to W. Smith, who in 1613 helped to celebrate the marriage of Princess Elizabeth to the elector Palatine with a historical romance called *The Hector of Germany*. This play was produced, not by a professional company, but by a group of London tradesmen. It is widely believed (though in the absence of any evidence) that *The Hector of Germany* was written by Wentworth, not a William, Smith. If so, *The Hector* is his sole surviving play, though he had a hand in writing as many as twenty others (many of which were collaborations).[6] Little is known of Wentworth Smith: the parish register of St. James Garlickhithe, London, reveals that Wentworth Smith, son of William Smith, was baptized on 9 March 1571. In September of 1594 he married Agnes Gimber at the church of St. Thomas the Apostle. From 1601 to 1603 he was employed by Philip Henslowe in writing for the Admiral's Men, doing what appears to have been primarily hackwork. Though he cannot be linked to any theatrical company after 1603, he was still alive on 15 May 1607, when he wedded Mary Potman, his second wife. It seems likely that he was still living in 1612. Although he may have written *The Hector of Germany,* we have, unfortunately, no poetry or prose that is certainly his with which to compare the Peter elegy.

Another possibility, which I have not explored, is that *The Hector* was written by William Smith, Rouge Dragon. This William Smith is the author of a British Library manuscript entitled, *The XII. Worshipfull Companies, or Misteries of London* (1605). He includes in the volume some verses in ballad meter:

What worldly wealth, what glorious state, can long on earth endure,
  But death doth make an end thereof, to mortal wights most sure.
Only one thing doth flourish still, though devil do disdain,
  And that is virtue, which for aye immortal shall remain.
                                                                  W. S.

It was possibly William Smith, Rouge Dragon, and not Wentworth Smith, who wrote *The Hector* for the wedding of Princess Elizabeth; this is a matter for further study. However, it is not terribly important who wrote the play. In the words of editor L. W. Payne, "The judgment that *The Hector of Germany* is worthless is too severe"[7]—yet the play contains little to recommend itself as literature. Either way, one can hardly imagine *The Hector* to have been written by the same W. S. who eulogized William Peter only a year earlier, unless in the interim he suffered an apoplexy. Nor are there any apparent ties between William Smith, Rouge Dragon, and the Peter elegy.

The last known versifier worth mentioning here is the friend or kinsman of Captain John Smith who wrote a commendatory poem for his *Sea Grammar* in 1627. The poem is titled "In Authorem" and signed "W. S." Neither he nor Captain Smith offers us further information concerning the poem's authorship.

For none of these several poets and playwrights have I been able to establish even a tenuous link to William Peter. Perhaps another will succeed where I have failed. In any case, those who find themselves unconvinced that the *Elegy* could have been written by either Strachey or Shakespeare will find here at least a few additional candidates to entertain their fancy, together with a dozen or more authors of prose works listed in the ensuing bibliography, any one of whom might well have sat down in February of 1612 to pen a last tribute to a slain friend.

Notes

1. It is possible that Breton wished his readers to suppose these verses to have been written by William Shakespeare. If so, it provides one more illustration of how well Shakespeare's contemporaries were able to imitate him.

2. Despite the intervention of different compositors, there are unusual spellings, such as "powre" (for *pour*), and unusual rhymes, such as *one:moan,* that appear in both texts. The two works share also a great number of quite ordinary spellings that are nevertheless worth note (e.g., a double -o- in such words as "foorth," "yoong," "woorse"; and -au- for -a- in such words as "chaunge," "chaunt," "graund," "daungerous"). The syntax of both texts is marked by frequent repetition and by extensive use of parallel structure. Smith's passionate shepherd is named *Corin;* while *Corineus,* Brute's general is presented in *Locrine* as the moral center of the play (wherein his name is sometimes abbreviated *Corin.*). Both writers borrow heavily from Spenser and Lodge; both texts were printed within a few months of one another, *Locrine* late in 1595, *Chloris* in 1596; and so on. Yet there is much contrary evidence, as for example Smith's insistent spelling of "hir" for *her,* which nowhere appears in the printed text of *Locrine*.

3. David Lake, *The Canon of Thomas Middleton's Plays* (Cambridge: Cambridge University Press, 1975), 109–35. See also Baldwin Maxwell, *Studies in the Shakespeare Apocrypha* (New York, 1956), 109–37.

4. Lake, *Canon of Middleton's Plays,* 117.

5. Though for what it's worth, the phase "mourning style" appears in both the *Elegy* and in *Locrine*.

6. Another possibility is that *Cromwell* and *The Puritaine* were written in whole or in part by Wentworth Smith, and that *The Hector* was written by some other person of the same last name, since the first two are closer chronologically to the years in which Wentworth Smith is known to have flourished; it is not known, however, that he wrote for either the King's Men or the Children of Paul's at any point in his career.

7. Leonidas Warren Payne, ed., *The Hector of Germanie, or the Palsgrave Prime Elector,* by W. Smith (Philadelphia: University of Pennsylvania Press, 1906), 36.

A Checklist of Works,
1570–1630
[Excluding William Shakespeare and William Strachey]

The place of publication is given for each title; see the *STC* for subsequent editions.

STC #

3705   S., W. "Ad Lectorem, de Authore." [By Nicholas Breton? In verse.] In Nicholas Breton, *The Will of Witt, Wits Wil, or Wils Wit*. 1597. Sig. A4v.

3793   S., W. "An Advertisement to the Reader, and Especially to the Perverted Catholics." In Georges Brisset, *A Letter Apologeticall of G. Brisse*. Edinburgh, 1616. Sigs. A2r–A3v.

21533.3   S., W. *Christs Unworthy Minister*. 1607.

6999   S., W. *A Declaration of the Reasons Which Moved M. A. de Dominis, to Depart from the Romish Religion*. 1617.

22761   S., W., ed. *Foure Sermons, Preached by Maister Henrie Smith*. 1602.

21526   S., W. *A Funerall Elegye in Memory of the Late Vertuous Maister William Peter of Whipton Neere Excester*. [In verse.] 1612.

22794   S., W. "In Authorem." [In verse.] In Captain John Smith, *A Sea Grammar, with the Plaine Exposition of Smiths Accidence for Young Sea-Men, Enlarged*. 1627. Sig. A3r.

21528   S., W. *The Lamentable Tragedie of Locrine, the Eldest Sonne of King Brutus . . . Newly Set Foorth, Overseene and Corrected, By W. S.* 1595.

18904   S., W. "Newes from Sea" and perhaps also "Newes to the Universitie," unsigned, which immediately precedes it. [Possibly by William Strachey, and sometimes attributed to him, but the evidence is inconclusive.] In Sir Thomas Overbury, *Sir Thomas Overbury His Wife*. 1614. Sigs. O3r–P1r.

21516   S., W.,, gent. "A Notable Description of the World." [Probably by Sir William Segar. In verse.] In R. S., ed. [Richard Stapleton?], *The Phoenix Nest*. 1593. 77–78.

21531   S., W. *The Puritaine, or the Widdow of Watling-Streete. Acted by the Children of Paules. Written by W. S.* 1607.

17816   S., M[aster] W. "Sonnet" and "The Saules Delight." [In verse.] In James Melville, *A Spirituall Propine of a Pastour to His People*. Edinburgh, 1589 [i.e., 1598]. Sigs. B2r, H2v.

21532   S., W. *The True Chronicle Historie of . . . Thomas Lord Cromwell. As It Hath Sundrie Times Been Acted by the Right Honorable the Lord Chamberlaine His Servants. Written by W. S.* 1602.

12714   S., W. "W. S. in Commendation of the Aucthor." [By William Seymour? (q.v.). In verse.] In John Grange, *The Golden Aphroditis.* 1577. Sig. B4r.

1500   Sa., William, gentleman. "William Sa. in Praise of the Author and His Work." [Probably by William Sammes. In verse.] In Robert Barret, *The Theorike and Practike of Modern Warres.* 1598. Sig. Prelim. [a]4v.

22375   Salter, William [Guilielmus Salter, *Templ.*]. "Ad Doctissimum . . . Theologum D. D. Leonellum Sharpe" and "Idemin Obitum Il- lustrissimi, Desideratissimique Principis." [Latin verse.] In Leonell Sharpe, *Oratio Funebris in Honorem Henrici Walliæ Principi.* 1612. Sig. A2r.

17401   Sampson, William, reviser (ca. 1600–1656?). *The True Tragedy of Herod and Antipater.* By Gervase Markham. 1622.

21529   Samuel, William [W. S.]. *A New Balade or Songe, of the Lambes Feaste.* [In verse.] Includes "A New Balade" and "Another, Out of Goodwill." 1574.

508   Savage, W[illiam]. *A New Almanack and Prognostication for York.* 1611.

21830   Sclater, William, the elder (1575–1626). *A Briefe Exposition with Notes, upon the Second Epistle to the Thessalonians.* 1627.

21833   ———. *The Christians Strength.* Oxford, 1612.

21834   ———. *An Exposition with Notes upon the First Epistle to the Thes- salonians.* 1619.

21838   ———. *A Key to the Key of Scripture: or an Exposition with Notes, upon the Epistle to the Romanes: the Three First Chapters.* 1611.

21841   ———. *The Ministers Portion.* Oxford, 1612.

21842   ———. *The Quæstion of Tythes Revised.* 1612.

21843   ———. *A Sermon Preached at the Last Generall Assise Holden at Taunton.* 1616.

21845   ———. *The Sick Souls Salve.* Oxford, 1612.

21846   ———. *Three Sermons . . . Now Published by His Sonne.* 1629.

21847   ———. *A Threefold Preservative against Three Dangerous Diseases of These Latter Times.* 1610.

21874   Scot, William [anon.], minister of Cupar. *The Course of Conformities, as It Hath Proceeded, Is Concluded, Should Be Refused.* [Amster- dam], 1622.

7487   ——— [Guilielmus Scotus]. "Quas gentes poterant. . ." [Latin verse.] In *Nostodia. In Jacobi Magnæ Britanniæ Regis Felicem in . . . Congratulatio.* Edinburgh, 1617. 41.

4508   Sedley, Sir William [Guilielmus Sydleius] (1558–1612?). "Ad Lec- torem." [Latin verse.] In William Camden, *Britannia Sive Florentissimorum Regnorum.* 1607. Sig. prelim. a4r.

22162   Segar, William (d. 1633), Garter king of arms. *The Blazon of Papistes.* [1587].

22163   ——— [anon.]. *The Booke of Honor and Armes.* 1590.

3219   ———. "From Sir William Segar . . . a Special Letter to the Author." In Edmund Bolton [anon.], *The Cities Advocate.* 1629. Sig. A3r–v.

22164   ————. *Honor Military, and Civill, Contained in Four Bookes.* 1602.

12500   ————. "Lenvoy to the Author by William Segar Garter, Principall King of Armes" [and perhaps also "An Epigram Explaining the Frontispiece," immediately preceding (addressed to Guillim, unsigned)]. [In verse.] In John Guillim, *A Display of Heraldrie.* 1610. Sigs. prelim. a2r–a3r.

3220   ————. "A Letter to the Author. . ." In Edmund Bolton [E.B.], *The Elements of Armories.* 1610. Sig. prelim. a3v.

NA   ————. "R. Iacobi I Delineatio Metrica." [Latin verse.] British Library MS. 12 G.ix.8.

24756   ————. "Sir William Segar . . . Principall King of Armes His Lenvoy to the Author of This Booke." [In verse.] In Augustine Vincent, *A Discoverie of Errours in the First Edition of the Catalogue of Nobility Published by Ralph Brooke.* 1622. Sig. prelim. [a]1v.

19511   ————. "Upon the Author and His Minerva." [In verse.] In Henry Peacham, *Minerva Britanna.* 1612. Sig. B3r–v.

14927   Seymour, William (ca. 1564– ?). "W. Seymour Gentleman of Grayes Inne in Commendation of the Author." [In verse.] In Timothy Kendall, *Flowers of Epigrammes.* 1577.

14646   Sh., W. [pseud.]. *Parts One and Two of the Troublesome Raigne of John, King of England.* 1611 [repr. of anonymous text of 1591].

22270.7   Shackley, William. *To the Right Honourable Assembly of the Commons. The Humble Petition of W. Shackley [against] the Commission for Buildings.* [1621?].

22375   Sharpe, William (1563–1623?). "Guilielmus Sharpus . . . de Obitu[m] Principis." [Latin verse.] In Leonell Sharpe, *Oratio Funebris in Honorem Henrici Walliæ Principi.* 1612. Sigs. A2v–A3r.

19019   Sheldon, William [Guilielmus Sheldon, Generos., Glocestr.] (ca. 1590–1659). "Candida florentes designant Lilia terras, . . ." [Latin verse.] In *Academiæ Oxoniensis Pietas Erga Jacobum.* Oxford, 1603. 136. [In the same volume, William Peter has some Latin verses on the accession (p. 145, signed "Guilielmus Petreus, Generos., Coll. Exon.").]

11207   Shute, W., trans. *The General Historie of Venice.* By Thomas de Fougasses. 2 vols. 1612.

7373.6   ————, trans. *Holy Meditations upon Seaven Penitentiall Psalmes.* By G.D.V. [Guillaume du Vair.] 1612.

17676   ————, trans. *The Triumphs of Nassau.* By J. J. Orlers and H. de Haestens. 1613.

11163   Singleton, William (1602– ?). "To His Worthy Friend, the Author, Master John Ford." [In verse.] In John Ford, *The Lovers Melancholy.* 1629. Sig. A3r–v. [Cf. "To My True Friend, and Kinsman: Philip Massinger," in Massinger, *The Emperor of the East* (1632), sigs. A3v–A4r.]

NA   Sk., W. [Sir William Skipwith?]. "As thys y^s endelesse, endlesse be yo[u]r joye, . . ." [In verse.] In John Marston, *The Ho[nora]ble Lorde and Lady of Huntingdons Entertainment . . . att the House of Ashby.* Huntington Library MS. EL 34 B9 (ca. 1607). Inside back cover.

22633	Slatyer, William (1587–1647). *Genethliacon . . . the Pedigree of James and Charles.* [Traces the descent of the royal line back to Adam; contains also six poems in English.] 1630.
22634	———. *Palæo-Albion, or the History of Great Britaine to This Present Raigne.* [In verse; Latin verso, English translation recto; includes also commendatory verses to King James and Prince Charles.] 1630.
22635	———. *Psalmes, or Songs of Sion, Intended for Christmas Carols.* [ca. 1630].
22636	———. *Threnodia . . . Elegies and Epitaphs* [for Queen Anne]. [In verse.] 1619.
22871	Smith, W. *The Hector of Germany. Or, The Palsgrave, Prince Elector.* [Usually ascribed, though perhaps incorrectly, to Wentworth Smith (fl. 1601–3).] 1615.
22872	Smith, William [the poet] (fl. 1596). *Chloris, or the Complaint of the Passionate Despised Shepheard.* [48 sonnets and a 20-line poem entitled "Corins Dreame of the Faire Chloris".] 1596.
NA	———. *A New Yeares Guifte: Made upon Certen Flowers.* [In verse.] British Library MS. Addit. 35,186.
22872.5	Smith, William [the priest]. *Qui non Credit Condemnabitur Marc. 16, or a Discourse [on] the Trinity.* 1625.
NA	Smith, William [W. S.], Rouge Dragon. *The XII. Worshipfull Companies, or Misteries of London.* Bodleian Library MS. Top. gen. e29 (1605). [Includes verses by Smith beginning "What worldly wealth, what glorious state. . ." (fol. 65).]
22882	Smyth, William [anon.] (ca. 1545–1615), chaplain to King James. *Ad Lectorem, Gemmi Fabri.* [Latin verse.] 1598.
22880.9	———. [W. S., Doct. in Divinite]. *The Black-Smithe. A Sermon Preached at White-Hall.* 1606.
19777	Sond, William [Guil. Sond] (ca. 1590–1637). "Annagramma Ionnes Bond." [Latin verse.] In Aulus Persius Flaccus, *A. Persii Flacci Satyræ Sex.* 1614. Sig. A7v.
4192	South, Warner [Warnerus South, Jurista Novi Collegii Socius] (1586–?), Canon of Wells. "Ad Authorem." [Latin verse.] In Charles Butler, *The Feminine Monarchie, or a Treatise concerning Bees.* Oxford, 1609. Sig. prelim. a4v.
24703	———. "De Nova Hac Editione. . ." [Latin verse.] In Thomas Vicars, *Cheiragogia. Manuductio ad Artem Rhetoricam.* 3rd ed. 1628. Sig. prelim. a4v.
23026	Sparke, William (ca. 1587–1641). *The Mystery of Godlinesse.* Oxford, 1628.
19018	——— [Guilel. Sparke Magd.]. "Si (quod Flaccus ait) melius nil coelibe vita;. . ." [Latin verse.] In *Oxoniensis Academiæ Funebre Officium in Memoriam Elisabethæ Reginæ.* Oxford, 1603. 154.
3194	——— [Guilel. Sparcke]. "Sic ego Mertonæ. . ." [Latin verse.] In *Justa Funebria Ptolemæi, Thomæ Bodleii.* Oxford and London, 1613. 105–6.
23028	———. *Vis Naturæ et Virtus Vitæ Explicatæ.* [In Latin.] 1612.

17229   Squire, William, trans. *Newes from Mamora*. 1614.
23138   Stallenge, William, trans. [W. S.] (ca. 1570– ?), comptroller of the Plymouth custom house. *Instructions for the Increasing of Mulberie Trees and Breeding of Silke Wormes*. 1609.
23212   Staney, William. *A Treatise of Penance*. 1617.
13381   Stansby, William (ca. 1573–1636?), London stationer. In *The Workes of Samuel Hieron*. 2 vols. 1624. Vol. 2, sig. prelim. [a]3r–v.
13716   —— [W. S.]. "To the Reader." In Richard Hooker, *Of the Lawes of Ecclesiasticall Politie*. 2 parts. 1617–18. Part 1, sig. A6r.
23256   Stepney, William. *The Spanish Schoole-Master. Containing Seven Dialogues*. [In Spanish and English.] 1591.
11684   Stewart, William, trans. *Ane Brief Gathering of the Halie Signes*. Edinburgh, 1565.
21527   Stinnet, William [W. S.]. (ca. 1586–ca. 1650). *An Hundred Heavenly Thoughts*. 1616.
23288   Stone, William (1603?–1661?). *A Curse Become a Blessing or a Sermon Preached at the Funeral of Paull Claybrooke, Esq*. 1623.
23318   Stoughton, William [anon.]. *An Assertion for True and Christian Church-Policie*. [Middleburgh] 1604.
NA   Strode, William (1600–1645). *The Poeticall Works*. Ed. Bertram Dobell. London: Charing Cross, 1907. [In addition to the printed works (none of which was published before 1635), Dobell includes the surviving manuscript poetry, some of which is earlier than 1630.]
NA   —— [W. S.]. "Oft when I look I may descry. . ." [Verse omitted from *The Poeticall Works,* ed. Dobell.] Bodleian Library MS. Rawl. Poet. 142, fol. 15v; British Museum MS. Sloane 1446, fol. 23v.
516   Strof, W. *A New Almanack and Prognostication for Cambridge*. Cambridge, 1626.
23367   Struther, William (1587–1633), minister at Edinburgh. *Christian Observations and Resolutions. I Centurie*. Edinburgh, 1628.
23368.5   ——. *Christian Observations and Resolutions. II Centurie*. Edinburgh, 1629.
7487   ——. "Ekpurēnismos tōn Kaloiōniston Onomatōn tou Megalou Iakōbou tēs Megalēs Bretanias." [Greek verse.] In *Nostodia. In Jacobi Magnæ Britanniæ Regis Felicem in . . . Congratulatio*. Edinburgh, 1617. Sig. G2v.
23370   ——. *Scotlands Warning, or a Treatise of Fasting*. Edinburgh, 1628.
23507.5   Sutton, William, Sr. [anon.] (1608?– ?). *A Seminary Priest Put to a Non Plus*. 1629.
23510   Swaddon, William (1572– ?). *In Obitum Serenissimæ Principis Annæ, Carmen Funebre*. [Latin verse.] [1619; repr. in *STC* 4523, William Camden, *Remaines of a Greater Worke concerning Britaine* (1623)].
6220   Swayne, William. "To the Right Honorable Sir William Cecil." In William Damon, *The Former Book of the Musicke Conteining All the Tunes of Davids Psalmes*. Edited by Swayne. 1591. Sig. A4r. [Repr. in *STC* 6221, William Damon, *The Second Book of the Musick* (1591), Sig. A4r.]

23526   Sweeper, Walter (ca. 1560– ?). *A Briefe Treatise Declaring the True Noble-Man and the Base Wordling.* 1622.

23527   ———. *Israels Redemption by Christ.* 1622.

23546   Swift, William (1566–1624), minister at St. Andrews, Canterbury. *A Sermon Preached at the Funerall of Mr. Thomas Wilson, in Canterbury.* 1622.

13260   Swift, William, master of Bristol Grammar School. "In Authoris Encomion." [Latin verse.] In John Hewes, *A Perfect Survey of the English Tongue.* 1624. Sig. A3r.

22791   Symonds, William [Wilhel. Simonides] (1556–1613?), minister at St. Saviors, Southwark. "Aliud Eiusdem ad Eundem Skenæum." [Latin verse.] In Sir John Skene, *Regiam Majestatem Scotiæ.* 2 parts. Edinburgh, 1609. Sig. prelim. a5v.

22624   ———. *A Heavenly Voice. A Sermon.* 1606.

23592   ———. *Pisgah Evangelica.* 1605.

22791   ———, ed. [W. S.]. "Proceedings of the English Colony in Virginia." Part two of Captain John Smith, ed. *A Map of Virginia.* Oxford, 1612. [Repr. 1624, with Symonds named as editor. The 1612 edition includes only a brief note signed by the editor, "W. S." (p. 110); the work is sometimes ascribed incorrectly to Strachey.]

23594   ———. *Virginia. A Sermon Preached at White-Chappel.* 1609.

23595   Sympson, William. *A Full and Profitable . . . Genealogie of Jesus Christ.* 1619.

23602   Symson, William [same as above?]. *De Accentibus Hebraicus.* [1617].

25210   ———. "To the Christian Reader." In John Wemyss [Weemes], *The Christian Synagogue.* 2 parts. 1623. Part 1, sig. A2r–v.

4660   Symson, William (ca. 1560–1620). Prefatory verses. In James Carmichael, *Grammaticæ Latinæ, de Etymologia, Liber Secundus.* Cambridge, 1587. [This volume was not available to me.]

APPENDIX B
WILLIAM STRACHEY, 1572–1621

MOST of what we know concerning the life of William Strachey may be found in S. G. Culliford's biography.[1] Little is known of the poet's youth. On 14 February 1588, at the age of fifteen, he was admitted as a pensioner to Emmanuel College, Cambridge. He did not stay for a degree, but proceeded to Gray's Inn, London, where he studied sometime between 1588 and 1595. On 9 June 1595, he married Frances Forster and withdrew from London to set up housekeeping with his in-laws, in Surrey. His first son, William, was christened in March 1596, at Crowhurst, followed by at least one other, Edmund, who was baptized there in February 1604.

Strachey's first publication appeared in 1604, when he prefixed a short poem to Robert Dallington's *View of Fraunce*. Francis Michell, who as a member of Gray's Inn was an old friend of Strachey, published the book without Dallington's permission. Strachey's measure of culpability in the theft is not clear, but he at least did not hesitate to wish Michell well in the venture, and his sentiment concerning "true English gain" seems a wry jest, given the circumstances of publication:

To his Worthy Friend, Francis Michell

Such as would travel without charge or pain
    And here in England take a view of France,
Read but this book and reap true English gain,
    By others' labors. What in due observance
You find in your contentments and lov'd ease,
    Give to his worthy pains. And worthiest friend,
With your own worth your own endeavors please:
    Virtue hath always in herself her end.
        The fortune of the press, then, ne'er respect.
        Sale and profane applause, mere fools affect.

William Strachey

The "press," or impression, nevertheless met with ill fortune, for Dallington moved quickly to prevent its unauthorized sale. The remaining copies were then reissued under Dallington's own name, with new front matter and a new title.

From its reopening in 1604, Strachey was one of six partners in the boys' company of Henry Evans, called the Children of the Queen's Revels, that "eyrie of children" scornfully alluded to, a few years earlier, in *Hamlet*. As a shareholder, Strachey worked closely with Jonson, Marston, Chapman, and Day, all of whom wrote for the company, and he must certainly have known Drayton, Daniel, and the Beaumont brothers, John and Francis. It may well be that he knew Shakespeare as well. Since Richard Burbage was landlord to the Children of the Queen's Revels, and since *Sejanus* had been acted by the King's Men at the Globe in 1603, it seems virtually certain that Shakespeare and Strachey were known to one another even if they were not well acquainted.

It is worth note in this respect that Shakespeare in *Twelfth Night* (2.5.40) makes a cryptic jest about "the Lady of the Strachey" who married "the Yeoman of the Wardrobe." The Strachey woman thus alluded to has never been identified. There appears to have been no such governmental post as "Yeoman of the Wardrobe," and no branch of the Strachey family at this time was of sufficient rank to merit the comparison to Countess Olivia. Charles J. Sisson has discovered that the "tyreman" of the Blackfriars Theatre was one David Yeomans (n. 1573).[2] This seems a promising lead, yet S. G. Culliford has searched in vain for evidence of a marriage between this keeper of the wardrobe and one of the Strachey women. Finding that the "Lady" could not have been Strachey's stepmother nor any of his sisters, Culliford concludes that "the most probable guess would appear to be a maidservant."[3] If so, the jest is pointless, and too obscure to have been understood even by Shakespeare's contemporaries. Another guess, perhaps no less implausible yet far more intriguing, is that William Strachey or a younger brother, had at some time played opposite Yeomans in a well-known, and perhaps comic, female role that had ended in a stage marriage, say, between a wealthy dowager and a penniless suitor. Malvolio's words might then have provoked laughter from a theatergoing audience. No other solution yet proposed has been at all convincing, much less funny. It is perhaps doubtful that Strachey could have played a female role as late as 1600–1601 (when *Twelfth Night* was brought to the stage), for he was by that time in his late twenties—indeed, it cannot be proven that Strachey ever acted at all—but the very absurdity of such a performance might well account for its topical interest to Shakespeare's audience, as a laugh line in *Twelfth Night*.

It was probably in the fall of 1604 or spring of 1605 that Strachey wrote a prefatory sonnet for the first edition of *Sejanus*. Jonson's tragedy, first acted in 1603 by the King's Men, quickly found its way into print on account of its failure on stage. *Sejanus* was registered to Thomas Thorp on

2 November 1604, and printed sometime after 25 March following. The volume includes commendatory verses by several of Jonson's best friends, including a sonnet in which William Strachey muses on "this cedar," the fallen Sejanus:

Upon Sejanus

How high a poor man shows in low estate,
    Whose base is firm and whole frame competent,
That sees this cedar made the shrub of fate.
    Th' one's little, lasting; th' other's confluence spent.
And as the lightning comes behind the thunder
    From the torn cloud, yet first invades our sense,
So ev'ry violent fortune, that to wonder
    Hoists men aloft, is a clear evidence
Of a vaunt-curing blow the fates have given
    To his forc'd state. Swift lightning blinds his eyes
While thunder from comparison-hating heaven
    Dischargeth on his height, and there it lies.
If men will shun swoll'n fortune's ruinous blasts,
    Let them use temperance. Nothing violent lasts.

William Strachey

During the early years of King James's reign, a gentleman in difficult financial straits could seek advancement in Constantinople or Virginia. Strachey, while struggling with his creditors, tried both. Unfortunately, his position as secretary to Sir Thomas Glover, ambassador to the Grand Signior at Constantinople, lasted only a year. As detailed by Culliford, the irascible Glover became embroiled in a vicious quarrel with Henry Lello, the former ambassador. Strachey was among those dismissed from Glover's service as punishment for having consorted with the more congenial Lello.

As a final alternative, Strachey volunteered—but without a commission—for service with the Virginia Company. The New World by 1609 had come to be viewed cynically as the last resort of desperate men. The colony had yet to earn its shareholders a single penny, and was not likely to produce a profit for anyone but the Indians at any time soon. Strachey, whose two shares cost him £25, was no exception.

On 15 May 1609, a fleet of six vessels left the Thames channel for the new world. Strachey traveled aboard the flagship, *Sea Venture,* which carried about 150 passengers, together with Sir George Somers, commander of the fleet, and Sir Thomas Gates, who was to act as deputy governor of the colony until the arrival of Lord De La Warr. The voyage was uneventful until 24 July when, in Strachey's words, a dreadfull storme and hideous began to blow from out the Northeast, which swelling, and roaring as it were by fits, some houres with more violence then others, at length did beate all light from heauen. . . .[4]

Six of the vessels eventually made it to Jamestown, a few of them badly damaged and with many injured crewmen. The *Sea Venture,* however, failed to appear, and after some weeks was given up for lost. In fact, though it had been wrecked in the Bermudas, all the passengers were saved. A year later, after eventually making it to Virginia, Strachey composed a record of his experience. His lively account of the wreck of the *Sea Venture,* and frank description of the Virginia colony, comes to nearly 23,000 words. The epistle is dated 15 July 1610, and is addressed to a lady of rank in England, possibly Dame Sara Smith, wife of Sir Thomas, treasurer of the Virginia Company in London. Fifteen years later his letter was published in *Purchas His Pilgrimes* (1625).[5]

Strachey's "True Reportory of the Wracke, and Redemption of Sir Thomas Gates" was used by Shakespeare as a source for *The Tempest* in 1610. How he came to read the report in manuscript has never been established. Leslie Hotson suggests, quite plausibly, that it was through the auspices of Shakespeare's friend, Thomas Russell, who was stepfather to Sir Dudley Digges, a member of the Council.

In September 1611 Strachey left Virginia. Upon returning home, he published a volume entitled *For the Colony in Virginea Britannia. Lawes Divine, Morall and Martiall.* This was a compendium of the rigorous statutes that governed the colonists under Sir Thomas Dale. Strachey's role was that of editor. He had no apparent hand in its composition. The volume was entered in the Stationers' Register on 13 December, and printed a month later at about the time that William Peter was killed. Strachey was then dwelling in the Blackfriars district.

The printed preliminaries for Strachey's edition of the *Lawes* include a prose dedication and three sonnets. The first of these is addressed "To the right honorable, the Lords of the Councell of Virginia":

> Noblest of men, though 'tis the fashion now
>   Noblest to mix with basest, for their gain,
> Yet doth it fare far otherwise with you
>   That scorn to turn to chaos so again,
> And follow your supreme distinction still,
>   Till of most noble, you become divine
> And imitate your maker in his will
>   To have his truth in blackest nations shine.
> What had you been, had not your ancestors
>   Begun to you that make their nobles good?
> And where white Christians turn, in manners, Moors,
>   You wash Moors white with sacred Christian blood.

This wonder ye, that others nothing make.
Forth, then, great lords, for your lords' Savior's sake.

By him, all whose duty is tributary
to your Lordships, and unto so
excellent a cause.

William Strachey

The second sonnet is addressed effusively "To the Right Honorable, His Singular Good Lord, the Lord La Warr, of the Heroic and Religious Plantation in Virginia-Britannia, the Sole Personal Advancer, His Majesty's Lord Governor and Captain General":

Of all things we enjoy, the founder's worth
    Is still most pray'd for. In attempts of war
The charger's fame is ever most set forth.
    Of all things founded, true religion far
Were worthiest palm, and merits holiest meed.
    This, then, heroic lord, your glory shrines,
That y'are sole personal lord of this great deed,
    Which more by all else shunn'd, the more it shines.
Scorn then all common aims and every act
    Where every vulgar thrusts for profit on.
Nor praise, nor prize, affect like the mere fact,
    Nor any other honor build upon
        Than only this: since 'tis for Christ's dear Word,
        You shall be surnam'd, the most Christian lord.

By an unworthy follower of the
same fortune, your lordship's
servant,
        William Strachey

The third sonnet is addressed "To the Much Honored, in All Nations Acknowledged the Most Renowned Famous Factor and Professor of All Actions That Have the Warrant of Religion, Honor, or Goodness, Sir Thomas Smith, Knight, and in this Pious Plantation of Virginia Britannia, the Unremovable Cordial Friend, and Right Bounteous and Well-Chosen Treasurer":

Sir, if the traffic with all nations,
    Vent'ring your purse for profit, hath renown'd
Your noble mind with all men's commendations
    For this divine gain, it is triple crown'd—
In which you traffic not with men, but God,
    Not venturing, but surely gaining, souls:

Not only such as idleness had trod
  As low as hell and given their flesh to fowls,
In our own country, but such souls beside
  As living like the son of earth, the mole,
Have never yet heaven's saving light descried.
  More than the world he gains, that gains a soul,
    Which, but yourself though few or none esteem,
    Assures your soul a heavenly diadem.

William Strachey

Copies of the *Lawes* were distributed to various shareholders and council members, with manuscript greetings from the editor, each signed "William Strachey." Several of these have been preserved, including those copies presented to Sir Anthony Aucher, Sir William Wade, Thomas Lawson, and William Crashaw. Strachey hoped that his labors in this respect would provide him with further advancement in the company. In his printed epistle to the Council he asks permission to return to Virginia or to help in some way from England. It appears that he was granted neither request.

As the *Lawes* came off the press, Strachey's attorney stood in the Court of Common Pleas, seeking to defend him from the writ of Jasper Tien, an impatient creditor. To stave off debtors' prison, the poet rushed to complete another book, a treatise that he had originally envisioned as the first grand chronicle of Virginia—*The Historie of Travell into Virginia Britania.* He paid a professional scribe to make three copies of the text (or perhaps more, but only three have survived). The first of these (preserved now in the Princeton Library) was dedicated to Henry Percy, Earl of Northumberland, in 1612. The second (Bodleian Library, MS. Ashmole 1758) was dedicated to Sir Allen Apsley, in the same year. Neither Percy nor Apsley offered to assist him with funds for publication. Six years later Strachey tried again, addressing a third copy to Sir Francis Bacon (British Library, Sloane 1622). Once again, he was disappointed. The *Historie of Travell* was not printed until 1849, when it was resurrected by the Hakluyt Society.[6]

The Historie of Travell begins with a six-line epigraph in verse, entitled "Ecclesiae et Reipub[lica]":

Wild as they are, accept them: so were we.
To make them civil will our honor be,
And if good works be the effects of minds
Which like good angels be, let our designs,
As we are Angli, make us angels, too.
No better work can church or statesman do.

W. Str.

In Book Two of the *Historie,* Strachey provides his own verse translation of a well-known quotation from Seneca:

> That age shall come, albeit in latter times,
>   When as the sea shall ope her lock'd-up bounds
> And mighty lands appear. New heavens, new climes,
>   Shall Typhis bring to knowledge, and new grounds,
>   New worlds, display. Then shall not Thule be
> The farthest nor'west isle our eyes shall see.

The volume contains no other poetry.

In 1613 Sir Thomas Overbury was murdered, a lurid story already told many times elsewhere. It cannot be said with certainty that Strachey was ever acquainted with Overbury, yet Strachey is one of many in Jonson's circle (Jonson excepted) who honored Overbury after his death (Overbury and Jonson, former friends, became estranged after 1610). *Sir Thomas Overbury His Wife* went through six editions in less than two years. In 1616, after the news broke of Overbury's murder (though before either Somerset or his wife was tried), there appeared a seventh edition, "With addition of many new Elegies upon his untimely and much lamented death," the "new elegies" having been contributed by various friends and admirers. These commendatory verses are in two parts, the first set in memory of Overbury, the second in praise of his *Wife.* Among the poems eulogizing Overbury is the tribute by his fellow Middle Templar, John Ford, that draws upon the Peter elegy. Also included is a 66-line poem, in the form of a prayer, signed "W. S.":

Upon the Untimely Death of the Author of this Ingenious Poem,
Sir Thomas Overbury, Knight, Poisoned in the Tower

	So many moons so many times gone round
	And rose from hell and darkness underground,
	And yet till now this dark'ned deed of hell
	Not brought to light? O tardy heaven! yet tell
5	If murther lays him down to sleep with lust,
	Or no? reveal, as thou art truth, and just,
	The secrets of this unjust secure act
	And what our fears make us suspect compact
	With greater deeds of mischief, for alone
10	We think not this and do suspect yet one,
	To which compar'd, this, but a falling star,
	That, a bright firmament of fire. Thy care,
	We see, takes meaner things: It times the world,
	The signs at random through the zodiac hurl'd,
15	The stars' wild wand'rings, and the glib quick hinges
	Which turn both poles; and all the violent changes
	It over-looks which trouble th' endless course

Of the high firmament. By thy blest force
Do hoary winter frosts make forests bare
20   And straight to groves again their shades repair.
By thee doth autumn's lion's flaming mane
Ripen the fruits and the full year sustain
Her burd'ned powers. O being still the same,
Ruling so much, and under whom the frame
25   Of this vast world weigh'd, all his orbs dost guide,
Why are thy cares of men no more applied?
Or if, why seem'st thou sleeping to the good,
And guarding to the ill? as if the brood
Of best things still must chance take in command
30   And not thy providence; and her blind hand
Thy benefits erroneously disburse
Which, so let fall, ne'er fall but to the worse?
Whence so, great crimes commit the greater sort,
And boldest acts of shame blaze in the court
35   Where buffoons worship, in their rise of state,
Those filthy scarabs whom they serve, and hate.
Sure things mere backward there: honor disgrac'd,
And virtue laid, by fraud and poison, waste;
The adult'rer up like Haman, and so sainted,
40   And females' modesty (as females) painted,
Lost in all real worth. What shall we say?
Things so far out of frame as if the day
Were come wherein another Phaeton,
Stol'n into Phoebus' wain, had all mis-won
45   A clean contrary way. O powerful God,
Right all amiss and set the wonted period
Of goodness in his place again: this deed
Be usher to bring forth the mask and weed
Whereunder blacker things lie hid perhap
50   And yet have hope to make a safe escape.
Of this, make known why such an instrument
As Weston, a poor serving-man, should rent
The frame of this sad good man's life. Did he
Stand with this court-bred learned Overbury
55   In strife for an ambass'dorship? No, no,
His orb held no such light. What did he owe
The prophet malice for composing this,
This cynosura in neat poesis,
How good, and great, men ought, and all, to choose
60   A chaste, fit, noble wife? and the abuse
Of strumpets friendly shadowing in the same,
Was this his fault? Or doth there lie a flame
Yet in the embers not unrak'd, for which
He died so falsely? Heaven, we do beseech,
65   Unlock this secret and bring all to view,
That law may purge the blood, lust made untrue.

W. S.

The seventh edition contains also, among the poems commending Overbury's *Wife,* a sonnet signed "W.Str.":

To the Clean Contrary Wife

Look here, and chide those spirits which maintain
  Their empire, with so strong command in you
  That all good eyes, which do your follies view,
Pity what you, for them, must once sustain:
O from those evils which free souls disdain
  To be acquainted with (and but pursue
  Worst minds), from them (as hateful as untrue),
By reading this, for fame's fair sake, refrain.
  Who would let feed upon her birth the brood
  Of lightness, indiscretion, and the shame
  Of foul incontinence, when the base blood
  Is careless only of an honor'd name?
Be all, that gentle are, more high improv'd,
For loose dames are but flatter'd, never lov'd.

W: Stra:

Both the sonnet by "W. Stra." and the longer poem by "W. S." have been accepted without debate as the work of William Strachey. The attribution can hardly be doubted: Strachey's ties to other contributors are well established. The phrase "clean contrary," appearing in line 45 of the first poem and in the title of the second, was characteristic of Strachey, as in the *Historie* when he speaks of "that dignity and Truith which aspires to a cleane contrary Comelynes."[7] More telling is that this "W. S." subtly compares Overbury to Strachey's well-bred friend, Henry Lello, while linking Overbury's assassin, Richard Weston, with Thomas Glover, Strachey's adversary: "Make known," prays W. S.,

    why such an instrument
As Weston, a poor serving-man, should rent
The frame of this sad good man's life. Did he
Stand with this court-bred learned Overbury
In strife for an ambass'dorship? No, no,
His orb held no such light.

(51–56)

The prosody, diction, syntax, and general manner are in perfect keeping with Strachey's other work. It is therefore doubtful that the attribution will ever be challenged, though it cannot, of course, be proven that Strachey had a hand in either.

The last known poem by Strachey was written, it appears, just before he died in 1621. These lines, preserved in the Bodleian Library (MS. Ashmole 781, fol. 135), are indexed by the scribe as "Mr Strachies Harke," and described as "Penitential Verses by W. Strachie just before his untimely death":

> Hark! 'Twas the trump of death that blew!
> My hour is come. False world, adieu,
> That I to death untimely go.
> Thy pleasures have betray'd me so,
> For death's the punishment of sin,
> And of all creatures I have been
> The most ungrateful wicked one
> That e'er the heavens did shine upon.
>
> Hark! I have sinn'd against earth and heaven,
> Early by date, late in the even;
> All manner sins, all manner ways,
> I have committed in my days.
> Hell and hell-fire is my due.
> O, but dear Christ, I humbly sue
> Thy blood may wash my red soul white.
> Mercy, not judgment, is thy delight.
>
> Hark! —at which mercy gate I knock.
> Let sobs and sighs the same unlock.
> Prostrate I fall, and beg for grace.
> O, do not turn away thy face!
> My crying sins beat at thy throne.
> Once bow the heavens, look down upon
> A wretch more overthrown than grief,
> That begs for mercy, not for life.

Finis

W. Strachey

On 21 June 1621, William Strachey was buried in the Parish church of St. Giles, at Camberwell.

The ten poems reprinted here, and the prose volumes as mentioned, are the only known works by Strachey. It seems unlikely that he is responsible for either *Thomas, Lord Cromwell* ("Written by W. S.," 1602) or *The Puritaine* (also "By W. S.," 1607). These two plays have much in common with one another, yet neither invites comparison with Strachey's work elsewhere.

Lastly, the Alderman Library of the University of Virginia owns a manuscript that has been catalogued as "William Strachey's Commonplace Book." The pages of this notebook are lettered from *A* to *Z*, with notations, in a seventeenth-century hand, on *Adam, Admonitions, Affliction, Africa, America,* and so through the alphabet. The volume has since been scribbled over with shorthand notes of a literature student in the early twentieth century. Several scholars mention this manuscript, and Culliford quotes from it. Yet it is clear that William Strachey the poet had nothing to do with "William Strachey's Commonplace Book." All or most of the seventeenth-century entries are from the 1650s, as is clear from frequent references to books first published as late as 1658. William Strachey the poet died in 1621. This William Strachey was apparently a student at Oxford University: he had access to the Bodleian Library and demonstrates a fair command of Latin (though no one of this name is known to have attended Oxford during the seventeenth century). He demonstrates an interest in the colonial enterprise, which is perhaps where the confusion arose. He was perhaps the son or grandson of the poet. The manuscript is, however, virtually worthless as an historical or literary document.

Critical Reputation

William Strachey today is known to historians chiefly for the role he played in colonizing Virginia, and to literary scholars for his "True Reportory," from which Shakespeare borrowed for *The Tempest.* As a poet he has been given short shrift, even by his biographer, S. G. Culliford. Six of the extant poems, Culliford mentions only in passing, and those few that he reprints are poorly edited. Yet Culliford accurately sums up the prevailing view of Strachey's poetry:

> Competently written, but no more, these occasional verses of Strachey's
> . . . reflect only the most commonplace of contemporary ideas: that
> virtue is its own reward; that moderation is good in all things; or that the
> spreading of the Gospel is a noble task. . . . Even the penitential verses,
> alone striking a personal note, read rather as a poetical exercise than the
> expression of a genuine and profound repentance. Once more the ideas
> are conventional in the extreme.[8]

Scholars treating of Strachey's verse are unanimous in dismissing him, somewhat too severely, as a poet of little talent and no originality.[9] Charles Sanders writes that Strachey's verses in *A View of Fraunce* and *Sejanus* "have no great poetic merit" but merely reflect "the gentleman-adventurer's affinity for poetry"; the tribute to Overbury is "highly cryptic," while his lines "To the Clean Contrary Wife" are "a cramped, awkward sonnet not much better or worse than the known efforts of William Strachey to write poetry." John St. Loe Strachey describes the *Sejanus* sonnet, curiously, as "one of the most cryptic things in English literature"; Culliford calls it merely "conventional." Wright and Freund describe Strachey's "Wife" in passing as a "moralistic sonnet" which is characteristic of his "moralizing piety." A. C. Gordon, in the *Dictionary of American Biography,* concludes that Strachey's verse was "second-rate . . . to judge from his surviving specimens."[10]

Only his friend, Thomas Campion, has praised Strachey's verse in print. In an epigram of uncertain date, titled "Ad Gulielmum Strachaeum" (published in 1619), Campion speaks of the "elegant little verses" penned by this "uncommon worshipper of the Muses":

Paucos jam veteri meo sodali
Versus ludere, musa, ne graveris,
Te nec taedeat his adesse nugis:
Semper nam mihi charus ille comptis
Gaudet versiculis facitque multos,
Summus Pieridum unicusq' cultor.
Hoc ergo breue, musa, solue carmen
Strachaeo veteri meo sodali.[11]

Strachey's verse has been too facilely dismissed. In addition to Campion's testimony, we have the indirect appraisal of William Shakespeare, who recalled Strachey's *Sejanus* sonnet when writing *King Lear.* As a prose stylist Strachey surpasses most writers of the age, and his surviving poems may compare favorably with commendatory verses by any other minor Jacobean poet. If Strachey is to be rejected as a candidate for authorship of the Peter elegy, it must be on other grounds that insufficient ability or lack of originality, measures which (in any case) are too subjective to tell us anything.

Notes

1. S. G. Culliford, *William Strachey, 1572–1621* (Charlottesville: University Press of Virginia, 1965). Except for the poetry and as otherwise noted, Culliford is my principle source for the ensuing biographical sketch. The poems are reproduced from the original texts, but orthography has been normalized.
2. Charles J. Sisson, *New Readings in Shakespeare* (London: Dawsons, 1956), 188–90.
3. Culliford, *Strachey,* 56.
4. William Strachey, "A True Reportory," in Samuel Purchas, *Purchas His Pilgrimes* (London, 1625), 1735.
5. Ibid., 1734–58.
6. The three surviving texts are described in detail by Wright and Freund, eds., *Historie of Travell* (1967), xiii–xvii.
7. Strachey, *Historie of Travell* (1967), 9.
8. Culliford, *Strachey,* 144–45.

9. For a just and thoughtful appraisal of Strachey's prose, see Howard Mumford Jones, *The Literature of Virginia in the Seventeenth Century* (Charlottesville: University Press of Virginia, 1968), 57–65.

10. Charles Richard Sanders, "William Strachey, the Virginia Colony, and Shakespeare," in *The Strachey Family, 1588–1932* (New York: Greenwood Press, 1968), 13, 16, 15; John St. Loe Strachey, *The Adventure of Living* (London, 1922), 27; Culliford, *Strachey,* 47; Freund and Wright, *Historie of Travell* (1967), xxix; A. C. Gordon, "William Strachey," *Dictionary of American Biography* (New York: Scribner's, 1927), 9.120.

11. Thomas Campion, *Epigrammatum Libri II. Umbra. Elegiarum Liber Unus.* (London, 1619), 1.224. In English, "Do not deny me, O Muse, the sport of a few verses for my old companion, nor let it pain you to enter into these trifles. For this man ever dear to me takes pleasure in elegant little verses and fashions many himself, a high and uncommon worshiper of the muses. Release then, O Muse, this brief song for my old companion Strachey." [Translation by Michael O'Connell.]

A Checklist of Strachey's Works

STC #

18904   S., W. "Newes from Sea." In Thomas Overbury, *Sir Thomas Overbury His Wife*. London, 1606. 237–39. Possibly by Strachey, and sometimes attributed to him, but the evidence is inconclusive. "Newes to the Universitie" (unsigned), which immediately precedes it (235–37), may be Strachey's as well.

23350   Strachey, W[illiam, ed.] *For the Colony in Virginea Britannia, Lawes Divine, Morall and Martiall*. London, 1612. Includes dedicatory verses "To . . . the Lords of the Councell of Virginia," "To the Right Honourable . . . Lord La Warr," and "To . . . Sir Thomas Smith" (sigs. A1r–A2v); with a prose dedication to the Council of Virginia (sigs. A3r–A4v). Surviving copies are variously dedicated in the poet's own hand to Thomas Lawson (Huntington Library copy), and to William Crashaw, Sir Anthony Aucher, and Sir William Wade (in copies owned by the British Museum).

NL   —————— [W. Strachie]. "Harke." Bodleian Library MS. Ashmole 781, fol. 135; Eng. poet. e.57, fol. 13.

NL   ——————. *The Historie of Travell into Virginia Britania*. The Percy MS [with a prose dedication to Henry Percy, earl of Northumberland]. Princeton Univ. Library. Edited by Louis B. Wright and Virginia Freund. 1953. Reprint. Nendeln, Liechtenstein: Kraus, 1967.

NL   ——————. [Another copy.] Bodleian Library MS. Ashmole 1758 [with a prose dedication to Sir Allen Apsley]. The dedication to Apsley is printed in Alexander Brown, ed., *The Genesis of the United States*. 2 vols. New York: Houghton Mifflin [1890]. 2.562–65.

NL   ——————. [Another copy]. British Library MS. Sloane 1622 [with a prose dedication to Sir Francis Bacon]. Edited by R. H. Major. London, 1849.

6202.   —————— "To his Worthy Friend Fraunces Michel." In Sir Robert Dallington, *The View of Fraunce* [anon.]. London, 1604. Sig. A2r.

20509   ——————. "A True Reportory of the Wracke, and Redemption of Sir Thomas Gates, Knight." Written in 1610; read in MS by William Shakespeare, who used it as a source for *The Tempest;* first published in Samuel Purchas, *Purchas His Pilgrimes. Microcosmus, or the Historie of Man*. London, 1625, 1734–58.

14782   ——————. "Upon Sejanus." In Ben Jonson, *Sejanus*. London, 1605. Sig. A3r.

18911   ——————. "Upon the Untimely Death of the Author of This Ingenious Poem, Sir Tho: Overbury, Knight, Poysoned in the Towre" [by "W. S."] (pre. 6r–7r) and "To the Cleane Contrary Wife" [by "W. Stra."] (pre. 14v). In Sir Thomas Overbury, *Sir Thomas Overbury His Wife . . . the Ninth Edition Augmented*. London, 1616.

Strachey may also have written "Newes to the Universitie," and "Newes from Sea" [by "W. S."], qq.v., in the same volume.

NL   ———. Letters to Peter Ferryman and to "Sir." In S. G. Culliford, *William Strachey, 1572–1621*. Charlottesville: University Press of Virginia, 1965. 94, 133.

APPENDIX C
THE ENGLISH ELEGY, 1570–1630

THE unusual sophistication of W. S.'s *Funeral Elegy* for William Peter will be obvious to those few scholars familiar with the bulk of Jacobean poetry. Other readers, however—whose acquaintance with the period may not extend beyond such names as Shakespeare, Donne, Tourneur, and Webster—may harbor an illusion that W. S.'s verse is typical for the period. An afternoon's reading from the ensuing bibliography will quickly dispel such a mistaken notion. Most contemporaneous memorial verse is crudely mechanical, a succession of hyperboles strung together in lumpish verse. The worst is given almost entirely to worn-out cliches and fresh absurdities. Few elegies of the age do more than to register the author's grief and the subject's virtue, while holding out a promise of eternal life in heaven. We find often a certain depth of feeling, but that alone is not enough to rescue such verse from a dusty oblivion.

There are, of course, exceptions. Donne's verse requires no defense, though one can hardly imagine two memorial poems more dissimilar than the Peter elegy and Donne's *Second Anniversary,* written within a few months of one another. Many of the shorter Jacobean elegies will likewise bear repeated reading—Jonson's well-known poem on Shakespeare is a fine example—as will a few of the longer works, such as the anonymous sonnet sequence *Great Brittans Mourning Garment* (possibly by George Sandys), or Sir Arthur Gorges's *Olympian Catastrophe;* while Daniel's memorial to the earl of Devonshire, and the tributes to Prince Henry by Tourneur, Webster, and Heywood are competent efforts. Among the Elizabethan elegies, Spenser's *Daphnaida* and "Astrophel" have found defenders (though it is well that Spenser's reputation does not rest on them), as have the other poems on the death of Sidney in *Colin Clouts Come Home Againe;* and even in the worst of the poems one sometimes finds a stunning line or effective image that lingers in the memory. If this seems a slim yield from a bibliography containing 82,000 lines of verse, it is good to bear in mind that English poetry in 1612 was still in short pants. It had been just fifty-five years since Tottel's *Miscellany,* twenty-two since *The Faerie Queene,* twelve since *Hamlet.* John Milton, at the time, was three years old. Aspiring Jacobean poets simply did not have a great number of English models to draw upon, especially when writing elegiac verse.

W. S.'s *Funeral Elegy,* if written by Shakespeare, is admittedly disappointing. The poem lacks the dramatic power of the great tragedies and romances, and is certainly less interesting poetically than Shakespeare's *Sonnets.* Nonetheless, as an elegiac poet W. S. has few competitors for the laurel. John Donne is perhaps the only contemporary who can boast to have surpassed W. S.'s achievement in an elegiac poem of more than two hundred lines. The verse of W. S. seems almost effortless beside the funereal labors of such noted poets as George Chapman, John Davies, or Thomas Heywood, and beyond comparison with the doggerel of such hacks as George Wither and Josuah Sylvester. With the possible exception of Shakespeare and one or two others, W. S.'s *Elegy* would add to the reputation of any Jacobean poet able to claim it as his own. Even where this poet shares certain concerns and generic conventions of the age, he does so with more originality and grace than most other Jacobean poets (including those who had been writing verse for more than twenty years). Yet the *Funeral Elegy* was written upon remarkably short notice. We may perhaps sympathize with the poet's expression of distaste for "exercise in this kind"; funeral elegies, after all, despite a few well-known exceptions, have never been an especially cherished genre. W S.'s tribute to William Peter is, nevertheless, an unusually fine elegiac poem, among the finest that the English Renaissance has to offer. If it is by Shakespeare, we might have hoped for better; but it is clear from the poems in the ensuing checklist that we could not have hoped for better from very many of his contemporaries.

A Checklist of English Memorial Verse, 1570–1630

Only verses in English are listed. Works first published after 1630 are omitted, even if written much earlier. Items in the 1610–13 Cross-Sample are marked with an asterisk before the author's name. Except as noted otherwise, the place of publication is London for all titles listed; and those works that appear to have been privately printed are marked with "/p" after the date. Original orthography in *u/v* and *i/j* has been normalized except where these letters appear as proper initials.

Anthologies are cross-indexed only for those poems that I have mentioned in the text. Except as noted otherwise, first publication only is given for each title. See the *STC* for subsequent editions.

STC#

12929   Anon. *The Crie of the Poore for the Death of the Earle of Huntington.* 1596. [96 ll.].

23224.5   Anon. *An Epitaph upon . . . Sir Edward Stanhope.* 1607 [i.e., 1608]/p. [48 ll.].

14423.3   Anon. *A Funeral Elegie upon the Lamentable Losse of Our Late King.* [1625]. [120 ll.].

13158   *Anon. *Great Brittans Mourning Garment [for] Prince Henry.* 1612. Includes "Great Brittans Mourning Garment" [sonnet sequence, 266 ll.] and "To the Sad Household of Prince Henry" [36 ll.].

5619   Anon. "His Epitaphs" [22 ll.]. In *The Funerall Obsequies and Buriall of Conchini Marshall d'Ancre.* 1617.

6791   Anon. *A Lamentable Dittie Composed upon the Death of Robert Lord Devereaux.* 1603. [200 ll.].

6792.3   Anon. *A Lamentable New Ballad upon the Earle of Essex Death.* [1620]. [96 ll.].

21224   Anon. *A Living Remembrance of Master Robert Rogers, Marchant Adventurer.* [1601]. [48 ll.].

14426.3   Anon. *Mirth in Mourning: or, Joyes Conquest of Sorrow.* [1625]. [116 ll.].

7589   Anon. *A Mourneful Ditty Entituled Elizabeths Losse.* [1603]. [100 ll.].

15645   Anon. *A Mornfull Dittie on the Death of Certaine Judges* [by William Painter?]. 1590 [88 ll.].

21456.5   Anon. *The Poor Peoples Complaint, Bewailing the Death of . . . the Worthy Earle of Bedford* [i.e., Francis Russell, d. 1586]. [ca. 1600?] /p. [110 ll.].

7594   Anon. *The Poores Lamentation for . . . Elizabeth.* 1603. [300 ll.].

13142   *Anon. *Three Precious Teares of Blood [for] Henry the Great* [doubtfully ascribed in the *STC* to Richard Niccols]. Edited by Jean Loiseau de Tourval. 1611. In three parts: "The First Teare" [48 ll.], "The Second Teare," [150 ll.], "The Third Teare" [90 ll.].

7604   Anon. *Tumulus Elizabethæ Reginæ Angliæ* [1610?]. [8 ll.].

22.7   Abbey, R. *An Elegie upon the Most Deplorable Death of Prince Henry
            . . . of Bohemia.* 1629. [128 ll.].

339   *Alexander, William (1567–1640). *An Elegie on the Death of Prince
            Henry.* Edinburgh, 1612. Two poems: "An Elegie on the Death of
            Prince Henrie" [116. ll.] and "To His Majesty" [10. ll.].

384   *[Allyn, Robert]. *Funerall Elegies upon . . . Henry, Prince of Wales.*
            1613. Eight poems: "Ebbe channels roare. . . ." [178 ll.], "In
            Effigiem Principis" [68 ll.], "Epitaphium" [6 ll.], "To the Kings
            Most Excellent Majestie" [20 ll.], "To the Queenes Majestie" [44
            ll.], "To Prince Charles" [18 ll.], "To the Lady Elizabeth" [16 ll.],
            and "To the Prince Palatine" [20 ll.].

991   Awdely, John (1559–77). *An Epitaph upon the Death of Master
            Fraunces Benison.* 1570. [76 ll.].

1057   B., R. *An Epitaph upon the Death of Master Benedict Spinola,
            Merchant.* [1580]/p. [88 ll.].

1546   *Basse, William (ca. 1583–1653?). *Great Brittaines Sunnes-Set Be-
            wailed, with a Shower of Teares.* Oxford, 1613. [170 ll.].

18911   *[Beaumont, Francis] (1584–1616). "An Elegie [for] Lady Rutland [d.
            1612]" [116 ll.]. In Sir Thomas Overbury, *Sir Thomas Overbury His
            Wife. With Addition of Many New Elegies upon His Untimely
            Death. The Ninth Edition Augmented,* q.v. 1616.

B1602   *————. "A Funeral Elegy on the Death of the Lady Penelope
            Clifton." *Poems.* 2d ed. 1653. [64 ll.].

1694   Beaumont, Sir John (1582?–1628). *Bosworth-Field: With a Taste of the
            Variety of Other Poems.* 1629. Includes epitaphs by Beaumont for
            King James [148 ll.], the Earl of Coventry [26 ll.], Elizabeth Nevill
            [14 ll.], the Marquess of Winchester [100 ll.], Sir William Skipworth
            [14 ll.], Francis Beaumont [10 ll.], Gervase Beaumont [20 ll.], Lord
            Chandos [42 ll.], Edward Stafford [32 ll.], Ferdinando Pulton [38 ll.],
            Lady Clifton [98 ll.], and two for Henry Wriothesley, earl of South-
            ampton [82 ll., 14 ll.]. Includes also memorial tributes to the poet
            himself by John Beaumont, Jr. (ca. 1612–44) [44 ll.], Ia. Cl. [James
            Cleland]? [22 ll.], Mi[chaell] Drayton [30 ll.], Thomas Hawkins (ca.
            1591–1640) [66 ll.], and Thomas Nevill (1605–28) [28 ll.].

1814   Bell, Thomas. "The Elogie of the Author [for] His Late Soveraigne"
            [60 ll.]. In *The Anatomie of Popish Tyrannie.* 1603.

3413   Bourman, Nicholas (ca. 1546–?). *An Epytaph of . . . Sir William
            Garrat.* 1571. [60 ll.].

3414   ————. *An Epytaphe upon . . . J. Juell, Bishop of Sarisburie.* 1571.
            [45 ll.].

3415   ———— [N. B.]. *An Epitaph upon . . . Lady Mary Ramsey.* 1602. Two
            poems: "An Epitaph. . . ." [120 ll.] and "In Obitum. . . ." [24 ll.].

3578   Brathwait, Richard. "Upon the Illustrate Prince Henry, the Authors
            Long Meditated Tears" [90 ll.]. In *The Poets Willowe: or the Pas-
            sionate Shepheard.* By Brathwait. 1614.

3633   Breton, Nicholas (1545?–1626?) [N. B.]. *Brittons Bowre of Delights.*
            1591. Includes "Amoris Lachrimæ . . . [for Sir Philip Sidney]" [366
            ll.] and "An Epitaph on the Death of a Noble Gentleman" [86 ll.].

3817   Broke, Thomas, the younger (ca. 1533–?) [T. Bro.]. *An Epitaph Declaryng the Life and End of Dom. Edmond Boner.* [1570]/p. [212 ll.].

3831   *Brooke, Christopher (?–1628). "A Funerall Elegie on the Prince" [400 ll.]. In *Two Elegies, Consecrated to the Never Dying Memorie of . . . Henry, Prince of Wales,* 1613. Includes also William Browne, "An Elegie on . . . Henry Prince of Wales," q.v.

18911   ——— [C. B.]. "To the Memory of . . . Sir Thomas Overburie" [50 ll.]. In Sir Thomas Overbury, *Sir Thomas Overbury His Wife. With Addition of Many New Elegies upon His Untimely Death. The Ninth Edition Augmented,* q.v. 1616.

3831   *Browne, William (1591–1643?) [W. B.]. "An Elegie on . . . Henry Prince of Wales" [144 ll.]. In Christopher Brooke, *Two Elegies Consecrated to the Memorie of Henry Prince of Wales.* 1613. Includes also Christopher Brooke, "A Funerall Elegie on the Prince," q.v.

18911   ——— [W. B.]. "An Elegie [on] Sir Thomas Overburie Knight" [150 ll.]. In Sir Thomas Overbury, *Sir Thomas Overbury His Wife, With Addition of Many New Elegies upon His Untimely Death. The Ninth Edition Augmented,* q.v. 1616.

3917   ———. *The Shepheards Pipe.* 1614. Includes two memorial poems: "The Fourth Eglogue" [180 ll.] and "To the . . . Sisters of Mr. Thomas Manwood" [22 ll.].

23077   [Bryskett, Lodowick] (ca. 1542– ?). "The Mourning Muse of Thestylis" [195 ll.] and [L. B.] "A Pastoral Eglogue upon . . . Sir Philip Sidney Knight" [162 ll.]. In Edmund Spenser, *Colin Clouts Come Home Againe,* q.v. 1595.

23578   *Burton, Henry (1578?–1648). "6. Elegie [for Prince Henry], A Pilgrims Sad Observation upon a Disastrous Accident" [194 ll.]. In Josuah Sylvester, *Lachrymæ Lachrymarum. Third Edition,* q.v. 1613.

4297a   C., R. *An Elegy Sacred to the Immortal Memory of Margaret, Lady Smith.* n.d./p. [188 ll.].

4519   [Camden, William, ed.]. *Reges, Reginæ, Nobiles et Alii in Ecclesia Collegiata B. Petri Westmonasterii Sepulti.* 1603. Includes twelve English epitaphs [293 ll.].

4546   *Campion, Thomas (1567–1620). *Songs of Mourning: Bewailing the Death of Prince Henry.* 1613. Includes "An Elegie upon the Untimely Death of Prince Henry" [72 ll.] and seven songs [124 ll.].

19043.5   *Carmina Funebria, in Obitum . . . Georgii de Sancto Paulo.* Oxford, 1614. Includes poems by T[homas] Andrews (ca. 1593–1617) [8 ll.], I. Hampton [140 ll.], I. S. [24 ll.], and two by T[homas] Holt (1596? – ?) [24 ll., 140 ll.].

4974   *Chapman, George (1559?–1634). *An Epicede or Funerall Song on . . . Henry, Prince of Wales* [with three epitaphs following]. 1612. [656 ll.].

4975   ———. *Eugenia. Or True Nobilities Trance, for the Death of . . . William Lord Russell.* [1614]/p. [1,205 ll.].

13624   ———. "To the Immortall Memorie of . . . Henry, Prince of Wales." In *The Whole Works of Homer.* By Chapman. [1616]. [16 ll.].

5121   Chettle, Henry (ca. 1560–1607?). *Englands Mourning Garment [for] Elizabeth*. [1603]. [collected poems, 258 ll.].

5250   Churchyard, Thomas (1520?–1604). *Churchyards Chance*. 1580. Includes twelve epitaphs [402 ll.].

5222   ———. *Churchyards Good Will . . . for the Archbishop of Canterbury*. 1604. [60 ll.].

5220   ———. "The Earle of Murtons Tragedy" [805 ll.]. In *Churchyards Challenge*. By Churchyard. 1593/p.

5227   ———. *The Epitaphe of the Honorable Earle of Pembroke*. 1570. [46 ll.].

5228   ———. *The Epitaph of Sir Phillip Sidney*. 1595. [85 ll.].

5231   ———. *A Feast Full of Sad Cheere*. 1592. Includes epitaphs for the Earl of Worcester [55 ll.], "Doctor Underhill" [58 ll.], "Sir James Acrofft" [46 ll.], "Maister William Holstock" [36 ll.], and "Sir William Winter" [50 ll.].

5235   ———. *A Generall Rehearsal of Warres . . . in Flaunders; or, Churchyardes Choise*. [1579]. Includes epitaphs for Edward VI [44 ll.] and the earl of Essex [40 ll.].

5253   ———. *A Revyving of the Deade by Verses that Foloweth*. 1591. Includes six epitaphs [249 ll.].

5254   ———. *A Sad and Solemne Funerall of Sir Francis Knowles*. 1596. [90 ll.].

5256   ———. *Sorrowful Verses Made on the Death of . . . Queene Elizabeth* [1603]. [30 ll.]

4489   Cole, Richard. "March 1" [18 ll.]. In *Lacrymæ Cantabrigienses, in Obitum Serenissimæ Reginæ Annæ*. Cambridge, 1619.

5679   Cooper, John (1580–1626). *Funeral Tears for the Death of the Earle of Devonshire Late Deceased*. 1606. Includes "In Honorable Memory of . . . the Earle of Devonshire" [80 ll.] and "Songs" [86 ll.].

23578   *Cornwallis, Sir William (ca. 1560–1631?). "3. Elegie on the Untimely Death of the Incomparable Prince Henry" [188 ll.]. In Josuah Sylvester, Lachrymæ Lachrymarum. Third Edition, q.v. 1613.

4481   *Cozen, John (1595–1672) [Io. Coz.]. "Scotia Alloquitur" [53 ll.]. In *Epicedium Cantabrigiense in Obitum Henrici Principis Walliæ*, q.v. Cambridge, 1612.

5958   Craig, Alexander (1567–1627). *The Poeticall Essayes of Alexander Craig Scotobritane*. 1604. Includes "Elizabeth . . . Her Ghost" [38.ll.] and "Scotlands Tears" [88 ll.].

5959   ———. *The Poeticall Recreations of Mr. Alexander Craig Scotobritaine*. Edinburgh, 1609. Includes three epitaphs [30 ll.].

6178   D., R. *An Epitaph on the Death of Richard Price*. [1587]/p. [42 ll.].

6199   Dallington, Sir Robert (ca. 1563–1638) [R. D.]. *A Booke of Epitaphs Made upon the Death of Sir William Buttes*. [1583?]/p. Seven epitaphs by Dallington [121 ll.], two each by Thomas Butts [4 ll.] and Henry Gosnold [58 ll.], one each by Robert Lawes (1560?– ?) [34 ll.] and Samuel Stalon [48 ll.].

6256   Daniel, Samuel (1562–1619). *A Funerall Poem uppon the Death of the Late Noble Earle of Devonshire*. [1606]/p. [388 ll.]. Rev. ed. 1607

	[422 ll.] in *Certaine Small Workes Heretofore Divulged by Samuel Daniel.*
6269	Darcie, Abraham. *Frances Duchesse Dowager of Richmond Her Funerall Teares.* [1624]/p. Includes "Upon the . . . Duke and Duchess of Richmond" [14 ll.], "Preface" [20 ll.], "The Duchesses Funeral Teares" [154 ll.], "Funeral Complaints and Consolations" [1,254 ll.], and "To Her Princely Grace" [12 ll.].
6272	———. *A Monumentall Pyramide to All Posterities Erected to . . . Lodwicke, Late Duke of Richmond.* 1624/p. [134 ll.].
6324	Davidson, John [I. D.]. *A Memorial of . . . Two Worthye Christians, Robert Campbel . . . and His Wife Elizabeth Campbel.* Edinburgh, 1595. [1,080 ll.].
6342	Davies, John, of Hereford (1565?–1618). "Divers Elegies Touching the Death of . . . Sir Thomas Overbury" [four memorial poems, 398 ll.]. In *A Select Second Husband for Sir Thomas Overburys Wife, Now a Matchless Widow.* By Davies. 1616.
6339	*———. *The Muses-Teares for the Losse of . . . Henry Prince of Wales.* 1613. Title poem [630 ll.], "Sobs for the Losse of . . . Prince Henry" [54 ll.], "An Epitaph on . . . Henry Prince of Wales" [26 ll.], "Another" [24 ll.], "Consolations for, and to, the King" [186 ll.], "To the Most Sacred Queen . . . after the Crosse" [160 ll.].
6338	*———. *Rights of the Living and the Dead.* [Includes "A Funeral Elegie on . . . Mirs. Elizabeth Dutton" (550 ll.), "An Epitaph on . . . Lady Leigh" (28 ll.), and "To the Lady Anne Glemman, upon the Death of Her Father" (14 ll.).] In *The Muses Sacrifice.* By Davies. 1612.
6341.	———. *The Scourge of Folly.* [1611]. Includes seven epitaphs [108 ll.].
6373	Davison, Francis, ed. *A Poeticall Rhapsody.* 1602. Includes anonymous verses on Sir Philip Sidney: "An Epigram to Sir Philip Sydney" [8 ll.] and "Hexameters upon . . . Sir Philip Sidney" [65 ll.].
6509	Day, Angel (ca. 1545– ?) [A. D.]. *Upon the Life and Death of Sir Philip Sidney.* [1586] [238 ll.].
6564	Deloney, Thomas (1543?–1600?) [T. D.]. *A Proper Newe Sonet Declaring the Lamentation of Beckles.* 1586. [112 ll.].
6674	Denton, John. *An Epitaph upon . . . Edward Earl of Derby.* [1572]. [156 ll.].
22273	Digges, L[eonard] (1588–1635). "To the Memorie of the Deceased Authour Maister W. Shakespeare" [22 ll.]. In William Shakespeare, *Comedies, Histories, and Tragedies,* q.v. [First Folio]. 1623.
7022	*Donne, John [anon.] (1573–1631). *An Anatomie of the World [for] Mistris Eliz. Drury* [The First Anniversary]. 1611. Includes "An Anatomie of the World" [474 ll.] and "A Funerall Elegie" [106 ll.].
23578	*——— [Mr. Donne]. "2. Elegie on the Untimely Death of the Incomparable Prince, Henry" [98 ll.]. In Josuah Sylvester, *Lachrymæ Lacrymarum. Third Edition,* q.v. 1613.
7023	*——— [anon.]. *The Second Anniversarie. Of the Progress of the Soule.* [Includes "The Harbinger to the Progress" (42 ll.) and "Of

the Progress of the Soule" (528 ll.).] In *An Anatomie of the World.* 2nd edition, 1612.

23580   Drayton, Mary. "A Funerall Pyramid Erected to the Honor of . . . Mrs. Elizabeth Grey . . . 1614" [21 ll.]. In Josuah Sylvester, *Panthea: or, Divine Wishes and Meditations.* 1630.

7190   Drayton, Michael (1536–1631). *The Battaile of Agincourt. The Miseries of Queen Margarite.* Includes "Upon the Three Sonnes of the Lord Sheffield Drowned in Humber" [86 ll.], "An Elegie upon the Death of the Lady Penelope Clifton" [126 ll.], "Upon the Death of His Incomparable Friend, Sir Henry Raynsford" [128 ll.], "Upon the Death of the Lady Olive Stanhope" [72 ll.], "Upon the Death of Mistris Elianor Fallowfield" [62 ll.]. 1627.

7205   ———. *Matilda the Faire and Chaste Daughter of the Lord Robert Fitzwater.* 1594. [1,134 ll.].

7214   ———. *Peirs Gaveston Earle of Cornwall. His Life, Death, and Fortune.* [1594?] [1,740 ll.].

7247   Drummond, William (1585–1649). *Flowres of Sion.* [Edinburgh], 1623. Includes "To the Memorie of . . . Countesse of Perth" [14 ll.] and "To the Obsequies of . . . James, King of Great Britaine" [14 ll.].

NL   ———. "On the Death of Godefrid Vander Hagen" [14 ll.]. In Godfried Vander Hagen, *Miscellanea Poemata.* Middlebourg, 1619.

7257   *——— [W. Dr.]. *Teares on the Death of Moeliades* [for Prince Henry]. Edinburgh, 1613. Includes "Teares on the Death of Moeliades" [196 ll.], "Of jet or porphyrie. . . ." [13 ll.], "Stay passenger. . . ." [14 ll.], and "Sonnet" [14 ll.].

7556   Elderton, William (ca. 1530–92). *An Epytaphe uppon the Death of J. Juell.* [1571]. [78 ll.].

4481   *Epicedium Cantabrigiense in Obitum Henrici Principis Walliæ.* Cambridge, 1612. Includes poems by A.B. [8 ll.]; William Farmer (ca. 1592– ?) [48 ll.]; Ed[ward] Gybson (ca. 1595–1653) [50 ll.]; L[aurence] Hawlett (ca. 1588–1626) [12 ll.]; Stephen Haxby (ca. 1584– ?) [8 ll.]; Thomas May (ca. 1592–1650) [18 ll.]; I. P. of Clare Hall [18 ll.]; Thomas Scampus (i.e., Thomas Scamp, 1573?–1631?) [12 ll.]; and Io[hn] Wilson, q.v. Includes also three poems used in the 1610–13 Cross-Sample: John Cozen, "Scotia Alloquitur"; Giles Fletcher, "Upon . . . Henrie Prince of Wales"; and Thomas Walkington, "A silver-winged cygnet brusling. . . ."; qq.v.

10798   F., I. [John Fenton?]. "A Sorrowfull Epitaph on the Death of Queene Elizabeth" [282 ll.]. *King James His Welcome to London.* By I. F., 1603.

19154.3   Field, Theophilus, ed. (1574–1636). *An Italians Dead Bodie, Stucke with English Flowers. Elegies, on the Death of Sir Oratio Pallavicino.* 1600. Memorial poems by I. Cecill of St. Johns College [12 ll.]; N. F. [20 ll.]; R. F. of Pembroke College [10 ll.]; S. H. [6 ll.]; Ed. Ma. of Pembroke Hall [Edward Maines?] [4.11.]; P. P. P. [84 ll.]; Han. Pemb. [anon., of Pembroke Hall] [78 ll.]; R. S. of St. John's College [19 ll.]; T. S. of Pembroke Hall [86 ll.]; R[ichard] Sen[house] (ca. 1575–1626) [26 ll.]; two each by Io[seph] Hall [42 ll., 10 ll.] and

Io[hn] May [56 ll., 20 ll.]; and three by Theophilus Field [48 ll., 222 ll., 42 ll.].

10943   FitzGeffrey, Charles (1576–1637). *Sir Francis Drake His Honorable Lifes Commendation.* Oxford, 1596. [1,995 ll.].

11038   Fleming, Abraham (1552?–1607). *Epitaph [on] Maister William Lambe, Founder of the New Conduit in Holborne.* [1580]. [184 ll.]

7598   Fletcher, Giles [G. F.] (1585?–1623). "A Canto upon the Death of Eliza" [96 ll.] and "She was, why?. . . ." [22 ll.]. In *Sorrowes Joy,* q.v. Cambridge, 1603.

4481   *———— [G. F.]. "Upon . . . Henrie Prince of Wales." In *Epicedium Cantabrigiense,* q.v. Cambridge, 1612. [84 ll.].

7598   Fletch[er], Phin[eas] (1582–1650). "Now did the sunne. . . ." [90 ll.]. In *Sorrowes Joy,* q.v. Cambridge, 1603.

1086   Fletcher, Robert. "An Epitaph or Briefe Lamentation for . . . Queene Elizabeth" [42 ll.]. In *A Briefe and Familiar Epistle Shewing His Majesties . . . Just Title to All His Kingdomes.* 1603.

11158   Ford, John (1586– ?). *Fames Memoriall, or the Earle of Devonshire Deceased.* 1606. Two parts: "Fames Memorial" [896 ll.] and "The Earle of Devonshire His Tombe" [252 ll.].

18911   ———— [Io: Fo:]. "A Memorial, Offered to that Man of Virtue, Sir Thomas Overburie" [28 ll.]. In Sir Thomas Overbury, *Sir Thomas Overbury His Wife. With Addition of Many New Elegies upon His Untimely Death. The Ninth Edition Augmented,* q.v. 1616.

11214   Fowler, William (ca. 1550– ?). *An Epitaph upon M. Robert Bowes, Esq., Ambassadour . . . to the King of Scotland.* [Edinburgh, 1597] / p. [28 ll.].

NL   ———— [W. F.]. *An Epitaph upon the Death of Sir John Seton.* [Edinburgh, 1594]/p. [14 ll.].

NL   ————. *A Funerall Sonet Written upon the Death of . . . Elizabeth Dowglas,* [Edinburgh, ca. 1595]. [14 ll.].

25118.4   Fraunce, Abraham, trans. (1587–1633). *The Lamentations of Amyntas for the Death of Phillis.* [By Thomas Watson]. 1587. [1,109 ll.].

23225   *Funerall Elegies, upon the Most Untimely Death of . . . Mr. John Stanhope, Son and Heir to . . . Lord Stanhope, Baron of Shelford.* 1624/p. Includes poems by Thomas Ballowe (1606– ?) [46 ll.]; Thomas Browne (1607–66) [30 ll.]; William Buckner (1603– ?) [30 ll.]; Richard Chaworth (1603–72) [158 ll.]; Edward Croke (1603– ?) [6 ll.]; Row[land] Crosbey (1604– ?) [40 ll.]; Thomas Fowler (1602– ?) [32 ll.]; Will[iam] Hemmings (1602– ?) [50 ll.]; I[ohn] Hodson (ca. 1594– ?) [60 ll.]; Henry Humberston (ca. 1602– ?) [190 ll.]; G. I. [70 ll.]; William Kitchen (1606– ?) [22 ll.]; Thomas Lockey (1602–79) [62 ll.]; Thomas Mot[t]ershead (1602– ?) [72 ll.]; Henry Pastilew (1604– ?) [30 ll.]; William Pennyman (1607–43) [8 ll.]; William Pickering (1602– ?) [48 ll.]; Edward Price (1605– ?) [22 ll.]; E. R. [46 ll.]; Sebastian Smith (1606–74) [12 ll.]; William Tresham (1604– ?) [14 ll.]; T[homas] Triplet (1602–70) [82 ll.]; Martin Tynley (1605– ?) [32 ll.]; and Gervase Warmstrey (1605–41) [38 ll.]. Latin poems by fifteen others, including John Donne.

11596   Gardyne, Alexander (1585?–1634?). *A Garden of Grave and Godlie Flowres.* Edinburgh, 1609. [43 memorial poems, 1,210 ll.].

11638   Gascoigne, George (1525?–77). "An Epitaph upon Captain Bourcher" [42 ll.]. In *The Whole Works of George Gascoigne.* 1587.

23578   *Goodyer, Sir Henry. "5. Elegie on . . . the Incomparable Prince, Henry" [74 ll.]. In Josuah Sylvester, *Lachrymæ Lachryarum. Third Edition,* q.v. 1613.

NL   *Gorges, Sir Arthur (1557–1625). *The Olympian Catastrophe* [ca. 1612]. [1,222 ll.]. In *The Poems of Sir Arthur Gorges,* edited by Helen E. Sandison. Oxford: Clarendon, 1953, pp. 135–82.

12271   Greene, Robert. *A Maydens Dream, upon the Death of Sir Christopher Hatton.* 1591. [378 ll.].

22533a.5   Gruffith, W[illiam]. "The Epitaph of Sir H. Sidney." In *A Very Godly Letter Made, by . . . Sir Henry Sidney.* 1591. [244 ll.].

12582   H., W., gent. "The Lamentation of Britaine" [1,852 ll.]. In *Englands Sorrow, or a Farewell to Essex.* 1606.

13817   Hall, Joseph (1574–1656) [Ios. Hall]. "Hermæ Eximii Viri D. Whitakeri" [in English, 102 ll.]. In *In Obitum Ornatissimi Viri, Guilielmi Whitakeri.* By Charles Horne. 1596.

12678   ———. [Ios. Hall]. *The Kings Prophecie: or Weeping Joy.* 1603. [384 ll.].

12312   ———. "On the Death . . . of Master Greenham" [14 ll.] and "Upon His Sabboth" [8 ll.]. In Richard Greenham, *Works,* edited by H. H[olland]. 1599.

12726   Hamilton, Francis. "King James His England" [678 ll.]. In *King James His Encomium.* By Hamilton. Edinburgh, 1626/p.

12749   Hannay, Patrick (ca. 1595–1629?). *Two Elegies upon the Death of Queen Anne. With Epitaphs.* 1619. Includes "The First Elegie" [202 ll.], "On the Queene" [14 ll.], "The Second Elegie" [226 ll.], and "An Epitaph" [14 ll.].

12751   Har, W[illiam] (ca. 1565– ?). *Epicedium, A Funerall Song upon Lady Helen Branch.* 1594/p. [144 ll.].

23578   *Herbert, Sir Edward (1583–1648). "4. Elegie on the Untimely Death of the Incomparable Prince, Henry" [66 ll.]. In Josuah Sylvester, *Lachrymæ Lachrymarum. Third Edition,* q.v. 1613.

12312   Her[r]ing, F[rancis] (1565– ?). "In Commendation of M. Greenham" [18 ll.]. In Richard Greenham. *Works.* 1599.

13323   *Heywood, Thomas (ca. 1575–1650). *A Funerall Elegye upon the Death of Henry, Prince of Wales.* 1613. [376 ll.].

13324   ———. *A Funeral Elegie upon the Death Of King James.* 1625. Three poems: "A Funerall Elegye" [194 ll.], "A Short Elegie upon the Anagram [for Henry Wriothesley, earl of Southampton]" [254 ll.], and "A Short Consolatorie Elegie" [42 ll.].

13550   Hodgson, William (Ca. 1600– ?). *The Plurisie of Sorrow [for] James King of England.* [1625]. Four poems: "The Plurisie of Sorrow" [95 ll.], "On the Learned and Pious Workes of King James" [12 ll.], "Illustrissimo Regi Fælix Faustumque Diadema" [in English, 36 ll.], and "The New Coines" [14 ll.].

13591   Holland, H[ugh] (ca. 1558– ?). *A Cypres Garland for the Forehead of Our Late King James.* 1625. [244 11.].

23578   *———. "1. Elegie on the Untimely Death of the Incomparable Prince, Henry" [164 11.]. In Josuah Sylvester, *Lachrymæ Lachrymarum. Third Edition,* q.v. 1613.

22273   ———. "Upon the Lines and Life of the Famous Scenicke Poet, Master William Shakespeare" [14 11.]. In William Shakespeare, *Comedies, Histories, and Tragedies,* q.v. [First Folio]. 1623.

13875   Howell, Thomas. *H. His Devises, for His Owne Exercise, and His Friends Pleasure.* 1581. Includes "An Epitaph upon the Death of the Lady Katherine, Countesse of Pembroke" [50 11.] and "An Epitaph" [12 11.].

14440   James, Richard (1592– ?). *The Muses Dirge, Consecrated to . . . James, King of Great Britaine.* 1625. Includes "The Muses Dirge" [368 11.] and "Certaine Anagrams Applied unto the Death of Our Late Sovereigne King James of Blessed Memorie" [36 11.].

14671   Johnson, Richard (1573?–1654?). *Anglorum Lacrimæ [for] Elizabeth.* 1603. [210 11.; plagiarized in part from Thomas Rogers, *Celestiall Elegies,* q.v.].

14674   ———. *The Golden Garland of Princely Pleasures, the third time printed.* 1620. Includes "The Woeful Death of Queen Jane [and of Elizabeth]" [72 11.], "A Short and Sweet Sonnet" [20 11.], "The Life and Death of Famous Tho. Stukely" [138 11.], "A Most Royal Song of . . . Queen Elizabeth" [152 11.], "A Lamentable Ditty on the Death of a Nobleman" [60 11.], "A Servants Sorrow for the Losse of Queene Anne [1619]" [130 11.], "The Good Shepherds Sorrow for the Death of His Beloved Son [Prince Henry, 1612]" [140 11.].

14691   * ——— [R. J.]. "A Mourners Passion." In *A Remembrance of Honours Due to Robert Earle of Salisbury.* By Johnson. 1612. [188 11.].

14685.5   ———, ed. *Musarum Plangores: upon the Death of Sir Christopher Hatton.* 1591. [234 11.].

14751   Jonson, Benjamin (1573?–1637). *Epigrammes* [includes eight epitaphs, 101 11.]. In *The Workes of Benjamin Jonson.* 1616.

22273   ———. "To the Memory of my Beloved, the Author Mr. William Shakespeare" [80 11.]. In William Shakespeare, *Comedies, Histories, and Tragedies,* q.v. [First Folio]. 1623.

3194   *Justa Funebria Ptolemæi Oxoniensis Thomæ Bodleii Equitis.* Oxford, 1613. Includes English poems by Peter Prideaux [18 11.], Guil. [i.e., William] Sparke (1587–1641) [14 11.], and G[eorge] Stanhope (ca. 1584–ca. 1645) [12 11.].

15189   Lane, John [I. L.]. *An Elegie upon the Death of . . . Elizabeth.* 1603. [244 11.].

15313   Lauder, G[eorge] (ca. 1600– ?). *Tears on the Death of Evander [Sir John Swinton].* The Hague, 1630. [112 11.].

15679   Lindsay, Sir David (1547?–1607). *The Historie of William Meldrum.* Edinburgh, 1594. Includes "The Historie of . . . William Meldrum" [1,594 11.] and "The Testament of . . . William Meldrum" [252 11.].

16620   Lloyd, Lodowick (fl. 1573–1610). *An Epitaph upon . . . Sir Edward*

Saunders. [1576]. [104 11.]. Reprinted in *The Paradyse of Daynty Devises* (1580 ed.), q.v.

17120   [Lyonn, John] (fl. 1608–22). *Teares for . . . Alexander Earle of Dunfermeling . . . Lord Chancellor of Scotland.* Edinburgh, 1622. [98 11.].

22273   M., I. "To the Memorie of M. W. Shakespeare" [8 11.]. In William Shakespeare, *Comedies, Histories, and Tragedies,* q.v. [First Folio]. 1623.

17175.3   Macguire, Patrick. *Teares for the Death of the Most Gracious Prince Lodovicke, Duke of Richmond.* [1624]. [98 11.].

19793   Markham, Jervis, trans. (1568?–1637). *Devoreaux. Vertues Teares for the Losse of . . . King Henry, Third, [and for] Walter Devoreux.* By Geneviève Pétau Maulette. 1597. [2,078 11.].

17385   ———. *The Most Honourable Tragedie of Sir Richard Grinvile.* 1595. [1,520 11.].

13160   *Mausoleum; or the Choicest Flowres of the Epitaphs on the Death of Prince Henry.* Edinburgh, 1613. Contains "Epit." by Walter Quin (1575?–1634?) [14 11.], and short excerpts from W. Drummond, *Teares;* G. Wither, *Prince Henries Obsequies;* R. Allyne, *Funerall Elegies;* G. Chapman, *Epicede;* and W. Rowley, "Lament"; qq.v.

17699   Maxwell, James (1581–1640?) [J. Anne-son]. *Carolanna.* [1620?]. Includes "Noble Queene Annes Epitaph" [26 11.], "Another Epitaph" [6 11.], "Carolanna" [543 11.], "Another Epitaph" [44 11.], "The Epitaph of Prince Charles" [24 11.], "Verses in Honour of . . . the Lady Honor Radcliffe" [24 11.], and "Verses in Honour of . . . Young Lady Penelope" [58 11.].

17701   * ———. *The Laudable Life, and Deplorable Death, of Prince Henry.* 1612. Four poems: "To Our Late Peerless Prince Henries Dear Brother and Sister" [12 11.], "To the Reader" [6 11.], "The Memorable Life and Death of Our Late Peerless Prince Henrie" [264 11.], and "Peerless Prince Henries Epitaph" [12 11.].

18248   Muggins, William. *Londons Mourning Garment, or Funerall Teares: Worn and Shed for the Death of Her Wealthy Cittizens . . . From 14 of July Last Past, 1603, to the 17. of November Following.* 1603. [679 11.].

18252   Mulcaster, Richard, trans. (1530?–1611) [R. M.]. "A Comforting Complaint." In *In Mortem Serenissimæ Reginæ Elizabethæ.* By Mulcaster. 1603. [277 11.].

18296   *Murray, David (1567–1629). *Cælia* [includes "Sonet on the Death of the Lady Cicily Weemes" (14 11.), "Epitaph on the Death of his Deare Cousin, M. David Murray" (72 11.), and "Sonet on the Death of His Cousin, Adam Murray" (14 11.)]. In *The Tragicall Death of Sophonisba.* By Murray. 1611.

7265   *Musarum Lachrymæ [for] Catharine, Comitissæ Corcagiæ.* Dublin, 1630. Includes poems by Thom[as] Andrewe [54 11.]; G. B. [8 11.]; Dudly Boswell [36 11.]; Ge[orge] Brady [226 11.]; Richard Brahan [38 11., 30 11.]; Ro[bert] Conway [28 11.]; Chr. Dav. [28 11.]; Guliel. [William] Donin [28 11.]; Will[iam] Ince [30 11.]; Alex[ander] S. [32 11.]; Dan[i]el Spicer [264 11.]; Ar[thur] Ware [16 11.]; Carol. [Charles] Wolsly [40 11.]; and anon., "Per Eundem" [22 11.].

24435.5   Musket, Anne. *The Much Afflicted Mothers Teares for Her Drowned Daughter* [52 11.]. [1624]. Published with Nathaniel Tyndale, *The Penitent Sonnes Teares*, q.v.

18424   Nelson, Thomas (ca. 1555– ?). *A Memorable Epitaph [for] Sir Francis Walsingham.* [1590]/p. [160 11.].

18513.5   Newton, Thomas, gent. (1542?–1607) [T. N. G.]. *Atropoion Delion, or the Death of Delia.* 1603. [364 11.].

13446   Niccols, Richard (1584–1616). *Englands Eliza, or the Victorious and Triumphant Reigne of Elizabeth, Queene of England* [ca. 1603. Includes "The Induction" (384 11.) and "Englands Eliza" (3,247 11.)]. In *A Mirour for Magistrates,* ed. Niccols. 1610.

18523   ———. *Monodia, or Walthams Complaint upon the Death of the Lady Honor Hay.* 1615. Two poems: "Monodia" [452 11.] and "Skie" [38 11.].

18524   ——— [R. N., Oxon.]. *Sir Thomas Overburies Vision.* Oxford, 1616. [1,154 11.].

18525   *——— [R. N.]. *The Three Sisters Teares [for] Henry, Prince of Wales.* 1613. In two parts [Pt. I, 176 11.; Pt. II, 426 11.] and "An Epitaph" [12 11.].

18520   ——— [anon.]. "A True Subjects Sorowe for the Losse of His Late Sovereign" [54 11.]. In *Expicedium: a Funeral Oration, upon . . . Elizabeth.* By Niccols. 1603.

18586   Nixon, Anthony (fl. 1602–16) [A. N.]. *Elizæs Memoriall. King James His Arrivall.* 1603. [246 11.].

18911   Overbury, Sir Thomas. *Sir Thomas Overbury His Wife. With Addition of Many New Elegies upon His Untimely Death. The Ninth Edition Augmented.* 1616. Includes memorials to Overbury by D. T. [46 11.]; B. G. of the Middle Temple [Bassingbone Gawdy? 10 11.]; Capt. Thomas Gainsford (?–1624?) [18 11.]; R. Ca. [Robert Carliel? 12 11.]; E. G. [38 11.]; F. H. [6 11.]; P. B. of the Middle Temple [Peter Ball? 28 11.]; and J. M., "An Elegie upon the Death of Sir Thomas Overbury Knight" [John Marston? 32 lines]; also an anonymous "Elegie on the Late Lord William Haward [*sic*], Barron of Effingham [1510–73]" [86 11.]. Includes also Christopher Brooke, "To the Memory of . . . Sir Thomas Overburie"; William Strachey, "Upon the Untimely Death of . . . Sir Tho: Overbury, Knight, Poysoned in the Towre"; William Browne, "An Elegie [on] Sir Thomas Overburie Knight"; John Ford, "A Memoriall, Offered to that Man of Virtue, Sir Thomas Overburie"; and Francis Beaumont, "An Elegie [for] Lady Rutland"; qq.v.

19078.4   P., S. *An Epitaph of the Virtuous Life and Death of Dame Helen Branch.* 1594/p. [112 11.].

19120.7   Painter, William, gent. (1540?–94) [Guil. P. G.] *A Moorning Diti upon . . . Earl of Arundell.* [1580]/p. [117 11.].

7518   *The Paradyse of Daynty Devises.* Enlarged ed., 1580. Includes F. G., "Having Marryed a Woorthy Lady . . . Taken Away by Death" [45 11.]; Lodowick Lloyd, "An Epitaph upon . . . Syr Edward Saunders," q.v.; H. D., "Written upon the Death of . . . John Barnabie [1579]" [28 11.]; and Barnabe Rich, "An Epitaph upon . . . William Drury [1579]" [78 11.].

19499   Peacham, Henry [the younger, 1576?–1643?]. *An Aprill Shower [for] Richard Sacville . . . Earle of Dorset.* 1624. Three poems: "His Monument" [12 11.], "An Elegie upon the Death of . . . Richard Sacville" [179 11.], and "A Double Vision upon the Death of that Noble Lord" [52 11.].

19513   *———. *The Period of Mourning. Disposed into Six Visions. In Memorie of the Late Prince.* 1613. Includes title poem [306 11.], plus "Epicedium" [126 11.] and "Elegiac Epitaph upon . . . the Hopefull Prince Henry" [48 11.].

19803.5   Petowe, Henry [H. P.]. *Elizabetha Quasi Vivens, Elizas Funerall.* 1603. Two parts: "The Induction" [30 11.] and "Eliza's Funerall" [112 11.].

19807.3   ——— [Mariscalus Petowb.]. *An Honourable President for Great Men. To the Memory of J. Bancks.* [1620]. [56 11.].

19863.7   Phillips, John (fl. 1570–91) [J. P.] *A Commemoration of the Life and Death of Dame Helen Branch.* [1594]/p. [356 11.].

19866   ———. *An Epitaphe on the Death of . . . Lady Margaret Duglasis.* [1578]. [140 11.].

19867   ———. *An Epitaph on the Death of . . . Lord H. Wrisley, Earle of Southhampton.* [1581]/p. [216 11.].

19868   ———. *An Epitaph on . . . the Ladie Maioresse.* [1570]. [68 11.].

19869   ———. *An Epytaphe . . . Wherein is Bewayled the Death of Sir W. Garrat.* 1571. [156 11.].

19864   ———. "A Freendly Farewell Geven to Honorable and Vertuouse Ladyes" [728 11.]. In *A Commemoration of . . . Ladye, Margrit Duglasis Good Grace.* By Phillips. [1578].

19871   ———. *The Life and Death of Sir Phillip Sidney.* 1587. [378 11.].

19876   ———. *Ut Hora, sic Fugit Vita. A Commemoration of . . . Sir Christopher Hatton.* 1591/p. [402 11.].

20169   Powell, Thomas (1572?–1634?) [T. P.]. *Vertues Due: or a True Modell of the Life of Katherine Howard.* 1603. Two poems: "Vertues Due" [300 11.] and "The Offering" [54. 11.].

20339   Prickett, Robert [R.P.]. *Honours Fame in Triumph Riding [for] the Earle of Essex.* 1604. Includes Prickett, "Honours Fame" [632 11.], and Ch[arles] Best, knight (?–1631), "Thou that true Honour from the grave doest raise . . ." [30 11.].

20393   *Primrose, W. [perhaps William Primrose of Cheshire, Canon of Lichfield]. *A Funerall Poeme upon the Death of the Learned Devine M. Hugh Broughton.* [1612]/p. [120 11.].

20566   Quin, Walter. *The Memorie of the Most Worthie Bernard Stuart, Lord D'aubigni Renewed.* 1619/p. Three poems: "The Memorie . . . of Bernard Stuart" [814 11.], "Of His Last Retiring to Corstorsin" [14 11.], and "Of His Burial in the Same Place" [14 11.].

20574   R., I. [John Rhodes?]. "A Flower for the Day" [108 11.]. In *An Epitaph on the Death of . . . John [Whitgift] Arch-byshop of Canterburie.* 1604.

23077   [Raleigh, Sir Walter] (1552?–1618). "An Epitaph upon . . . Sir Philip Sidney, Knight" [60 11.]. In Edmund Spenser, *Colin Clouts Come Home Againe,* q.v. 1595.

20788   Raymond, Henry. *The Maiden Queene Entituled the Britaine Shep-
           herdes Tears for the Death of Astrabomica.* [1607]. [656 ll.].

20961.5   Rhodes, Matthew. *The Dismall Day, at the Black-fryers.* 1623. [98 ll.].

21010   Richards, Nathaniel. *The Celestiall Publican.* 1630. Includes epitaphs
           for King James [17 ll.], the Duke of Richmond [50 ll.], the Mar-
           quess of Hamilton [13 ll.], Lord Chichester [16 ll.], Sir Francis
           Carew [12 ll.], the Lady Francis [10 ll.], and Margaret Brograve [9
           ll.].

21080   Roberts, Henry. *Fames Trumpet Soundinge. Or Commemorations of
           . . . Sir Walter Mildmay and Sir Martin Calthorp.* 1589. Two poems:
           "The Honorable Life and Death of . . . Sir Walter Mildmay" [196
           ll.] and "Londons Lamentation for . . . Syr Martin Calthorp
           Knight" [161 ll.].

21225   Rogers, Thomas, esq. [of Bryanston] (ca. 1553–1616). *Celestiall Ele-
           gies of the Goddesses and the Muses [for the] Countesse of
           Hereford.* 1598. Two parts (in sonnets): "Celestiall Elegies" [400
           ll.] and "Funerall Lamentacions upon the Death of . . . Maister
           Mathew Ewens" [84 ll.].

21241.5   *Rogers, Thomas [of Tewkesbury]. *Gloucesters Myte . . . for the
           Remembrance of Prince Henry.* 1612. Two poems: "Gloucesters
           Myte" [132 ll.] and "Our Happinesse under the Late Queene . . .
           Our Remisnisse Afterward. Our Punishment by Losse of . . . our
           Most Gracious Prince" [48 ll.].

21406   Rowlands, Samuel (1570?–1630?). *Sir Thomas Overbury, or the
           Poysoned Knights Complaint.* [1614?]. [76 ll.].

21420.5   Rowley, William (1585?–1642?). *For a Funerall Elegie on the Death of
           Hugh Atwell, Servant to Prince Charles.* [1621]/p. [34 ll.].

23760.5   * ———. "Lament. Heu, Heu, Mortuis Lachrymæ Non Prosunt [for
           Prince Henry]" [in English, 88 ll.]. In John Taylor, *Great Britaine
           All in Blacke,* q.v. 1612.

23077   [Roydon, Matthew] (ca. 1560–1622?). "An Elegie, or Friends Passion,
           for His Astrophill" [234 ll.]. In Edmund Spenser, *Colin Clouts
           Come Home Againe,* q.v. 1595.

21497   S., H. *Queene Elizabeths Losse, and King James His Welcome.* 1603.
           [212 ll.].

21526   S., W. *A Funerall Elegye in Memory of the Late Vertuous Maister
           William Peter of Whipton Neere Excester.* [1612]/p. [578 ll.].

22210   Sempill, Rob[ert]. *The Tragical End and Death of the Lord James,
           Regent of Scotland.* Edinburgh, 1570. Two poems: title poem [75 ll.]
           and "The Tragedies Lenvoy" [72 ll.].

22273   Shakespeare, William. *Comedies, Histories, and Tragedies* [First Fo-
           lio]. 1623. Includes memorial poems by Leonard Digges, "To the
           Memorie of the Deceased Authour"; Hugh Holland, "Upon the
           Lines and Life of . . . William Shakespeare"; Ben Jonson, "To the
           Memory of My Beloved, the Author Mr. William Shakespeare";
           I. M., "To the Memorie of M. W. Shakespeare"; qq.v.

22636   Slatyer, William (1587–1647) [W. S.]. *Threnodia . . . Elegies and Epi-
           taphs [for Queen Anne].* 1619/p. Includes "Elegia" [28 ll.] and seven
           epitaphs [203 ll.].

7598   *Sorrowes Joy, or a Lamentation for Our Late Deceased Sovereign
           Elizabeth.* Cambridge, 1603. Includes poems by R. B. of Pembroke
           College [16 ll.]; I[ohn] Bowle (ca. 1579–1637) [52 ll.]; Thomas Brad-
           bury (1578– ?) [14 ll.]; Thomas Byng [T. B.] [four poems, 123 ll.];
           Henry Campion [48 ll.]; Th[omas] Cecill (ca. 1578–1628) [30 ll.];
           Theophilus Field [7 ll.]; L. G. [12 ll.]; T. G. of King's College [14 ll.];
           I. Jones of Pembroke College (ca. 1570–1605) [40 ll.]; Edward Kellet
           (ca. 1582–1641) [30 ll.]; E. L. of Clare Hall [40 ll.]; Th. Mills (ca.
           1579– ?) [12 ll.]; Ri. Parker (1572–1629) [76 ll.]; Thomas Walkington
           [24 ll.]; and anon., "A Stay-Grief for English Men" [46 ll.]; two
           poems each by I. G. of Trinity College [84 ll., 18 ll.] and Thomas
           Goodrick [28 ll., 42 ll.]. Includes also Giles Fletcher, "A Canto upon
           the Death of Eliza" and "She was, why? . . ."; and Phineas
           Fletcher, "Now did the sunne. . . ."; qq.v.

22972   Southwell, Robert (1561?–95) [R. S.]. "Of Howards stemme a glorious
           branch is dead . . ." [24 ll.]. In *The Triumphs over Death.* By
           Southwell. 1596 [i.e., 1600?].

23077   Spenser, Edmund [1552?–95]. *Colin Clouts Come Home Again.* 2
           parts. 1595. Part 2, *Astrophel,* includes Ed. Spenser, "Astrophel. A
           Pastoral Elegie upon the Death of . . . Sir Philip Sidney" [216 ll.];
           anon., "The Doleful Lay of Clorinda" [by Mary, Countess of
           Pembroke?] [108 ll.]; Lodowick Bryskett, "The Mourning Muse of
           Thestylis" and "A Pastoral Eglogue upon . . . Sir Philip Sidney,
           Knight," qq.v.; and [Fulke Greville, Lord Brooke?], "Another of the
           Same" [40 ll.].

23079   ——— [Ed. Sp.]. *Daphnaida. An Elegy upon the Death of [Lady]
           Douglas Howard.* 1591. [567 ll.].

23089   ———[Immerito, pseud.]. "November" [208 ll.]. In *The Shepheardes
           Calender.* 1579.

23100   Spicer, Alexander (1575– ?). *An Elegie on . . . Sir Arthur Chichester.*
           1625 [362 ll.].

18911   Strachey, William (1572–1621) [W. S.]. "Upon the Untimely Death of
           . . . Sir Tho: Overbury, Knight, Poysoned in the Towre" [66 ll.]. In
           Sir Thomas Overbury, *Sir Thomas Overbury His Wife. With Addi-
           tion of Many New Elegies upon His Untimely Death. The Ninth
           Edition Augmented,* q.v. 1616.

13162   *Sundry Funeral Elegies on the Untimely Death of . . . Henry, Late
           Prince of Wales.* See Josuah Sylvester, *Lachrymæ Lachrimarum.*

23575.5   Sylvester, Josuah (1563–1618). *All the Small Workes of That Famous
           Poet Josuah Silvester.* 1620. Includes "Honours Fare-Well . . . or,
           Lady Hays Last Will" [214 ll.]; "Honors Epitaphs" [6 ll.]; and
           Josuah Sylvester, trans., "Henrie the Great (the Fourth of that
           Name) Late King of France . . . His Trophies and Tragedie" [642
           ll.]. By Piere Mathier.

21653   ———. "A Funerall Elegie . . . in Pious Memory of . . . Margarite
           Wyts" [190 ll.] and "To God's Glory in Pious Memory of . . .
           Margarite, Wife of Robert Hill" [32 ll.]. In *Du Bartas His Divine
           Weeks.* Translated by Sylvester. 1620.

23578   *———. *Lachrymæ Lachrymarum, or the Spirit of Teares Distilled* *for the Untimely Death of Prince Panaretus. Third Edition, with Addition of His Owne and Other Elegies.* 3 parts. 1613. Part 1 includes Sylvester, "Lachrymæ Lachrymarum" [177 ll.], "An Epitaph" [8 ll.], "Another" [4 ll.], "Against the Papist Upbraiding Us with the Sixt of November" [16 ll.]; and I[oseph] Hall, "Upon the Unseasonable Times" [26 ll.] and "Upon the Rain-bowe" [12 ll.]. Part 2, "Sundry Funerall Elegies on the Untimely Death of . . . Henry, Late Prince of Wales" includes G. G., "An Elegie on the Untimely Death of the Incomparable Prince, Henry" [34 ll.]; Sir P. O., "An Epitaph" [14 ll.]; Mr. [Hugh] Holland, "1. Elegie," q.v.; Mr. [John] Donne, "2. Elegie," q.v.; Sir William Cornwallis, "3. Elegie," q.v.; Sir Edward Herbert, "4. Elegie," q.v.; Sir Henry Goodyer, "5. Elegie," q.v.; and Henry Burton, "6. Elegie. A Pilgrim's Sad Observation upon a Disastrous Accident," q.v. (Part 2 was also issued as an independent quarto [*STC* 13162].) Part 3: Sylvester, "An Elegiac Consolatorie against Immoderate Sorrow for . . . Sir William Sidney" [166 ll.]. The brief poems by Joseph Hall (in Part 1) and by G. G. and Sir P. O. (in Part 2) are omitted from the 1610–13 Cross Sample.

23579   ———. *Monodia. An Elegie in Commemoration of Dame Helen Branch.* [1594]. [164 ll.].

17661   *———, trans. [Jos. Syl.]. "The Trophies of . . . Henry the Great, Late of France and Navarre" [642. ll.]. In P. Mathieu, *The Heroyk Life and Deplorable Death of . . . Henry the Fourth.* Translated by Edward Grimeston. 1612.

23758   Taylor, John (1580–1653). *For the Sacred Memoriall of . . . Charles Howard, Earle of Nottingham.* 1625/p. [180 ll.].

23760.5   *———. Great Britaine All in Blacke. For the Incomparable Losse of Henry, Our Late Worthy Prince.* 1612. Includes Taylor, "Henricus Principis" [8 ll.], "Great Britaine All in Blacke" [106 ll.], and "Great Britaines Greatest Woe" [98 ll.]. Includes also R[ichard] Leigh (1590– ?), "Epitaph" [14 ll.] (not in Cross-Sample); and William Rowley, "Lament," q.v.

23772   ———. *A Living Sadnes, in Duty Consecrated to . . . Our Late Sovereigne James, King of Great Britaine.* [1625]/p. [318 ll.].

23775   ———. *The Muses Mourning, or Funerall Sonnets for the Death of John Moray, Esq..* [1615]/p. [196 ll.].

23808.5   ———. *True Loving Sorrow [for] Prince Lewis Steward Duke of Richmond and Linox.* 1624. [95 ll.].

15561   *Threnodia in Obitum D. Edouardi Lewkenor Equitis, and D. Susannæ. Funerall Verses.* 1606. Includes English verses by G. B. [12 ll.], W. B. [8 ll., 28 ll.], S. P. [44 ll.], and W. Firmage [60 ll.], and five anonymous poems in English: "Ye learned Sisters, which mount Helicon . . ." [189 ll.], "Ten thousand thanks ye Muses . . ." [12 ll.], "Upon the Death of . . . Edward Lewkenor" [8 ll.], "Deaths Apologie" [222 ll.], and "A Rejoinder to Death" [96 ll.].

24148   Tourneur, Cyril (1575?–1626). *A Funerall Poeme. Upon the Death of Sir Francis Vere.* 1609. [604 ll.].

24148.3   *———. A Griefe on the Death of Prince Henrie.* 1613. Three poems:

"A Griefe on the Death of Prince Henrie" [140 ll.], "On the Representation of the Prince at His Funerall" [8 ll.], and "On the Succession" [8 ll.].

24435.5   Tyndale, Nathaniel. *The Penitent Sonnes Teares for His Murdered Mother* [52 ll.]. [1624]. Published with Anne Musket, *The Much Afflicted Mothers Teares,* q.v.

21653   Vicars, John (1580–1652). "Sacrum Memoriæ . . . Josuah Sylvester" [88 ll.]. In *Du Bartas His Divine Weeks.* Translated by Josuah Sylvester. 1620.

24918   W., T., Gent. *The Lamentation of Melpomene for the Death of Belphœbe Our Late Queen.* 1603. [266 ll.].

4481   *Walkington, Thomas (ca. 1577–1621). "A silver-winged cygnet brusling . . ." In *Epicedium Cantabrigiense,* q.v. Cambridge, 1612. [62 ll.].

23071   [Wastell, Simon] (ca. 1564–1631?). *The Muses Thankfulnesse, or a Funerall Elegie [for] Robert, Baron Spencer, of Wormleighton.* [1627]/p. [614 ll. (plus prose passages)].

25121   [Watson, Thomas, trans.]. *An Eglogue upon the Death of Sir Francis Walsingham.* 1590. [426 ll.].

25174   * Webster, John (1586?–1625?). *A Monumental Column Erected to the Memory of Henry, Late Prince of Wales.* 1613. [328 ll.].

25342   Whetston, George (1544?–87). *A Mirrour of Treue Honour and Christian Nobilitie . . . the Earle of Bedford.* 1585/p. Includes "A Mirrour of Treue Honour" [630 ll.]. and "An Epitaphe upon . . . Francis, Earle of Bedford" [14 ll.].

25343   ———. *A Remembraunce of the Life of Sir Nicholas Bacon.* [1579]. [371 ll.].

25344   ———. *A Remembraunce of the Life of Thomas Late Earle of Sussex.* 1583/ p. [287 ll.].

25345   ———. *A Remembraunce of the Vertues of Sir James Dier.* [1582]. [273 ll.].

25346   ———. *A Remembraunce of the Wel Imployed Life of George Gaskoigne, Esq.* [1577]. Includes "The Wel Imployed Life, and Godly End of G. Gascoigne Esquire" [348 ll.] and "An Epitaph of M. G. Gaskoigne" [14 ll.].

25349   ———. *Sir Phillip Sidney, His Honourable Life, His Valiant Death, and His True Vertues.* [1587]. Includes title poem by Whetstone [350 ll.], and two poems by B. W. of the Inner Temple, "A Commemoration of . . . Sir Phillip Sidney" [68 ll.] and "Of . . . Sir Philip Sidney the Epitaph" [6 ll.].

NL   Williams, Richard. *A Lamentable Motion or Mour[n]full Remembrance for the Deathe of Roberte Lorde Deverox.* 1603. [396 ll.].

4481   Wilson, Io[hn] (1591– ?). "Full true it is. . . ." [30 ll.]. In *Epicedium Cantabrigiense in Obitum Henrici Principis Walliæ,* q.v. Cambridge, 1612.

25915   *Wither, George (1588–1667). *Prince Henries Obsequies or Mournefull Elegies upon His Death.* Four parts: "To the Whole World in

Generall" [24 ll.]; "Prince Henries Obsequies" [630 ll., in sonnets]; "An Epitaph . . . upon Henrie, Prince of Wales" [14 ll.]; and "A Supposed Interlocution betweene the Spirit of Prince Henrie, and Great Brittaine" [202 ll.]. 1612. Rvd. in *Juvenilia.* 1622.

Total: 549 poems, 81,602 lines.

Also of Interest:

B1602   Beaumont, Francis. "Elegy on the Death of the Lady Markham [ca. 1609]." In *Poems. By Beaumont.* 2d ed. 1653.

12747   Brathwait, Richard, ed. (1588?–1673). "Remains After Death . . . a Discourse of Epitaphs and Epicedes" [a collection of anonymous epitaphs, mostly humorous, including the epitaph for John Combe of Stratford alleged to have been written by Shakespeare]. In *The Good Wife, or a Rare One amongst Women.* Published as part 2 of Patrick Hannay, *A Happy Husband.* 1618.

4523   [Camden, William, ed.] (1553–1623). "Epitaphs" [a collection of short, mostly humorous, epitaphs]. In *Remaines of a Greater Worke Concerning Britaine. Third Impression.* Edited by Camden. 1623.

14754   Jonson, Benjamin. *The Underwood* [includes epitaphs on Vincent Corbet (d. 1619), Philip Gray (d. 1626?), Elizabeth Chute (d. 1627), and Henry, Lord La Warr (d. 1628)]. In *The Workes of Benjamin Jonson* [Second Folio]. 1640.

21654   Sylvester, Josuah. *Posthumi, or Sylvesters Remains.* In Guillaume de Salluste Du Bartas, *Bartas His Divine Weekes and Workes, Trans. J. Sylvester. With a Compleate Collection of All the Other Workes Trans. and Written by J. Sylvester.* 1620; enlarged 1633 [1633 edition includes various memorial verses published here for the first time, though written as early as 1603].

24326   Turberville, George. *Epitaphes, Epigrams, Songs and Sonets.* 1567. Reprint. 1570.

Note also the following items, none of which has been available to me:

4270.5   C[hettle], H[enry]. *A Dolefull Ditty, or Sorowfull Sonet of the Lord Darly* [sic] [1586?].

NL   Godschalck, J. *Elegy upon His Honoured Friend Mr. James Herrewyn.*

17329   *Lachrymæ Academiæ Marischallanæ.* 1623.

17308.5   Marcelline, George. *A Funerall Elegie upon the Death of Lodovick Duke of Lenox, and Richmond.* 1624.

19120.3   Painter, William, Gent. [W. P. G.]. *Luctus Consolatorius [for Christopher Hatton].* 1591.

Addenda:

6030   Anon. "An Elegie, or Mournefull Meditation." [116 ll.] In William Crashawe, ed., *The Honour of Vertue,* q.v. 1620.

6030   Anon. "Her Answer to Them All." [6 ll.] In William Crashawe, ed., *The Honour of Vertue,* q.v. 1620.

6030   Boothe, R. "A Poore Memoriall of the Rich Worth of That Matchlesse Mistress Crashaw." [28 ll.] In William Crashawe, ed., *The Honour of Vertue,* q.v. 1620.

21070   Brydges, Elizabeth. "The Offering." [14 ll.] In Thomas Powell, *A Welch Bayte to Spare Provender.* 1603.

4746   Casaubon, Isaac. *A Letter of Mr. Casaubon. With a Memoriall of Mris. Elizabeth Martin, Late Deceased.* 1615. Issued also as Part 2 of James Martin, *Via Regia. The Kings Way to Heaven. With a Letter of I. Casaubon.* 1615 [*STC* 17509]. Includes verses by Mary (Grey) Drayton, Penelope Grey, and Anne Grey, qq.v.

6030   Crashawe, William, ed. *The Honour of Vertue [for] Mrs. Elizabeth Crashawe Who Dyed in Child-birth and Was Buried in Whit-Chappell Octob. 8. 1620. In the 24 Yeare of Her Age.* 1620. Includes verses by R. Booth; Timoth. Leucadelph.; H. P.; Fr. Smith; C. W.; George Williams; and anon. verses entitled, "An Elegie, or Mournefull Meditation" and "Her Answer to Them All"; qq.v.

4746   Drayton (n. Grey), Mary. "On the Decease of My Incomparable Sister, Mistresse Elizabeth Martin." [21 ll.] In Isaac Casaubon, *A Letter,* q.v. 1615.

4746   ——— [Mary. q. G.] "To the Soule." [28 ll.] In Isaac Casaubon, *A Letter,* q.v. 1615.

4746   Grey, Anne. "To Her Soule-Loved Sister, Mris. E. M." [12 ll.] In Isaac Casaubon, *A Letter,* q.v. 1615.

4746   Grey, Penelope. "Parodia." [36 ll.] In Isaac Casaubon, *A Letter,* q.v. 1615.

6238   Herbert (n. Sidney), Mary, Countess of Pembroke (1561–1621). "To the Angell Spirit of the Most Excellent Sir Phillip Sidney." [75 ll. Wrongly ascribed to Daniel.] In *The Whole Workes of Samuel Daniel Esquire in Poetrie.* 8 pts. 1623.

6030   Leucadelph., Timoth. "A Word of Consolation." [10 ll.] In William Crashawe, ed., *The Honour of Vertue,* q.v. 1620.

17403   Markham, Robert. *The Description of That Ever to be Famed Knight, Sir John Burgh.* 1628. [640 ll.].

6030   P., H. "To the Memorie of That Worthy Wife" [18 ll.] and "An Epitaphe uppon That Thrise Gentlewoman Mrs. Elizabeth Crashawe" [16 ll.]. In William Crashawe, ed., *The Honour of Vertue,* q.v. 1620.

20388   Primrose, Lady Diana. *A Chaine of Pearle, Or a Memoriall of the*

             Peerless Graces, and Heroick Vertues of Queene Elizabeth. 1630.
             Includes "The Induction" [24 ll.] and title poem, 10 parts [316 ll.].

6030   Smith, Fr[ancis]. "A Consolatorie Elegie." [20 ll.] In William
             Crashawe, ed., *The Honour of Vertue,* q.v. 1620.

22928   Soowthern, John. *Pandora, the Musyque of the Beautie of His Mis-*
             tresse Diana. 1584. Includes "Foure Epytaphes [on] the Lord
             Bulbecke" [64 ll.], ascribed to Lady Anne Vere, Countess of Ox-
             ford; and an "Epitaph [on] the death of the Princesse of Espinoye"
             [14 ll.] ascribed to Queen Elizabeth; all of which were probably
             written by Soowthern himself.

6030   W., C. [of the Inner Temple]. "A Dolefull Description, and Yet a
             Joyfull Commemoration." [20 ll.] In William Crashawe, ed., *The*
             Honour of Vertue, q.v. 1620.

6030   Williams, George. "To the Never Dying Memory of . . . Mrs. Eliza-
             beth Crashawe." [20 ll.] In William Crashawe, ed., *The Honour of*
             Vertue, q.v. 1620.

INDEX